The
Trials
of
Persiles
and
Sigismunda

The Trials of
Persiles and Sigismunda,
A Northern Story

Miguel de Cervantes

Translated from the Spanish by

Celia Richmond Weller
and
Clark A. Colahan

UNIVERSITY OF CALIFORNIA PRESS
Berkeley   Los Angeles   London

The publisher wishes to acknowledge the generous assistance of The Program for Cultural Cooperation between Spain's Ministry of Culture and United States Universities in the publication of this book.

University of California Press
Berkeley and Los Angeles, California

University of California Press, Ltd.
London, England

Library of Congress Cataloging-in-Publication Data

Cervantes Saavedra, Miguel de, 1547–1616.
    [Trabajos de Persiles y Sigismunda, English]
    The trials of Persiles and Sigismunda: a northern story = Los trabajos de Persiles y Sigismunda: historia setentrional / Miguel de Cervantes: translated from the Spanish by Celia E. Weller and Clark A. Colahan.
        p.   cm.
    Bibliography: p.
    ISBN 0–520–06315–5
    I. Title.   II. Title: Trabajos de Persiles y Sigismunda.
PQ6329.P4   1989   863'.3—dc19   88–28187

Printed in the United States of America

1 2 3 4 5 6 7 8 9

For
Dick and Nathan,
Pati and Benjamín,
these trials also were theirs.

Contents

Introduction

I magine that Don Quixote had a little-known son born just after his death who continued his quest and achieved it. In *The Trials of Persiles and Sigismunda, A Northern Story,* his last book, Cervantes does indeed give us Don Quixote's spiritual and literary heir. The hero is crown prince to an ancient northern island kingdom; the heroine, crown princess of her own northern land. While Don Quixote had his evil enchanters who thwarted his glorious deeds and kept him from his beloved yet unattainable Dulcinea, on their journey Persiles and Sigismunda meet no less fearful trials in the form of ravaging sea serpents, werewolves, barbarous islands of human sacrifice, masters of astrology, and witches complete with deadly hexes. But their travels leading them away from home, unlike those of Don Quixote, do not end in disillusionment and death. On the contrary, the long and complicated process of their triumph over all hardships and obstacles leads Persiles and Sigismunda to a knowledge of themselves as individuals and to an understanding of each other that prepares them not only for their Christian marriage but allows them to return to their homelands to rule together in new harmony and peace.

Cervantes' life, too, mirrors the difference between the *Quixote* and *Persiles and Sigismunda.* He knew long years of humiliating defeat before achieving the spectacular triumph of the *Quixote.* The importance that *Persiles and Sigismunda* had for him can be fully appreciated only in the context of his personal struggle and final victory. Born in 1547, he was christened Miguel de Cervantes Saavedra in Alcalá de Henares, a small university town not far from Madrid. Little is known about his early youth, but he did go to Italy around 1569 in the service of Cardinal Aquaviva and there not only became familiar with the country itself but increased his knowledge of Renaissance art, architecture, literature, and philosophy. He eventually enlisted in the Spanish military forces of the Holy Roman Empire and in 1571 fought with John of Austria's fleet in the famous naval encounter at Lepanto. In the battle he received a wound in the chest and another that permanently crippled his left arm. His bravery in combat stood out in his mind as perhaps the most glorious event of his life, and throughout his writings he heaps praise on skillful, valiant soldiers. On the voyage back to Spain in 1575, Cervantes was captured by Barbary pirates and sold as a slave, finally becoming the property of the Viceroy of Algiers. After many attempted escapes, he was ransomed in 1580 at a cost that brought subsequent financial ruin to himself and his family. The Captive's story included in the *Quixote* seems to be an autobiographical account/fantasy of these experiences in North Africa.

On his return to Spain Cervantes married Catalina de Palacios, very possibly for her dowry and evidently with so little love (or perhaps with a love as idealized as that seen in his early pastoral novel, *The Galatea*) that their married life was a disaster. There were no children, though it is probable that he had one illegitimate daughter born before his marriage. Working then as a government purchasing agent—whose charge included outfitting the ill-fated Spanish Armada—he proved anything but successful; and when his inept practices resulted in deficits he was more than once imprisoned. His lack of business acumen and his poverty in general may have been a blessing for us, however, for he seems to have written most during these times in prison and later in Madrid when he was at court desperately trying to secure any position—in either the New World or in Italy—which might make his and his family's life easier.

Between 1582 and 1587 he wrote more than twenty plays, only two of which survive. He always wanted to be known as a dramatist and poet, and discovered only late in life his gift for prose fiction. Prior to the great popular success of *Don Quixote* (Part I, 1605; Part II, 1615), his career as a writer was characterized primarily by dogged determination. After 1605 publication became easier, and in the ten years between publishing the two parts of the *Quixote* he produced the *Exemplary Tales* (1613), twelve original stories—some ironically critical of society and human passion, others nobly idealistic and probably drawn more from his own aspirations—and the *Journey to Parnasus* (1614), a topical poem in epic style evaluating contemporary writers, including himself. During the decade before his death in 1616 Cervantes seems to have found the Christian world view more compelling and the teachings of the Church more important in his concept of what society could and should be. One indication of this concern is that he joined the Franciscan lay order; an even stronger one is the nature of *The Trials of Persiles and Sigismunda, A Northern Story,* published a year after his death. The protagonists, a young couple in love, journey south from the imperfectly Christianized or pagan lands of remote Northern Europe and then across the continent to Rome—the center of civilization and Christianity. Through their symbolic journey—a religious pilgrimage and life passage—Cervantes echoes the resolution of his personal trials and suggests solutions for the problems of his and all other ages. The ideals of love so incompletely dealt with in *The Galatea,* the wrenching pull of soaring idealism versus disillusioning realism in the *Quixote,* the twisted emotions of jealousy and deceit of many of the *Exemplary Tales,* all come together in a clear and steady final vision in *Persiles and Sigismunda.*

Many twentieth-century readers have found it difficult to understand why Cervantes and his first highly enthusiastic readers considered *Persiles and Sigismunda,* which is so different from *Don Quixote* in some ways, not only the very model of late Renaissance fiction but a brilliant literary experiment as well. Still, this last book did not appear at all unexpectedly or without parallels in his earlier writing. We can guess at its growth in Cervantes' mind through indications in earlier works, just as Beethoven's late quartets innovate boldly but along an observable creative trajectory. As a point of departure, we know that the second part of *Don Quixote* was published ten years after the first part, and that there are unmistakable differences between them. For example, there is no fundamental change in the protagonist either during or at the end of the first part, while in the sequel, of course, he regains his sanity, drops his disguise as a knight, refuses his former squire's plea that they become stylized shepherds, and makes his final peace with family, friends, and church. The reader, like Sancho, may be saddened by the outcome of the second part of *Don Quixote,* still, the hero is now himself again, his real self, Alonso Quijano the Good, not the appealing, romantically striving but invariably counterproductive paladin of justice he made of himself for a while. Persiles and Sigismunda, too, will travel toward their destiny through the hardships and trials of living in disguise. When at the end they cast aside this disguise, there is no question: shedding it means a triumphant return to the most authentic possibilities that life, affection, and the human community can offer. Order, even a measure of satisfaction, can emerge from the daily chronicle of madness. It is a fleeting peace for Alonso Quijano, the old country gentleman at death's door, but there is a greater promise of happiness for a young couple just come of age, their struggle crowned with virtue and self-knowledge.

This movement toward order is reflected also in the structures of the texts. While the first part of *Don Quixote* wanders through a couple of false starts and the author, like the protagonist, seems not fully aware at first where he is going with his series of ludicrous adventures, in the second part the episodes and characters while just as abundant are more clearly woven together in the Baroque manner of themes with variations. The perils encountered by Persiles and Sigismunda are even more diverse—indeed they proliferate as fast as the pirates and werewolves—but as the story unfolds all the surface confusion only serves by contrast to bring out more forcefully an underlying thematic unity. While the hero's life in Part I of *Don Quixote* seems to amount to a random collection of disastrous deceptions and the narrator himself—confused about something as basic as who the author really is—seems to share the characters' uncertainty about the facts, the situation in Part II is different. Rather than getting into trouble because of his own misperceptions, the Knight of the Mournful Countenance is more often than not the victim of others' deception. Rather than the "What is truth?" of Part I, the theme that materializes ever more visibly from beginning to end of this second half is the Don's gradual recognition—in episodes like Montesino's Cave and Sancho's "enchantment" of Dulcinea—that he is not effectively bringing chivalry back to life or helping to restore mankind's lost Golden Age.

It is precisely such a certainty about final truth that characterizes—almost defines—Persiles and Sigismunda. Unlike the would-be knight errant, they are, in fact, once and future kings, struggling against the odds within the context of faith in their identity and in their place in the world. They know their long journey out is ultimately the effort to come home at last, just as Don Quixote's finally proved to be.

This is true for Cervantes' own journey, too, for his last book is a celebration of the idealism of his youth and an acceptance of his civilization, despite the real flaws inherent in the human condition that he never overlooked. Likewise, in contrast with the chaotic violence of the far-flung barbaric peoples into whose hands they fall early in their journey, the European Christian society toward which Persiles and Sigismunda make their patient way in Cervantes' final artistic statement is immeasurably closer to what we would call Camelot, but which he called Rome. So by viewing Spain from without, by putting it in a much larger context, Cervantes becomes less a novelist—less concerned with the ironies and abuses of his here and how—and more a maker of timeless myth. He sets the story in other times and places rich in possibilities for observing the whole range of human behavior, where we see virtues and vices beyond those encountered in our everyday lives. And finally, precisely because he strives to get beyond time, this last work of his attempts and achieves a conjunction of symbols left incomplete in *Don Quixote*.

This change in Cervantes' outlook is understandable, whether or not the various explanations for it are fully convincing. It has been pointed out that many other writers—Shakespeare, Mann, and Conrad, for instance—also conceived their darkest or saddest visions in middle life, then in later years told more tempered, reconciled tales. We have already mentioned that Cervantes drew the cloak of religion tighter around himself at the end of his life. Whether this can be explained as maturity, a renewal of faith, or simply success, there is evidence that after the immediate and overwhelming triumph of Part I of *Don Quixote* Cervantes, though materially in straits as tight as ever, put life in a new perspective. He believed that his last book was his best, barring none. Even while the work was still in progress we know he felt great pride in it and had high hopes for its success, for he proclaimed in the Dedication to Part II of *Don Quixote* that it "will be the worst or the best that's ever been written in our language, I mean, of those written to entertain—and now I wish I hadn't said 'the worst' because my friends feel it will achieve the highest possible excellence."

A more mature work, then, but wherein lies this excellence? And in what way was *Persiles and Sigismunda* a literary experiment? The Renaissance abounded in theories, of course, and Cervantes was unquestionably familiar with authoritative ideas on what made for worthwhile fiction. In *Don Quixote* Parts I and II, for instance, there is plenty of talk about the pros and cons of those best-selling books of chivalry. There is even a well-developed outline—in the long conversation with the Canon of Toledo—of an ideal narration, a perfected story of chivalry and a true "epic in prose." That ideal, his personal working out of the ideas of counterreformation literary theorists, would become *Persiles and Sigismunda*. It is also important to realize that this literary theorizing did not contradict his hopeful final vision; the two, of course, were inextricably tied together.

In the sixteenth-century confluence of neo-classicism and the emphasis on morality by a Church under attack and insisting on discipline, Aristotle's *Poetics* and Horace's *Art of Poetry* were taken as gospel but interpreted with a stress on truth—or at least the appearance of it—and on useful information and edifying examples. We find, accordingly, that Persiles and Sigismunda are themselves highly exemplary, and that little nuggets of wisdom are interspersed throughout the course of their adventures. Not so perfect, in fact often fascinating in their gross defects, are many of the minor characters. But like the hero and heroine, they, too, are intended to represent typical or "typified" human experience, valid—if indeed "preprepared"—data from which the reader is expected to generalize

5

and draw valuable conclusions. From the popularity of the books of chivalry the rule makers did learn to appreciate the role of attention-getting but frankly unbelievable (and so unacceptable) details: magic, exaggerated combat heroics, dragons, omens, witches' prophecies fulfilled, and the like, all of which were referred to as "the marvelous." These strategies—today they might be called gimmicks—were certainly effective. Could there not be a way to legitimize them, that is, to keep their impact without the blatant reminder that fiction is basically a lie—a recounting of something that never happened and consequently the contrived prologue to a moral one is much freer to accept or reject than "the verdict of history"? Yes, it was felt this best-of-fiction, best-of-history combination could legitimately be achieved, and one of the recommended methods was choosing a setting in a far-off land, somewhere unfamiliar but presumably strange and unpredictable. After all, it was the century of exploration of the New World with all its fresh and striking material waiting to be examined by early modern science, or to amaze the public.

For such critics, a shining star out of the past was the fourth-century Byzantine writer Heliodorus, who had sent his brave young fictional couple off to wander through the wilds of an Ethiopia extravagantly portrayed but in fact little known to Greek readers of the time; in the Prologue to the *Exemplary Tales* Cervantes specifically mentions competing with Heliodorus as an important goal in writing *Persiles and Sigismunda*. The Italian Renaissance poet Tasso had written that the mysterious lands of Europe's far north would also make an excellent setting for adventures. Cervantes seems to have taken his suggestion to heart, for his persevering pilgrims find themselves astray in frozen seas and stranded on snow-covered islands whose strange names, as well as other exotic details of circumstance and action, are taken from sources such as Olaf the Great's colorful *History of the Northern Peoples*. It is in the setting of this twilight zone of midnight sun and midwinter blackness that many of the "marvelous" turns of plot occur. Some, such as the episode involving skiing and a ship caught in the ice, seem less startling now than they did to the first wave of readers, while others that we summarily dismiss, such as flying witches and geese generated from barnacles, were then much closer to popular belief.

It is in just such matters as these that Cervantes' ironic wit makes its appearance. He knew that much of the material considered by theorists to be objectionable in chivalric fiction was, in fact, a major factor in that genre's popularity and questioned whether it really needed to be entirely eliminated. Playing with the experts' ideas, Cervantes pushed the limits of credibility, trying to show just how far the reader or listener is prepared to go for the sake of a good story. We discover only at the end of one of the most fantastic and intricately described scenes, for example, that it was a dream Persiles had one night aboard ship. And by having the hero himself, rather than the narrator, tell many of his adventures to groups of other characters, the author is able to introduce discussions among them about whether or not the events recounted are believable. Some of the characters uncritically accept even far-fetched details, emphasizing how much they like hearing them, while others take a hard, scornful line echoing the literary rule makers. It is a brilliant game foretelling the Romantics' nineteenth-century "willing suspension of disbelief" and their stress on imaginative literature. In broader philosophical terms, it also reflects the importance of things unseen in a world-view posited on faith.

The other experimental aspect of the book is found in its solution to the Renaissance writer's dilemma of being caught between the claims of unity and variety—the attraction of a simple, straightforward plot with clarity and coherence versus a labyrinthine story line detoured through secondary characters and events designed to enrich and enliven, but carrying the danger of confusion. Arthur, Lancelot, Gawain, Amadís, and their peers led storybook lives of notorious complexity, at least as far as action was concerned, and we immediately discover that Cervantes, Don Quixote's companion in addiction to such reading material, has opted for the excitement of diversity over the plain, ordered narration called for by authoritative proponents of an unmistakable moral to every story. So richly woven is the tapestry, in fact, that only after many chapters does the reader begin to piece the puzzle together. The complexity is compounded by the fact that in order to build gripping suspense from the very beginning, Cervantes has made wholehearted use of *in medias res*—starting in the middle of the action and explaining the background later—the classic formula for opening an epic.

But while the structural unity, that is, the story line, is as branching and intertwined as a Spanish wrought-iron balcony, many of the varied and seemingly unrelated episodes are tied together in another way, one related to the later Romantic use of recurring themes, or the *leitmotivs* of musical composition. As the Baroque evolved out of the Renaissance, overarching themes characteristically replaced plot details as the structure holding the narrative together. But here again, as with the role of the imagination, Cervantes pushed on ahead of his time, for it is not just simple ideas that keep coming

7

back but symbols rich in traditional connotations and whole cycles of events, many of which, moreover, reproduce in some way the one large cycle that takes in the whole book. That integrating pattern is repeated in actions large and small like an illuminating and purifying ritual. It begins with hardship, often including darkness and bondage, and leads to a trial that must be endured—often a close glimpse of death—but which is followed triumphantly by a rebirth of light, vital energy, and hope. Many times a character's weakness, of a clearly identifiable kind, contributes to the crisis or hardship, and several minor players do not survive their vices. But a goodly number, not just Persiles and Sigismunda, do grow in wisdom and in strength, the trajectory of their stories tracing the Christian belief in mankind's movement toward God, as well as the myth of rebirth found in so many world religions. More important than the myriad connections within the plot is this vision of completion emerging from confusion. Like a musical theme it is what carries the reader through the work on waves of feeling leading at the end to a response that is both intellectual as well as emotional.

The emphasis of much recent literary criticism in English on *Persiles and Sigismunda* has been on these innovations by Cervantes as he gave his Christian Baroque interpretation to the Classic ideas about truth and moral purpose in literature. Alban K. Forcione, for example, examines Cervantes' concerns regarding Renaissance literary theory in *Aristotle, Cervantes and the Persiles* (Princeton: Princeton University Press, 1970), while in *Cervantes' Christian Romance* (Princeton: Princeton University Press, 1972) he focuses on *Persiles and Sigismunda* and provides a thorough analysis of the major themes, symbols, and narrative techniques. Ruth El Saffar's *Novel to Romance* (Baltimore: Johns Hopkins University Press, 1974), although centered on the *Exemplary Tales,* examines and argues for the importance of an evolution toward spiritual harmony in all of Cervantes' work during the last years of his life. Her *Beyond Fiction: The recovery of the Feminine in the Novels of Cervantes* (Berkeley, Los Angeles, London: University of California Press, 1984), continues her work with what she calls the patterns of unity in Cervantes' long narratives. At the same time she focuses on the symbolic movement toward oneness uniting Persiles with Sigismunda and their growth toward a closer identification as trials and encounters with other characters force them to share and blend the best and the worst of their traditionally masculine or feminine qualities. El Saffar stresses that through these experiences they come to value and understand themselves and each other, and at the end are truly prepared for an endur-

8

ing union within Christian marriage. Other critics, such as Diana de Armas Wilson and Mary Gaylord Randel, focus on the strong female characters in *Persiles and Sigismunda,* pointing out that they question, judge, and often reject masculine assumptions. Their analyses show specifically the ways in which many of Cervantes' women manage to escape becoming either victims or merely objects of desire.

But whatever these distinguished critics—or we ourselves in this brief introduction—can add, of course, is secondary to the actual experience of reading and participating in the *Trials of Persiles and Sigismunda.* In the Prologue Cervantes himself invites the student he meets on the road to join him "in pleasant conversation" as he makes his final journey home. Now, that same master of both wisdom and laughter invites us to become fellow travelers with Persiles and Sigismunda and to hear his last word on art and life.

Translators' Note

We first considered translating *Persiles and Sigismunda* into English out of our desire as teachers to present the whole trajectory of Cervantes' work to American students. Believing a careful reading of the work is necessary for an understanding of how Cervantes' writing matured, and seeing that the value of his last, great effort has recently received fresh recognition, we looked for translations. Although they are numerous and up-to-date in the other major European languages, we found that only three English versions have been done. Unfortunately the latter not only are inaccurate and more or less incomplete, they are also very inaccessible. The 1619 rendering, although the best of the three, still suffers from the unavoidable problems of not having been translated directly from Spanish but rather through French. What is more, three hundred and fifty years later much of the language is archaic and hard to understand. The 1741 text, like many eighteenth-century translations, was really more a rewriting; it takes great liberties in changing not only names but the plot itself. The nineteenth-century version published in 1854, the only one not anonymous, was the work of Margaret Stanley. Although the most recent, it is unquestionably the one most plagued by errors and omissions. So, with the encouragement of colleagues eager to be able to read and study *Persiles and Sigismunda* in English, four years ago we undertook the quixotic task.

As the basis for our translation we have used Juan Bautista Avalle-Arce's standard edition in Spanish (Madrid: Clásicos Castalia, 1969) and a copy of the original 1617 printing, with some references to other earlier editions including that of R. Schevill and A. Bonilla (Madrid: Bernardo Rodríguez, 1914). Rather than attempt to touch on all the criticism of the novel in elaborate notes, we chose to comment on the text itself only when the language was problematic or we felt a specific aspect of Spanish culture needed to be clarified. Both of us translated the work in its entirety, though at the end of each chapter and for each draft we brought our versions together to redraft and polish. Every minute of our collaboration was greatly enjoyed, and we hope that readers are as delighted with this translation of *Persiles and Sigismunda* as we are to present it.

The rendering of Cervantes' seventeenth-century Spanish into accessible modern English demanded that several important stylistic decisions be made. The first edition, for example, has far fewer paragraph divisions than a modern writer would feel necessary, while

Professor Avalle-Arce has introduced substantially more than current English usage calls for. We hope to have reached a middle ground defined by our own sense of the natural breaks in the flow of the narrative. The long Baroque sentences posed a similar challenge to keep the flavor and intellectual complexity without drastically distorting or prejudicing the reaction of contemporary readers accustomed to simpler syntactic units and a more linear presentation of ideas. As for the vocabulary—particularly at the formal, stately end of Cervantes' varied stylistic register—we have aimed above all for clarity and naturalness, and have chosen language our readers will feel most at home with in the many marvelous moments—suspenseful, sad, solemn, and ironic—that with enthusiasm and humility we invite you to share with Cervantes through our words.

We would like to express our sincere thanks to Alban K. Forcione and J. B. Avalle-Arce for their encouragement and inspiration; to Ruth El Saffar for her support from beginning to end of the project; to Diana de Armas Wilson for her generous contribution of time and her valuable editorial scrutiny and suggestions; to René Girard for his interest and comments on the text of the final version; and to Patrick Henry of Whitman College for urging us to take on the project in the first place.

Celia E. Weller
Clark A. Colahan

Whitman College
Walla Walla, Washington

The Trials of Persiles and Sigismunda
A Northern Story

Prologue

It so happened, dearest reader, as two friends and I were coming from the famous town of Esquivias, famous for a thousand reasons, one of them being its illustrious families and another its even more illustrious wines,[1] that I perceived someone behind me spurring his mount on in a great hurry. He apparently wanted to overtake us and soon made that clear by calling out for us not to spur on so urgently. We waited for him, and on a she-ass up came a drab student, drab because he came dressed all in rustic brown[2] with leggings,[3] round-toed shoes, a sword in a chaped scabbard,[4] and a starched lace collar with its matching ties;[5] the fact of the matter is that he had only two of these ties to hold it on, so every other minute the collar kept falling over to one side and he was at great pains to keep it straight.

Catching up to us he said, "You, sirs, must be on your way to court to obtain some office or benefice—for his Most Illustrious Grace of Toledo[6] and His Majesty themselves are doubtless there—judging by the hurry with which you're traveling, since even my ass, which has been praised more than once for her speed, couldn't catch you." To this one of my companions replied, "It's the fault of Señor Miguel de Cervantes' nag, which is somewhat long-stepping."

Scarcely had the student heard the name Cervantes when he dismounted from his pack animal, sending his saddlebags flying in one direction and his valise in another—he traveled so completely outfitted—and rushed up to me, seizing my left hand and saying, "Yes, yes, this is the complete cripple, the completely famous and comic writer, and lastly, the delight of the muses!"[7]

I, who in so short a space of time saw such great compliments in my praise, felt it would have been discourteous not to respond to them. And so, embracing him around the neck, whereby I destroyed his collar altogether, I said to him: "That is an error into which many of my uninformed admirers have fallen. I, sir, am Cervantes, but not the delight of the muses or any of the other foolish things that you mentioned. Round up your ass, mount up, and let's pass the brief remainder of our journey in pleasant conversation."

The obliging student did just that, we reined in slightly, and then resumed our trip at a more leisurely pace. As we traveled we talked about my illness and the good student immediately diagnosed me a hopeless case, saying: "This sickness is dropsy, incurable even if you were to drink all the waters of the Ocean Sea[8] made sweet.

15

Señor Cervantes, sir, you should limit your drinking and don't forget to eat, for thereby you will recover without any other medicine."

"That's what many have told me," I replied, "but I just can't give up the pleasure of drinking all I want, for it almost seems I was born to it. My life's race is slowing at the rate of my pulse and by this Sunday at the latest it will complete its course and with it my life.[9] You, sir, have made my acquaintance at a difficult moment, for there isn't enough time left to express my gratitude for the goodwill you've shown me."

At this point we arrived at the Toledo bridge where I crossed into the city and he rode off to enter by the Segovia road. As to what may be said of this incident, fame will take care to report it, my friends will take pleasure in telling it, and I even more pleasure in hearing it. Once again we embraced each other, he spurred his mount and left me just as ill at ease as he was in trying to be a gentleman on that ass. He had afforded my pen a great opportunity to be witty, but you can't always make of one moment what you can of another. A time may come, perhaps, when I shall tie up this broken thread and say what I failed to here and what would have been fitting. Goodbye, humor; goodbye, wit; goodbye, merry friends; for I am dying and hope to see you soon, happy in the life to come!

Book One of The Story of
The Trials of Persiles and Sigismunda
A Northern Story

Chapter One

At the top of his voice Corsicurbo the barbarian was shouting into the narrow mouth of a deep dungeon which seemed more a tomb than a prison for the many living bodies buried there. And although the terrible and frightening din could be heard both near and far, no one clearly understood his words except the miserable Cloelia, whose misfortunes held her locked in those depths. "Have that young man we committed to you two days ago, Cloelia," the barbarian was saying, "hauled up here bound by this rope I'm letting down and keep his hands tied behind his back just as they are; and see if among the women of the last group of prisoners there might be one who deserves our company and the pleasure of the light of the clear sky above us and the fresh air surrounding us."

At this he let down a thick hemp rope, and after a short time he and four other barbarians pulled up a youth with the rope tied tightly under his arms. He seemed to be about nineteen or twenty years old and was dressed in rough linen like a sailor, but handsome beyond all possible exaggeration. First the barbarians checked his manacles and the cords that tied his hands behind his back. Then they shook out his hair, which covered his head with countless rings of pure gold. When they had cleaned his face, which was covered with dust, such marvelous beauty was revealed that it amazed and softened the hearts of those who were to be his executioners. The countenance of the gallant youth showed no signs of distress; on the contrary, with eyes that even seemed happy, he lifted his face and surveyed the sky, saying in a clear and calm voice: "I give thanks to you, oh immense and merciful Heavens, for you've brought me out here to die where your light may shine upon me and you didn't leave me in those dark cells where my death would have been shrouded in black shadows. For I am a Christian and shouldn't want to die in despair, but my misfortunes are such that they lead and, indeed, almost compel me to desire death."

None of these words meant anything to the barbarians for they were spoken in a language different from their own. And so, after first closing off the mouth of the dungeon with a large stone and taking hold of the youth without untying him, the four of them took him to the water's edge where there was a raft made of logs tied together with strong vines and flexible willows. It immediately became apparent that they used this contrivance as a boat to get to another island that appeared to be no more than two or three miles distant.

The barbarians promptly leaped onto the raft and seated the prisoner in their midst. Then one of them seized an immense bow that was on the raft and, fitting a huge arrow with a flint point to the string, quickly drew it back and faced the youth, making it clear that he was the target and indicating that he intended to shoot him in the chest. The remaining barbarians grabbed three thick poles cut to be used as oars, one of them acting as helmsman and the other two setting the raft in motion toward the other island.

The handsome youth, who at any moment expected and feared to be struck by the threatening arrow, drew up his shoulders, pressed his lips together, arched his eyebrows, and in the profound silence of his heart asked Heaven, not that he be saved from that danger so cruel and close at hand, but that he be given strength to bear it. Seeing this, and realizing it wasn't with a death such as this that they were to take his life, the barbarous archer, whose hardness of heart had been softened by the youth's beauty, chose not to prolong the threat of death by keeping the arrow aimed at his chest. He threw the bow aside and approached the youth, making it known as best he could by signs that he didn't wish to kill him.

While they were thus occupied the raft reached the center of the strait formed by the two islands. Suddenly a squall blew up and the inexperienced sailors being powerless to prevent it, the timbers of the raft broke into several pieces. The youth, who only a short time earlier had feared another death than drowning, was left on a piece made up of perhaps as many as six logs.

The water rose in whirlpools, the opposing winds fought among themselves, the barbarians drowned, and the logs carrying the bound prisoner were swept out to the open sea, while all the while the waves were pouring over him, not only preventing him from seeing the sky but also making it impossible for him to ask Heaven to show mercy on his misfortune. But Heaven did have compassion, for even though his hands were tied behind him and he couldn't hold on or help himself in any way, the continual and furious waves that engulfed him didn't tear him from the timbers but carried him out to deep water.

In this manner he came out into the open ocean, which, however, became somewhat more quiet and calm as he passed a point on the island toward which the logs miraculously floated and where they were protected from the fury of the sea. The weary youth sat up and, looking all around, discovered almost by his side a ship that was taking refuge in that tranquil spot in the angry sea as if it were in a serene harbor. Those aboard the ship saw the logs and some object resting on them, so they launched the ship's dinghy to find out what it might be. On drawing close and finding the youth with such a beautiful but disheveled appearance, they quickly and compassionately took him to their ship where the new discovery filled everyone aboard with amazement. The exhausted young man—who had not eaten in three days and had been battered and beaten by the waves—was carried on board and, unable to stand, collapsed to the deck. The ship's captain, moved by a generous spirit and natural compassion, ordered the crew to help him.

Some men quickly came forward to remove his bonds, and others brought food and fragrant wines that helped the fainting youth regain consciousness as if from death to life. Setting his eyes on the captain, whose noble manner and rich attire captivated his gaze while it untied his tongue, he said to him: "May merciful Heaven repay you, kind sir, for the favor you've done me, for one can scarcely bear the sorrows of the soul if the body's weaknesses aren't strengthened. My misfortunes have left me in such a state that I can offer you no reward for this kindness except my gratitude. But if such a poor soul may be allowed to boast, I know that no one in the world will be able to outdo me when it comes to being grateful."

With this he attempted to get up and kiss the captain's feet, but he was too exhausted; three times he tried and three times he fell back onto the deck. Seeing this, the captain ordered him taken below and laid on two hammock mattresses, and further, that after his wet clothes had been removed, he should be dressed in dry clean ones and made to rest and sleep. The captain's orders were obeyed. The youth silently complied, and once again the captain was amazed when he saw him, in a display of gallant character, rise to his feet. This awakened in the captain a strong desire to know more about the young man, to know as soon as possible who he was, what his name was, and how he had come to be in such a predicament. But since his compassion exceeded his desire, he preferred to respond to the youth's needs before satisfying his own wishes.

Second Chapter of the First Book

The seamen who were taking care of him left the youth to rest just as the captain had ordered. But, since several sad thoughts assailed him, he could not sleep and was further prevented from doing so by some distressing sighs and anguished moans that seemed to him to come from between the planks of another compartment next to his. And, moving closer to listen more carefully, he heard someone saying:

"It was a sad and wretched sign under which my parents conceived me and it was under no benign star that my mother cast me out to the light of the world. I truly say 'cast out' because a birth like mine is more a casting out[1] than being born. I thought that I would freely enjoy the light of the sun in this life; but my thoughts deceived me since I see myself about to be sold as a slave,[2] a misfortune incomparably worse than any other."

"Oh you, whoever you may be," the young man said at this point. "If it's true, as often said, that adversities and trials can be eased by telling them to others, come over here and through the chinks in these boards tell me your troubles; for even though I may not be able to help you, you'll find that I can be sympathetic."

"Listen then," came the reply, "and I'll try in a few words to do justice to the injustices that fate has dealt me. But first I'd like to know to whom I'm telling my story.

"Are you by chance the young man found half dead a short time ago floating on some timbers lashed together and said to be used as boats by the barbarians of the island where we anchored to take refuge from the squall that blew up?"

"Yes, I'm the one," answered the youth.

"Well, then, who are you *really*?" asked the person speaking.

"I'll tell you, but first please tell me the events of your own life, which, judging from the few words I heard you say, must not have turned out as well as you'd have wished."

This was the reply that he received:

"Listen, and I'll briefly tell you of my misfortunes. The captain and commander of this ship is called Arnaldo, and he's the son and heir of the king of Denmark. By diverse and strange events a high-born young lady who was my mistress fell into his hands. It seems to me that her beauty surpasses that of all women who now live in the world and even all those the keenest minds might imagine. Her prudence and insight are equal to her beauty and her misfortunes match all three. Her name is Auristela. Her parents are rich and of the lineage of kings. She, then, for whom all this praise falls short, found herself sold and then bought by Arnaldo who loved and loves her with such earnestness and devotion that he's offered a thousand times to make her—instead of his slave—his legitimate wife. This offer had the consent of the king, Arnaldo's father, who believed that Auristela's rare virtues and grace made her worthy of even more than being queen. But she herself resisted, saying that it wasn't possible to break a vow she'd made to remain a virgin all her life, and she had no intention of breaking it in any way even if they tried to convince her with promises or threaten her with death. But, nevertheless, Arnaldo didn't stop entertaining his hopes with questionable fantasies, trusting them to the passage of time and to the changeable nature of women; until one day it happened that my mistress Auristela was walking along the seashore, relaxing not as a slave but like a queen, when some pirate ships landed, and they seized her and carried her off to who knows where. Prince Arnaldo believed that these pirates were the same ones who'd sold her in the first place—the same pirates that roam all these seas, islands, and shores, stealing and purchasing the most beautiful maidens they find in order to bring them to sell for a profit on the island where they say we are now. The island is inhabited by barbarians, a savage and cruel people who hold as a certain and inviolable truth (being persuaded either by the Devil or by an ancient sorcerer they consider the wisest of men) that from among them a king will come forth who will conquer and win a great part of the world. They don't know who this king is that they await, but, in order to find out, the sorcerer gave them the following order: they must sacrifice all the men who come to their island, grind the hearts of each of them into powder, and give these powders in a drink to the most important barbarians of the island with express orders that he who should drink the powders without making a face or showing any sign that it tasted bad would be proclaimed their king. However, it wouldn't be this king who'd conquer the world, but his son. The sorcerer also commanded them to bring to the island all the maidens they could buy or steal and hand the most beautiful one over to the barbarian whose heroic succession would have been determined by drinking the powders. These purchased or stolen maidens are well treated by the barbarians (in this alone they aren't barbarous) and they're bought at the highest of prices paid with pieces of uncoined gold and the most precious of pearls that abound in the seas around these islands. Many men have been led by these gains and profits to become pirates and merchants.

"Arnaldo, however, as I've told you, thinks Auristela (that part of his soul without whom he can't live) must be on this island, and to prove this theory he's ordered me sold to the barbarians. For, while I'm among them, I may serve as a spy to find out what he wants to know. He's only waiting until the sea calms to make a landing and conclude the sale. Don't you think I have reason to complain since the fate awaiting me is to live among barbarians? Even with my beauty, I can't hope to become a queen, especially if bad luck has brought my incomparable lady Auristela to this land. The sighs you've heard come from me are for this reason and the complaints that torment me arise from these fears."

After saying all this she fell silent. The youth, feeling a lump in his throat, pressed his face against the boards, which he dampened with copious tears, and after a short time asked her if, by chance, she had any idea whether Arnaldo had taken advantage of Auristela, or if Auristela had scorned Arnaldo and his offer of a kingdom because she was pledged to another—for it seemed possible to the youth that the laws of human pleasure might be stronger than religious vows.

She answered that although she understood past events had given Auristela reason to love a certain Periandro, a gentleman generously endowed with every good quality to make him beloved by all who might meet him, and who had taken Auristela from her homeland, she'd never heard her name him in the continual complaints her misfortunes caused her to lift up to Heaven, nor at any other time.

He asked her if she knew the Periandro she'd mentioned. She told him no, only that she'd heard it said he was the one who'd taken her lady away with him, and she herself had come into Auristela's service only after Periandro had left her as the result of some strange event.

They were in the midst of this conversation when from above came a call for Taurisa[3]—for this was the name of the woman who had related her misfortunes—and she, hearing her name called, said: "Without doubt, the sea is calm and the squall quiet, for they're calling me so they can hand me over. May God be with you, whoever you are, and may Heaven not only keep you from being handed over but keep the ashes of your burnt heart from testifying to this vain and senseless prophecy, for the insolent inhabitants of this island are looking for hearts to burn as well as maidens to keep for their purposes."

They parted. Taurisa went up on deck. The youth thought for a while; then asked for clothes, wanting to get up. They brought him a suit of green damask cut in the same style as the one made of coarse linen he had been wearing. He went on deck.

Arnaldo was glad to see him and sat the youth down beside him. They dressed Taurisa richly and elegantly in the style that water or mountain nymphs usually dress themselves. The youth looked on with admiration while this was being done, and Arnaldo told him all about his love and his intentions and even asked his advice about what he should do. He asked him if the methods he was using to get news of Auristela were steps in the right direction.

The youth, whose soul was full of a thousand imaginings and suspicions from his conversation with Taurisa and from what Arnaldo had told him, quickly reflecting on what could happen if Auristela were found among those barbarians, answered him: "Sir, I'm not old enough to know how to advise you; but I have a will that moves me to serve you, for the life you've given me by so kindly rescuing me obliges me to use it in your service. My name is Periandro, I was born of noble parents and my bad luck and misfortunes, too numerous to relate at this time, are equal to my nobility. The Auristela you're looking for is a sister of mine whom I also am seeking, for through various events we lost each other a year ago. By her name and the beauty you describe in such glowing terms, I know without a doubt that she's my lost sister, and I'd give not only the life I possess to find her, but the happiness I expect to feel on once having done so, which is the greatest I can imagine. Therefore, since I'm so interested in finding her, I choose, among the many methods my imagination devises, this one that—although the most dangerous to my life—will be the most sure and swift. My lord Arnaldo, are you determined to sell this maiden to the barbarians so once in their power she can see if Auristela is there? And do you then plan to get this information by going back to sell another maiden to the same barbarians, thereby giving Taurisa a way to communicate or signal whether or not Auristela is with the others whom the barbarians are keeping and eagerly buying up for the purpose of which we're aware?"

"That's right," Arnaldo said, "and I've chosen Taurisa rather than any of the other four young women on board for this purpose because she, having been her handmaiden, knows her."

"All that is very well considered," said Periandro, "but it seems to me that no one else could carry out the plan as well as I, for my age, my looks, and my personal interest in the matter, plus the fact that I know Auristela, are all urging me to undertake this task. Think it over, sir, and if you agree then don't delay, for in difficult and trying circumstances the plan and its execution should come one on the heels of the other."

Periandro's proposal made sense to Arnaldo and, without stopping to consider the disadvantages for him it implied, he put the plan to work. He dressed Periandro in rich women's raiment he had come provided with in case Auristela should be found, and Periandro then seemed to be the most elegant and beautiful woman human eyes had ever seen, for if it weren't for Auristela's beauty, certainly no other woman's could equal it. The ship's crew was astonished, Taurisa amazed, and the prince confused. Indeed, had the latter not thought Periandro was Auristela's brother, the thought that he was a man would have pierced his soul with the cruel lance of jealousy whose point dares penetrate the facets of the sharpest diamond. I mean to say that jealousy breaks through all security and prudence, the armor of love-stricken hearts. Finally, with Periandro's metamorphosis complete, they put out to sea a little way to make sure they would be seen by the barbarians.

His haste to know about Auristela had left Arnaldo no time to ask Periandro who he and his sister were and through what dangerous circumstances they had come to arrive at the miserable one in which he had found him; good sense would have required all these questions to be asked before Arnaldo placed his confidence in Periandro, but since it's the normal condition of those in love to occupy their thoughts first with the means of reaching their desires rather than with other curiosities, he didn't allow himself time to ask what it would have been good to know and what, when he found it out later, did him no good to know then.

So having stood a short distance off the coast of the island, as has been said, they decorated the ship with streamers and pennants that, whipping the air and kissing the waves, made a very beautiful sight. The tranquil sea, and the clear sky, together with the sound of the flageolets[4] and other instruments as military as they were cheerful, were breathtaking. The barbarians, who were looking on from

24

a short distance, were even more astonished by the spectacle; and armed with bows and arrows they quickly crowned the shore.

When the ship came within a mile of the island it shot off all its artillery, which was plentiful and heavy, and a dinghy was launched carrying Arnaldo, Taurisa, Periandro, and six sailors. They placed a piece of white linen on a lance as a signal they came in peace, a custom observed in almost all the lands on earth; and what happened to them in this land will be told in the following chapter.

Third Chapter of the First Book

As the dinghy neared the shore, the barbarians crowded together, each one wanting to be the first to see and find out what was coming in on it. And as a sign they would receive the boat in peace and not war, they took out many strips of cloth and waved them in the air. They shot countless numbers of arrows into the wind and leaped about with incredible agility.

The dinghy couldn't come right up to shore because the tide was out—for in those parts the sea ebbs and flows just as in ours—but twenty barbarians entered the wet sand on foot and came within touching distance of the dinghy. On their shoulders they carried a woman, a barbarian but nevertheless very beautiful, and before any one else could speak, she said in Polish:

"To all of you, whoever you are, our prince or, I should say, our chief, bids you tell him who you are, why you came, and what it is you're looking for. If by chance you bring another maiden to sell, you'll be very well paid. But, if your cargo is something else, we don't need it because on this island of ours, thanks to Heaven, we have everything necessary for human life, without having to go elsewhere to look for it."

Arnaldo understood her very well and asked her if she was a native barbarian or if perhaps she was among the maidens purchased on the island.

"Just answer the questions that I've asked," she replied. "My masters don't like me to get off onto other topics of conversation, rather to stick to their business."

"We're natives of the kingdom of Denmark," answered Arnaldo. "Our livelihood is trade and piracy; we barter what we can, sell what people will buy from us, and dispose of what we steal. Among the other booty that's come into our hands is this maiden"— and he pointed to Periandro—"who, being one of the most beautiful, or I should say, *the* most beautiful in the world, we wish to sell her to you, for we already know why you buy maidens on this island. And if the prediction your wise men have made should turn out to be true, you can easily expect that she who is without equal in beauty and noble spirit will give you handsome and valiant sons."

Hearing this exchange, some of the barbarians asked the woman to tell them what he'd said. She repeated it and immediately four of them left and went—it seemed—to inform their chief. In the time it took them to return, Arnaldo asked her if they had some women who had been purchased on the island, and if there was among them one of such beauty that it might possibly equal that of the woman they had brought to sell.

"No," she said, "even though there are many such women, none of them is equal to me, and, in fact I'm one of the unhappy ones destined to become queen of these barbarians, which would be the worst misfortune that could befall me."

The barbarians who had gone inland returned with many others including their chief whose rich finery indicated that he was their leader. Periandro had thrown a thin, transparent veil over his face so that the light of his eyes might suddenly without warning—like lightning bolts—strike the barbarians' eyes, which were fixed on him.

The chief spoke with the woman who then told Arnaldo that he wanted the maiden's veil lifted, and it was done. Periandro stood up, uncovered his face and lifted his eyes to the sky, showing that his fate was grieving him. The light of his eyes swept across the group like rays of the sun and, meeting the eyes of the barbarian chief, knocked him to the ground; at least it seemed to, since he kneeled down, and in that position worshipped the beautiful image he thought was a woman. Then, speaking through the interpreter, he closed the sale with only a few words and paid everything Arnaldo demanded without argument.

All the barbarians left for the island and in a wink returned with countless numbers of gold pieces and long strings of very fine pearls that were handed over to Arnaldo untallied in a jumbled pile. Then Arnaldo, taking Periandro's hand, turned him over to the barbarians and instructed the interpreter to tell her chief that within a few days he'd return to sell him another maiden, and though not as beautiful as this one, she was at least beautiful enough to merit purchase.

Periandro embraced everyone on the dinghy, his eyes almost overflowing with tears—not from an effeminate heart but from thinking about the perils they had undergone for his sake.

Arnaldo signaled the ship to shoot off the artillery while the barbarian gave a sign for his men to play their instruments, and so the artillery and the music of the barbarians thundered into the sky at the same instant, filling the air with confused and discordant sounds. With this acclaim and carried on the shoulders of the barbarians, Periandro came to stand on dry ground and Arnaldo and his men arrived back at the ship. Periandro and Arnaldo had arranged between them that, if the wind weren't too strong, Arnaldo would try to stand off from the island, but only far enough to keep the ship from being seen. Later, they could return to sell Taurisa if necessary. They also planned that Periandro would signal the "yea" or "nay" of Auristela's presence on the island and, in case she wasn't there, a scheme to liberate Periandro would be devised using all Arnaldo's power and that of his friends—even though it might mean war against the barbarians.

Fourth Chapter of the First Book

Among those who came with the barbarian chief to settle the purchase of the maiden was Bradamiro, one of the most valiant and important men of the island. He scorned all laws, was arrogant above all arrogance, and was as insolent as only himself, for no one could compare to him in that. This man, then, from the moment he saw Periandro, believing, as everyone did, that he was a woman, decided in his heart to choose "her" for himself without waiting for the laws of the prophecy to be tested and carried out.

As soon as Periandro set foot on the island, many of the barbarians, pushing and shoving, took him on their shoulders and with signs of great happiness carried him to a large tent set in a pleasant and peaceful meadow among many other smaller ones, each one covered with the skins of domestic or wild animals. The barbarian woman who had served as interpreter for the buying and selling never left Periandro's side and consoled him with words in a language he didn't understand.

The chief then ordered some of his men to go to the prison island and bring forth a man, if there was one, in order to test their mistaken prophecy. He was obeyed at once and at the same time fragrant, clean, and smooth tablecloths made of tanned animal skins were spread out on the floor, and in no particular order or arrangement they tossed and scattered many kinds of dried fruits over them. The chief and some of the important barbarians seated themselves, and as the chief began to eat, he gestured to Periandro to do the same. Only Bradamiro remained standing, leaning on his bow and staring at the person he took to be a woman. The ruler bade him sit down but he refused; instead, heaving a great sigh, he turned his back and left the tent.

At this point a barbarian arrived and told the ruler that when he and four others had gotten down to the shore to prepare to go to the prison island, a raft had arrived carrying a man and the woman guard of the dungeon. This news put an end to the meal and the chief and all those with him got up and went to see the raft. Periandro wanted to accompany him, and that greatly pleased the chief.

When they got there, the prisoner and the guard were already on shore. Periandro looked carefully to see if by chance he knew the unfortunate one placed by bad luck in the same desperate situation in which he himself had been. But Periandro couldn't see all of the man's face because he held his head down, and it seemed that he purposely wasn't allowing anyone to look at him. But Periandro couldn't help but recognize the woman said to be the prison-keeper. When he saw and recognized her, he was amazed and excited, because, clearly and without a doubt, he recognized her as Cloelia, his beloved Auristela's maidservant. He wanted to speak to her but dared not because he didn't know if it was the right thing to do. And so, silencing his desires as well as his lips, he waited to see how the situation would resolve itself.

The chief, wanting to get on with the tests, the sooner to enjoy Periandro's companionship, ordered the youth sacrificed immediately and his heart made into powder for the ridiculous and fraudulent test. Several barbarians immediately took hold of the youth and with no more ceremony than blindfolding him, made him kneel down, tying his hands behind him. Not saying a word and like a gentle lamb, the young man waited for the blow to take his life.

When old Cloelia saw this, she raised her voice and with more vigor than might be expected at her age, she spoke up: "Consider, great chief, what you're doing, for that man you're ordering sacrificed isn't one at all, nor can he be of any use or serve you in any way you intend, because he's a woman, the most beautiful imaginable. Speak, beautiful Auristela, and don't—swept away by your

28

misfortunes—let them take your life, for that would limit Heaven's providential power, which can yet save and protect you and bring you future happiness."

On hearing this, the cruel barbarians stayed their hands just as the shadow of the knife marked the throat of the kneeling figure. The chief ordered him untied, his hands put at liberty, and his eyes given light. Examining him carefully it seemed to the chief that he beheld the most beautiful woman's face he had ever seen and, even though he was a barbarian, he judged that unless it were Periandro's, no other face in the world could equal it.

What tongue could say or pen write what Periandro felt when he knew Auristela was the condemned person now set free! His eyes dimmed and his heart stopped, and with weak and faltering steps he went to embrace Auristela, to whom he said as he held her tightly in his arms, "Oh, beloved half of my soul, oh, strong pillar of my hopes, oh, treasure now found though I don't know whether for good or ill, though surely it can only be for my good, since no evil can possibly come from the sight of you! Behold your brother Periandro!"

These words were said in a voice so low that he could be heard by no one else, and he went on saying, "Live, my lady and my sister, for on this island there's no death for women, and you wouldn't want to be more cruel with yourself than the people who dwell here. Trust in Heaven, since having spared you until now from the countless dangers you must have seen, it will surely save you from any you may face in the future."

"Ah, brother," responded Auristela, who, indeed, was the person about to be sacrificed as a man. "Ah, brother," she repeated once more, "I believe this danger in which we find ourselves is the worst that can befall us! What happy fortune to have found you, but how unhappy the place and in such clothing!"

While they were both crying Bradamiro saw their tears and, believing Periandro spilled them out of pain for the death of the other who he thought some acquaintance, relative, or friend, the barbarian decided to free him regardless of all obstacles and consequences. And thus, approaching the two, he grabbed Auristela with one hand and Periandro with the other, then with a threatening expression and arrogant gesture said in a loud voice, "Let no one dare, if he values his life at all, touch these two, not even a hair on their heads. This maiden is mine because I love her, and this man must go free because she loves him."

Scarcely had he spoken when the barbarian chief, indignant and impatient beyond measure, put a huge and sharp arrow in his bow. Bending it away from him to the full length of his left arm, with his right hand he put the string to his right ear and shot the arrow with such steady aim and such fury that in an instant it had arrived at Bradamiro's mouth and closed it, stopping the movement of his tongue, freeing his soul, and leaving everyone there amazed, shocked, and bewildered.

But he didn't get away with this shot, as daring as it was accurate, for his audacity was soon repaid in kind. A son of Corsicurbo, the barbarian who had drowned during Periandro's passage from prison, thinking his feet were swifter than his arrows, was upon the chief in two leaps and raising his arm, pierced the other's breast with a dagger that, even though it was made of stone, was stronger and sharper than forged steel.

The chief closed his eyes in eternal night. His death avenged Bradamiro's and stirred the passions and hearts of the relatives of both men. Incited to revenge and fury, they all immediately took up arms and began to send death on their arrows in every direction. All the arrows having been spent, they still attacked each other with their hands and daggers, son showing no respect for father, or brother for brother. On the contrary, as if many ancient outrages had made them mortal enemies, they clawed each other with their fingernails and wounded each other with daggers, and there was no one to put them at peace. Filled with confusion and fear, Periandro, Auristela, old Cloelia and the woman who had served as their interpreter were all huddled together among these many arrows, wounds, blows and deaths.

In the midst of this fury, a group of barbarians—most probably ones from Bradamiro's side—got carried away, left the fray, and went out to set fire to a nearby woods belonging to the chief. The trees began to burn, the wind fanned the wrath of the blaze, adding to the flames and smoke, and everyone was afraid of being blinded and burned.

Evening was coming on and even if it had been a clear night, it would have been quite dark; but as it happened, it was overcast and gloomy, and the darkness promised to be complete. The cries of the dying, the voices of those threatening each other, and the crackling of the fire didn't put any fear into the hearts of the barbarians since they were too filled with anger and revenge. Those who were miserably huddled together and didn't know what to do, where to go, or how to protect themselves were, indeed, very frightened. But even in this confused time, Heaven didn't forget to aid them, and by an occurrence so unusual they took it for a miracle.

With night closing in and, as has already been noted, it being dark and fearsome, the flames of the burning woods alone shed enough light to distinguish things, when a young barbarian came up to Periandro and spoke to him in Castilian[1] that he understood very well: "Follow me, beautiful maiden, and tell the rest of the people with you to do the same so I can save you, if Heaven helps me."

Periandro didn't answer but had Auristela, Cloelia, and the interpreter get up and follow him. And so, stepping on dead bodies and treading on weapons, they followed the young barbarian who led them away. The flames of the burning wood were at their backs and served as a wind to hasten their steps. Cloelia's age and Auristela's youth didn't permit them to match the guide's pace and, realizing this, the vigorous and strong barbarian grabbed Cloelia and threw her up on his shoulders while Periandro did the same with Auristela. The interpreter, being hardier and not so tender, followed them with manly courage. Thus, after many ups and downs, as the saying goes, they reached the shore and, having walked about a mile along it toward the north, the barbarian went into a spacious cave where the surf ran in and out. They walked through the cave for a while; the path, twisting from side to side, sometimes narrow sometimes wide, caused them alternately to crouch, stoop, creep along the floor, and walk erect, until it seemed they had come out of the cave into an open field where their guide told them they could safely stand up straight. They couldn't see this for themselves due to the darkness of the night and because the light from the burning woods, though now burning even stronger, couldn't reach them there. "Praise God," said the barbarian, once again speaking in Castilian, "who's brought us to this place where, though we may fear some danger, at least we'll no longer have to fear for our lives."

Then they saw a great light coming quickly toward them almost like a comet, or perhaps like a shooting star racing through the air. They would have waited in fear if the barbarian hadn't said, "This is my father, coming to meet me." Periandro, who knew how to speak Castilian, though not very fluently, said to him, "May Heaven reward you, angel in human form or whoever you may be, for the good you've done us. Although it may come to nothing more than delaying our death, we consider it an extraordinary act of kindness."

The light arrived at this moment carried by one who seemed to be a barbarian a little more than fifty years old. Coming up, he immediately put the light, a thick-handled torch, on the ground, and with open arms went up to his son asking him in Castilian what had happened to him that he was returning in such company.

"Father," answered the youth, "let's go to our camp for there are many things to tell and even more to think about. The island is on fire, almost all of its inhabitants have either been reduced to ashes or charred, and with Heaven's help I've stolen the remaining few you see here from the flames and the sharp edge of the barbarians' daggers. Come on to our camp, sir, as I said before, so my mother and sister may show and tenderly practice their kindness by caring for my tired and fearful guests."

The father led on and they all followed him. Cloelia, feeling somewhat revived, traveled on foot, but Periandro refused to put down the beautiful burden he carried, since Auristela, who was all he had in the world, could never weigh him down.

They had walked only a little way when they arrived at a very high crag, at the base of which they found a broad space or cave whose roof and walls were formed by that same rock. Two women dressed like barbarians came out with burning torches in their hands. One of them was a girl about fifteen years old and the other a woman of thirty; the woman was beautiful, but the girl was exceedingly so. "Oh, my father and brother!" exclaimed one, while the other said only: "Welcome, my dearest son."

The interpreter was amazed to hear the women who seemed to be barbarians speaking a language different from the one used on the island. Going over to ask them to clear up the mystery of how they came to know that language, she was stopped by the father who bade his wife and daughter spread out fleecy skins on the floor of the rough cave. They obeyed him, placing the torches against the walls, eagerly and quickly bringing out goat, sheep, and other animal skins from a second inner cave to decorate the floor and check the cold that had begun to bother them.

Chapter Five

Concerning the Account of Himself the Spanish Barbarian Gave to His New Guests

The meal was promptly served and quickly consumed, but just being able to eat it without fear made it tasty. The torches had been renewed and although the room was smoky, it was warm. The dishes used for dinner were neither of silver nor fine china;[1] the barbarian brother's and sister's hands were the serving platters and the glasses were pieces of tree bark somewhat nicer than cork. Candía[2] wine was far away, so clean, clear, icy cold water was served in its place.

Cloelia fell asleep because old age is more a friend to sleep than to any kind of conversation, however pleasing it might be. The older barbarian woman made her comfortable in the second room, using animal skins as quilts and blankets, and then returned to seat herself with the others, to whom the Spaniard was saying the following in Castilian:

"Although it would be reasonable enough, ladies and gentlemen, for me to ask you about the deeds and events of your lives, I first prefer to tell you about myself so, being obliged by having heard my story, you won't later keep yours from me.

"As good luck would have it, I was born in Spain, in one of her best provinces. I was brought into the world by parents belonging to the lesser nobility, and they reared me as the wealthy do their children. When I arrived at the gates of grammar,[3] which lead to the other branches of knowledge, I was inclined by the stars somewhat toward letters, though much more toward arms.[4] I wasn't friendly in my tender years either with Ceres or Bacchus and so for me Venus was always cold.[5] Led by my natural inclination, I left home and went away to the war that his majesty Charles V, another Caesar, was waging in Germany[6] against some of the rulers there. Mars favored me, I gained a reputation as a good soldier, the emperor honored me, I had friends, and above all, I learned to be generous and well-mannered, for these are virtues learned in the school of Christian warfare.

"I returned to my home rich and honored, intending to stay there for a while to enjoy my parents who were still living and my friends who were waiting for me. But she whom others call Fortune, though I don't know what she is, jealous of my peace of mind and turning the wheel they say she has, cast me down from its heights where I thought I was settled, to the depths of misery where I now find myself, using as her instrument a gentleman, the second son of a titled nobleman who had his estate near where I lived.

"This gentleman, then, came to my town to observe some celebrations. While he was standing in the square among the hidalgos[7] and noblemen who formed a circle of spectators, myself being one of them, he turned to me with an arrogant smile and said: 'You're looking gallant,[8] Señor Antonio. His experiences in Flanders and Italy must have done him a lot of good for he truly looks very fine.[9] And good Antonio should know that I like him very much.'

"I answered him, 'Since I'm that Antonio, I kiss your Lordship's hands a thousand times for the grace you've shown me. After all, your Lordship acts like the person he is in honoring his countrymen and servants, but despite all this, I want your Lordship to know that I took my gallantry with me from my home to Flanders and my good upbringing has been with me from birth. Therefore I deserve neither praise nor reproach for them; nevertheless, however good or bad I may be, I'm very much your Lordship's servant and I beg you to honor me as my good wishes for you deserve.'

"A gentleman and great friend of mine at my side told me—and not in such a low voice the nobleman couldn't hear it—'Watch what you say, friend Antonio, for here we don't call Don So-and-So, "your Lordship."'[10] To which the nobleman replied before I could— 'The good Antonio speaks well for he's addressing me as they do in Italy, where, instead of "your Grace" they say "your Lordship."'

"'I know very well the polite usages and ceremonies that go with good breeding, and I call your Lordship, "Lordship," not because I'm following an Italian practice but because I know that anyone who calls me the common "you" must be a "Lordship" according to the Spanish custom. What's more, as I'm the son of my own deeds as well as my noble parents, I deserve a "your Grace" from any "Lordship" and anyone who says otherwise'—here, putting hand to my sword—'is a long way from being well-bred.'

"Then, speaking and acting at the same time, I gave him two such slashes on the head that he was left so stunned he didn't know what had happened to him, nor did he do anything in his own defense to satisfy the affront, which I insisted on by standing there with my naked sword in my hand. Finally coming to his senses, however, he took up his sword and with noble spirit began to avenge the insult. But neither I nor the blood which flowed from one of his head wounds let him carry out his honorable resolution.

"The bystanders became alarmed and intervened against me. I fled to my parents' house. I told them what had happened and, aware of the danger I was in, they provided me with money and a good horse, advising me to find a place of refuge, for I had made many strong and powerful enemies for myself. I did as they advised and in two days crossed the border into Aragón,[11] where I caught my breath a little from my unprecedented haste. To make a long story short, with almost the same speed, I proceeded to Germany and returned to the service of the Emperor. There they told me that my enemy, accompanied by several others, was looking for me and intended to kill me by any means. I feared the danger, as well I might. I returned to Spain, as there's no better refuge than one right under the nose of one's enemy. I saw my parents by night and they again provided me with money and jewels, which I took with me to Lisbon. I embarked on a ship that had all sails set to leave for England. On board there were some English gentlemen who, out of curiosity, had come to see Spain, and now having seen all of it, or at least its major cities, were returning to their homeland.

"It so happened that I had a quarrel with an English sailor over something of little importance and had to slap him in the face. This blow provoked the anger of the rest of the sailors and of all the riff-raff on the ship who began to throw at me anything that wasn't nailed down. I fled to the sterncastle[12] and sought protection behind the back of one of the English gentlemen, who kept me from losing my life then and there. The rest of the gentlemen were able to calm the rabble, but only on condition that I be thrown into the sea or put into the ship's boat or dinghy,[13] in which I could return to Spain or go wherever Heaven might carry me. And so it was done.

"They gave me the boat supplied with two barrels of water, one of lard, and some hardtack. I thanked my defenders for the kindness they were showing me, entered the little boat with only two oars, the ship sailed away, dark night fell, and I found myself alone in the middle of the immensity of those waters, taking only the road not opposed by either wind or waves. I raised my eyes to Heaven, commended myself to God with all the devotion I could muster, and looked toward the north where, although I could make out the way I was going, I couldn't figure out where I was. I drifted like this for six days and six nights, trusting more in Heaven's goodwill than in the strength of my arms, which by now were so tired and weak from

continual work that they abandoned the oars, which I removed from
the oarlocks and put inside the boat so I could use them when the
sea permitted or when I regained some strength.

"I lay down flat on my back in the boat, closed my eyes, and
there wasn't a saint in Heaven to whom in my innermost heart I
didn't call for help. But such is the power of our physical needs and
requirements that in the midst of this danger and in the middle of
this need . . . it's hard to believe, but . . . a drowsiness so heavy
came over me that it swept away all sensation and I fell asleep. Yet
during that sleep my imagination conjured up a thousand kinds of
frightening deaths—all of them in the water—and in some of them
it seemed to me I was eaten by wolves and torn apart by wild animals, so that asleep or awake my life was a prolonged dying.

"I woke with a start from this uneasy rest when a furious wave
passed over the boat and filled it with water. I saw the danger and,
as best I could, dumped the seawater back into the sea. I took up the
oars again but they got me nowhere. I saw that the sea was getting
rough, whipped and wounded by a south wind from Africa, which
in that region seems to show its strength more than in other waters.
I knew it was foolish to try to oppose the fury of the seas with my
fragile boat and its harshness with my own frail and feeble forces.
And so I again put away the oars and let the boat go where the waves
and wind might carry it. I repeated my prayers, added promises, and
increased the waters of the sea with some that poured from my eyes,
not from fear of death that seemed so near, but rather from dread
of the punishment my evil deeds deserved. Finally, at the end of I
don't know how many days and nights that I drifted over the sea becoming increasingly disturbed and agitated, I found myself close by
an island with no human inhabitants, although it was full of wolves
that roamed in packs.

"I reached the shelter of a huge rock at the water's edge and
didn't dare jump to land for fear of the animals I'd seen. I ate some
of the now water-soaked hardtack, for need and hunger can't be
particular. Night fell, though it wasn't as dark as the night before. It
appeared the sea was quieting and the coming day promised more
tranquility. I looked to the Heavens and saw that the stars seemed to
promise fair weather on the water and calm in the air.

"While I was thus occupied it seemed to me, as I peered through
the dim light of the night, that the rock serving as my harbor was
now crowned with the same wolves I'd seen on the shore, and that
one of them . . . I swear it's true . . . told me with a clear and distinct voice and in my own language: 'Spaniard, go away and look

elsewhere for your fate, unless you wish to die here torn apart by our claws and teeth; and don't ask who it is telling you this, just thank Heaven you've found mercy even among wild animals.'

"I'll let you decide whether I was frightened or not—but I wasn't so confused that I didn't follow the advice given me. I set the oars in the oarlocks and tied them in place, pulled with all my strength, and rowed out to the open sea. And since it's usual for misfortunes and afflictions to confuse the memory of those who suffer from them, I can't tell you how many days I drifted through those seas, swallowing not one but a thousand deaths at every wave until, when my boat was snatched up by a terrible storm, I found myself next to this very island, at just the spot where the cave you came through opens out. The boat almost ran aground inside the cave, but the surf started to pull it out again. Seeing what was happening, I threw myself out of the boat and, sinking my fingers into the sand, prevented the receding waters from carrying me out to sea. Although the sea took my life with it when it took the boat, since it thereby deprived me of all hope of being saved, I took pleasure in changing the manner of my death and in being on land, for as long as there's life, there's hope."

When the Spanish barbarian—his clothing gave him away— arrived at this point in his story, soft moans and sobs were heard coming from the inner room where they had left Cloelia. Auristela, Periandro, and all the rest immediately rushed in with torches to see what could be the matter and found that Cloelia, sitting on the skins with her back against the rock, was gazing at Heaven with eyes whose light was fading. Auristela went up to her and with compassionate and sorrowful voice said, "What's this, my old nursemaid? Can it be possible you'd want to leave me alone and at a time when I have most need of your advice?"

Cloelia became a little more lucid, and taking Auristela's hand, said to her, "Here, daughter of my soul, are the things I've kept for you.[14] I would have liked my life to last until yours found the peace that it deserves; but since Heaven isn't allowing that, my will bows to Heaven's and I freely offer up my life with as much goodwill as is in my power to give. What I ask of you, my lady, is, when good fortune permits you—and it will—to take your rightful place again, if my parents or any of my relatives should still be alive, that you tell them I died a Christian, believing in Jesus Christ, and—what amounts to the same thing—believing in the Holy Roman Catholic Church. Now I tell you no more, for I cannot."

After saying this and pronouncing the name of Jesus over and over, she closed her eyes in darkest night; Auristela also closed hers at this sight and fell into a deep faint. Periandro's eyes filled with tears like two fountains, while those of the others present overflowed like rivers. Periandro hurried to help Auristela who, regaining consciousness, added her tears to those of all the others and added sighs of her own, saying things that would move stones to pity.

They decided to bury Cloelia the next day; the barbarian girl and her brother stayed to watch over the body while the others went away to rest during the small portion of night still remaining.

Sixth Chapter

Where the Spanish Barbarian Continues His Story

That day was later than usual in revealing itself to the world, it seemed, because the smoke and haze rising from the still burning island prevented the rays of the sun from reaching the earth there. The Spanish barbarian told his son to leave the place, as he often did, to discover what was happening on the island.

The others spent a restless night because the sadness and grief at the death of her nursemaid prevented Auristela from sleeping and this in turn kept Periandro awake. The two of them went out into the open air and saw that the place was constructed by nature as if man's art had designed it. It was round, encompassed by very high, bare cliffs, and they estimated that it measured a little more than a league in circumference. It was full of wild trees that offered fruit, which, though somewhat sour, was edible nonetheless; the grass was very tall because of the great amount of water that ran off the rocks and kept it perpetually green. All of this surprised and amazed them.

The Spanish barbarian arrived at this moment and said: "Come along, good people, and we'll give rest to the dead woman and an end to the story I began." They did what he said and buried Cloelia in a hollow place in a rock, covering her with earth and small rocks. Auristela asked the barbarian to place a cross on top to indicate that a Christian's body lay there. The Spaniard replied that he would bring a large cross he had in his shelter and place it atop the grave. They all paid her their last respects and Auristela, whose tears immediately brought forth others from Periandro's eyes, renewed her weeping.

38

Meanwhile, since the young barbarian had yet to return, everyone went back into the hollow of the rock where they had slept, to take refuge from the cold that threatened to become severe. When they had seated themselves on the soft skins, the barbarian called for silence and continued his story in this manner:

"When the boat I came in left me on the sand and the sea took it back again—I said earlier that my hopes for freedom went with it, hopes that to this moment I still lack—I came inside this place, looked at it, and it seemed to me that nature had made and formed it as the theatre where the tragedy of my misfortunes would be played out. I was surprised not to see any people, only some mountain goats and small animals of different kinds. I wandered all around, found this cave dug out of the rocky cliffs and chose it for my dwelling. Finally, having explored it all, I returned to the entrance through which I'd come, hoping to hear a human voice or come across someone who might tell me where I was. Good luck and merciful Heaven, which still had not totally forgotten me, provided me with a barbarian girl about fifteen years old who was walking around hunting for colorful seashells and tasty shellfish among the cliffs, boulders, and rocks on the beach.

"She was stunned to see me, her feet took root in the sand, she let go of the little shells she held and the shellfish all scattered; clasping her in my arms without saying a word to her, nor she to me, I went straight into the cave and brought her to this same spot where we are right now. I placed her on the ground, kissed her hands, caressed her face, and made every sort of gesture and sign I could to show her I was gentle and loving. Once she got over her first fright, never taking her eyes off me, she touched me all over my body and, from time to time, all fear now forgotten, she would laugh and embrace me, and then taking from her clothes a special kind of bread not made of wheat, she put it in my mouth and spoke to me in her language, asking me, I later learned, to eat it. I ate because I really needed to. She took me by the hand and led me to that stream right over there where, also with gestures, she asked me to drink. I couldn't get enough of looking at her, for she seemed to me more an angel from Heaven than a barbarian from earth.

"I returned to the entrance of the cave and there with gestures, as well as with words she didn't understand, I begged her—as though she did understand—to come back and see me. After this, I embraced her again while she kissed me innocently on the forehead and made unmistakable signs that she would indeed be back. Having done this, I returned to walk around this place and investigate and taste the fruit with which some of the trees were laden, finding walnuts, hazelnuts, and some wild pears. I gave thanks to God for the discovery and renewed my flagging hopes of being saved. I spent that night in this very place awaiting the day, and when it came I waited for the return of my beautiful barbarian, who, I began to fear and suspect, might have revealed my hiding place and turned me over to the barbarians who I imagined filled the island. But I was freed from this fear by the sight of her returning somewhat later in the morning, beautiful as the sun, gentle as a lamb, and not accompanied by barbarians who might capture me, but loaded down with supplies that would sustain me."

The gallant Spaniard had arrived at this point in his story when the youth who had gone to find out what was happening on the island returned and told them that almost everything was burned up and all or most of the barbarians dead, some by the sword, others by fire, and if there were any still left alive, they had probably put out to sea on wooden rafts, escaping on the water from the fires on land. Their group, too, would do well to leave their refuge and walk around that part of the island not cut off to them by the fire. Meanwhile, each one of them should be thinking about what they might have to do to escape that accursed land, for nearby there were other islands inhabited by less barbarous people, and perhaps by changing location, they could change their luck.

"Calm down a little, son, for I'm giving an account of the events of my life to these good people and not much is left to tell, although my misfortunes are countless."

"Don't wear yourself out, my husband," said the older barbarian woman, "by telling everything in detail, for you may well become tired or tiresome. Let me tell what's left, at least up to the present moment." "It will be my pleasure," answered the Spaniard, "for it will give me exactly that to hear how you tell it."

"The thing is, then," responded the barbarian woman, "that my many comings and goings from this place gave him such pleasure that this girl and boy were born to me and to my husband. I call him my husband for before he slept with me he promised to be my husband in the manner he says is customary among true Christians. He's taught me his language, as I've taught him mine, in which he also taught me the laws of the Catholic Christian faith. He baptized me in the water from that creek over there, although not with the same ceremonies he's told me are usually performed in his country. He explained as much of his religion to me as he knows and I gave it a place in my heart and soul where I've accepted it with all the belief

40

I can. I believe in the Holy Trinity, God the Father, God the Son, and God the Holy Spirit, three separate persons who are all the one true God and, although they're God the Father, God the Son, and God the Holy Spirit, they're not three distinct and separate gods but the one true God. Finally, I believe in everything the Holy Roman Catholic Church holds to and believes, for it is ruled by the Holy Spirit and governed by the Supreme Pontiff, vicar and viceroy of God on earth, legitimate successor to Saint Peter, its first shepherd after Christ, who in turn is first and universal shepherd of his wife the Church. He told me of the greatness of the perpetual Virgin Mary, Queen of Heaven and Our Lady and Lady of the Angels, treasure of the Father, sanctuary of the Son, and beloved of the Holy Spirit, help and refuge of sinners. Along with these he's taught me other things that I won't repeat, for it seems to me I've said enough for you to understand that I'm a Catholic Christian. I, simple and compassionate, turned my rustic soul over to him, and he, with Heaven's grace, has returned it to me wise and Christian. I surrendered my body to him, not thinking that in so doing I might offend anyone, and this surrender resulted in the two children you see here who add to the number of those who praise the true God. At various times I've brought him pieces of gold that abound on this island, and some pearls that I've stored away waiting for the day, bound to be a happy one, that will take us out of this prison and to a place where, freely and surely and with nothing to worry us, we'll be among the flock of Christ, whom I adore through the image of the cross you see over there. What I've said seems to me all my husband Antonio (that was the Spanish barbarian's name) had left to say." Then he added, "What you say is true, dear Ricla." (This was the barbarian woman's name.) They amazed everyone present with the twists and turns of their story and were rewarded with a thousand praises and a thousand good wishes, especially from Auristela, who was very fond of the two barbarian women, mother and daughter.

The barbarian youth, who like his father was also called Antonio, said it wasn't good for them to be idle at this time without a way and plan for getting out of the trap they were in, for if the fire raging fiercely on the island should pass over the high rocks, or be carried by the wind and fall there, everyone would burn up. "You've got it exactly right, son," responded the father.

"It seems to me," said Ricla, "we should wait a few days, because people who dwell on an island very near here, one that can sometimes be seen when the sun is bright and the sea tranquil, come to sell and trade their goods for ours. I'll go out, and now that there's no one to hear or stop me—since the dead neither hear nor prevent anything—I'll arrange for them to sell me a boat at whatever price they want, saying I need it to escape with my children and husband now hidden in a cave for protection from the fire. You should know, however, that even though these boats are made of wood and covered with enough strong animal skins to prevent water from coming in through the sides, from what I've seen and observed, they never venture out on the sea unless it's calm, and they don't use those pieces of canvas I've seen on other boats that often come to our shores to sell maidens or men to fulfill the vain superstition you must have heard about and that's been practiced for a very long time on this island. All of this makes it clear to me that these boats aren't to be trusted on the open sea with the squalls and storms they say happen frequently there."

In response Periandro asked, "Hasn't Señor Antonio tried that plan in all the many years he's been confined here?" "No," replied Ricla, "for there have always been too many eyes watching for me to be able to bargain with the owners of the boats and because I couldn't find a good excuse to give for the purchase." "That's right," said Antonio, "and it wasn't because I didn't trust the seaworthiness of the boats; but now that Heaven has given me this advice I plan to take it, and my beautiful Ricla will be on the lookout for the next time the traders come from the other island. Then, not worrying about the price, she'll buy a boat with all the necessary supplies and equipment, saying she wants it for the reason she already mentioned."

In short, they all agreed to this plan, and when they left that place they were astonished to see the damage the fire and weapons had done. They saw a thousand different kinds of death commonly invented by fury, rage, and anger. Likewise they observed that the surviving barbarians had retreated to their rafts where they were watching the cruel burning of their homeland from afar, and apparently some of them had gone over[1] to the island which had served as a prison for the captives.

Auristela wanted them to go over to the island to see if anyone had been left in the dark dungeon; but it wasn't necessary, for they saw a raft approaching that contained about twenty people whose clothing led them to believe were the miserable prisoners who had been in the dungeon. They reached the shore and kissed the ground, almost seeming to worship the fire. The barbarian who had let them out of the dark jail had told them it was consuming the island and had added that therefore they no longer needed to fear the barbarians.

The people who had been freed earlier gave them a friendly welcome and consoled them as best they could. Some told their woes and others left them unspoken, unable to find words to express them.

Ricla was surprised that there had been a barbarian kind enough to release them and that none of the barbarians who had taken refuge on the rafts had gone over to the prison island. One of the prisoners said that the barbarian who had freed them had told them in Italian all about the calamitous burning of the island, advising them to go over and compensate for their trials with gold and pearls they'd find there, saying that to keep them company and help them plan their escape he'd come over on another raft left on the prison island. The events they related were so varied, so strange, and so unhappy that some of them brought tears to their listeners' eyes while others inspired hearty laughter.

At this point they saw some six boats of the kind Ricla had described coming toward the island. They landed but didn't take out any trading goods, for there were no barbarians on hand to buy them. Ricla arranged to buy all the boats with all their merchandise, though she had no intention of taking the goods. They refused to sell her any more than four of the boats so that two would be left for them to return in. A remarkably generous price was arrived at with very little haggling about such and such being worth this or that. Ricla went to her cave and with the previously mentioned pieces of uncoined gold, paid them all they asked. They gave two boats to the people who had gotten out of the dungeon, while they themselves embarked in the other two; one was filled with all the provisions they could gather along with four of the newly freed people. Meanwhile, Auristela, Periandro, Antonio the father and Antonio the son, along with the beautiful Ricla, the prudent Transila,[2] and the striking Constanza, daughter of Ricla and Antonio, got into the other boat. Auristela wanted to go and say farewell to her dear Cloelia's remains and everyone accompanied her; she wept at the grave and then, shedding tears of grief but also showing signs of happiness, they embarked once again, first kneeling on the beach and asking Heaven with heartfelt and devout prayers to give them a happy voyage and to show them the way they should go.

Periandro's boat acted as flagship for the others to follow and just as they were about to put the oars into the water (they had no sails), a handsome barbarian came down to the water's edge and shouted in Tuscan:[3] "If by chance those of you leaving in those boats are Christians, I beg you by the true God to take this one with you." One of the people in the other boats said: "This barbarian, gentle-

43

men, is the one who let us out of the dungeon. If you want to put the goodwill you seem to have into practice"—this remark was directed to those on the first boat—"it would be well if you repaid him for the good he did us by letting us take him into our company."

On hearing this, Periandro commanded the speaker to return to land in the boat carrying the supplies and pick up the man on shore. This done, they shouted for joy, and taking the oars in their hands happily began their journey.

Chapter Seven of the First Book

The four boats must have sailed four miles more or less when they caught sight of a powerful ship that seemed to be heading straight for them, running before the wind with all its sails set. When he had seen it Periandro said: "This ship is sure to be Arnaldo's, who's returning to find out what's happened to me; I think it would be a very good thing not to see him right now." Periandro had already told Auristela about everything that had happened to him with Arnaldo and the plan the two of them had agreed upon.

Auristela became alarmed, for she didn't want to return to Arnaldo's control, and she had related, though only quickly and in a few words, what had happened to her during the year she was in his power. She didn't like the idea of seeing the two suitors together, for even though Arnaldo could probably be counted on to believe the pretense that she and Periandro were brother and sister, she was still afraid the truth of their relationship might come out and, what's more, what would keep Periandro from being jealous if he found himself face to face with such a powerful rival? For no amount of prudence avails and no amount of loving faithfulness can reassure the love-stricken heart when, to its misfortune, jealous suspicions creep in. But the wind saved her from all these worries for in an instant it turned and blew the sails full in the opposite direction; therefore, quickly and right before their eyes the ship's sails were dropped and then within a short, almost imperceptible space of time hoisted again all the way up the masts, so that the ship began to turn to and run in the opposite direction, moving away from the boats at full speed.

Auristela breathed a sigh of relief and Periandro, too, breathed easy again; but the others traveling in the boats would have liked to

44

go over to the ship that, because of its size, promised more safety for their lives and a happier journey. They would have tried to follow it had they been able, but it was out of sight in less than two hours and they could do nothing but make for an island whose high and snow-covered mountains made it seem near, though in fact it was more than six leagues[1] away. Night had begun to fall and it was already getting dark, but a brisk breeze blowing from astern brought some relief for their arms as they took up the oars again and hurried to reach the island.

It must have been about midnight, as well as Antonio the barbarian could judge from the North Star and the watches,[2] when they reached the island; since the surf was breaking gently on the beach and the pull of the receding waves was nothing to worry about, they brought the boats directly to shore and beached them by hand.

It was such a cold night that they were obliged to seek protection from the icy air, but there was none to be found. Periandro told all the women to get into the lead boat, where by crowding closely together they would be able to take the edge off the cold. They did just that and the men stood guard around the boat, walking back and forth like sentries and waiting for the dawn before sizing up where they were, since for the time being they had no way of knowing whether or not the island was inhabited. As it's only natural for worries to drive away sleep, no one in that apprehensive band could close his eyes; when Antonio the barbarian realized this he asked the Italian barbarian if, to pass the time and take their minds off the discomfort of the terrible night, he would please entertain them by telling his life's story, which couldn't help but be strange and unusual judging by his clothes and the place where they'd picked him up.

"I'll be very glad to do that," answered the Italian barbarian, "though I fear my misfortunes are so many, so novel, and so extraordinary that you won't believe them at all." Periandro replied: "After all that's happened to us we're accustomed and prepared to believe whatever anyone might tell us, even though it might seem more impossible than true to life."

"Let's gather around here," responded the barbarian, "right beside the boat where the ladies are; perhaps the sound of my voice will put one or two of them to sleep, while perhaps another, banishing drowsiness, will be led to show me pity, for it's a relief to someone telling his misfortunes to see or hear that there's someone else who shares his sorrow." "I for one," answered Ricla from inside the boat, "despite my sleepiness, have tears of compassion to offer for your short luck and long-lasting hardships."

45

Auristela repeated almost the same sentiments. And so all the men gathered around the boat and began listening attentively to what was being said by the seeming barbarian, who began his story as follows.

Chapter Eight

Where Rutilio Tells the Story of His Life

My name is Rutilio, my homeland Siena, one of the most famous Italian cities, and my profession, dancing master, in which I could have been unmatched and highly successful had I so wished. There was a rich gentleman in Siena to whom Heaven had given a daughter more beautiful than bright; he was trying to marry her off to a gentleman from Florence, and in order to present her to him adorned with all the social graces—in place of the mental ones she lacked—he asked me to teach her to dance. For refinement, elegance, and bodily grace are shown off to better advantage in modest dances than in other actions, and it's a good thing for illustrious ladies to know how to dance in order to be prepared for those obligatory social situations they'll find themselves in. I began to teach her the movements of the body but instead I moved her soul; since she wasn't wise, as I've said, she surrendered her soul to mine and luck, which had set my misfortunes in motion long before, arranged for me to take her out of her father's house and carry her away to Rome so we could fully enjoy each other. But since love doesn't sell its pleasures cheaply and punishment dogs the frightened heels of indiscretion, the two of us were caught on the road by officers of the law her father had sent to find us. Her defense and mine, too, was to claim I had my wife with me and that she was traveling with her husband, but this was so ineffective that it not only didn't lessen my guilt but compelled, moved, and convinced the judge to sentence me to death.

"I was placed on death row with others already condemned for crimes not nearly so honorable as mine. I was visited in my cell by a woman said to be imprisoned for *fatucherie,* which in Castilian means witchcraft. She'd been let out of her cell by the wife of the warden who'd taken her to her own room so with herbs and magic spells she could cure one of her daughters of an illness the doctors weren't able to heal. Finally, to make my story short—for there's no account, however good it may be, that seems so if it's long—seeing myself tied with the noose around my neck and sentenced to death, with no stay or hope of reprieve, I said 'yes' to what the sorceress asked me, which was to be her husband if she got me safely through that ordeal. She told me not to worry, for that very night following the day this conversation was taking place she would break the chains and the stocks and, in spite of any and all obstacles, would set me free and put me in a place where my enemies couldn't harm me even though they might be numerous and powerful.

"I thought of her not as a sorceress but rather an angel sent by Heaven for my salvation. I waited for night and in the midst of its silence she came to me and told me to take hold of the end of a cane she placed in my hand and to follow her. I felt somewhat apprehensive, but since there was a lot at stake I moved my feet to follow her and found that they were free from shackles and chains; the doors throughout the prison were wide open, and the prisoners and guards were sunk in a very deep sleep.

"When we got out into the street my guide spread a cloak out on the ground and ordered me to step onto it; she told me to be of good courage and to stop praying. I immediately took that as a bad sign and realized she intended to carry me through the air, and although as a well-instructed Christian I've been taught to treat all this witchcraft as a trick—which, after all, is the right way to approach it—still, the threat of death, as I've said, made me push everything aside. As a result, I stepped into the middle of the cloak and she, with no further ado, began muttering some phrases I couldn't understand and the cloak began to rise into the air. I was seized by a powerful fear and in my heart there wasn't a single saint in the whole litany to whom I didn't call out for help.

"She must have realized I was afraid and suspected I was praying for aid, for she again commanded me to give it up. 'Oh, what a miserable mess I'm in!' I said. 'What possible good can I hope for if I'm forbidden to pray to God, from whom all blessings flow?' In short, I closed my eyes and let myself be carried off by devils, for surely they and no others act as witches' steeds. Thus, it seems, I'd flown for four hours or a little more when I found myself in the twilight of dawn in an unknown land.

"The cloak touched the ground and my guide said to me: 'You're in a place, my friend Rutilio, where no one in the whole human race will be able to harm you.' After saying this, she began to embrace me in a manner less than modest. I pushed her away from

47

me and saw, as nearly as I could make out, that I was being embraced by something in the shape of a wolf,[1] the sight of which chilled my soul, confused my senses, and undid my great courage. But as it often happens that during the greatest dangers the slight hope of conquering them draws desperate strength from the spirit, what little hope and strength I had put a knife that by chance I carried in my clothes into my hand, and with fury and rage I drove it into the chest of the woman I thought was a she-wolf. Falling to the ground, she changed back from that shape and I beheld the wretched sorceress dead and bleeding.

"Consider, ladies and gentlemen, how all this left me—in an unknown land and with no one to guide me. For many hours I waited for daybreak but it never completely arrived; there was no sign on the horizon that the sun was, in fact, going to come up. I got away from the corpse because having it near filled me with fear and horror. Time after time I raised my eyes to Heaven and studied the movement of the stars; judging by the course I'd seen them run, it seemed to me that it should already be day.

"While in this confused state, I thought I heard the sound of conversation coming from some people walking nearby, and it indeed turned out to be the case. Going out to meet them, I asked them in my Tuscan language to tell me what land I was in. One of them, also speaking Italian, answered me, 'This land is Norway.[2] But, who are you asking this, and in a language very few people in these parts understand?'

"'I'm a miserable wretch,' I responded, 'who by fleeing death has fallen into its hands.' And in a few words I told him about my trip, even including the sorceress' death. The man I was talking with proved to be sympathetic and said to me, 'My good man, you can give countless thanks to Heaven for having saved you from the power of the wicked witches that abound in these northern lands. It's said they turn themselves into wolves, males as well as females, for there are sorcerers and enchanters of both sexes. How this can be, I don't know, and as a Catholic Christian I don't believe it, but experience demonstrates just the opposite. As nearly as I can understand it, all these transformations are illusions created by the Devil—with God's permission—as punishment for the abominable sins of these accursed people.'

"I asked him what time it might be because it seemed to me night was lasting too long and day was never coming. He answered that in those remote areas the year was divided into four seasons: there were three months of dark night during which the sun didn't appear at all; there were three months of morning twilight during which there was neither night nor day; there were another three months of continuous daylight during which the sun never set; and three more of evening twilight. At that time they were in the season of morning twilight, so waiting for the sun to shine brightly was an empty hope, just as it would be useless for me to expect to return soon to my homeland, unless it would be during the season of the long day when ships leave those regions for England, France, and Spain with certain kinds of trading goods.

"He asked me if I knew some trade with which I could earn my keep while waiting for the time to return to my homeland. I told him I was a dancer, a very nimble fellow, and quite skillful at juggling and sleight-of-hand. He laughed heartily and told me those skills or occupations—or whatever I might want to call them—just weren't practiced in Norway or in any of those parts. He asked me whether I might know the goldsmith's craft and I replied that I had the ability to learn whatever he might teach me. 'Then come along with me, brother, though first it would be a good idea to bury this miserable creature.' We did so, and he took me to a city where everyone went around the streets with burning wooden torches in their hands, carrying on the business affairs that most concerned them. On the way I asked him how or when he'd come to that land and if he were truly Italian.

"He replied that one of his ancestors had married there when he came from Italy on business, had taught his language to his sons, and it had passed down through all his descendants until it had come to him, one of the great-, great-, great-, great-grandsons. 'And so, since my family has lived here so long, and moved by the affection of my children and wife, I've stayed and become flesh and blood with these people, not remembering either Italy or the relatives my parents said they had there.'

"If I were to describe now the house I went into, the wife and children I found there, the servants—of which he had many—the great wealth, the kind reception and hospitality they showed me, I'd have to go on indefinitely. Suffice it to say, in short, that I learned his trade and within a few months I was paying for my food with my work.

"By then the season of the long day arrived and my master and teacher—for I can call him that—ordered a large quantity of his merchandise taken to other islands, some nearby, others quite distant. I went with him as much out of curiosity as to sell some of the things I had acquired, and on that trip I saw some things that amazed and startled me, as well as others that made me laugh and feel glad. I saw customs and observed ceremonies never before seen nor practiced by any other people. Finally, at the end of two months we ran into a storm lasting about forty days, after which we came to the island we just left today and ran upon some rocks where our vessel broke up, leaving no one on board alive except me."

Chapter Nine

Where Rutilio Continues the Story of His Life

The first thing in sight, before I saw anything else, was a barbarian hanged from a tree, which made me realize I was in a land of savages. My fright immediately brought to mind a thousand kinds of death, and not knowing what to do I feared and expected to meet each one or all of them together. In short, since necessity, as the saying goes, is the mother of invention, something very extraordinary occurred to me, and it was this: I took the barbarian down from the tree and, having taken off all my clothes and burying them in the sand, I dressed myself in his, which fit me well enough since they had only the shape of animal skins, not sewn or cut to size but just wrapped around the body, as you've seen. To keep from speaking my native language and to avoid being recognized as a stranger because of it, I pretended to be deaf and dumb; then with this artifice, which included capering and jumping in the air, I began to walk inland.

"A short time later I came upon a great number of barbarians who surrounded me, and right away some of them began to ask me in their language—I learned later—who I was, what I was called, where I was coming from, and where I was going. I answered by keeping silent and making all the most obvious signs I could; then I repeated the leaps and multiplied the capers. I walked away from the crowd but was followed by the boys, who wouldn't leave me alone no matter where I went. By using this strategy I passed as a barbarian and a mute, and the boys, since they enjoyed seeing me jump and gesture, would give me some of their food. Living this way, I spent three years among them and could easily have lived all the rest of my life like that without being found out. I payed careful and curious attention to their language, learning a great deal of it; I heard of the prophetic plan to insure the continuation of their kingdom as foretold by an ancient and wise barbarian to whom they all gave great credence. I've seen men sacrificed to put the prophecy's fulfillment to the test and have seen maidens bought for the same purpose, up to the time of the burning of the island, which you, ladies and gentlemen, have seen. I kept away from the flames and went to inform the prisoners in the dungeon, where I'm sure you were all once kept. I saw these boats, hastened to the shore, and there my supplications found a place in your generous hearts. You picked me up in the boats and for that mercy I give you countless thanks; now I hope for the same mercy from Heaven. Since it's saved us all from so much suffering, most surely it shall give us good fortune on this journey we're attempting." Here Rutilio came to the end of his story, which left his listeners amazed and delighted.

The day turned out to be bitterly cold, unsettled, and with sure signs of snow. Auristela gave Periandro the things Cloelia had given her the night she died, which were two balls of wax; one, they saw, covered a diamond cross so rich they didn't even try to appraise it for fear that very act would minimize its value, and the other covered two round pearls, also of inestimable worth. Seeing these jewels the others realized that Auristela and Periandro were important people, although this truth was even better expressed by their gracious manner and pleasant ways.

At daybreak Antonio the barbarian went a little way inland on the island, but he found nothing more than mountains and ridges of snow. Returning to the boats he reported that the island was uninhabited and said it would be wise to leave then and there to look for another place to take refuge from the menacing cold and where they might provide themselves with the supplies they would soon need. They quickly threw the boats into the water, everyone embarked, and they turned the prows toward another island visible not far away. As they were moving forward at the slow pace made possible by two oars, for that's all each boat had, a voice was heard coming from one of the other two boats, a voice so soft and sweet that it made them listen with rapt attention. They all noticed—but especially Antonio the barbarian, who knew Portuguese very well— that the song was being sung in that language. The voice fell silent but soon after began singing again, this time in Castilian, with no other accompanying instruments than the oars that moved the boats smoothly through the calm sea, and this was the song they heard:

Calm sea, fair wind, the bright and shining stars,
a path untried but one most sweet and sure—
all these will lead our rare and wondrous ship
to find a pleasant, safe, and spacious port.

Our ship fears neither Scylla nor Charybdis,
nor does it stay its pure and virtuous course
for fear of dangers that the sea may hide,
but steers its way through open waters wide.

But if your hopes for anchor in this port
should start to waver, hesitate, or pale,
only a fool would think of shifting sail.

For love is steadfast enemy to change
and only he who's constant as a gem
comes safely to a rich and worthy end.[1]

As the voice became quiet, Ricla the barbarian said, "The singer of that song must be very lazy and idle to raise his voice to the winds at a time like this." But Periandro and Auristela judged the singer differently, believing him more lovestruck than idle; for lovers feel a common bond and make friends easily with those they know are suffering their same disease. And so, with the permission of the others traveling in their boat (though it wasn't necessary to ask it), they had the singer come aboard, both to enjoy his voice at close range and to find out what had befallen him, since anyone singing at such a time either felt deeply or was beyond feeling.

The boats came together, the musician crossed over to Periandro's, and everyone in it gave him a warm welcome. As the musician came aboard he said, half in Portuguese and half in Castilian, "I'm grateful to Heaven, and to you, ladies and gentlemen, as well as to my voice, for this change and improvement in vessel, though I believe I'll soon relieve it of the burden of my body, for the pain I feel in my soul keeps warning me that my life is coming to an end." "Heaven will make things better for you," responded Periandro, "for I'm living proof that trials can't kill a person."

"Hope that can be checked and destroyed by misfortune," said Auristela at this point, "isn't really hope at all, for just as light shines more brightly in darkness, so hope should be more steadfast in trials. Despair is the act of a cowardly heart and there's no greater evidence of cowardice or meanness than when a person, no matter how sorely tried, surrenders to hopelessness."

"The soul," said Periandro, "keeping a stiff upper lip and even when caught by the skin of its teeth—if I can put it that way—must never stop hoping for rescue, for that would be to do an injustice to God (to whom none must ever be done), by putting a limit and boundary to his infinite mercies." "That's all true," responded the musician, "and I believe it, in spite of and notwithstanding the many experiences that have meant trouble for me during the course of my life."

Meanwhile, they did not stop rowing during this conversation, and so, two hours before nightfall they reached another uninhabited island. It wasn't devoid of trees, however, for there were a great many of them full of fruit that was fit to eat, though past its season and rather dry. They all leaped ashore and beached the boats; then they quickly hurried to break off branches of trees and make a large hut to shelter themselves from the cold of the coming night. They also made a fire by rubbing two dry sticks together, a common and well-known technique. Because they were all working, it wasn't long before they saw the rough structure raised; everyone gathered inside, and with the fire making up for the discomfort of the place, the hut seemed to them a spacious palace. They satisfied their hunger and then would have settled down to sleep if Periandro's desire to hear the musician's story hadn't intervened, for he asked him, if it were possible, to tell them about his misfortunes, for, indeed, it couldn't have been good fortune that had brought him to those parts. The singer was obliging and therefore, without having to be begged, said:

Chapter Ten

What the Love-Stricken Portuguese Told Them

With fewer words than might seem possible I'll put an end to my story, as well as to my life, if I'm to believe a certain dream that troubled my spirit last night. I, ladies and gentlemen, am Portuguese, of noble blood, rich in worldly goods and not poor in the natural gifts. My name is Manuel de Sousa Coutinho,[1] my home is Lisbon and I'm a soldier by profession. Very close to the estate of my parents, adjoining it, in fact, was that of another gentleman of the ancient Pereira lineage who had an only daughter, the sole heir to all his goods, which were many, and the comfort and hope of her parents' prosperity. Due to her noble family, her riches, and her beauty, she was sought after by the best men in the kingdom of Portugal. As her closest neighbor, I had the best opportunity to see her. I observed her, made her acquaintance, and adored her with a hope founded more on doubts than on any certainty that she might become my wife. To save time and because I knew that words of love, promises, and gifts would have little effect on her, I decided that a relative of mine should ask her parents for her hand in marriage for me, since we didn't differ at all in lineage, worldly goods, or even in age.

"The answer brought back was that their daughter Leonora wasn't yet of marriageable age, and that I should let two years pass. They gave their word not to make any arrangement for their daughter during that entire time without informing me. This first blow struck at the shoulders of my patience and the shield of my hopes. Nevertheless, it didn't stop me from courting her publicly, though within the bounds of my honorable intentions, which were soon known to the entire city. But she, taking refuge in the fortress of her prudence and in the inner chambers of her modesty, accepted my courting both with moderation and the permission of her parents, making it known that even though she didn't return my feelings, at least she didn't reject them.

"It happened that at this time my king named me captain-general of one of the forts he has in Barbary,[2] a position of distinction and trust. The day of my departure arrived; the fact that it wasn't also that of my death shows there's no separation that can kill nor any pain that can destroy. I spoke with her father and once again had him give me his word to wait the two years. Being understanding, he took pity on me and allowed me to bid farewell to his wife and his daughter Leonora, who, in her mother's company, came out to the great hall to see me. With her came modesty, grace, and silence.

"I was overcome when I saw such beauty so near me; I wanted to speak but my voice caught in my throat and my tongue stuck to the roof of my mouth. I didn't know what to do, nor could I do anything but keep still and let silence express my confusion. Her father, seeing the state I was in and being as polite as he was understanding, embraced me and said: 'On days of departure, Señor Manuel de Sousa, the tongue should never say too much, and it may be that this silence speaks more in your favor than any other eloquence. May you go forth to perform your duty and return in the allotted time, for I shall never fail in anything related to my promise to you. My daugh-

54

ter Leonora is obedient, my wife wishes to please me, and I intend to do what I have said. It seems to me that by counting on these three things you can expect to obtain your heart's desire.'

"All these words stuck in my memory and were so stamped on my soul that I haven't forgotten nor will I forget them as long as I live. Neither the beautiful Leonora nor her mother spoke a word to me; neither could I, as I've said, say a thing. I departed for Barbary and for two years performed my duty to my king's satisfaction. I returned to Lisbon and found that Leonora's fame and beauty had traveled beyond the limits of the city and the kingdom, stretching throughout Castile and other places from which came delegations of princes and gentlemen who aspired to marry her. But her will was so tied to that of her parents that she showed no interest in whether or not she was being courted. Finally, seeing that the two-year term was up, I returned to beg her father to give me her hand in marriage. But oh, what grief! Still, I musn't dwell too long on these matters, for death is knocking at my life's door and I fear it will leave me no time to relate my misfortunes; yet, if death truly is waiting for me, I won't think my misfortunes so unfortunate!

"Finally one day they told me they'd give me my beloved Leonora on an approaching Sunday and I almost died of happiness at the news. I invited my relatives, informed my friends, made preparations for festivities, sent gifts, and did everything necessary and possible to show I was getting married and that Leonora was to be my wife. The day came and, accompanied by all the best people of the city, I went to a convent called the 'Mother of God.' They told me that my bride had been waiting for me there since the day before, because it had been her wish to celebrate her betrothal in that convent with the permission of the archbishop of the city."

The aggrieved gentlemen paused for a little while as if to catch his breath before continuing his story, and then said: "I arrived at the convent, which was royally and magnificently decorated. Almost all the illustrious people of the kingdom, including many of the most important ladies of the city, were there waiting and came out to welcome me. The sanctuary was overflowing with the music of voices and instruments as the incomparable Leonora came out the cloister door accompanied by the prioress and many other nuns. She was dressed in white satin, her long skirt was slashed in the Castilian fashion, and the slashes were filled with large rich pearls. The skirt was lined with green cloth of gold.[3] Her hair, worn loose about her shoulders, was so blond it outdazzled the sun and so long it almost kissed the ground. Some were of the opinion that the belt, necklace, and rings she wore were worth a kingdom, and again I repeat that she came out looking so beautiful, so costly, so elegant, and so richly dressed and adorned that she was the envy of all the women and the admiration of all the men. As for myself, I can only say I was so impressed by the sight that I felt unworthy of her; moreover, it seemed that even had I been the emperor of the whole world, I wouldn't have deserved her.

"A kind of platform had been made in the center of the church where our vows were to be solemnized freely and without hindrance. The beautiful maiden went up on the platform first where everyone could see her noble grace. To all the eyes gazing upon her she seemed like a beautiful dawn, or, as the ancient stories say, like pure Diana in the forest; but some of those present, I think, were wise enough to feel she could be compared only to herself. I went up on the platform, thinking I was going up to my Heaven, and kneeling before her, showed that I practically worshiped her. Then in one resounding voice many in the church said, 'Live long and happy years in the world, oh happiest and fairest lovers! May beautiful children soon grace your table like a crown, and as you walk together through life may your love grow and extend to your children's children. May the dwelling place of your hearts never know furious jealousy nor doubting suspicions. May envy surrender at your feet and may good fortune never leave your house.'

"All these blessings and holy good wishes filled my soul with happiness, seeing that everyone was so pleased at my good fortune. At this point the beautiful Leonora took me by the hand, and as we were standing side by side she raised her voice slightly and said to me, 'You know very well, Señor Manuel de Sousa, that my father gave you his word not to promise me to anyone for two years, to be counted from the day you asked for me as your wife; and also, if I remember correctly, seeing myself pursued by your entreaties and obliged by the countless favors you'd done me, more because of your courtesy than because I deserved them, I told you I'd take no other husband on earth but you. My father has kept his word to you, as you can see, and I, also, want to keep mine. Therefore, because I know that deception, even when done for honorable and beneficial purposes, has something of treachery about it when protracted and delayed, I want to tell you right now the truth about a treason you'll feel I've committed against you. I, dear sir, am married, and there is no way, since my husband is alive, I can marry another. I'm not leaving you for another here on earth, but for one in Heaven, who is Jesus Christ, true God and man. He is my bridegroom, I gave Him my word before I gave it to you. I gave it to Him without deception and of my own free will; I gave it to you with hypocrisy, with no sincere intent. I confess that if I were to choose a husband on earth, none could equal you, but having Heaven to choose from, who is better than God?[4] If this seems like treason or unjust treatment, give me whatever punishment you wish and call me any name that comes to your mind, for there is no death, promise, or threat that can separate me from my crucified husband.'

"She stopped talking and at the same time the prioress and the other nuns began to disrobe her and to cut off her lovely locks. I was struck dumb; I was careful to curb the tears that came to my eyes so as to show no sign of weakness, and, kneeling once again before her, I pressed her hand to my lips and she threw her arms around my neck with Christian compassion. I stood up and, raising my voice so everyone could hear me, said, 'Maria optimam partem elegit.'[5]

"After saying this, I went down from the platform and accompanied by my friends I returned home, where I almost lost my mind by constantly going over and over this strange happening. Now, for the same reason, I'm about to lose my life." And heaving a hugh sigh, his soul left his body and he fell to the floor.

Chapter Eleven of the First Book

Periandro hurried over to examine him and found that he was in fact dead, and this sad and unheard-of event filled everyone with confusion and amazement. "This final dream," said Auristela then, "has excused this gentleman from telling us what happened to him last night and the dangers, surely as desperate as they were strange, through which he came to the barbarians' prison and to such a disastrous end." To this Antonio the barbarian added: "Is there by some strange chance anyone miserable only through his own misfortune? Afflictions always bring companions with them, and wherever they all turn up so do trials that only cease when they end the life of the afflicted."

Right away they gave the order to bury him as best they could. His own suit served as his shroud, the snow as earth, and for a cross they used the one they found over his heart on a scapular[1] of the Order of Christ,[2] and although he wore its habit it wasn't necessary to find this sign of honor on him to recognize his nobility, for his serious demeanor and intelligent conversation made it perfectly clear. His burial was accompanied by many tears, for compassion used its ability to bring them to the eyes of everyone present.

By this time it was dawn and they put the boats back in the water, for it seemed a calm and gentle sea was awaiting them; between feelings of sadness and happiness, between fear and hope, they renewed their course without knowing exactly where they were going. All the seas in that region are practically covered with islands, all or the majority of them uninhabited, while the inhabited ones shelter a backward and half-barbaric people, scarcely civilized, with hard and arrogant hearts. Still, despite all this, our travelers hoped to find an island to take them in, for they thought any people who might dwell in the area couldn't possibly be as cruel as the mountains of snow and the hard, rugged cliffs of the islands they had left behind.

They sailed for ten more days without reaching any harbor, beach, or shelter at all, leaving behind them on both sides, right and left, small islands that showed no signs of settlement. Setting their gaze on a great mountain now in sight, they struggled with might and main to reach it as soon as possible, for their boats had begun to leak and provisions would soon run out. Finally, less with their own arms' help and more with Heaven's, as one ought to believe, they arrived at the coveted island and saw two people walking along the shore. In a loud voice Transila called out and asked what land it was, who governed it, and if the people were Catholic Christians.

In a language she understood they answered that the island was called Golandia[3] and it belonged to Catholics, even though so few people occupied it that it was virtually uninhabited; all of them lived in a single building that also served as an inn for people arriving at the harbor located behind a huge rock that they pointed out. "And if you, whoever you may be, would like to stock up on needed supplies, then keep us in sight and we'll get you into port."

The people on the boats gave thanks to God and though still at sea followed those guiding them on land; on rounding the rocks pointed out to them they saw a sheltered bay that might be called a harbor, and in it as many as ten or twelve vessels, some of them small, others medium-sized, and even some large ones. They were delighted to see them, for it gave them some hope of changing vessels and confidence that they could safely travel on to other places.

They touched land, and people from the ships as well as from the inn came out to greet them. Auristela, wearing the dress and adornments that Periandro had worn when Arnaldo had sold him to the barbarians, went ashore on the shoulders of Periandro and the two barbarians, father and son. Along with her came the striking Transila and the beautiful barbarian Constanza with her mother Ricla, and all the rest of the people on the boats also accompanied the handsome band.

This beautiful troop caused such admiration, surprise, and astonishment among those on the sea and on land that they all got down on the ground and seemed to be worshiping Auristela. Everyone looked at her in silence and with such respect that they were unable to move their tongues, so absorbed were they in gazing. The beautiful Transila, seeing they understood her language, was the first to break the silence, saying to them, "Our fortune, adverse until today, has brought us to this, your kind reception. By our dress and by our gentleness you can tell we seek peace and not war, for neither women nor men in distress do battle. Take us, friends, under your protection and into your ships, for the boats that carried us to this place have given up their daring ways and will never return to the restless sea. If we can exchange gold or silver here for needed provisions then you will be well paid for whatever you may provide us, and no matter how high your selling price, we'll accept it as though it were a gift."

Though miraculously strange to say, someone who seemed to be from the ships answered in Spanish: "Anyone would be foolish, indeed, to doubt that what you say is the truth, beautiful lady, for though lies can be hidden and harm disguised behind a mask of truth and goodness, it's impossible for them to find a place and take shelter within beauty such as yours. The host of this inn is most courteous, though no more so than all the people on these ships. Choose whether you prefer to go on board the ships or come into the inn, for in both will you be welcomed and treated as your importance deserves." Then, seeing, or rather hearing his language spoken, Antonio the barbarian said, "Since Heaven has brought us to a place where the sweet language of my country sounds in my ears, I can almost believe my misfortunes are at an end. Let's go to the lodge, ladies and gentlemen, and after resting a little while we'll be better able to return to our journey in greater safety than we've had so far."

At this point a cabin boy who was perched above a topsail shouted in English, "Ship ahoy, with all sails spread and sea and wind astern, heading straight for the harbor!" Everyone got excited and right where they were, without moving a step, set themselves to wait for the vessel that could be seen approaching. When it was closer they saw its swelling sails were spanned by some red crosses and recognized that a flag flying from the end of the yardarm of the topsail carried the coat-of-arms of England painted on it. As it arrived two pieces of heavy artillery were fired and then perhaps as many as twenty muskets. From the land, where they had no artillery with which to respond, they signaled back with happy voices and signs of peace.

Chapter Twelve of the First Book

Wherein Is Related Who the People on the Ship Were and Where They Came from

After the salutes had been given from both the ship and the shore, as has been described, those on board dropped anchor and launched a boat into the water. The first person to leap into it, following four sailors who furnished it with carpets and set themselves at the oars, was an old gentleman who appeared to be about sixty years of age, dressed in a robe of black velvet that reached down to his feet; it was lined with black plush and belted with a silk sash called a colony; on his head he wore a tall, pointed hat, which also seemed to be made of plush. Next to get down into the skiff was a handsome and lively young man about twenty-four years old; he was dressed like a sailor, but in black velvet with a golden sword in his hand and a dagger at his belt. Then, as if they were throwing them from the ship into the boat, they pushed in a man loaded down with chains and a woman entangled and bound by the same fetters; he was around forty years old, she more than fifty; he was feisty and testy, she melancholy and sad. The sailors began to row the skiff. They promptly ran aground then brought ashore the old man, the young man, and the two prisoners on their shoulders and on those of some other musket soldiers who had been traveling on the ship.

Transila, who like the others had been very carefully observing those arriving in the boat, turned to Auristela and said: "If you please, lady, cover my face with that veil you have over your arm, for unless I guess wrong, I know some of the people arriving in that boat, and they know me." Auristela did what she asked, and at that moment the group from the boat came up to them, everyone greeting each other politely.

The old man in plush went straight to Transila saying, "If my science doesn't deceive me and luck isn't against me, then good fortune must be mine in this happy discovery." And no sooner said than done, he lifted the veil from Transila's face and then fainted dead away into her open arms that she held out for him so he wouldn't collapse on the ground. You can believe beyond any doubt that such an unusual and unexpected event astonished everyone present, and they were astounded even further to hear Transila say, "Oh my dear father! How can you be here? What has brought your venerable gray head and your tired years out here to lands so far from your own?"

"What else could bring him out here," said the lively young man at this moment, "but to search for his good fortune, which is lost without you? Both he and I, my sweet lady and wife, come searching for our North Star, which will lead us to the harbor of our rest. But since thanks to Heaven, we've now found it, help your father Mauricio come to, my lady, and let me share in his happiness; welcome him as your father and me as your lawful husband." Mauricio did come to, but Transila promptly fainted. Auristela stepped forward to help her, but Ladislao—this was her husband's name—didn't presume to go up to her since he respected her too much for that. However, since fainting spells produced by happy and unexpected events either kill instantly or don't last long, Transila was unconscious for only a short time.

The owner of the inn or lodging said, "Come inside, all of you, where it's more comfortable and not as cold as out here, and where you can tell each other your stories." They took his advice and went off to the inn that they found to be large enough to lodge a whole fleet. The two people in chains went in with their feet linked together while the musketmen, coming along as guards, helped them carry their chains. Some of the people went back to their ships, quickly and gladly bringing back what good things they had to offer. They lit a fire, set the tables, and before doing anything else satisfied their hunger, though more with several kinds of fish than with much meat, which was represented only by the flesh of the many birds they raise in those parts. They are grown in such a strange way, so odd and curious, that I'm obliged to describe it:

They sink some sticks into the seashore at the water's edge and between the rocks in pools that fill up with water. In a short time those parts of the sticks covered by water turn to stone, while the parts out of the water rot and corrode. This rotting material engenders a tiny bird that flies to land, grows large, and becomes so very tasty that it's one of the finest foods eaten there. The greatest abundance of these is found in the provinces of Hibernia and Ireland,[1] and the bird is called a barnacle.[2]

Everyone's desire to hear the stories of the new arrivals made the meal seem long, but when it was over old Mauricio slapped the table loudly as a signal that he wanted everyone to pay careful attention to him. They all became quiet, silence sealed their lips, and curiosity opened their ears; seeing this, Mauricio raised his voice to give the following account: "I was born on an island, one of seven near that of Hibernia, and my ancestry had a beginning just as ancient as that of the Mauricios,[3] a name synonymous with the highest praise. I am a Catholic Christian and not one of those beggars who go around looking for the true faith in other people's opinions.[4] My parents brought me up in the study of arms as well as letters—if one can say that arms are studied. I am a devotee of the science of judicial astrology, for which my name has acquired a certain fame. Having come of age to take a wife, I married a beautiful and important woman of my city, with whom I had this daughter you see before you. I followed the customs of my country, at least insofar as they seemed to be reasonable, while I gave the appearance of following those that didn't, for sometimes pretense is to one's advantage. This girl grew up in my own shadow, for two years after she was born she lost her mother and I lost someone to care for me in my old age. The duties of raising my daughter were too much for me, so to free myself of this responsibility—which is a heavy burden for tired, old shoulders to bear—when she had almost reached the age to be given a husband as her support and companion, I did just that. And the one I chose for her was this good-looking youth called Ladislao here at my side, having first obtained the consent of my daughter, for it seems wise and even in their own best interests for parents to find husbands for their daughters in harmony with the girls' likes and wishes, since they're not giving them a companion for just one day but for all the rest of their lives. By not handling it in this manner, thousands of difficulties have been produced, are produced, and shall be produced, most of them leading to disaster.

"You should know, then, that in my country there's a custom, the worst among many bad ones. Once a marriage has been arranged and the wedding day has arrived, in a large house designated for this purpose the bride and groom gather with their brothers and sisters, if they have them, and all their close relatives on both sides along with the city officials, some to act as witnesses and others to be the executioners, which I can and should call them. The bride is in an elegant chamber waiting for something I don't know how to describe

without my tongue stammering in shame. She's waiting, I was saying, for the groom's brothers, if he has any, and some of his closest
male relatives to come in one by one to pick the flowers of her garden
and paw the bouquet she would have wanted to save untouched for
her husband. It's a damned barbarous custom that goes against all
laws of honor and decency! For what more priceless dowry can a
maiden offer than being one; and what purity can and should please
a husband more than that which his wife brings to him complete?
Chastity always goes hand and hand with modesty and modesty with
chastity. If either one or the other of them begins to crumble and
collapse into ruin, then the whole edifice of beauty will fall to the
ground and be considered cheap and repulsive. I had often tried to
convince my people to stop this monstrous custom, but as soon as
I'd try, I'd run head on into many death threats and so came to understand the truth of the well-known old adage that habit is second
nature and kicking it hurts like Hell. Finally, my daughter had been
shut away in the private room I've mentioned, awaiting her ruin; but
when one of her husband's brothers tried to go in to begin the disgraceful business, just imagine her coming out into the great hall
where everyone was gathered, holding a spear before her in both
hands. She was as fair as the sun, as brave as a lioness, and as angry
as a tigress."

Old Mauricio had gotten this far in his story, everyone hanging
on his words, when Transila, caught up again in the same spirit that
had moved her at the time of the original act and event her father
was describing, rose to her feet with her voice trembling in anger.
With her face as red as glowing coals and her eyes like fire—that is,
with a look that could have rendered her less beautiful if distressing events had the power to impair great beauty—taking the words
right out of her father's mouth she said those found in the following
chapter.

Chapter Thirteen

Where Transila Continues the
Story which Her Father Began

I came out," said Transila, "into the great hall, as my father has said, and looking all around, in a loud and angry voice I cried out, 'Come forward, you whose indecent and barbarous customs are at odds with those practiced in any well-ordered republic. You, I say, who are more lustful than religious, who under the appearance and protection of empty ceremonies like to cultivate other peoples' fields without the permission of the legitimate owners. Here I stand before you, you who are badly misguided and worse informed; come, come on, for reason, placed on the point of this spear, will defend my position and sap the strength of your evil thoughts, the enemies of decency and morality.'

"On saying this I sprang into the middle of the crowd and breaking through it went out into the street accompanied only by my anger, then continued on down to the shore. There, with a thousand possibilities running through my head in that moment, I rolled them all into one and threw myself into a small boat that Heaven had doubtless provided for me. Seizing two small oars I put as much distance between myself and the shore as I could; but seeing that they were hurrying to follow me in many better-equipped and more powerfully driven boats and that it was impossible for me to escape, I dropped the oars and again took up my spear intending to wait and let them take me by force, thinking that even if I didn't lose my life I'd first avenge my injury on whomever I could. I repeat that Heaven, moved by my misfortune, quickened the breeze and, without my moving the oars, carried the boat out to sea until it came to a current or stream that practically snatched it out of the water, carrying it farther out to sea and dashing the hopes of those coming to overtake me, for they didn't dare enter the raging current prevailing in that part of the sea."

"That's true," said her husband Ladislao at this point, "but since you were taking away my soul, I couldn't help but follow you. Night overtook us and we lost you from sight; we also lost even the hope of finding you alive, unless it would be on the tongues of fame, which from that moment would take charge of celebrating your heroic deed for all eternity."

"The fact is, then," continued Transila, "that night a wind blew from the sea and carried me to land. On the shore I found some fishermen who kindly took me in and gave me refuge, even offering me a husband if I didn't have one, and I think it wouldn't have been with the conditions put on me by the husband from whom I was fleeing. But human greed, which rules and has its dominion even among the rocks and reefs of the sea and in hard and uncivilized hearts, crept that night into those of the rustic fishermen; they plotted among themselves that, since I was the prisoner of all of them and couldn't be divided into pieces to be shared, they'd sell me to some pirates they'd sighted that afternoon not very far from their fishing grounds. I probably could have offered them more than they got from the pirates for me, but I didn't want to be in any way indebted to anyone from my barbarous land; so at dawn when the pirates had arrived, they sold me for I don't know how much, having first stripped me of all my bridal jewels. All I do know and can tell you is that the pirates treated me better than my own countrymen; they told me not to be melancholy for they weren't taking me away to be a slave but rather to a place where I had hope of becoming a queen and even mistress of all the universe, if the barbarians of that island weren't lying in certain prophecies of theirs much discussed throughout the world.

"How I arrived there, the reception the barbarians gave me, how I learned not only their language during the time I've been away from you, but their rituals, ceremonies, and customs, including the subject of their vain prophecies, my meeting these people I'm traveling with, the burning of the island, now reduced to ashes, and our being freed, are all things I'll talk about at another time. But enough has been said for the present and I want to give my father a chance to tell what change of fortune has brought him here to turn my luck around when I least expected it." Transila finished speaking at this point, everyone hanging on her deft words and admiring her extreme beauty, second only to Auristela's.

Her father Mauricio then said: "You already know, my lovely Transila, dearest daughter, that among my many enjoyable and praiseworthy studies and intellectual pursuits I was particularly attracted by judicial astrology, it being the sort of pursuit that when successful satisfies the natural desire all men have to know not only everything about the past and the present but also about the future. Seeing then that you were lost, I noted the exact point in time, observed the stars, looked at the planets' aspects, and identified the signs and houses necessary for my work to produce what I desired, for no science deceives if it's truly science. Deception lies in the person who hasn't mastered it, and this is especially true in the science of astrology, because the velocity of the heavens carries all the stars along and they don't influence here the same way they do there nor there the same as here. And thus, if the judicial astrologer is sometimes correct in his conclusions, it's because he sticks to what's most probable and likely on the basis of past experience. Therefore, the best astrologer in the world (although he, too, often makes mistakes) is the Devil, because he predicts the future not only from the science he knows but also from premises and conjecture; since he has long experience with previous happenings and so much knowledge of present events, it's easy for him to come to rapid conclusions about those to come, an advantage that we the apprentices of this science don't have, being always obliged to grope uncertainly to make these judgments.

"Still, in spite of all this, I managed to predict that you'd be lost for two years and I'd recover you on this day and in this place, thereby giving new youth to my gray head and good cause for giving thanks to Heaven for finding my treasure. I foresaw that my spirit would be gladdened with your presence, but I know that it will be at the cost of some unpleasant and unexpected events; for good times don't usually come without the counterbalance of misfortunes, which have jurisdiction and a kind of permission to mix themselves among good events in order to remind us that neither are good times eternal nor do misfortunes last forever." "Heaven will be pleased to give us a prosperous journey," said Auristela at this point after having been quiet for a long while, "if such a good meeting as this is any assurance."

The woman prisoner, who had been listening with rapt attention to Transila's story, got to her feet in spite of her chains and in spite of the effort made by the man to whom she was chained to prevent it, and in a loud voice said:

Chapter Fourteen of the First Book

Where the Identity of the Two Who
Arrived Loaded Down with Chains Is Made Known

If those who suffer should ever be allowed to speak in the presence of the fortunate, grant your permission to me this one time, for the brevity of my words will temper any annoyance you might experience in listening to them. You've complained, Mrs. Virgin," she said, turning to Transila, "of the 'barbarous custom' of the people of your city, as if that were the correct term for what's in fact lightening the work of the needy and removing a burden from the weak; for how can it be a mistake, however fine the horse may be, to let him walk the course before he begins the race? Nor does any practice or custom go against decency if honor is not thereby lost, and such a practice must be considered correct even though it might not seem so; for surely the helm will be best governed by someone who's been a sailor, not one who comes straight out of the pilot schools on land. Since experience in all things is the best teacher of skills, it would be better for you to come to your husband with some experience under your belt—then you won't turn out to be a coarse and clumsy companion."

The man shackled to her had scarcely heard this last idea when he said, putting his closed fist right up into her face and threatening her, "Oh, Rosamunda, or, I should say, filthy rose, for you never were clean,[1] nor are you now, nor shall you ever be in your life if you should live more years than time itself, so I'm not surprised that the decency and modesty to which honorable maidens are obliged would seem bad to you.

"I want all of you to know, ladies and gentlemen," he continued, looking around at everyone present, "that this woman you see here shackled like a crazy person yet outrageously loose, is the famous lady Rosamunda who's been the king of England's concubine and mistress and whose immodest habits have been the subject of long stories and even longer historical accounts by people all over the world.[2] This woman ruled the king and all the kingdom to boot. She imposed laws, repealed them, raised up the vicious who had fallen, and threw down the virtuous who had risen. She indulged her vices disgracefully and publicly with contempt for the king's authority; and to prove just how lascivious her appetites were—there were so many demonstrations of them and her indecencies were so disgusting and so numerous—they broke the diamond chains and bronze nets with which she held the king's heart bound, and they caused him to reject her and to revile her to the same degree that he had prized her previously. When this woman was on top of the world and had firmly seized the moment,[3] I was indignant and filled with desire to show the world just how misplaced the desires of my king and natural lord were. I have a certain genius for satire and slander, a quick pen and a loose tongue; malicious quips delight me and to express just one I'd risk losing not only one friend but a hundred thousand lives. Prisons didn't tie my tongue nor banishments quiet it nor threats frighten me nor punishment reform me. Finally the day of reckoning caught up with both of us at once. For her, the king ordered that no one in the whole city nor in all of his kingdoms and dominions should give her, either as a gift or for money, any nourishment except bread and water; furthermore, they should take me along with her to one of the many islands around here, and, making sure it was uninhabited, leave us there. This punishment has for me been worse than taking my life, for the life I spend with her is worse than death."

"Look here, Clodio," Rosamunda said at this point, "it's so terrible to be in your company that a thousand times I've considered throwing myself into the depths of the sea and if I haven't it's only because I didn't want to take you with me, for if I could be in Hell without you, my suffering would be relieved. I confess that my indecencies have been many, but they've injured only the weak and imprudent; yours, on the other hand, have fallen like a weight on gentlemanly shoulders and on those with seasoned judgment, while you've gained no more profit from them than a pleasure flimsier than that of the smallest straw blown about by fickle whirlwinds. You've injured a thousand honors that didn't concern you, you've destroyed illustrious reputations, you've uncovered hidden secrets and contaminated pure lineages; you've been insolent with your king, your fellow citizens, your friends, and your own relatives; by way of saying clever things you've cleverly disgraced yourself with everyone. I only wish that as punishment for my crimes the king had wanted to end my life with another kind of death in my own land and not with these wounds your tongue sticks me with at every step and from which it seems neither Heaven nor the saints are safe."

"In spite of all you've said," spoke Clodio, "my conscience has never accused me of having told a single lie." "If you had a conscience," replied Rosamunda, "you'd have plenty to accuse yourself of, considering the truths you've told, for not every truth should be revealed in public for all eyes to see."

"Yes," said Mauricio at this point, "yes, Rosamunda's right, for no one should dare bring out publicly the truth of wrongs committed in secret, especially those of the kings and princes who govern us. Indeed, it's not a common man's place to censure his king and lord nor to fill the ears of his vassals with their prince's shortcomings; for this won't be the way to reform him but will only make his people lose respect for him. And if reprimand in private is everyone's right, why should a prince, too, not enjoy this privilege? Why should his defects be publicly thrown in his face? For as often as not thoughtless public censure will only tend to harden the offender's heart and make him more obstinate, not more yielding. And since censure necessarily condemns faults, whether real or imagined, no one wants to be censured in public. Therefore satirists, slanderers, and the malicious are justly banished and thrown out of their homes dishonored and in disgrace, stripped of all praise except being able to call themselves cleverly knavish and knavishly clever. For as the saying goes: treason pleases but the traitor displeases.[4] And there's more—since reputations ruined in writing pass from person to person like the wind, they can't be restored, and without restitution being made for them, sins can't be forgiven."

"I know all that," responded Clodio, "but if they don't want me to speak or write they should cut off my tongue and my hands, and even then I'll put my mouth to the bowels of the earth and speak however I can, hoping to make King Midas' reeds appear there."[5]

"All right now," said Ladislao at this juncture, "make your peace. Let's marry Rosamunda to Clodio. Perhaps with the blessing of the marriage sacrament and putting together what good sense they have, between them they may change their lives by changing their situation." "That's easy for you to say," said Rosamunda, "but I have here a knife with which I can open one or two doors in my breast for my soul to get out, for it's already hanging by the skin of its teeth just from hearing about such a disastrous and absurd marriage."

"I won't kill myself," said Clodio, "because even though I'm a backbiter and slanderer the pleasure I derive from slander, when I do it well, is so great that I want to live because I want to go on slandering. It's true I plan to watch my step with princes, for they have long arms and reach wherever and whomever they want. Experience has already taught me it's not wise to offend the powerful, and Christian charity teaches that you should pray to Heaven for the life and health of good princes, asking also that the bad ones may improve and reform."

"Anyone who knows all that," said Antonio, "is himself close to reforming. There's no sin so great nor any vice so powerful that it can't be erased or removed altogether through repentance. A slanderous tongue is like a double-edged sword that cuts to the bone, or like a lightning bolt from the sky that smashes and shatters the steel without breaking the scabbard that covers it. And although the salt of gossip spices conversations and amusements—still, most of the time—it leaves a bitter and vexing aftertaste. The tongue is as loose as thought itself, and when the conceptions of thought are evil, then their births on the tongue are even worse, for words are like stones: once released from one's hand they can never be recalled or returned to their source until they've had their effect, and regret at having said them rarely outweighs the wrong done by the speaker, even though I've already said that sincere repentance is the best medicine for the diseases of the soul."

Chapter Fifteen of the First Book of This Great History

They were in the middle of all this when a sailor entered the inn shouting, "A big ship's heading for this port with sails set and so far I haven't been able to see any sign to tell me where it's from."

These words were scarcely spoken when the horrible sound of many pieces of artillery fired by the ship as it entered the port reached their ears; but the firing was harmless since it carried no load of shot, and thus was a sign of peace and not war. Mauricio's ship and all the musket soldiers aboard fired similar shots in reply.

Immediately all the people at the inn went down to the shore. On seeing the newly arrived ship, Periandro recognized it as that of Arnaldo, Prince of Denmark, and not only was he not pleased but his stomach began to churn and his heart to pound in his chest. In her heart Auristela felt equally upset and frightened, knowing from long experience what Arnaldo wanted of her, and she couldn't think for the life of her how Arnaldo and Periandro's purposes could be reconciled and how their souls could not be pierced by jealousy's cruel and desperate arrow.

Arnaldo was already in the ship's boat, indeed already reaching shore, when Periandro stepped forward to welcome him. But Auristela didn't move from the spot where she had first set foot; in fact, she would have liked her feet to sink into the ground and turn into twisted roots like those of Peneus' daughter when the swift runner Apollo was pursuing her.[1] Arnaldo recognized Periandro as soon as he saw him, and without waiting for his men to carry him to shore on their shoulders, he jumped from the stern of the boat onto the beach and into Periandro's arms, which were open to welcome him. Arnaldo then said to him, "If I were so fortunate, Periandro my friend, as to find your sister Auristela with you, I'd have no evil to fear nor anything better to hope for." "She *is* with me, valiant sir," replied Periandro, "for Heaven, quick to favor your virtuous and honest intentions, as well as her own chaste resolve, has kept her for you as untouched as she deserves."

By this time word of the identity of the prince arriving on the ship had spread through both the newcomers and those on land. Auristela was still standing like a statue, speechless and motionless; near her were the beautiful Transila and the two seeming barbarians, Ricla and Constanza. Arnaldo came forward and kneeling before Auristela, said to her: "Well found, unchanging star of the North that guides my honorable thoughts and leads me to the port where all my good intentions will find their resting place." Auristela gave no answer to all this, but tears came to her eyes and began to bathe her rosy cheeks.

Arnaldo was very confused by her reaction and couldn't figure out if it came from distress or happiness. But Periandro, who was watching everything and had his eyes fixed on Auristela's every move, cleared up Arnaldo's doubts by telling him, "Sir, my sister's silence and tears are born of astonishment and pleasure; astonishment at finding you in so unexpected a place and tears of pleasure at the sight of you. She's grateful, as all well-born ladies should be, and recognizes the obligation she has to serve you with the same graciousness and decent treatment she's always received from you."

With this they all went back to the inn; again the tables were heaped with food and their hearts swelled with pleasure as their cups were filled with choice wines, which, from traveling the seas from one end to the other, get so good that no nectar can equal them. This second dinner was given in honor of Prince Arnaldo. Periandro told the prince what had happened to him on the Barbarous Isle, including the freeing of Auristela and all the other events and details told so far. Arnaldo was astonished, and all those present were pleased and amazed once again.

Chapter Sixteen of the First Book of Persiles and Sigismunda

At this point the innkeeper said, "I don't know whether I should say I'm sorry to see the good sailing weather promised by the signs in the sky; the sun is going down clear and clean and not a cloud can be seen near or far, while the waves softly and gently strike the shore and the birds playfully fly to and fro over the sea. All these are signs of sure and lasting calm, and that means the most honored guests fortune has ever brought to my inn will be leaving me."

"Right you are," said Mauricio, "for even though we consider your generous hospitality agreeable and pleasing, our desire to return to our homelands won't let us enjoy it for very long. As for myself, I can say that tonight during the first watch I'll set sail, provided my pilot and the soldiers attached to the ship agree." To this Arnaldo added, "Lost time can never be regained, and time lost during an ocean voyage is irretrievable."

And so it was that all those in port agreed to set out that night to return to England, where everyone was bound. Arnaldo got up from the table, took Periandro by the hand, and led him out of the inn; when they were alone and no one else could hear him, he said to Periandro, "It's not possible, Periandro my friend, that your sister Auristela hasn't told you of the intentions I made known to her in the two years she was in the hands of my father the king, intentions that so respected her own honorable wishes that no words ever came out of my mouth that could have disturbed her pure resolve. I never tried to find out more about her social status than she chose to tell me, picturing her in my imagination not as a common person of low estate but as the queen of the whole world, for her modesty, her dignified manner, and her extraordinarily extraordinary mind wouldn't let me think anything else. A thousand times I offered myself to her as her husband—with my father's consent—but it still seemed to me that my offer fell short of what it should be. She always replied that until she got to the city of Rome, where she was going to fulfill a vow, she couldn't give herself to anyone. She never consented to tell me her social rank or that of her parents, nor did I, as I've said, beg her to tell me; for she alone, just for herself, with no need of any other nobility, deserves not only the crown of Denmark, but that of the whole world. I'm telling you all this, Periandro, so that as a reasonable and perceptive man, you'll realize that the opportunity knocking at the doors of your and your sister's interests is not insignificant, for I'm offering myself here and now as her husband and promise to make this offer good whenever and wherever she wishes, here under these poor roofs or under the golden ones of fabled Rome. And likewise I promise you to contain myself within the bounds of decency and correct behavior even though I may be consumed by the urges and desires that accompany unbridled lust and hopes soon to be fulfilled, for hopes near at hand are more trying than distant ones."

Here Arnaldo finished speaking and then listened intently for what Periandro was going to say in response, which was this: "I know very well, valiant Prince Arnaldo, that my sister and I are obligated to you for the favors you've done us prior to this moment and for the one you're doing for us now. I myself owe you in that you've offered to be my brother, and she for your offer to be her husband. But although it may seem madness for two miserable pilgrims exiled from their homeland not to immediately accept this offered favor, I can only tell you that it's just as impossible to accept it as it is possible to be grateful for it. My sister and I are led by destiny and choice to the holy city of Rome, and until we reach there it seems we have no identity at all nor any liberty to use our free will. If Heaven leads us to walk that holy ground and worship its sacred relics, then we'll again be able to exercise our now restrained wills, and mine will be totally in your service. I can also tell you that if you should see your good intentions fulfilled, you'll have a wife born of a very illustrious family line and a brother who'll be more a brother than a brother-in-law. And along with the many favors both of us have received from you, I beg you one more, which is not to ask me anything else about our social status or our life so that I won't be obliged to lie, inventing dishonest and false fantasies to avoid telling you the truth of our story."

"You can count on me, my brother," Arnaldo responded, "for whatever you wish and desire; think of me as the wax, and you as the seal may imprint on me whatever you please. If it's all right with you, let's leave for England tonight. We can easily get to France and Rome from there, and no matter how you decide to travel, I'll plan to accompany you on that journey, if you like." Although this last offer worried Periandro, he accepted it hoping that with time and delay perhaps things might turn out better. Then after the two brothers-in-law-in-hope embraced each other, they returned to the inn to arrange their departure.

Auristela had seen Arnaldo and Periandro go out together and was apprehensive about what their talk might lead to. And although she was aware of Prince Arnaldo's restraint and Periandro's prudence, a thousand kinds of fears assaulted her; she felt that since Arnaldo's love was as great as his power, he might resort to force to secure compliance with his requests, for sometimes patience can turn to rage and courtesy to rudeness in rejected lovers' hearts. But when she saw them return so calm and peaceful she felt her spirits lift a little.

Clodio the slanderer, who by then had learned who Arnaldo was, threw himself at his feet and begged him to give orders to take off the chains and separate him from Rosamunda's company. Mauricio then described to him the characters, the crimes, and the shared punishment of Clodio and Rosamunda. Moved by pity Arnaldo had the captain in charge of them unshackle and hand them over to him, for he was taking it upon himself to obtain a pardon from their king, a good friend of his. Seeing this, Clodio the slanderer said, "If all those in power would make it their business to do good works there'd be no one who'd make it his business to speak ill of them; how can someone who does wrong expect good things to be said of him? And if, after all, works which are right and virtuous are slandered by human malice, why not evil deeds? Why should he who sows the bad seed of discord and malice expect to reap a harvest of good fruit? Take me with you, oh prince, and you'll see how I praise you to the moon!"

"No, no," replied Arnaldo. "I don't want you to praise me for deeds that come naturally to me. And what's more, praise is only as good or as vicious and evil as the one who gives it; for if praise is the reward of virtue, then when he who praises is virtuous it's truly praise, but if he's vicious it's a condemnation."

Chapter Seventeen of the First Book

Arnaldo Tells What Happened to Taurisa

Auristela was very anxious to know what had passed between Arnaldo and Periandro in the conversation they had outside the inn. She was waiting for the right moment to ask Periandro about it and to find out from Arnaldo what had become of her maid Taurisa. Then, as if Arnaldo could read her mind, he told her, "The misfortunes you've suffered, beautiful Auristela, must have swept some others from your mind that you ought to have remembered, and I could only wish that among them you had forgotten those involving me, for if I could just imagine I was once in your memory, I'd be content, since it's impossible to forget someone who's never been remembered; to forget in the present you have to have some remembrance of the past. But be that as it may, whether you remember me or not, I'll be happy with whatever you do, for Heaven has destined me to be yours and won't let me do anything else; my free will is only free to obey you.

"Your brother Periandro had told me many things that have happened to you since you were stolen from my kingdom; some of them have amazed me, others were astonishing, and here and there they frightened me. I see, moreover, that misfortune has the power to erase from one's memory some seemingly powerful obligations. You've not asked me about my father nor about Taurisa, your maid. I left him well and wanting me to look for you and find you; her I brought with me to sell to the barbarians so she could act as a spy and see if fortune had carried you into their hands. Periandro must have already told you how he came into mine and the agreement the two of us made; but even though I've tried many times to return to the Barbarous Isle, contrary winds have not allowed me to do so. Just now I was returning with that same intention and desire, and Heaven has fulfilled it with the special bonus of having you, the universal remedy for all my cares, here with me. It must have been two days ago that I left your handmaiden Taurisa, who was very ill and her life in danger, with two gentlemen friends of mine whom I met on the open sea on a powerful ship heading for Ireland. This vessel I'm traveling in, on the other hand, could better be described as a pirate ship than one belonging to a king's son, and seeing that it had neither the comforts nor medicines sick people need, I gave her to them to take to Ireland and hand over to their prince who will take good care of her, cure, and keep her safe until I come for her personally.

"Today I informed your brother Periandro that we'll sail tomorrow either for England or for Spain or France, but wherever we get to, there will certainly be some convenient way to put into effect your virtuous plans described to me by your brother. I, meanwhile, will carry my hopes on the shoulders of my impatience, sustained by the support of your understanding. All in all, I beg and entreat you, my lady, to decide whether our plan is what you have in mind, and if it's out of tune in any way with yours, we won't do it."

"I have no other will," answered Auristela, "than that of my brother Periandro, and he, being wise, won't want to stray from yours in the slightest." "Well, if that's the way things are," replied Arnaldo, "I don't want to command, but to obey, lest people say of me that I want to better myself by giving orders to my betters." This is what happened between Arnaldo and Auristela, who told it all to Periandro. That night Arnaldo, Periandro, Mauricio, Ladislao, the two captains, and the crew of the English ship, with all the people who had left the Barbarous Isle, conferred and arranged their departure in the following manner.

Chapter Eighteen of the First Book

Where through Astrology Mauricio Learns of a
Misfortune which Then Befell Them on the Sea

Everyone who had been released from the dungeon and prison on the Barbarous Isle embarked on the ship on which Mauricio, Ladislao, and the captains and soldiers who brought Rosamunda and Clodio had come, while Ricla and Constanza, the two Antonios (father and son), Ladislao, Mauricio, and Transila[1] were lodged on Arnaldo's ship, nor would Arnaldo allow Clodio and Rosamunda to be left ashore. Rutilio, too, found a place with Arnaldo.

That night they took on water, gathering up and buying all the provisions they could from the innkeeper; after he had consulted all the signs most relevant to their departure Mauricio said that if good fortune helped them escape from a single case of bad luck posing an immediate threat to them their voyage would be successful. And this danger, even though it had to do with water, would not come about, if it did happen, because of any squall or storm on sea or land, but rather through treachery mixed with and possibly even totally forged from lustful and lascivious desires.

Periandro, always apprehensive in Arnaldo's company, began to fear that the treachery might have been planned by the prince to make off with the beautiful Auristela, since he was going to have her on his ship. But his generous spirit vigorously rejected this unworthy thought and he refused to believe what he feared, since it seemed to him that the hearts of valiant princes shouldn't harbor any kind of treachery. However, this didn't prevent him from asking and even pleading with Mauricio to take a closer look to see where the harm that threatened them might come from. Mauricio responded that he didn't know where the danger would come from, saying only he was sure it would happen, although its severity would be tempered by the fact that none of those affected would lose their lives, only their peace of mind and tranquility, and they would see their best hopes and half their plans destroyed.

To this Periandro replied that they should delay their departure for a few days; perhaps after a delay the strong influence of the stars would change or moderate. "No," replied Mauricio, "it's better to place ourselves in the hands of this danger that won't take our lives than to try another road on which we might lose them." "All right, then," said Periandro, "the die is cast; let's get an early start and let Heaven do what it has ordained, since our efforts can't prevent it."

Arnaldo generously settled accounts with the owner by giving him many gifts in return for his good accommodations; then, as each thought best, some people in some ships and others in others, they emptied the harbor and set sail. Arnaldo's ship set out decorated with fluttering streamers and banners and showy, colorful pennants. After pulling up the chains and weighing anchor they fired both the heavy and light artillery; the air was split by the sounds of recorders and other festive musical instruments, and one could hear the voices of those who kept saying "Bon voyage, have a good trip!" The beautiful Auristela didn't raise her chin from her chest during any of this, but in what seemed to be a premonition of the misfortune that was to befall her, she remained wrapped in thought. Periandro was constantly looking at her and Arnaldo was always gazing at her, each of them making her the target of his glances, the end toward which his thoughts were directed, and the beginning of his joy.

Day was done and a clear and serene night fell, with a soft breeze clearing broken clouds and preventing their tendency to gather. Mauricio raised his eyes to the sky and again began to turn over in his mind the signs of the horoscope he had drawn, once more confirming the danger threatening them; but he never was able to figure out where it would come from. Filled with confusion and apprehension he fell asleep on deck, but he awoke shortly thereafter terrified and screaming, "Treachery! Treachery! Treachery! Wake up, Prince Arnaldo, your men are killing us!"

Hearing the shouts, Arnaldo, who wasn't sleeping although he was stretched out near Periandro on the same deck, got up and said, "What's the matter, friend Mauricio? Who's attacking us, or who's killing us? Aren't all of us on board this ship friends? Aren't most of them my vassals and servants? Isn't the sky clear and serene, the sea calm and smooth? And isn't the ship sailing clear of reefs and shoals? Surely there aren't any suckerfish[2] holding us up, are there? Since it's none of these, what is it you fear so much that you frighten us with your terror?"

"I don't know," replied Mauricio, "but please, sir, have the divers go down into the bilge, because unless this is a dream, I believe we're about to sink." No sooner were these words spoken than about four to six sailors who were known as good divers lowered themselves into the depths of the ship and inspected everything. They found no openings with water leaking in and on coming back on deck said that the ship was sound and whole and the bilge water murky and stinking, a sure sign that water from outside wasn't getting in.

"That may well be," said Mauricio, "but I, old as I am and regularly struck by fear, am frightened even by dreams; and I pray to God that my dream was just that, for in this case I'd be more pleased to be taken for an old coward than a canny astrologer." Arnaldo said to him, "Calm down, good Mauricio, for the dreams in your sleep are preventing these ladies from getting any." "I'll do just that if I can," responded Mauricio. They all stretched out once more on the deck with the ship full of very peaceful silence in the midst of which Rutilio, who was seated at the foot of the mainmast, prompted by the serenity of the night, the pleasant weather, or by his voice—for he had an extremely good one—and accompanied by the wind that sweetly strummed the sails, began to sing this song in his own Tuscan language, and translated into Spanish it went like this:

Forewarned, the world's great patriarch did flee
the never-conquered Hand's severity

and with him shut away within the ark
surviving remnants of the human race.

The spacious sovereign sanctuary broke
the laws of Fate,[3] who, fierce and unrestrained
held sway in that same hour o'er everything
that drew in breath and breathed the empty air.

Behold, within that vessel most sublime
the lion and the lamb lie down together,
while dove and hawk unite in peace secure;

No miracle turns discord into love;
but common danger and misfortune shared
force all the baser instincts from the mind.[4]

The one who best understood what Rutilio had sung was the elder Antonio who said to himself, "Rutilio sings well and if by chance the sonnet he sang was his, then he isn't a bad poet. But how could someone with such a common occupation be a good poet? Still, I must be mistaken, for I remember having seen poets of all occupations in Spain, my homeland."

He said this loudly enough to be heard by Mauricio, the Prince, and Periandro, who weren't asleep. Then Mauricio said, "It's quite possible for a person with a common occupation to be a poet because poetry isn't in one's hands but in the mind, and the soul of a tailor is just as capable of poetry as that of a field marshall, for all souls are equal and have their origins in the same material, created and shaped by their Maker. Depending on the form and temperament of the body that encloses them, they seem more or less intelligent and show aptitude for and take pleasure in learning the sciences, arts, or skills toward which the stars most incline them. But more important and most correct is the saying 'the poet *nascitur*.'[5] Thus, it isn't surprising that Rutilio should be a poet, even though he's been a dancing teacher."

"And such a dancer," replied Antonio, "that he's made leaps in the air higher than the clouds." "That's right," responded Rutilio who was listening to all of this, "for I leaped almost to Heaven when that sorceress carried me riding on her cloak—as though on horseback—from my homeland of Tuscany to Norway where I killed her, for she'd taken on the shape of a she-wolf, as I've already described more than once before."

"This business of some people in these northern parts changing into wolves and she-wolves is a very great error," said Mauricio, "although a lot of people accept it as true." "But then, how can it be," said Arnaldo, "that it's commonly commented and taken for the truth that bands of wolves, formerly human beings, roam the countryside in England?"

"That can't be in England," replied Mauricio, "for not only are wolves not found on that mild and most fertile island, but no other harmful animals such as serpents, vipers, toads, spiders, or scorpions are either. On the contrary, it's obvious and plain to see that if any venomous animal is brought from other places to England it dies as soon as it arrives there. Furthermore, if soil from that island is taken elsewhere and used to encircle a viper, the snake doesn't dare nor is it able to leave the circle imprisoning and surrounding it, and so it dies. The truth of this business of changing into wolves is that there's a disease doctors call "lycanthropy"[6] and by its nature the person suffering from it feels he has changed into a wolf and so howls like one and joins with others suffering from the same disease. They roam in packs through the fields and mountains, sometimes barking like dogs and sometimes howling like wolves, tearing trees to pieces, killing whomever they come across and eating the raw flesh of the dead. And I know that to this very day on the island of Sicily, the largest in the Mediterranean Sea, there are people of this type, called by Sicilians 'werewolves,' who get a feeling before they break out with the foul disease and tell everyone around them to get away and run from them or else tie them up and lock them away, for if they aren't controlled they'll bite others to pieces and tear them to shreds with their claws—if they can get to them—while making horrible and frightening howling noises.

"This is so true that when couples are about to be married an investigation is made to prove that neither one of them is touched by this disease, and if later with the passage of time the opposite proves to be true, then the marriage is annulled. It's also Pliny's opinion, according to what he writes in Book 8, Chapter 22,[7] that among the Arcadians there's a kind of people who after crossing a certain lake hang the clothes they're wearing on an oak tree and then set out naked inland to find and join another group of people to whom they're related and who have the shape of wolves. They stay with them for nine years at the end of which they again cross the lake and resume their original shapes. But all this must be considered a lie, and if there's any truth to it, must occur only in their imaginations and not in real life."

"I don't know about that," said Rutilio; "all I know is that I killed the she-wolf and found the sorceress dead at my feet." "All that may well be," replied Mauricio, "because the force of the spells cast by witches and enchanters—who do exist—makes us see one thing for another, and we may all be certain that there are no people at all who can change their original nature into something else."

"It has given me great pleasure," said Arnaldo, "to learn the truth, for I was one of those who believed that error. Then the same must hold true for what the legends tell about King Arthur of England changing into a crow, something so strongly believed by that sensible nation that they refrain from killing crows throughout the whole island."[8] "I don't know," responded Mauricio, "how this legend, as widely believed as it is ill conceived, could have gotten started."

They spent practically the whole night in this discussion, and at daybreak Clodio, who up until then had been listening and keeping quiet, said, "I'm a man who doesn't give two cents for finding out about such stuff. What's it to me whether or not there are werewolves or whether kings go around in the shape of crows—or eagles, for that matter? Nevertheless, if they have to change into birds, I'd rather they be doves than birds of prey."

"Watch your step, Clodio," warned Prince Arnaldo, "don't speak ill of kings, for it seems to me you're honing your tongue to cut them down to size."

"Not really," answered Clodio, "for punishment has put a muzzle on my mouth, or, I should say, on my tongue, that won't let me move it; and so from now on I'd rather burst from keeping quiet than give in and indulge in blabbing. Sharp-witted sayings and long involved gossip amuse some while saddening others; but there's no punishment or rebuke for silence. I want to live the remainder of my days in peace and in the shadow of your generous protection, since at times I'm plagued by certain malicious impulses that make my tongue dance in my mouth while I chew on gobs of truths just dying to get out into the marketplace of the world. May God's will be done in all things!" This prompted Auristela to say, "Oh, Clodio, the sacrifice you're making to Heaven with your silence is so commendable!"

Rosamunda, one of the women who had just joined the conversation, turned to Auristela and said, "The day Clodio's silent will be the day I turn good; for lust in me, like backbiting in him, comes naturally; however, I may have more hope of reform than he, for beauty ages with the years and lewd desires diminish when beauty fades, but time has no jurisdiction over the slanderer's tongue. And so old backbiters talk more the older they get, for they've seen more, and have gathered and concentrated all the other sensual pleasures in their tongues."

"Things are bad all over," added Transila, "and everyone takes his own road to damnation." "The one we're taking now," said Ladislao, "must be prosperous and happy, judging by the favorable wind and calm sea." "So it seemed last night," said Constanza the barbarian, "until Lord Mauricio's dream confused and upset us so that I began to think the sea had already swallowed us all up."

"To tell you the truth, lady," responded Mauricio, "if I hadn't been taught the truths of Catholicism and if I didn't remember what God says in Leviticus—'You shall not divine nor observe dreams,'[9] since it's not given to everyone to understand them—I'd hazard a prediction from the dream that so frightened me. But I feel it didn't come to me from any of the usual sources of dreams, for when dreams aren't divine revelations or delusions from the Devil, they usually come from eating too much which sends vapors to the brain and disturbs common sense, or from whatever the person most had on his mind during the day.

"Neither does the dream that disturbed me fall under the category of astrological observation, for without noting the exact time or observing the stars, without fixing my bearings or looking at constellations, it seemed to me I was actually seeing a great palace made of wood, and all of us now present were there. Lightning bolts were raining down from the sky and breaking everything up, while from the openings they were making in the clouds out dumped not only one sea, but a thousand seas of water. So much water that, believing I was drowning, I began to shout and make the same movements a drowning man makes. I'm still not so free of this fear that some remnants of it don't remain in my soul. But since I know there's no more certain astrology than prudence, from which right reasoning is born, is it surprising that while sailing in a wooden ship I'd fear lightning bolts from the sky, clouds in the air, and water from the sea? But what most confuses and perplexes me is that if some harm threatens us it won't come from any natural element destined and specifically prepared for that purpose, but from treachery forged, as I've already mentioned, in some lustful hearts."

"I can't believe," Arnaldo said at this point, "that those who sail the sea would let Venus' weaknesses or the appetites of her lewd son[10] slip into their hearts; moreover, pure love can walk through grave dangers saving itself for better times." Arnaldo said this so Auristela and Periandro and all those aware of his passion would know how strictly reasonable all his actions were. And he went on, saying, "A prince can with full confidence live secure among his vassals, for the fear of treason is born only when he leads an immoral life." "That's so," replied Mauricio, "and what's more, it's a good thing it's so. But why don't we let this day go by, and if then night comes on with no alarms I'll be the first to report the good news and give thanks for the happy event."

It was about time for the sun to go down into the arms of Tethys,[11] and the sea remained as calm as before. There was a favoring breeze and no clouds in sight to worry the sailors. The sky, the sea, the wind—all of them together and each one by itself—were promising a very successful journey, when wise Mauricio said in a loud voice full of alarm, "We're definitely sinking! We're sinking without a doubt!"

Chapter Nineteen of the First Book

Where We Learn What the Two Soldiers Did and of Periandro and Auristela's Separation

To these shouts Arnaldo responded, "How can this be, great Mauricio? What waters are sucking us down and what seas swallowing us? What waves are crashing into us?" Arnaldo was answered when he saw a terrified sailor come up from below deck spraying water from his mouth and eyes and saying in distraught and disjointed words, "This ship has opened up all over, and the sea has been coming in at such breakneck speed that you'll soon see it covering this deck! Everyone look out for yourself and save your own life! Take refuge, Prince Arnaldo, in the dinghy or in the ship's boat, and take with you the things you value most before these bitter waters take full possession of them!"

At this point the ship stalled, unable to move because of the weight of water that had already filled it. The pilot abruptly lowered all the sails and all the terrified, frightened people rushed around looking for a way to save themselves. The prince and Periandro went over to the dinghy and, pushing it into the sea, put Auristela, Transila, Ricla, and Constanza the barbarian aboard. Rosamunda, seeing that no one remembered her, threw herself in after them, and Arnaldo ordered Mauricio to go in after her.

At this time two soldiers were unslinging the ship's boat from where it was tied to the side of the ship, and one of them, seeing that the other wanted to get in first, took a dagger out of his belt and sheathed it in the other's chest, shouting, "Since we've gained so little from our crime, let this punishment serve as warning for you and an example for me, at least for the short time left in my life." On saying this, not wishing to take advantage of the refuge the ship's boat offered them, he threw himself desperately into the sea shouting out these barely intelligible words: "Listen, Arnaldo, to the truth this traitor tells you, for at a time like this it's good to speak the truth. Along with that fellow you saw me stab in the chest I opened and drilled holes all over the ship, intending to rape Auristela and Transila after making off with them in the dinghy; but seeing my plan turn out so differently from what I had in mind, I've taken my partner's life and now am killing myself." With this last word he let himself sink into the depths of the water, which cut off his breathing and buried him in perpetual silence.

And although they were all running around confused and engrossed in looking, as has been said, for a way to save themselves from their common danger, this didn't prevent Arnaldo from hearing the suicide's words. He and Periandro ran to the ship's boat and before getting into it ordered the younger Antonio to board the dinghy. Not remembering to gather any supplies whatsoever, Arnaldo, Ladislao, the elder Antonio, Periandro, and Clodio got into the boat and tried to pull it close to the dinghy, which had become somewhat separated from the ship, now covered by water except for the mainmast which was still visible like a marker over the ship's grave.

But night fell before the boat could reach the dinghy, from which Auristela was shouting, calling to her brother Periandro, who was answering her, repeating over and over again her name so dear to him. Transila and Ladislao were doing the same, and the cries of "My sweetest husband!" and "My beloved wife!" met each other in midair, where their plans were breaking apart and their hopes coming undone, for it was impossible for them to be united in that night wrapped in darkness with the wind beginning to blow from several different directions. In short, the boat moved away from the dinghy and since it was lighter and less heavily loaded it flew away to wherever the sea and the wind wanted to take it. The dinghy, more from the burden of grief than the weight of those traveling in it, stayed behind as if they were willing it not to move. When night closed in darker than before, once again they began to grieve over the misfortune that had occurred. They found themselves on an unknown sea, threatened from the sky by all kinds of severe weather, and lacking the comforts land could offer. The dinghy was without either provisions or oars, and only the sorrow they felt held their hunger at bay.

Mauricio, acting as the skipper and sailor on the dinghy, had nothing to steer it with nor did he know how; not only that, but considering all the weeping, groans, and sighs coming from those traveling aboard, there was reason to fear they alone might sink it. He kept looking at the stars, and although all weren't completely visible, the fact that some of them shone through the darkness indicated to him that calm was approaching, although they didn't show him from which direction it was to come.

They spent the night awake, for their emotions wouldn't let sleep relieve their anguish. And day came moving them not to forward progress, but to tears, as the saying goes, because at dawn they searched the sea everywhere around them, both near and far, to see if they might spy the boat carrying away the souls dear to them or some other vessel that might bring promise of help and aid in their time of need. But they didn't spot anything except an island to their left, which made them glad and sad at the same time; they were glad to see land nearby and sad to realize it would be impossible to get there if the wind didn't carry them toward it. Mauricio had the most faith that everyone would be safe because, as has been said, in the horoscope he had cast as a judicial astrologer, he had found that their circumstances threatened near-fatal hardships, but not death.

Finally the kindness of Heaven, together with the winds, little by little carried the dinghy to the island and allowed them to come ashore on a spacious beach where they were welcomed by no one at all, only by large quantities of snow covering everything. But the stormy fortunes of the sea are so miserable and frightening that those who suffer them rejoice to exchange them for the greater misfortunes that may present themselves on land. The snow on that deserted beach seemed like soft sand to them and the solitude companionship. Some carried by others, they disembarked; the younger Antonio was Auristela's and Transila's Atlas, and Rosamunda and Mauricio also disembarked on his shoulders. They all huddled together in the shelter of a huge rock visible not far from the water's edge, having first beached the dinghy as best they could, placing their hopes in it second only to God.

Antonio, thinking hunger would begin its work and might be enough to take their lives, prepared his bow, always kept hanging on his back, and said he wanted to go explore the land to see if he could find some people or any game to help meet their needs. Everyone agreed with his idea and so he went inland at a fast pace, stepping not on earth but on snow frozen so hard that it seemed to him he was walking on flint. Without him noticing and without her being stopped by the others, who thought a call of nature obliged her to leave them, the disgraceful Rosamunda followed him. Antonio didn't look back until he was too far away for anyone to see them, and then finding Rosamunda next to him, said to her, "The thing I need least, in this time of need we're suffering, is your company. What do you want, Rosamunda? Turn back, for you don't have a weapon to kill any kind of game and I can't slow down to wait for you. Why are you following me?"

"You're green, boy," answered the lustful woman, "and far from recognizing my true intentions in following you, not to mention the debt you owe me!" With this she drew near him and went on, saying, "You see here, my young hunter more handsome than Apollo, a new Daphne who not only doesn't flee but actually follows you. Forget that my beauty is already fading through the cruelty of ever-rushing time and see in me the Rosamunda who was—destroyer of the pride of kings and of the most distinguished men's freedoms. I adore you, noble youth, and here among this ice and snow love's flame is turning my heart to ashes. Let's give ourselves over to pleasure, make me yours, and I'll take you to a place where you can fill your hands with treasures, gathered and hidden away by me for you—you can count on it—for if we reach England, where a thousand death warrants threaten my life, I'll lead you secretly to where you can take possession of more gold than Midas ever had and more riches than even Crassus stored up."[1]

At this point she put an end to her talking but not to the movement of her hands, which reached out to grasp those of Antonio, who for his part was pushing them away; and while this struggle between decency and lust was going on, Antonio was saying, "Stop, you harpy! Don't make an ugly, filthy mess of Phineus' table![2] Don't force yourself on me, you barbarous Egyptian,[3] and don't tempt modesty and purity, for I'm no slave of yours! Bite your tongue, you damned serpent, and don't expose your heart's indecent desires in equally indecent words! Consider the short time we have left from this moment to the end of our lives; for hunger and the uncertainty of whether we'll be able to leave this place threaten death at any moment. But even if escape were certain, you should greet that prospect with other intentions than those you've shown toward me! Get away and don't follow me, or I'll punish your audacity and tell everyone about your madness! If you go back I'll relent and keep your shame to myself, but if you don't leave me alone I'll take your life."

When the lustful Rosamunda heard this her heart was so heavily burdened there was no more room in it for sighs, entreaties, or tears. Wisely, the sensible Antonio left her. So Rosamunda went back and he continued on his way, but he found nothing to reassure him, because the snow was abundant, the paths rough, and the people non-existent. Realizing that if he went any farther he might not be able to find his way back, he turned around and went to rejoin the company, where they all lifted their hands to Heaven and lowered their eyes to the ground, as if amazed by their misfortune. Then they told Mauricio they should launch the dinghy again since it was utterly impossible to get the help they needed on such a barren and deserted island.

Chapter Twenty

Concerning a Remarkable Event
that Occurred on the Snowy Isle

Before much of the day had gone by, seeing a large ship in the distance raised their hopes of getting help. It lowered sail and seemed to be dropping anchor. Not wasting any time, those on board launched the boat and headed toward the beach, where the sad company had already boarded their dinghy. Auristela said it would be best to wait there for those coming in to find out who they were.

The ship's boat arrived and ran aground on the icy snow: out of it jumped two attractive and vigorous young men, visibly strong-willed and spirited, carrying on their shoulders an exceedingly beautiful young woman so weak and faint it seemed she might not live to reach land. They called out loudly to those who had already embarked in the dinghy and begged them to disembark to serve as witnesses to an event requiring their presence.

Mauricio responded saying there were no oars to row the dinghy, unless they loaned them theirs. So the sailors guided the dinghy with their oars and the travelers again set foot on the snow. The valiant young men immediately took up two square shields and covered their chests; then with dueling swords in their hands they again leaped ashore.

Auristela, fearful and anxious, and practically sure of some new misfortune, stepped forward to see the now unconscious and beautiful young woman, and everyone else did the same. But the gentlemen said, "Wait, ladies and gentlemen, and listen carefully to what we want to tell you." "This gentleman and I," said one of them, "have agreed to fight for possession of that sick young woman you see there; death will have to decide the winner, for there's no other way at all to settle our amorous dispute unless she, of her own free will, should pick one of us as her husband; that alone would make us sheathe our swords and calm ourselves. What we ask is for you not to interfere in any way in our quarrel, which we would carry through to its end without fear of anyone hindering us if we didn't need you to watch. Even though this deserted place might offer some way to extend the life of this young woman, who has the power to end ours, the haste we feel to conclude our business doesn't give us time, for now, to ask you who you are or how it is you're in such a deserted place and without oars—or so it seems—necessary to help you get away from this island, so deserted not even animals live here."

Mauricio responded that they wouldn't deviate a hair's breadth from what the young men wished; then the two of them laid hands to their swords, without first asking the sick young woman to state her choice, submitting their dispute to arms rather than to the lady's wishes. They rushed at each other without a thought for the rules, studied movements, thrusts, retreats, and parries of fencing; with the first strokes one of them was run through the heart and the other had his head split open. Heaven granted just enough life to the latter to make his way over to the young woman and place his face near hers, saying to her, "I won, my lady! You're mine, and although the benefit of possessing you will last only a short time, the thought that I can have you for my own, if only for an instant, makes me feel like the luckiest man in the world. Take this soul, lady; I send it to you wrapped in these last breaths; make a place for it in your heart without asking your modesty's permission, for the word 'husband' allows it."

Blood from his wound flowed over the woman's face, but being unconscious she didn't answer a word. The two sailors who had rowed the ship's boat jumped to land and went quickly to examine both the man dead from the sword thrust and the one wounded in the head, who with his mouth placed against that of his so dearly purchased wife sent his soul out into the air and let his body fall to the ground.

Auristela had been observing these activities and so had not uncovered and looked closely at the sick lady's face; now she went up purposefully to look at her and, wiping away the blood the love-stricken corpse had rained on her, she recognized her handmaiden Taurisa, who had served her during the time she was in the hands of Prince Arnaldo; he in turn had told Auristela he'd left her in the care of two gentlemen who were to take her to Ireland, as has been related. Auristela felt stunned, amazed, and sadder than sadness itself, and even more so when she realized the beautiful Taurisa was dead.

"Oh no!" she said then, "Heaven keeps giving me such powerful demonstrations of my misfortune that if it would conclude by ending my life I'd call it happy, for provided they aren't drawn out and prolonged, evils that come to an end in death do, indeed, make for a happy life! What sweeping net is this in which Heaven catches all my paths toward peaceful rest? What insurmountable obstacles are these I uncover at every step I take toward help? But since tears are useless here and moans are pointless, let's show pity in the time that might be wasted on them, burying the dead instead; I won't make the living suffer for my sake."

She immediately requested that Mauricio ask the sailors with the boat to return to the ship for tools to make the graves. Mauricio did so, going to the vessel himself intending to arrange with whatever pilot or captain might be aboard to get them off that island and take them wherever the ship was heading. Meanwhile Auristela and Transila had time to prepare Taurisa for burial, Christian piety, pity, and modesty not permitting them to undress her. Mauricio returned with the tools, having negotiated everything he wanted. Taurisa's grave was dug; but the sailors, being Catholics, didn't want any made for the two men killed in the duel.[1]

Rosamunda, who after returning from declaring her evil intentions to Antonio the barbarian hadn't lifted her eyes from the ground, her sins keeping them cast down, lifted her head when they were going to bury Taurisa and said, "If you feel you're charitable, ladies and gentlemen, and if justice and mercy walk hand in hand in your hearts, use those two virtues with me. Ever since I've been old enough to know right from wrong, I've never chosen right and have always been bad. What with my green youth and great beauty, too much freedom and abundant wealth, vices began taking possession of me in such a way that they have been and are an integral part of me. You already know, since I've told you before, that I've had my foot on the neck of kings and have held men's wills in my hands whenever I wished; but time, the thief and robber of women's physical beauty, stole in for mine while I was so unsuspecting that I've become ugly before giving up my illusions of beauty. Since vices make their place in the soul, which doesn't age, they won't leave me; and since I don't try to resist them, rather let myself be swept away on the current of my desires, I've allowed myself to be swept away by a desire caused just by seeing this barbarian youth. Although I made my desires plain, he doesn't return my feeling, which is made of fire, while his is of frozen snow. I find myself rejected and despised, instead of respected and well loved, blows that can't be fended off with so little patience and so much desire. Now death is already stepping on my skirts and stretching out its hand to snatch me from life. By whatever you feel a heart filled with goodness owes a miserable one who entrusts herself to it, I beg you to cover my fire with ice and bury me in that grave; for although you mix my lustful bones with those of this pure young woman, they won't contaminate them, for good relics are always good wherever they may be."

Turning to young Antonio, she continued, "And you, proud youth, who are reaching or about to reach the borders and boundaries of pleasure, ask Heaven to guide you in such a way that neither old age nor fading beauty will search you out; and if I've offended your fresh ears—I'll call them that—with my thoughtless and indecent words, forgive me, for those who ask forgiveness at a time like this deserve to be pardoned out of simple courtesy, and if not pardoned at least heard." Having said this, and letting a long sigh escape, she was engulfed in a mortal swoon.

Chapter Twenty-One of the First Book of Persiles and Sigismunda

I don't know," said Mauricio at this point, "what this thing they call love is doing in these mountains, in these deserted and rocky places, among all this snow and ice, leaving behind Paphos, Cnossus, Cyprus, and the Elysian Fields,[1] places from where hunger flees, where there's no discomfort at all. Delightful love finds a dwelling place in peaceful hearts and calm spirits, but not in tears nor in unpleasant surprises."

Auristela, Transila, Constanza, and Ricla were stunned by this turn of events and silence was the expression of their astonishment; finally, with no few tears they buried Taurisa, and after Rosamunda regained consciousness they gathered together and embarked in the ship's boat. They were welcomed and treated warmly by those on board the ship, and then promptly satisfied the hunger afflicting them all; only Rosamunda didn't eat, for her condition had her continually knocking at death's door.

They hoisted the sails, some of them wept for the two dead captains, and right away they appointed one man to be captain over them all; then they continued their voyage with no planned destination, for they were pirates (not Irishmen as they had told Arnaldo) from an island in rebellion against England. Mauricio, uneasy in that company, was constantly afraid some misfortune might result from the pirates' fast living and evil ways of life; and since he was old and experienced in the ways of the world his heart kept pounding in his chest for fear that Auristela's great beauty, his daughter Transila's attractive and striking good looks, and Constanza's youth and unusual attire would awaken evil thoughts in the pirates. The young Antonio acted as their Argus,[2] serving them like the shepherd by the Anfriso.[3] The two men's eyes were like unsleeping sentries keeping vigil during the night watch over gentle and beautiful lambs sheltered beneath their care and vigilance.

Rosamunda, suffering from rejection, wasted away until one night they found her entombed in perpetual silence in one of the ship's cabins. They had already wept a great deal, but still felt grief and Christian compassion for her death. The wide sea served as her grave, although even it didn't have enough water to quench the fire kindled in her heart by the attractive Antonio.

Like everyone else Antonio often begged the pirates to take them once and for all to Ireland, or to Hibernia,[4] if they didn't want to take them to England or Scotland. But the pirates always replied that until they had taken a good, rich prize, they weren't going to touch land, except to take on water or get necessary supplies. Ricla the barbarian gladly would have paid pieces of gold for them all to be taken to England, but she didn't dare bring them out for fear the pirates would steal rather than accept them in payment for safe passage.

The captain gave them separate quarters and made arrangements that provided safety from the insolence they might have had to fear from the soldiers. Under these circumstances they traveled from one place to another on the sea for almost three months; now they landed on one island, now on another; sometimes they would go out to the open sea—normal behavior for pirates looking for profit; at other times when the sea was peaceful and they were becalmed, they couldn't move at all.

To amuse himself the ship's new captain would go to his passengers' cabin, entertaining them with intelligent conversation and humorous but always decent stories, and Mauricio did the same. But Auristela, Transila, Ricla, and Constanza were busier thinking about the absence of their souls' better halves than listening to the captain or to Mauricio. Nevertheless one day they did pay careful attention to a story told them by the captain, and related in the next chapter.

Chapter Twenty-Two

Where the Captain Tells of the Elaborate Festivals
King Policarpo Was Accustomed to Holding in His Kingdom

Heaven gave me as my homeland one of the islands near that of Hibernia; it's so large it's called a 'kingdom,' though one not inherited or passed down by succession from father to son. Its inhabitants choose as their ruler whomever they think best, always striving to insure he's the best and most virtuous man to be found in the kingdom. Without the intervention of pleadings and negotiations, and without being wooed by promises or bribes, the king emerges from the common consensus and takes up the scepter of absolute command, which lasts as long as he lives or until his virtue diminishes. Because of this, those who aren't kings try to be virtuous in order to become one, while those already kings strive to be even more virtuous so they won't be obliged to stop ruling. Thanks to this, soaring ambition's wings are clipped, greed is grounded, and although hypocrisy is everywhere at work, in the long run its mask falls off and it fails to win the prize. As a result the people live in peace, justice triumphs and mercy gleams, and the petitions of the poor are handled with dispatch while those of the rich are not dispatched one bit better because of their wealth. The scale of justice is not tipped by bribes nor by the flesh and blood of kinship, and all business dealings proceed reasonably according to the rules. Finally, it's a kingdom where everyone lives free from the threat of insolence and where each person enjoys what is his.

"This custom (in my view a just and holy one) placed the kingdom's scepter in the hands of Policarpo, a gentleman as distinguished and famous in the practice of arms as of letters. When he became king he had two extremely beautiful daughters; the elder was called Policarpa and the younger Sinforosa. They no longer had their mother with them, but at her death they lost only her companionship, for thanks to their own virtues and sweet manner they became their own governesses, setting a marvelous example for the whole kingdom. These good qualities made both them and their father well loved and respected by everyone.

"The kings there, believing melancholy often awakens negative thoughts in their subjects, try to keep the people happy and entertained with public festivals and occasional light comedies; above all they would celebrate the day of their coronation, reinstituting as best they could the festival the pagans called the 'Olympic Games.' They designated a prize for the runners, honored the skilled, crowned the marksmen, and praised to the sky those who threw others to the ground. They would hold this spectacle at the shore on a spacious beach, sheltered and shaded from the sun by countless interwoven branches; in the center they placed a sumptuous dais on which the king and the royal family would sit to watch the entertaining contests.

"One of those days rolled around and Policarpo tried to outdo the magnificence and grandeur of all the other previous celebrations. When his royal highness along with the most important people of the kingdom were already on the dais, when the musical instruments of peace and war were about ready to signal the beginning of the festival, and when four runners—agile and swift youths—already had their left feet planted in front of them and their right feet raised—with nothing holding them back from springing into the race except a cord used as the starting mark and dropped as a signal that they were to sprint to a point marked as the finish line—I repeat, at this very moment they saw a boat whose sides gleamed white from recent caulking coming over the sea cutting smartly through the water aided by six oars on each side, rowed by what were observed to be twelve attractive young men with bulging shoulders and chests and sinewy arms. They were all dressed in white except for the one steering the rudder, who was dressed in red like a sailor.

"The boat reached the beach at a furious speed and its running aground and everyone on board leaping ashore was accomplished in a single motion. Policarpo ordered the race not to begin until they found out who those people were and why they had come, although he imagined they were probably there to join in the festival and put their skills to the test in the games.

"The first to step forward to speak to the king was the one who had acted as helmsman; he was a very young man whose smooth, clean cheeks were snowy white and blushing red, his locks of hair like golden rings, and his face perfect in every detail; the parts altogether were so handsome they formed a marvelous whole. The beautiful figure cut by the youth captured the attention and even the hearts of everyone who looked at him and naturally, I too, began to take a strong liking to him.

"He said to the king, 'My Lord, my companions and I, hearing of these games, have come to serve you and participate in them, and we come not from distant lands but from a ship we left off the isle of Scinta, not far from here. Since the wind was of no help to head the ship in this direction we made use of this boat, the oars, and the strength of our arms. We're all noblemen and want to win fame. So, appealing to the respect that as king you should show to strangers who come before you, we request your permission to demonstrate our strength and intelligence for our own glory and gain as well as your pleasure.'

"'Certainly, my fair young sir,' replied Policarpo, 'since you ask for what you want with so much grace and courtesy, it would be unfair to deny it to you. Honor my festival in any way you wish; leave me the responsibility of rewarding you for it, for if your striking figure is any indication, you leave very little hope for anyone else to win the best prizes.'

"The handsome youth bent his knee and bowed his head showing both his good breeding and his gratitude; then in two bounds he placed himself at the cord holding back the four swift runners, while his twelve companions moved to one side as spectators of the race. A trumpet sounded, they dropped the cord, and the five leaped forward at flying speed; but before they'd taken twenty steps the newcomer was leading by more than six and after thirty steps he was ahead of them by more than fifteen; finally, when the others were little more than halfway and seemed like motionless statues, he finished the race to the admiration of all present, especially Sinforosa, who didn't take her eyes off him whether he was running or standing still, for the youth's good looks and agility were enough to attract not only the eyes but the hearts and goodwill of everyone watching him. (I happened to notice this because my own eyes were attentively following Policarpa, the sweet object of my desires, and as they gazed after her Sinforosa's movements also came into view.)

"On seeing how easily the stranger had carried off the prize for running, envy began to take possession of his competitors' hearts. The second event was fencing. Our man on the winning streak took up the foil; using it against six others who came out against him one by one, he closed their mouths, flicked flies off their noses, sealed their eyes, and blessed their heads, without their touching a single hair on *his* head, as the saying goes.

"The crowd raised their voices and awarded him the first prize by acclamation. Then six others got ready to wrestle, and against them the youth showed even more skill; he bared his broad shoulders, his wide and extraordinarily solid chest, and the sinews and muscles of his powerful arms; with these and with skill and incredible dexterity—to their despair and sorrow—he pinned the shoulders of the other six fighters to the ground. Then he grabbed hold of a heavy bar thrust into the ground, for they told him throwing it was the fourth event. He hefted it, and signaling to the crowd in front of him to make room for the throw, taking the bar by one end and without even drawing his arm back, he hurled it with such force that it flew past the boundary marked by the beach, and the sea had to provide one, for the bar ended up buried well out into the water.

"Seeing this prodigious throw his opponents became discouraged and didn't dare compete in the event. Next they put a crossbow and some arrows into his hands and showed him a very tall, smooth tree at the top of which was driven a short spear; on it, tied by a string, was a dove to be shot at no more than once by those wishing to prove themselves in that event. One fellow who claimed to be a marksman stepped forward and took the first turn, planning, I believe, to get the jump on them and bring down the dove before anyone else; he shot and drove his arrow into almost the very end of the spear, the blow startling the dove and causing it to spring up into the air. Then another, no less sure of himself than the first, shot with such skillful marksmanship that he broke the string by which the dove was tied; she, loosed and set free from the restraining bond, entrusted her freedom to the wind and flapped her wings rapidly. But the one now accustomed to winning all the first prizes shot his arrow and, as if he were ordering it what to do and it had understanding to obey him, that's what it did; splitting the air with a long, rasping whistle, it reached the dove and pierced its heart, thus depriving it in the same instant of flight and life. At this the voices of those present renewed their shouts and praises for the stranger who in the race, in fencing, in wrestling, in the bar throw, in the crossbow shoot, and in many other contests I haven't described, had made off with all the first prizes by very large margins, saving his companions the trouble of competing at all.

"It was close to sundown when the games were finished; King Policarpo, along with the judges who were with him, was just getting up from his seat to reward the victorious youth when he saw him kneeling before him saying, 'Our ship was left all alone and unprotected, and a rather dark night is falling. I wish, great Lord—since the prizes I'm expecting will come from your hand and should be given the highest esteem—that you would defer the awards for another occasion, for I'm planning to return to serve you when there's more time and I'm in a better position to do so.'

"The King embraced him and asked his name; he said he was called Periandro. With this the beautiful Sinforosa removed a garland of flowers adorning her uncommonly beautiful head and placed it on that of the handsome youth, saying to him with modest grace as she put it there, 'When my father is lucky enough to have you return to visit him, you'll see that you've come not only to serve him, but to be served.'"

Chapter Twenty-Three

What Happened to Jealous Auristela When She Found Out It Was Her Brother Periandro Who Had Won the Prizes in the Competition

Oh, powerful force of jealousy! Oh, sickness that so infects the soul that only a person's death will get rid of you! Oh, most beautiful Auristela! Stop! Don't rush to let this raging disease take its place in your mind! But who can keep thoughts within bounds? They tend to be light and airy, have no body, can pass through walls, pierce hearts, and see into the most hidden recesses of the soul.

The above has been said because when Auristela heard her brother Periandro's name mentioned—having already heard the praises of Sinforosa and about the favor she showed by putting the garland on him—her suffering yielded to suspicion and patience surrendered to moans; heaving a deep sigh and embracing Transila, she said, "My dear friend, pray to Heaven that my brother has been lost without you losing your husband Ladislao. Don't you just see him (as described by this gallant captain) honored as a conquerer, crowned for his bravery, and more attentive to a maiden's favors than to the worries his sister's exile and wanderings should be causing him? Isn't he off looking for palm branches[1] and trophies in strange lands, leaving his sister among the steep rocks, crags, and mountains heaped up by the raging sea? And, isn't it true that because of his advice and wishes there's no mortal danger in which I haven't found myself?"

The ship's captain listened very carefully to these words but didn't know what conclusion to draw from them. He started to speak but didn't say anything in response to Auristela because a wind came up so suddenly and so strong that it snatched the words out of his mouth in an instant or a split second, bringing him to his feet to yell to the sailors to lower the sails, furl, and secure them. They all rushed to their tasks and the ship began to run before the wind over the rough seas toward wherever the gale wanted to carry it.

Mauricio retired into the cabin with his companions so the sailors could do their jobs without hindrance. Once there Transila asked Auristela what had so upset her, for to her whatever it was seemed to have been caused by hearing Periandro's name, and she couldn't imagine why hearing a brother praised for his successes should cause distress. "Oh, friend!" answered Auristela. "I'm obliged to keep perpetual silence concerning a pilgrimage I'm on, so much so that until I finish it, although my life may end first, I'm forced to keep silent about it. When you learn who I am, as you surely will if God wills it, you'll see the reasons for my distress, and on learning its cause you'll see pure thoughts under attack but not defeated; you'll see unsought-for misfortunes and know that we've escaped from labyrinths thanks to unimagined and fortunate turns of events. Don't you know how strong family ties to a brother are? Well, I have an even stronger tie than that to Periandro. And don't you also know how natural it is for those in love to be jealous? Well, I'm even more than naturally jealous of my brother. Didn't this captain, my friend, glowingly describe Sinforosa's beauty and didn't Periandro, as she crowned his brow, look her over? Yes, I'm sure of it. As for my brother, haven't you yourself seen the extent of his merits and good looks? Then would it be surprising if he'd awakened a thought in Sinforosa's mind that might make him forget his sister?"

"Stop and think, my lady," responded Transila, "everything the captain has related happened before your imprisonment on the Barbarous Isle and since then you've both seen each other and talked together, so you must know that not only does he not love anyone else, but he doesn't care about anything except making you happy; I just can't believe jealousy's power is so far-reaching that it can make a sister feel jealous about her own brother."

"Look here, Transila my daughter," said Mauricio, "love's manifestations are as diverse as they are inscrutable and its laws as numerous as they are variable; try to be wise enough not to pry into other peoples' thoughts nor attempt to find out more about someone than he or she may want to tell you. It's fine to be curious about the details and fine points of one's own business, but don't even think of minding other people's, which doesn't concern us." Hearing Mauricio say this made Auristela put her discretion and her tongue on guard, for Transila's rather foolish talk was on its way to making her let her whole story out of the bag.

Meanwhile the wind slacked before there was time for the sailors to become fearful or the passengers upset. The captain went to see them again to continue his story, for his curiosity had been piqued by the alarm Auristela had shown on hearing Periandro's name. Auristela also wanted to get back to the earlier conversation to learn from the captain whether the favors Sinforosa had done for Periandro had gone beyond just crowning him with flowers, and so she asked about it coyly and cautiously so as not to reveal her thinking. The captain replied that Sinforosa hadn't had time to be more gracious to Periandro—and that's what it should be called when ladies grant their favors. Still, in spite of Sinforosa's goodness, he was troubled by certain indications leading him to believe she couldn't entirely free her mind of Periandro: after his departure, whenever his accomplishments were mentioned, she would praise them to the skies. His suspicions had been further confirmed when she ordered him to set out on a ship to search for Periandro and make him return to see her father.

"What? Is it possible," asked Auristela, "that great ladies, kings' daughters, sitting high and mighty on Fortune's throne, will bring themselves down to the level of admitting that their thoughts are fixed on humble subjects? And even if that's true—just as it is that greatness and majesty don't mix well with love, love and greatness instead repelling each other—it still must follow that Sinforosa, being a beautiful and unattached queen, wouldn't allow herself to be captivated at first sight by an unknown young man whose social position wasn't very promising, since he arrived steering the rudder of a boat accompanied by twelve naked companions, as are all those who ply the oars."

"Be still, Auristela my daughter," said Mauricio, "for in no other natural phenomena does one see greater or more frequent miracles than in those having to do with love, for its wonders are so many and so great that they go unmentioned and unnoticed however extraordinary they might be. Love unites scepters with shepherd's crooks, greatness with lowliness, makes possible the impossible, equalizes different social ranks, and becomes as powerful as death. You already know perfectly, lady, and I'm well aware of it too, the nobility, good looks, and worth of your brother Periandro, whose separate elements compose a figure of singular beauty; and it's the privilege of beauty to subdue wills and attract the hearts of all who come to know it; the greater and more recognized the beauty, the more it's loved and esteemed. Therefore it would be no miracle if Sinforosa, however important she might be, should love your brother, for she wouldn't be loving him just as Periandro, but as a handsome, brave, swift, and skilled individual in whom all the virtues are collected and held up for display."

"What?! Periandro is this lady's brother?" said the captain. "Yes," replied Transila, "and because of his absence she lives in perpetual sadness; all of us join in her bitter weeping, for we love her dearly and knew him." Then they told him everything about the sinking of Arnaldo's ship, the separation of the dinghy from the boat, and everything necessary for him to understand what had happened up to that point.

At precisely this point the author leaves the first book of this great story and moves on to the second, where things will be related that, though they stay within the bounds of truth, will surpass those of the imagination, for the wildest and most ingenious one could scarcely conceive of its events.

THE END OF THE FIRST BOOK
OF THE TRIALS OF PERSILES AND SIGISMUNDA,
A NORTHERN STORY

Book Two of The Story of The Trials of Persiles and Sigismunda
A Northern Story

First Chapter

*Which Tells How the Ship
Capsized with Everyone on Board*

It seems the author of this story knew more about being in love than being a historian, because he spends almost all this first, opening chapter of the second book on a definition of jealousy, prompted by the jealousy Auristela felt regarding what the ship's captain told her; but in this translation—for that's what it is[1]—it has been removed because it's too tedious—besides being a topic often aired and discussed; instead we go straight to the truth of the matter, that is, as the wind changed and clouds gathered, a dark and gloomy night fell; and thunder, sending lightning as its messenger then followed after it; the sailors began to worry and everyone on the ship was bewildered; the squall began with such fury that even the efforts and skill of the sailors couldn't withstand it, and so, confusion and the storm struck them at the same time. But this didn't keep anyone from manning his post and doing the tasks he thought necessary, perhaps not to escape death but at least to prolong life; the daring souls who entrust theirs to a few ships' planks defend themselves as best they can, even putting their hopes in a timber perhaps torn from the ship in a storm, clinging to it and thinking its hard embrace a great good comfort.

So, too, Mauricio clung to his daughter Transila, and Antonio embraced Ricla and Constanza, his mother and sister. Only poor Auristela was left with no refuge except the anxiety that comes with the approach of death, to which she would gladly have given herself if it were permitted by the Christian and Catholic religion she tried very sincerely to observe. And so she huddled with them, and knotted together—or rather cowering in a ball—they let themselves be

101

pushed down into the stern of the ship to escape the frightening noise of the thunder, the intermittent flashes of lightning, and the confused shouting of the sailors. In that limbo they were prevented from seeing that at times, when the ship was flung above the clouds, they could have touched the sky, while at others the topsail was sweeping the sands at the bottom of the sea. They waited for death with their eyes closed, or to be more exact, they feared it without seeing it, for the figure of death, no matter how it comes dressed, is terrifying, and an unexpected death that comes for someone still having all his strength and health is truly horrible.

The storm so worsened that the sailors' skills, the captain's diligence, and finally everyone's hopes of being saved were all exhausted. Now no voices were heard shouting to do this or that, only prayers and vows being made and sent up to Heaven. This suffering and distress was so great that Transila no longer thought of Ladislao nor Auristela of Periandro, for one of death's powerful effects is to erase everything having to do with life from one's memory, even keeping people from feeling jealousy's passion (which is another way of saying it can do the impossible). There was no hourglass there to count the hours, no compass to indicate the direction of the wind, nor any way to guess where they were. All was confusion, all screams, all sighs and prayers. The captain blacked out, the sailors gave themselves up for lost, human strength was overcome, and in the midst of their laments silence took possession of the voices of the suffering folk as one by one they lost consciousness.

The insolent sea dared stroll over the deck of the ship and to visit even the highest topsails that as if to avenge this insult kissed the sands in the depths of the ocean. Finally at daybreak—if one could call "day" something bringing no light whatsoever with it—the ship stopped and stalled, not moving at all, one of the greatest dangers, aside from sinking, that can happen to a sailing ship. Finally, beaten by a furious hurricane and flipped over as though by some trick, it plunged its topsail into the depths of the water, exposing its keel to the sky and becoming a tomb for everyone on board.

Farewell, Auristela's modest thoughts; goodbye, best-laid plans; rest in peace, conduct as honored as it is saintly; don't expect any other mausoleums, pyramids, or obelisks than those offered you by these poorly tarred planks! And you, Transila, shining example of chastity, may now celebrate your wedding in the arms of your wise and aged father; although not with your husband Ladislao, at least you will be wedded to the faith, which by this time must have led you to a better bridal bed. And you, Ricla, whose desires were leading you toward a peaceful sanctuary, gather your children Antonio and Constanza to you and put them in the presence of Him who has taken your life now in order to give you a better one in Heaven.

In conclusion, the overturning of the ship and the certainty that those on board would die put the preceding words into the pen of the author of this great and sad story, as well as those to be heard in the next chapter.

Second Chapter of the Second Book

Where a Strange Event Is Related

It seems the ship's turning over overturned, or to be more exact, confused the mind of the author of this story since he wrote four or five beginnings for this second chapter, almost as if he doubted his purpose in it. He finally made up his mind, saying that happiness and unhappiness usually come so close together that perhaps there's no middle ground to separate them. Sorrow and pleasure are so closely linked that it's equally foolish for the sad to despair and the happy to feel secure, as this strange event clearly shows.

The ship was entombed, as has been said, in the water; the dead were buried without earth, their hopes undone and all help impossible for them; but merciful Heaven, which long ago set the course to help our misfortunes, ordained that the ship, gradually pushed toward shore by the waves now grown gentle and mild, should come to a beach that for the time being was calm and peaceful enough to serve as a safe harbor. Not far away was a very spacious port filled with many vessels, and reflected in its waters—as if in a clear mirror—a populous city with fine buildings climbed up a high hill.

The townspeople saw the hulk of the ship and thought it a whale or some other great fish done in by the earlier squall. Many came out to see it and on ascertaining it was a ship informed King Policarpo, lord of the city; then he, accompanied by his two beautiful daughters Policarpa and Sinforosa and several others, also came out and ordered the ship secured all over by means of capstans, winches, and boats, so it could be taken in tow and brought to port. Some of the people, having jumped onto the ship, told the king they could hear pounding and perhaps even human voices inside.

An elderly gentleman who happened to be next to the king said to him, "My Lord, I remember having seen a Spanish galley along the Genovese coast in the Mediterranean Sea; when the sail made it heel over too sharply it flipped, leaving it just like this vessel with the mast in the sands and the keel up to the sky; before they turned it over or righted it, hearing noises like the ones coming from inside this one, they sawed into the keel, making a hole so they could see what was inside, and no sooner had light entered that opening than the captain of the galley and four of his company came out through it. I myself saw this and the case is written up in many Spanish histories; even now it's quite possible there are people still alive who were born for a second time from the womb of that galley. If the same thing should happen here it won't have to be thought of as a miracle, but a mystery, for miracles happen outside the laws of nature while mysteries are things that seem like miracles but really aren't, rather merely events that rarely happen."

"Well, what are we waiting for?" said the king. "Saw a hole right now and let's see this mystery, but if this belly disgorges living people, I'll consider it a miracle." Great was the haste with which they set to sawing through the hull and great the desire they all had to see the birth. Finally a large opening was made which revealed dead people—in reality dead ones and living ones who only seemed so; someone stuck in his arm and grabbed hold of a young woman, and putting his hand over her heart he could feel signs of life; others reached in, each one of them fishing out his own prize; some of them, thinking they were getting live ones, brought out the dead, for fishermen aren't always lucky. Finally, on contact with the air and light, those who were half-alive caught their breath and began to breathe, wiped their faces, rubbed their eyes, stretched their arms and, as though waking from a heavy sleep, looked all around; Auristela found herself in Arnaldo's arms, Transila in Clodio's, Ricla and Constanza in Rutilio's, though the elder Antonio and his son weren't in anyone's, for they got out by themselves, as did Mauricio.

Arnaldo was still feeling more stunned and dazed than those who had been revived, deader than the dead. Auristela looked at him, but not recognizing him the first thing she said was—for she was the first to break the general silence—"By any chance, brother, is the very beautiful Sinforosa among these people?"

"Good God, what's this?" said Arnaldo to himself. "How can she be thinking about Sinforosa at a time when it's unreasonable to think of anything except giving thanks to Heaven for its recent mercies?" But despite all that, he answered her saying, yes Sinforosa was there, then asked how she knew her, for Arnaldo wasn't aware the ship's captain had told Auristela about Periandro's triumphs and thus he couldn't fathom why she was asking for Sinforosa. Had he understood it perhaps he would have said jealousy's power is so great and so cunning that it can join and enter with the sharp knife of death itself, haunting the love-stricken soul even in the last critical moments of life.

Then, when both the fear felt by those brought back to life (yes, they really were!) as well as when the astonishment of the living who'd fished them out had somewhat subsided and everyone began to speak rationally again, they all began asking each other at the same time how those from land happened to be there and how those on the ship had gotten there. At this point Policarpo, seeing that after the hold had been opened in the ship the air space inside had been filling with water, ordered it towed to shore and beached by mechanical means; all of this was done with great dispatch.

At the same time all the people who had been on the ship's keel went ashore and were greeted with as much delight as astonishment by King Policarpo, his daughters, and all the most important citizens. But what astonished them most, especially Sinforosa, was seeing Auristela's incomparable beauty; Transila's beauty also contributed to this astonishment, as did Constanza the barbarian's attractive and unusual dress, plus her youth and elegance, which did not totally overshadow her mother Ricla's good looks and grace. Then, since the city was nearby they all walked there, not bothering to arrange for someone to take them.

By this time Periandro had managed to talk with his sister Auristela, Ladislao with Transila, and the barbarian father with his wife and daughter, and they were giving one another accounts of their adventures. Only Auristela, totally occupied in watching Sinforosa, was quiet. But finally she spoke to Periandro, saying, "By any chance, brother, is this exceptionally beautiful maiden walking with us Sinforosa, King Policarpo's daughter?" "She is," replied Periandro, "and she's a person in whom beauty and courtesy make their home." "She must be very courteous," responded Auristela, "for she's very beautiful."

"Even if she weren't so beautiful," answered Periandro, "the obligations that place me in her debt, my dear sister, would make her seem so to me." "If it's a question of obligations, and you measure beauty by them, then you should think my beauty the greatest on earth, considering how much you owe *me*." "Divine attributes," replied Periandro, "shouldn't be compared with human ones; hyperbole and praise, no matter how lavish, do have their limits. To say that a woman is more beautiful than an angel is a courteous exaggeration, not a binding statement. For you alone, my sweetest sister, are rules broken, and hyperbole offered up to your beauty takes on the force of truth."

"If my trials and anxieties, dear brother, hadn't taken their toll on my beauty, perhaps I could believe the praises you give it are sincere. But I hope to merciful Heaven that someday my unrest will be laid to rest and my storms turned to clear skies; in the meantime, as strongly as I can I beg you not to let the beauty of strangers or other obligations remove or erase from your mind what you owe me, for my beauty and your obligations to me should satisfy your desires and fill the empty niche in your heart; and you'll see that in joining the beauty of my body—such as it is—to that of my soul, you'll find an even more satisfying combination of beauties." Periandro was confused by Auristela's words; he thought she must be jealous, something new for him, for throughout his long experience with her he had never known Auristela's good sense to let her go beyond the limits of modesty; her tongue never moved except to express virtuous and pure thoughts, nor had she ever said anything to him either in public or in private which would be improper to say to a brother.

Arnaldo was feeling envious of Periandro; Ladislao was happy with his wife Transila, as was Mauricio with his daughter and son-in-law and the elder Antonio with his wife and children; Rutilio rejoiced at their all being found, while the slanderer Clodio was glad for the opportunity now available to him to tell of the wonderful strange event wherever he might find himself.

They reached the city where the generous Policarpo honored his guests regally and magnificently, ordering that they all be lodged in his palace and outdoing himself in his treatment of Arnaldo, whom he now knew was the heir of Denmark and whose love for Auristela had taken him from his kingdom. As soon as Policarpo had seen Auristela's beauty, in his heart he, too, understood Arnaldo's pilgrimage.

Policarpa[1] and Sinforosa lodged Auristela practically in the same room with them; Sinforosa didn't take her eyes off Auristela, thanking Heaven for having made her Periandro's sister and not his beloved; therefore, as much for her great beauty as for the close family ties she had to Periandro, Sinforosa adored Auristela and couldn't bear to leave her side for a moment. She observed her actions intently, took note of her every word, reflected on her charm, and even the sound and timbre of her voice gave her pleasure. As for Auristela, she was watching Sinforosa in almost the same way and with the same intensity. The two had different intentions, however, for Sinforosa was watching with sincere goodwill, but Auristela with jealousy.

They spent some days in the city recovering from their earlier trials, Arnaldo was plotting a course to return to Denmark or wherever Auristela and Periandro wanted to go, and he was making it obvious, as he always did, that the brother and sister's wishes were all he, too, wanted. Clodio, who had been watching Arnaldo's actions with the idle and curious eyes and had seen how the yoke of love was choking him, found himself alone with him one day and said, "I've always censored the vices of princes in public, not observing the proper decorum owed to their greatness and not fearing the harm done by slander; now I beg you to listen patiently—even though you may not want to hear it—to something I wish to tell you in secret, for unpleasantness told in the form of advice can be excused by virtue of its good intentions."

Arnaldo was confused, not knowing where Clodio's preamble was going to lead, but he decided to listen and find out, telling him to say whatever he wanted. With this promise of safe-conduct Clodio proceeded, saying, "You, my Lord, love Auristela; not just 'love,' but I should say 'adore'; and to the best of my knowledge you know no more about her social position or who she is than what she's been willing to tell you, which is nothing. She's been in your power for more than two years, during which time, according to what we're supposed to believe, you've made every possible effort to soften her firmness, tame her sternness, and subject her will to yours through the honorable and effective method of matrimony; yet she's just as firm in her resolve today as the first day you began to court her, from which fact I conclude that, just as you have too much patience, she shows too little gratitude; you need to consider that there must be some great mystery involved when a woman rejects a kingdom and a prince worthy of her love.

"There's also something mysterious about a young vagabond woman wandering from land to land, from island to island, exposed to inclement weather from the sky as well as hazards on land, which are usually worse than those on the stormy sea. All this, while cautiously concealing her lineage and accompanied by a young man who, although she says he's her brother, may not in fact be so. Of all the good things Heaven distributes among mortals, those having to do with honor should be the most esteemed, for honor should be placed before life itself; the wise measure their desires by the rule of reason and not by the desires themselves."

Clodio had reached this point and showed every sign of wanting to continue with this serious philosophic discourse when in came Periandro; at his arrival Clodio grew silent despite his wishes to continue and Arnaldo's to hear him. At the same time Mauricio, Ladislao, and Transila also came in, and with them Auristela, leaning on Sinforosa's shoulder and feeling so indisposed that it was necessary to take her to bed; her illness so startled and frightened Periandro and Arnaldo that if they hadn't prudently concealed their feelings they would have needed the doctors just as much as Auristela.

The Third Chapter of the Second Book

As soon as Policarpo learned of Auristela's illness he sent for doctors to examine her, and since the pulse like a tongue tells what illness a person is suffering, Auristela's let them know her affliction was of the soul, not of the body. Periandro recognized her illness before they did, Arnaldo understood it in part, but Clodio knew what it was better than anyone. The doctors ordered them not to leave her alone for a minute and to try to entertain and amuse her with music—if she wished—or with other cheerful kinds of entertainment. Sinforosa took charge of Auristela's health and offered to keep her company at all times, an offer Auristela didn't like very much, for she would have preferred not to have so close at hand what she considered the cause of her illness. She didn't expect to recover from this illness for she was determined not to tell anyone what was wrong. Her modesty tied her tongue and her dignity resisted her desire to speak.

Finally everyone cleared out of Auristela's room leaving Sinforosa and Policarpa alone with her. With an obvious pretext Sinforosa soon sent her sister out; no sooner was she alone with Auristela than, putting her mouth to Auristela's squeezing her hands tightly between her own and sighing ardently, she seemed to try to transfer her soul into Auristela's body. These signs of affection once more upset Auristela who said to her, "What's this, my lady? Should I interpret this behavior to mean you're sicker than I and your soul more wounded than mine? Try and think whether I can be of any help to you, for even though my body is sick my will is still strong."

"My sweet friend," replied Sinforosa, "I appreciate your kind offer with all my heart, and in the same spirit of goodwill with which you offer your help I'll respond, not out of any pretended politeness or lukewarm feelings of obligation. My sister—that's what I'll call you—for as long as my life may last, I'll love, desire, and adore. Did I really say that? No, because shame and being who I am always tie my tongue. But, must I keep still till I die, or will my affliction be cured by some miracle? Can silence speak, by any chance? Can two modest and shy eyes have both the ability and strength to proclaim the countless thoughts of a soul in love?"

Sinforosa went on talking like this and her many tears and sighs moved Auristela to dry her eyes for her, then to embrace her and say to her, "Don't let your words, my passionate lady, die in your mouth. Dismiss confusion and embarrassment for a short time and make me your confidante; for when misfortunes are told to others, they may at least find some relief, if not a cure. If your passion comes from love, as I have good reason to believe, then there's no doubt in my mind that you're made of flesh—although you seem to be of alabaster—just as I also know the soul of each of us is always in continual movement, unable to avoid wanting that someone toward whom the stars incline us, though it's wrong to say they force us to love. Tell me, my lady, whom you want, whom you love and whom you adore, for as long as you haven't succumbed to the madness of falling in love with a bull[1] or to the craziness of the man who adored a banana tree,[2] and as long as it's a man you adore—as you put it— it won't shock or amaze me. I'm a woman like you and have my own desires; until now, in order to protect my soul's honor, they haven't left my mouth, though it's true I easily could have let them slip out during my fever; but in the end they'll surely break through all prohibitions, and I'll say the unthinkable and make known the cause of my death, if only in my last will and testament."

Sinforosa was looking at Auristela intently. She weighed every word she said as if it were a pronouncement from the mouth of an oracle. "Oh, my lady," she cried, "I can't tell you how firmly I believe that Heaven, feeling pain for my pain and sorrow for my sorrow, has brought you to this land, and by such a strange roundabout route that it seems a miracle. From the dark womb of the ship Heaven brought you forth into the light of the world so my darkness might have light and my desires a way out of their confusion. And so, to keep neither myself nor you in suspense any longer, you should know that your brother Periandro came to this island . . . ." Then she told in succession about his arrival, his triumphs, the opponents he'd beaten, and the prizes he'd won, as has already been related. She also told her how first her brother Periandro's charms had awakened a sort of desire in her that wasn't love, rather more a friendly interest. But later when she was alone and idle she began going over and over his charms in her head and love began to portray him to her not as an ordinary man, but as a prince, for if he wasn't one he certainly deserved to be. "This picture was engraved on my soul and without realizing it I let it be, not putting up any resistance at all, and so little by little I came to want him, to love him, and even to adore him, as I've said."

Sinforosa would have gone on if Policarpa hadn't returned planning to entertain Auristela by singing to the accompaniment of a harp she was carrying. Sinforosa fell silent and Auristela felt lost, but the silence of the one and the confusion of the other didn't keep them from listening closely to Policarpa, who was a matchless musician. In her own language she began to sing a song that Antonio the barbarian later said meant the following in Castilian:

> Oh Cynthia,[3] if seeing now with opened eyes
> cannot restore your former freedom lost;
> 'tis neither brave nor honest to restrain,
> so loose the reins of pain that bind your life.
>
> That very same but noble passion true
> which holds your free will captive in its grip
> will bring your long-held silence to its death
> just when you think it must forever last.
>
> May feeble voice come to your aching soul,
> for it is wise and good to let the tongue
> say what the poor soul in its anguish feels.
>
> If you can grieve aloud, at least the world
> will know how hot love's fever burned in you,
> for smoking words came signaling from your mouth.[4]

No one else understood as well as Sinforosa the verses sung by Policarpa, who knew all about her desires; and although she had decided to bury them in the darkness of silence, now she resolved to take her sister's advice and continue telling Auristela her thoughts, as she had already begun to do. Sinforosa had often stayed with Auristela, making it appear she was keeping her company more out of kindness than because she enjoyed it. Finally, taking up the thread of the earlier conversation she said to her, "Hear me once again, my lady, and don't let my words tire you, for the ones boiling up from my soul won't let my tongue rest. I'll explode if I don't say them, and the fear of just that forces me to tell you—in spite of what it may do for my reputation—that I'm dying for your brother; when I noticed his good qualities I was attracted to him and fell in love; not bothering to find out who his parents are, what his homeland is, the extent of his wealth, or how high fortune has lifted him, I care only about the generous endowments given him by the hand of nature. For himself alone I want him, for himself alone I love him, for himself alone I adore him; and for your own sake, I beg you to remember who you are and not to speak ill of my hasty thoughts but to help me in any way you can. Without my father's knowledge my mother left me countless riches when she died; I'm the daughter of a king who, even though he was chosen by election, is after all a king. You can already see my age; my beauty hasn't been hidden from you and, such as it is, may not deserve to be highly regarded, but neither does it deserve to be viewed with contempt. Give me, my lady, your brother for my husband; I'll give myself to you as a sister, I'll share my wealth with you; I'll try to find you a husband who after (and perhaps even before) the end of my father's days as king may himself be elected king by the people of this kingdom; and if this cannot be, my riches will buy you other kingdoms."

Sinforosa was holding Auristela by the hands, bathing them in tears, while expressing these tender feelings. Judging by her own experience of the many intense pressures felt by a heart in love, although she considered Sinforosa an enemy, Auristela wept with her and felt sorry for her, for a generous heart refuses to take revenge even when it can, and especially in this case since Sinforosa hadn't committed any offense against her she might need to avenge. Sinforosa's fault was one with hers, her thoughts the same ones, her intentions the very ones that bewildered Auristela, too. Above all, Auristela couldn't accuse her without first finding herself guilty of the same crime. But what she did try to find out was if Periandro— even in some small way—had given Sinforosa any sign of favoring her, or whether Sinforosa's tongue or eyes had ever revealed her loving desires to him. Sinforosa replied she'd never been so bold as to raise her eyes to look at Periandro, except within the bounds of modest reserve that she—being who she was—was obliged to observe, and that her tongue's reserve had kept pace with that of her eyes.

"I do believe you," replied Auristela, "but is it really possible he hasn't shown any signs of loving you? Yes, he must have, for I don't think he's made of such hard stone that a beauty like yours couldn't soften and melt him; so it seems to me that before I tackle this problem you should try to talk with him; you can provide an opening for conversation by giving him some kind of modest token of your esteem, for unexpected favors sometimes kindle and inflame the most lukewarm and unconcerned hearts; then once he responds to your longings it will be easy for me to convince him to satisfy your every desire. All beginnings, my friend, are difficult, and those of love are extremely so. I'm not advising you to compromise yourself or to throw yourself at him, for the favors—however innocent they might be—bestowed by young women on those they love aren't always taken as such, and honor shouldn't be risked for pleasure. Nevertheless, discretion can get you far, and love, a past master at thinking up ways and means, can offer—even to the most bewildered—a time and place to declare love without damaging reputations."

Chapter Four of the Second Book

Wherein Sinforosa's Story and Love Continue

The love-stricken Sinforosa listened attentively to Auristela's wise words but didn't reply to them; instead she resumed her earlier topic, saying: "Consider, my lady and friend, that the love planted in my heart by the qualities I recognized in your brother was so strong I sent a captain of my father's guard out to search for him and bring him back to me either by force or by his own free will, and the ship that captain set out in is the same one in which you arrived, for he was found inside it among the dead." "I'm sure that's right," answered Auristela, "for he told me a great deal of what you've said and I already had some idea, although a rather confused one, of your thoughts; but, if possible, I want you to keep them under control until you make them known to my brother or until I've taken charge of helping you. And that will be as soon as you've disclosed to me whatever may happen now between you and him, for you're sure to have chances to talk to him, and I will, too."

Once again Sinforosa thanked Auristela for her offer of help and once again Auristela offered her sympathy. While this was going on between the two women Arnaldo was talking to Clodio, who was dying to upset or undo Arnaldo's amorous plans. And finding Arnaldo alone—if anyone whose soul is occupied with love's desires can be said to be alone—Clodio addressed him saying, "The other day, sir, I told you how little one can rely on the fickle nature of women, and Auristela is indeed a woman, even though she seems to be an angel, just as Periandro is a man even though he may be her brother. Now, I'm not saying this to plant some evil suspicion in your heart but so you can cultivate some sensible caution. And if this caution by some chance leads you down the road of reason, I'd like you to reflect on who you are, your father's loneliness, the fact that your subjects need you, and the risk you're running of losing your kingdom, which is the same risk run by a ship without a pilot to guide it. Remember that kings have an obligation to marry not for beauty but for blood, not for riches but for virtue—out of the obligation they have to give their kingdoms good successors to follow them. The respect one should feel for a prince diminishes and decreases when he's seen limping along on a weak blood line, and it's not enough just to say a king's greatness can by itself make any woman he might choose his equal. The horse and mare of distinguished and illustrious breeding promise offspring of exceptional worth, much more so than those with an unknown and lowly pedigree. Among the common people personal taste is very powerful, but it shouldn't be among the nobility. Therefore, my lord, either return to your kingdom or try to be cautious and not let yourself be deceived. And pardon my being so bold, for since I already have the reputation of being a slanderer and a gossip I don't want to get another for harboring evil intentions; you hold me under your protection, my life takes refuge behind the shield of your valour, and as long as I remain in your shadow I shall fear no storms from the heavens, for my nature, depraved until now, seems to be improving under the influence of better stars."

"Clodio, I appreciate the good advice you've given me," said Arnaldo, "but Heaven won't consent to it nor allow me to take it. Auristela is good, Periandro is her brother, and I don't want to believe anything else, for she's said it's so, and—for me—whatever she says must be the truth. There's no question I adore her, for the almost infinite depths of her beauty draw to them the depths of my desire, which can't be fulfilled except in her. For her sake I have lived, I do live, and I will live. Therefore, Clodio, don't advise me anymore, for your words will just be swept away with the wind and my actions will show you just how useless your advice is to me." Clodio shrugged his shoulders, lowered his head, and left Arnaldo's presence resolved not to try anymore to be an advisor, for whoever wants to be a good one should have three qualities: first, authority; second, good judgment; and third, patience to wait for someone to ask for his advice.

These amorous disturbances, schemes, and machinations were on the move in Policarpo's palace and in the hearts of the confused lovers: Auristela was jealous; Sinforosa, infatuated; Periandro, disturbed; and Arnaldo, obstinate. Mauricio was making plans to return to his homeland against Transila's wishes, for she didn't want to return to the people of her country, for she considered them avowed enemies of decent conduct. Her husband Ladislao neither dared nor wanted to contradict her. The elder Antonio was dying to see himself with his wife and children in Spain, while Rutilio felt the same about his native Italy. All of them had desires, but no one's desires were fulfilled, for it is a condition of human nature that, although God created it perfect, we all, through our own fault, always find it lacks something, and that something will always be lacking unless we stop wanting things.

It happened then that Periandro had the opportunity to be alone with Auristela, thanks to the efforts of Sinforosa, who wanted Auristela to start negotiating her cause and suit right away, for its verdict would mean her life or death. The first words Auristela spoke to Periandro were, "Our pilgrimage, my brother and my lord, so full of trials and shocks, so full of threatening dangers, makes me fear death every moment of every day, and I'd like us to give some thought to making our life more secure by settling in one place. I can think of none better than this one where we are now, for here riches are offered you in abundance—not just the promise of riches but real riches—along with a noble and extraordinarily beautiful woman who shouldn't have to court you, as she's doing, but whom instead, you should court. Ask for her hand and strive to win her."

While Auristela was saying this Periandro was gazing at her with such rapt attention that he didn't bat an eyelash; his mind was racing ahead to try and understand where this speech could possibly be heading. But, going on with it, Auristela brought him back from his confusion. "I'm saying, brother—and I'll call you this whether you marry or not—I'm saying Sinforosa worships and wants you for her husband; she says she has unbelievable wealth, and I say she's very believably beautiful, believable because her beauty is so great it doesn't need exaggerations to heighten it or hyperbole to enhance it. And insofar as I've been able to see, she has a gentle nature and a sharp mind, while she behaves with as much good judgment as modesty. All that I've said doesn't mean I've forgotten how much you deserve—being who you are—but under the present circumstances this alliance wouldn't be a bad idea. We're away from our homeland, you're pursued by your brother, and I by my bad luck. The more we try to follow our road to Rome, the more difficult and longer it becomes. My intention is unchanged, but it's wavering, and since I wouldn't want death to come upon me while immersed in these fears and dangers, I plan to spend the rest of my life in religious orders; I'd like you to finish yours in the happy state of matrimony."

At this point Auristela finished her speech and began to weep tears that undid and erased everything she'd just said. She took her arms modestly out from under the covers, stretched them on the bed, and turned her face away from Periandro, who, seeing her desperation and having already heard her words, was powerless to keep his eyes from growing dim, his throat from catching, and his tongue from sticking to the roof of his mouth; he fell to the floor on his knees and leaned his head against the bed. Auristela turned her head toward him and, seeing he had fainted, put her hand on his face and dried the tears that, without his feeling them, were running down his cheeks in two cascading ribbons.

Chapter Five of the Second Book

Concerning What Happened between
King Policarpo and His Daughter Sinforosa

We see effects in nature for which we do not know the cause; one's teeth go to sleep or go numb on seeing a knife cut cloth; a man may shake with fear at a mouse; I've seen one shudder at seeing a radish sliced, and another get up from a table out of respect for some olives placed there. When one asks the cause there is no way to explain these things, and those most convinced they can explain them say only—on observing the phenomena just mentioned and similar things we see at every turn—that the stars clash with those people's personalities in such a way to influence or move them to do those things or have those fears and phobias.

One of the definitions of man says he is a laughing animal, because man alone of all the animals laughs; I maintain it can also be said he is a weeping animal; but just as too much laughing shows little sense, too much weeping also reveals deficient rational thought. There are three reasons for which a sensible man may legitimately weep: first, because he has sinned; second, because he has obtained pardon for it; and third, because he is jealous; all other tears are out of place on a dignified countenance.

Let's look again, then, at the dazed Periandro, and since he can't be weeping either as a sinner or a penitent, he must be weeping out of jealousy, and so his tears can be pardoned and even dried, as they were by Auristela, who with more playacting than sincerity had reduced him to that state. At last he came to; on hearing footsteps in the room he turned his head and over his shoulder saw Ricla and Constanza coming in to visit Auristela; he thought it was a lucky thing, too, for if they had been left alone he wouldn't have found words to answer this lady. But as it turned out he left to think them through and to consider the advice she had given him.

Sinforosa was also anxious to find out what opinions had been handed down at the first hearing of her suit in the court of love; doubtless she rather than Ricla and Constanza would have been the first to go in to see Auristela, had she not been delayed by the receipt of a message from her father the king commanding her to appear before him immediately, with no excuses accepted. She obeyed, went to see him, and found he had withdrawn to a room by himself. Policarpo had her sit next to him and at the end of a long silence and in a low voice, as if he were worried he might be overheard, he said to her, "Daughter, although your tender years shouldn't have to feel this thing they call love, and my advanced ones should no longer be subject to its jurisdiction, sometimes nature seems to stray from its normal course, for girls still green and tender catch fire and burn, while decrepit old men dry up and are consumed."

When Sinforosa heard this she thought there was no doubt her father knew about her desires, but though she thought this she kept quiet and refrained from interrupting him until he had more fully explained himself, even though the whole time he talked her heart was pounding. He continued, saying, "After I lost your mother, my

116

daughter, I took refuge in the shelter of your affection, wrapped myself in your loving concern, and lived my life according to your advice. I've observed, as you know, the laws governing widowers, and I've done so honorably and to the letter, as much for the sake of my reputation as to keep the Catholic faith I profess. But since these new guests arrived in our city the clock of my good sense hasn't kept time, I've veered from my life's good course, and finally I've fallen from the heights of my presumed good sense to the depths of I don't know what kind of desires, for if I keep quiet about them they'll kill me but if I talk about them they'll dishonor me. No more suspense, daughter, no more silence, my friend—no more; but if you must have something more it must be to tell you I'm dying for Auristela. The heat of her touching beauty has kindled love's flame in the marrow of my old bones; my eyes, already dim, have taken new spark from the stars in hers; seeing her graceful body has breathed new life into my feeble one. I would like, if possible, to give you and your sister a stepmother, but one whose worthiness will justify my doing so. If you feel the same, I won't care what others may say; should this be judged madness and my kingdom taken away from me, then let me reign in the arms of Auristela, and there will be no monarch on earth equal to me.

"My plan is, daughter, to have you tell her this and get from her the affirmative answer so important to me; I believe she won't find it very hard to give, provided she puts my authority on the scales of her good sense and counterbalances it against my advanced years, recognizing that my great wealth outweighs her youth. It's good to be a queen, good to command, honors are pleasing, and not all forms of amusement depend on the marriage partners being evenly matched. In reward for the good news of that 'yes' answer you'll bring me on this mission, I hereby decree a step up in your fortunes, and if you're wise—as you are—you won't be able to think of anything you'd rather have.

"Listen well; a worthy man should strive to have and hold these four things: a good wife, a good house, a good horse, and good weapons. A woman is just as obliged as a man to strive for the first two—and perhaps even more so, since a woman can't raise a man's social status but a husband can improve his wife's. Majesty and grandeur are not destroyed by marriage with common people, because when great men marry they confer equality of rank upon their wives; thus, whoever Auristela may be, once she's my wife she'll be queen and her brother Periandro my brother-in-law; I'll give him to you for your husband, honoring him with the title brother-in-law of the king; you, too, will be highly regarded, both as his wife and as my daughter."

"But, how do you know, my lord," asked Sinforosa, "that Periandro isn't married, or even if he isn't that he might want to marry me?" "The fact that he isn't," replied the king, "seems obvious to me when I see him wandering on a pilgrimage through strange lands, something that marriage among the great prevents; the fact that he'll want to be yours is certified and guaranteed by his abundant good sense, for he'll realize what he stands to gain with you; and since his sister's beauty makes her a queen, it's not too much to expect that yours can make him your husband."

With these last words and with that great promise the king sweetened Sinforosa's hopes and whetted the appetite of her desires. Thus, not only did she not oppose her father's desires but she also promised to be a matchmaker, taking for granted the reward for bringing good news of something she hadn't yet arranged. The only thing she said to him was to think carefully before giving her Periandro as her husband, for even though his abilities were an indication of his worth, still, to be sure of him, it would be wise not to leap into anything until the experience of dealing with him for a few more days could guarantee it. To tell the truth, of course, could she have received him as her husband at that very moment she would gladly have given all the happiness she could ever want if she lived for centuries, for virtuous and highborn young women say one thing with their tongues but feel another in their hearts.

While this went on between Policarpo and his daughter, in another room another conversation and discussion was in progress between Rutilio and Clodio. As what has been written about his life and habits shows, Clodio was perceptive as well as inclined to think the worst of people, a combination that made him a polished slanderer, for stupid and simple people don't know how to gossip or malign; and although it is wrong to be good at speaking ill—as was said earlier—still, people do praise a clever slanderer. Any conversation is mellowed and spiced by a keen malicious wit—like salt on your food—and while people criticize and censure the witty slanderer for being harmful, that doesn't stop them from pardoning and praising him for being clever.

So this gossip of ours, whose mouth exiled him from his homeland in the company of the disgraceful and wanton Rosamunda when the king of England imposed equal punishment on her lewdness and his malicious tongue, finding himself alone with Rutilio said to him,

"Look here, Rutilio, it's a stupid man, a very stupid one indeed, who when revealing a secret to someone else begs him earnestly to keep it quiet since his life depends on what he's telling him not becoming known to others. I say to such a man, come here, tattler of your own thoughts and spiller of your own secrets; if you, with your life depending on it, as you say, reveal them by telling them to someone who doesn't care whether they come out or not, how can you expect him to shut them up and stash them away under the lock and key of silence? What better insurance can you take out against what you know not becoming known than not telling it?

"I know all this, Rutilio, and nevertheless certain thoughts keep coming to my tongue and into my mouth just dying for me to tell them and let them out of the bag before they fester in my heart or make me burst. Come here, Rutilio, and tell me: What is this Arnaldo doing following Auristela's beautiful body around as if he were her own shadow, leaving the governing of his kingdom to the whim of his aged and perhaps senile father—getting himself lost here, sinking there, weeping over here, sighing over there, and bitterly complaining about the luck he's made for himself? What can we say about this Auristela and this brother of hers, young vagabonds who conceal their lineage, perhaps to cloud the question of whether or not they're highborn people? Anyone away from his homeland where no one knows him can easily give himself any parents he wishes, and with cleverness and finesse can give the impression by his behavior that he's the son of the sun and the moon. I don't deny it's a praiseworthy virtue for people to better themselves, but improvement must come without harm to any third party. Honor and praise are rewards conferred on steadfast and firm goodness, not on false and hypocritical virtue.

"Just who is this wrestler, this fencer, this runner and leaper, this Ganymede,[1] this handsome devil, sold here, bought over there, this Argus watching over Auristela as if she were a heifer[2] and who will hardly let us take a good sighting on her? We don't know nor have we been able to find out where this peerless pair of beauties comes from or where they're going. But what bothers me most about them is—and I swear to you by the eleven circles of Heaven[3] said to exist, Rutilio—that I'm not convinced they're brother and sister; and even supposing they might be, it doesn't seem right to me that this pair of siblings should go around so closely together over seas, through lands, wildernesses, wars, and in lodgings and inns.

"What they spend comes out of the saddlebags, knapsacks, and packs full of pieces of gold belonging to the barbarians Ricla and

Constanza. It's easy for me to see that the diamond cross and those two pearls Auristela's carrying are worth a fortune, but they're not possessions that can be used for everyday trading and bartering. To believe they'll always find kings to take them in and princes to do them favors is just wishful thinking.

"And what can we say next, Rutilio, about Transila's fantastic story and her father's astrology? She's bursting with bravery and he considers himself the best astrologer in the world. I'll bet that right now Transila's husband Ladislao would rather be in his own country, relaxing at home—even though he might have to submit to the laws and customs of his countrymen—than in a strange land at the mercy of whoever might feel like giving them what they need.

"And this Spanish barbarian of ours, whose arrogance is an abridged version of all the pride in the world, I'll lay odds that if Heaven takes him back to his country he'll have people lined up to see his wife and children wrapped in their animal skins, with the Barbarous Isle painted on a backdrop and him pointing out with a stick there—where he was captive for fifteen years—and here—the prisoners' dungeon. He'll be talking about the vain, ridiculous hopes of the barbarians for their future, and the unexpected burning of the island—just like those people who, freed from Turkish slavery and in Christian lands again, take their chains off their feet and hang them over their shoulders to tell the story of their misfortunes with pitiful voices and humble appeals. But let's not be *too* hard on them, for although it may seem that what they're telling is impossible, the human condition is subject to incalculable dangers and those suffered by the banished—no matter how extreme—may well be believed."

"Where will you stop, Clodio?" asked Rutilio. "I'm going to end," he replied, "by saying you'll be hard pressed to use your talents in these parts, where the inhabitants don't dance or have any pastimes other than those Bacchus offers them smilingly and lasciviously as they drink; I'll end with me, too, who having escaped death through Heaven's grace and Arnaldo's mercy thank neither one nor the other; what I'd rather like to do—even though it might be at the expense of Arnaldo's happiness—is try to improve our own luck. Friendships among the poor can last because a common lot in life links their hearts, but there can't be any lasting friendships between the rich and the poor due to the differences separating wealth from poverty."

"You sound like a philosopher, Clodio," responded Rutilio; "but I can't imagine what path we could possibly take to improve our luck—as you say—when it began to be bad from the time we were born. I'm not as learned as you, but I do see that those born of

120

humble parents can rarely pull themselves up by their own boot-straps to be singled out by others unless Heaven gives a lot of help and virtue also lends a hand. But you—who's going to lend you a hand if the best you can do is slander virtue itself? And who's going to pull me up when, no matter how hard I try, I can't get any higher than a dancer's leap? I'm a dancer, you're a gossip; I'm condemned to the gallows in my country and you're banished from yours for slander. Just how much hope do you think we have of bettering our-selves?" Rutilio's words struck Clodio dumb, and with his surprised silence the author of this great story brought the chapter to a close.

Chapter Six of the Second Book

They all had someone to share their thoughts with; Policarpo had his daughter and Clodio had Rutilio; only the perplexed Periandro was reflecting alone, for Auristela's words stirred up so many thoughts he didn't know which one to concentrate on, which one would make him feel better. "Good God! What is this?" he said to himself. "Has Auristela lost her mind? She, my match-maker? Can she have forgotten our agreements? What's Sinforosa to me? What kingdoms or riches could make me leave my sister Sigis-munda, unless I stopped being Persiles?"

On saying this word he bit his tongue and looked all around to see if anyone was listening to him and, assuring himself that no one was, continued, "Auristela is unquestionably jealous; when two people love each other very much jealousy is stirred up just by the touch of the passing breeze, by the sunlight that falls on them, and even by the ground on which they walk. My lady, think what you're doing; don't wound your dignity or your beauty and don't deprive me of the glory of my steadfast intentions, whose decency and con-stancy are forging me the priceless crown of a true lover! Sinforosa is beautiful, rich, and highborn, yet in comparison with you she's ugly, poor, and common. Remember, my lady, love is conceived and born in our hearts, either by choice or by destiny: love that comes from destiny is always at its fullest while love based on choice may wax or wane when the causes that lead or move us to love each other likewise wax or wane. And this is so true that I find no boundaries able to enclose my love nor any words to express it. I can practically say I've loved you sincerely ever since I was in swaddling

121

clothes, and here's destiny's rhyme and reason: as I grew older and more rational, my understanding grew and those qualities that made you lovable were also growing; I saw them, studied and grew to know them, engraving them on my soul and then blending our souls into such a unified whole that I'm prepared to say death will be hard pressed to divide it.

"So, my love, forget all those Sinforosas; don't offer me other beauties, don't ask me to accept empires or kingdoms, and let's not hear this sweet-sounding name of brother come to my ears anymore. All this that I'm saying to myself I'd like to say to you, and in the very same way I'm shaping it in the forge of my imagination, but that won't be possible because the light of your eyes—especially if they look at me in anger—will cloud my vision and silence my tongue. Better to write it down for you on paper, where the thoughts will ever stay the same and you'll be able to see them over and over, always finding in them the same truth, a reassurance of my faithfulness and my commendable and trustworthy intentions; so I'm resolved to write you." At this he fell silent for a while, thinking he could more skillfully put his soul into his pen than onto his tongue.

Let's leave Periandro to his writing and go hear what Sinforosa is saying to Auristela, for she managed to get Auristela alone, wanting to find out how Periandro had answered and to tell her at the same time about her father's plans, thinking she would only have to make them known to get the "yes" to bring them about and convinced that riches and titles are rarely rejected—especially by women—most of whom are by nature greedy, and proud and arrogant, too.

When Auristela saw Sinforosa coming she wasn't very pleased because since she hadn't seen Periandro again, she didn't have an answer for her. But Sinforosa, before bringing up her own case wanted to introduce her father's, thinking that bringing news so likely to please Auristela would put her on her side, the very thing she considered the key to her good fortune. And so she said to her, "There's no doubt, my most beautiful Auristela, that Heaven loves you dearly, for it seems to me it wants to shower you with more and more good fortune. My father the king adores you and has sent me to tell you he wants to be your husband; as reward for the 'yes' you'll give and I'll take to him, he's promised me Periandro for my husband. Now, my lady, you're a queen and Periandro is mine; now you have more than enough riches, and if my father's gray hair doesn't thrill you that much, the joy of command and of having vassals always attentive to your needs will leave you nothing to desire.

"I've told you a great deal, my friend and lady, and now you must do a great deal for me, for when one gives a gift of great value one expects nothing less than comparable gratitude. Let the world begin to see there can be two sisters-in-law who truly love each other and two women who share a friendship free from deceit, and see them it will if you don't forget your good sense. Now tell me how your brother replied to what you told him about me; I'm sure it was the right answer since anyone would really be foolish not to accept your advice as if it came from an oracle."

To this Auristela replied, "My brother Periandro, a well-bred gentleman, is grateful, just as being a wandering pilgrim makes him wise, for observing a great deal and reading widely quickens men's minds. My trials and those of my brother are a book continually teaching us how much we should value tranquility, and since that's what you offer us I think we'll certainly accept; but Periandro hasn't yet given me any answer, nor do I know anything about his wishes to either encourage your hopes or dash them. Beautiful Sinforosa, give the matter some time and us a chance to consider the advantages of your offers, so after we've accepted them we'll be able to fully appreciate what we have. Actions that are to be taken only once clearly can't be remedied the second time around if they should go awry, as there's no second chance; marriage is just such an act and so it's vital to think carefully before entering into it. However, I believe the time for thinking is already past and I'm sure you'll satisfy your desires, just as I'll accept your promises and advice. Now go, sister, and have Periandro called on my behalf, for I want to hear from him and report to you his happy news, and also get his advice—as an older brother to whom I owe respect and obedience—about what's best for me." Sinforosa embraced her and left to go get Periandro to come see her.

He, meanwhile, had taken up his pen in a room by himself and, after several starts, he scratched out and rewrote, made deletions from and added to, finally coming up with a sheet that they say said the following:

> I've not dared rely on my tongue as I do on my pen, nor can I count on my pen too much since it's impossible to write about matters of moment when one is awaiting death momentarily. I now realize not all wise people know how to offer counsel in all situations, although indeed, some of them, having had experiences similar to those about which they are asked to give advice, may do so. Forgive me for not accepting yours, but it seems to me that either you don't know me or have forgotten yourself. Come to your senses, my lady, and don't let an empty and jeal-

ous suspicion make you forget the wisdom of your level-headed judgment and exceptional mind. Remember who you are and don't forget who I am; in yourself you'll recognize the greatest good any man could desire and in me all the steadfast love anyone could imagine. Then holding fast to this wise thought you'll never fear that other beauties might inflame me, nor imagine your incomparable beauty and virtue eclipsed by any other. Let's continue our journey, fulfill our vow, and lay aside fruitless jealousy and unfounded suspicions. I'll request our departure from this land with all diligence and dispatch, for it seems to me that on leaving it I'll leave behind the Hell of my torment and come out into the Heaven of seeing you free from jealousy.

This was what Periandro wrote and what was left after he'd made six rough drafts. Then folding the paper he went to see Auristela, on whose behalf they had already called him.

Chapter Seven of the Second Book, divided in two parts

[First Part]

Rutilio and Clodio, those two who wanted to better their humble fortunes, one confident in his wit and the other in his gall, imagined themselves worthy, one of Policarpa and the other of Auristela. Rutilio very much appreciated Policarpa's voice and grace and Clodio Auristela's peerless beauty, and they were looking for an opportunity to reveal their feelings without getting into trouble. For indeed, it's right for a lowborn and common man to feel afraid if he dares tell a highborn woman what he shouldn't have even dared think in the first place. But sometimes it happens that the boldness of a less than honorable lady, even though she may be highborn, gives a lowborn commoner cause to look at her boldly and declare his feelings. An important lady has to be serious, self-possessed, and modest but without becoming arrogant, rude, or inconsiderate; the more she's a lady, the more she'll behave in a humble and reserved manner. Now in the case of these two gentlemen and new suitors, their desires weren't inspired by any flirtation or lack of reserve on the part of their ladies; yet wherever the inspiration came from, the upshot was that Rutilio wrote a note to Policarpa and Clodio wrote another to Auristela in the following style:

RUTILIO TO POLICARPA

Lady, I'm a foreigner and although I might tell you great things about my lineage, since I have no witnesses to confirm them you might judge them less than believable—although the fact that I dare tell you I adore you is sufficient to confirm I come from an illustrious line. Decide what proofs you might want me to provide to confirm this truth, for your wish is my command; and since I want you for my wife, you can believe that what I want matches who I am and I deserve as much as I desire: it's natural for lofty spirits to aspire to lofty things. Give me some answer to this letter if only with your eyes, for in the leniency or harshness of your gaze I'll read the sentence of my life or death.

Rutilio folded the paper intending to give it to Policarpa, confident of the old saying: "A word to the wise is sufficient." First he showed it to Clodio, who in turn showed him the one he'd written to Auristela, which follows:

CLODIO TO AURISTELA

Some fall into love's net by taking beauty's bait, some by swallowing the hook of grace and charm, while others are lured by the worth they perceive in the person to whom they decide to surrender their will; but I have another reason for putting my neck under its yoke, my shoulders in its harness, my will under the weight of its laws, and my feet in its shackles, and that reason is pity. Who could be so hardhearted, beautiful lady, as not to feel some on seeing you bought and sold and put in such heartrending straits that you've been only a heartbeat away from death? Iron and merciless steel have threatened your neck, fire has burned the fabric of your clothing, snow has practically frozen you stiff, hunger has made you waste away and turned the roses of your cheeks yellow, and finally, the waters have swallowed you up and spit you back out. I just don't know where you find the strength to bear these trials, for you can't draw any from a vagabond king who follows you around only because he's interested in your body, nor does your brother—if that's what he is—have enough strength of his own to inspire you in

125

your wretchedness. Don't rely on distant promises, my lady, but take shelter in nearby hopes, choosing a life sure to be the one Heaven would like you to have. I'm young and clever enough to know how to live in the farthest corners of the earth; I'll find a way to get you out of this land and free from Arnaldo's insistence; and once I've gotten you out of this Egypt, I'll take you to the promised land of Spain or France or Italy (since I can't live in England, my sweet and beloved homeland); above all, I offer to be your husband and naturally accept you as my wife.

Having heard Clodio's letter, Rutilio said, "We're truly out of our heads, for we're trying to convince ourselves we can fly up to Heaven on just the wings given us by our ambition—and they're ants' wings. Look, Clodio; I think we should tear up these sheets of paper, for no loving impulse has led us to write, only idle and empty wishes; love can neither be born nor grow without hope to lean on, and lacking that support it collapses entirely.

"Why should we want to gamble on losing and not on winning in this venture? Declaring our intentions and seeing our necks in a noose or up against a knife will occur virtually simultaneously; what's more, by letting it out we're in love, we'll appear not only ungrateful but out-and-out traitors. Don't you see the distance that separates the daughter of a king from a dancing master who bettered his trade by learning to be a silversmith? And the gulf between an exiled slanderer and a woman who tosses aside and scorns kingdoms? Let's bite our tongues and let our second thoughts catch up with our foolishness. As for me, my letter will end up in the fire or on the wind rather than reaching Policarpa."

"Do whatever you wish with yours," responded Clodio; "as for mine—even though I may not give it to Auristela—I'm thinking of keeping it in honor of my wit, though I'm afraid if I don't give it to her my conscience will gnaw at me all the rest of my life for having changed my mind, for there's not always harm in trying." These words passed between the two would-be lovers, who were also truly foolish and foolhardy.

At last the time came for Periandro and Auristela to talk privately, and he went in to see her intending to give her the letter he'd written; but as soon as he saw her, forgetting all the speeches and apologies with which he'd come prepared, he said, "My lady, take a good look at me, for I'm Periandro, who was Persiles and whom you want to be Periandro. No one but death itself can untie the knot that links our wills; this being so, what good does it do you to give me advice so at odds with that truth? For Heaven's sake and for yours—for you're more beautiful than Heaven itself—I beg you not to mention Sinforosa again, nor even imagine her beauty or riches could persuade me to forget the treasure of your virtue and your incomparable beauty, both of body and soul. This soul of mine—which draws its very breath from yours—I offer you again, though with no greater advantages than those when first I saw and offered myself to you; no clause remains to be added to the contract of obligation in which I agreed to serve you the very minute the knowledge of your virtues was imprinted on my mind. Try to regain your health, my lady, as I'll try to the best of my ability to secure our departure from this land and arrange for our journey. For although Rome is Heaven on earth, it isn't located in the Heavens, and there'll be no trials or dangers to prevent us finally from reaching it, though some may slow us down. Hold fast to the trunk and branches of your great merits and don't imagine anyone in the world could be your rival."

All the while Periandro was saying this Auristela was gazing at him tenderly with eyes full of tears of jealousy and compassion. But at last Periandro's loving arguments began to take effect on her soul and she made room in it for the truth contained in his words, answering him briefly as follows. "It's not difficult for me, my sweet love, to believe you, and fully trusting in you I ask that we leave this land soon; perhaps in another I'll recover from the disease of jealousy keeping me in this bed."

"If I'd been in any way the cause of your illness, my lady," replied Periandro, "I'd patiently bear your reproaches and my apologies would bring relief to your complaints, but since I haven't offended you there's no need for me to apologize. I beg you to act like your true self and gladden the hearts of all who know you, and do so quickly, for since there's no cause for your illness neither is there any reason for you to kill us with it. I'll do as you command; we'll leave this land as soon as possible."

"Don't you know how much is at stake for you, Periandro?" replied Auristela. "You should be aware they're coaxing me with promises and pressuring me with gifts. And it's not just any small bribe; to start with, they're offering me this kingdom. King Policarpo wants to be my husband; he's sent his daughter Sinforosa to tell me so, and she, thinking that as her stepmother I'll be on her side, wants you to be her husband. You can judge for yourself just how impossible all this is; give some thought to how much danger we're in, and after taking stock use your good sense and look for the remedy our situation calls for. And forgive me, for suspicion overpowered me and forced me to hurt you, but, then, love easily forgives mistakes like these."

"They say," responded Periandro, "that love cannot exist without jealousy; but when produced by weak and flimsy suspicions jealousy itself can make love grow, serving to spur on the will to love, which when it's overly confident of itself, turns lukewarm or at the least seems to fade. In the name of your good sense, I beg you from now on to look at me, not with more loving eyes, for there can be none in the world lovelier than yours, but with a will freed from needless anxieties, not making some oversight of mine the size of a grain of mustard seed into a mountain of jealousy reaching up into the sky. As for everything else, use your good judgment and play along with the king and Sinforosa, for you won't offend her by insincere words designed to fulfill our right desires. And peace be with you, for I must go lest our long conversation plant some mean suspicion in someone's evil heart."

With this Periandro left her, and on leaving the room he came upon Clodio and Rutilio; Rutilio was just finishing tearing up the letter he had written to Policarpa and Clodio was folding his to put it away in his shirt. Rutilio had thought better of his crazy idea while Clodio still felt self-important in his cleverness and conceited about his audacity; but time will pass and the moment will come when he will be willing to give half his life not to have written it, if it can be said that lives are divisible.

Chapter Seven of the Second Book

[Second Part]

King Policarpo was enjoying his amorous thoughts and was also anxious to know Auristela's decision. He was so confident and sure she would return his feelings that he was already planning the betrothal in his mind, arranging for the festivities, thinking up gala events, and even imagining himself bestowing favors in honor of the forthcoming marriage. But among all these calculations he failed to take the pulse of his age, nor did he wisely judge the gap that separates seventeen from seventy years (which even if he were sixty, would still have been a great distance). Thus lascivious desires flatter and cajole the will, thus imagined pleasures deceive keen minds, thus sweet imaginings tug and drag after them all those who can't hold their ground in love's encounters.

Sinforosa was having different thoughts for she wasn't so sure of her fate, and it's natural for one who has intense desires to have intense fears; she banished from her mind the very things that could have given wings to her hope, such as her worth, her noble descent, and her beauty, since those deeply in love characteristically think they have no qualities worthy of being loved by those whom they want very much. Love and fear go so hand in hand that wherever you look you'll see them together; nor is love proud, as some say, but rather humble, agreeable, and gentle, for it often gives up its rights so it won't cause the beloved any harm. What's more, since all lovers value and esteem the ones they love, they always try to avoid being the cause of losing them.

Beautiful Sinforosa considered all this with a clearer head than her father, and torn between fear and hope went to see Auristela to learn from her what she hoped and feared. Finally Sinforosa found herself alone with Auristela—which was what she most wanted—and was so anxious to hear the news of her good or bad fortune that as soon as she went in to see her, not saying a word, she began to gaze at her eagerly to see if she could detect any signs of her own life or death in the expression on Auristela's face.

Auristela understood her feelings and half laughing, or perhaps I should say with a cheerful look on her face, said to her, "Come closer, my lady, for fear hasn't laid an axe to the root of the tree of your hopes to chop it down. It's quite true your happiness and mine will have to be postponed for a little while but they'll come in the end, for even though obstacles often block the fulfillment of right desires, not even desperation will be strong enough to keep us from hoping. My brother says his knowledge of your worth and beauty not only obliges but compels him to love you, and he's pleased and considers it a special favor that you want to be his. But before such a happy possession is possible, it will be necessary to spoil Prince Arnaldo's hopes of taking me as his wife, as I will doubtless become if your marriage to my brother doesn't prevent it; for you must know, my sister, that I can no more live without Periandro than a body can live without a soul. I have to live wherever he lives, for he's the spirit that moves me and the soul that gives me life; now since this is true, if my brother marries you here in this country how could I live so far from him in Arnaldo's? To avoid this catastrophe threatening me, command us to go with Arnaldo to his kingdom and from there we'll ask his permission to go to Rome to keep a vow, the fulfillment of which took us from our country. It's clear—and experience has always taught me—that he won't stray an inch from what I want done. Then, when we're at liberty, it will be a simple matter for us to return to this island, where spoiling his hopes, we'll see the fulfillment of our own—with me marrying your father and my brother, you."

To this Sinforosa replied, "I don't know the words, sister, to adequately describe the kindness you've shown me in what you've just said, and since I can't express it I'll just let it drop. But please take what I want to tell you now more as words of caution than as advice; right now you're in this country and under the power of my father, who's willing and able to protect you from the whole world, so it's not a good idea to put your personal security at risk. It won't be possible for Arnaldo to drag you and your brother away by force; rather he'll be forced, if not to want the same things then at least to comply with whatever my father might want, since he's in his house and kingdom. Promise me, dear sister, that you intend to become my lady by becoming my father's wife and that your brother won't scorn becoming my lord and husband, and I'll smooth out all difficulties and surmount all obstacles Arnaldo may use to achieve his ends."

To this Auristela replied, "Wise men judge the future on the basis of past and present cases. If your father persists either openly or secretly in keeping us here by force, Arnaldo's bound to be offended and his anger aroused, for he is, after all, a powerful king—or at least more powerful than your father—and frustrated and deceived kings can easily find ways to take revenge. Then, instead of taking pleasure from our kinship, you may be harmed, for because of us war will come into your very homes. You may reply that this fear will always be with us whether we remain here now or come back later, but remembering that Heaven never presses misfortunes down around us so tightly that some glimmer of light doesn't get through them to show us the way out, I think we should go with Arnaldo and you yourself, making use of your intelligence and good judgment, should request our departure, for thereby you'll also request and shorten the time till our return. Then—if not in kingdoms as grand as Arnaldo's, but here where at least we'll have a more secure peace—I'll enjoy your father's wisdom and you my brother's charms and goodness, without splitting and separating our souls."

On hearing those words a deliriously happy Sinforosa threw herself at Auristela, wrapped her arms around her neck, and took the measure of her mouth and eyes with her own beautiful lips. At this moment they saw the two seeming barbarians, father and son, come into the room along with Ricla and Constanza and after them Mauricio, Ladislao, and Transila, all eager to see and talk to Auristela and to find out the status of her illness, which was making them all sick with worry. Sinforosa took leave of them happier and more deceived than when she had come in, for lovers' hearts easily believe even the shadows of their pleasure's promises.

Old Mauricio, having exchanged with Auristela the usual questions and answers between the sick and their visitors, then said, "If poor people, even beggars, grieve on finding themselves exiled from their homeland where they left nothing but the poor clods of earth that supported them, how must those people far away from home feel who left behind all the good things fortune could possibly promise them? I say this, my lady, because my age, which with rapid steps is hurrying me toward my final rest, makes me long to be back in my homeland where my friends, relatives, and children can close my eyes and bid me their last farewell. All of us here want to enjoy this same blessing and mercy, since we're all foreigners and far away from home, and all of us, it seems to me, have something in our homelands we won't find in any others. Therefore, my lady, please request our departure or at least consent to our trying to arrange it, for we won't be able to leave without you. Your noble nature and extraordinary beauty, together with your dazzling intelligence, is the lodestone that attracts our souls." "At least," said the elder Antonio at this time, "they are to me and to my wife and children, and so much so I'd sooner take leave of my life than leave Lady Auristela's company, provided she doesn't scorn ours."

"Sirs," replied Auristela, "I appreciate the goodwill you've shown me, and although it's not in my hands to respond directly to it as I ought, I'll have Prince Arnaldo and my brother Periandro put your wishes into action, for my illness—which now has turned to health—won't stand in the way. In the meantime, then, until the happy day and hour of our departure, lift up your hearts, don't let melancholy dwell in them and don't think of the dangers to come; since Heaven has brought us through so many of them, letting none overtake us, it will surely lead us to our sweet homelands, for misfortunes too weak to end our lives shouldn't be strong enough to exhaust our patience." Everyone admired Auristela's answer, which revealed her kind heart and excellent mind.

At this very moment King Policarpo came in feeling exceedingly happy since his daughter Sinforosa had just told him about the promising hopes for the fulfillment of his desires, which were at once pure and lustful. In old men amorous impulses are usually covered and disguised with the cloak of hypocrisy; and since there's no hypocrite—even if not publicly recognized as such—who harms just himself, old men often conceal their depraved appetites under the cover of marriage.

Arnaldo and Periandro came in with the king; after congratulating Auristela on her health the king commanded that, in recognition of the mercy from Heaven everyone had received with Auristela's improvement, festival lights would be lit in the city that night, to be followed by celebrations and rejoicing for an entire week. Periandro expressed his gratitude as Auristela's brother and Arnaldo as one who loved her and wanted to be her husband. Policarpo rejoiced inwardly to see just how easy it was to deceive Arnaldo, who, pleased with Auristela's improvement and being unaware of Policarpo's designs on her, was searching for ways to get out of his city, for the longer their departure was delayed, the longer, it seemed to Arnaldo, it would be until his desires were satisfied.

Mauricio, also anxious to return to his homeland, consulted his science and discovered through it that great difficulties would block their departure. He made this known to Arnaldo and Periandro, who by that time had learned of Sinforosa's and Policarpo's intentions and were very concerned, knowing for certain that when love's desire exerts its power over the hearts of the powerful it usually breaks through every obstacle to reach its goal; respect is not shown, promises not kept, and obligations not honored; so there was no reason to be sure Policarpo would feel even the slightest obligation toward them.

In conclusion, the three agreed that Mauricio should look among the many vessels in the port for one to take them secretly to England, for a suitable way of embarking would surely be found. In the meantime, no one should give any hint of knowing anything about Policarpo's intentions. This whole plan was communicated to Auristela, who concurred with their views and made fresh efforts to care for her own health, and with it that of the others as well.

Chapter Eight of the Second Book

Clodio Gives His Letter to Auristela
and Antonio the Barbarian Kills Him by Mistake

The story next records that Clodio's insolence, or rather shamelessness, made him so bold he dared place in Auristela's hands the shameful letter he'd written her, misleading her as he did so by saying it contained some pious verses worth being read and admired. Auristela opened the letter, and her curiosity was so strong that despite her anger she read it to the very end. When she had finished she folded it up again and with her eyes fixed on Clodio—sending out from them not loving radiance as she usually did, but sparks of furious fire—she said to him, "Get out of my sight, you perverse, shameless man! If I thought the origin of your insolent madness lay in some carelessness on my part that could diminish my good reputation and honor I'd punish myself for your audacity, which won't go unpunished unless my pity intercedes with my patience for your madness!"

Clodio was stunned and would have given half his life, as has already been said, not to have been so daring. Immediately he felt surrounded by a thousand fears and didn't give himself any longer to live than the time it would take for Arnaldo or Periandro to find out about his knavery. Without answering a word he lowered his eyes, turned his back, and left Auristela alone. Her mind was troubled by the fear, far from groundless but rather very reasonable, that Clodio, being desperate, would turn traitor and take advantage of Policarpo's intentions if he should happen to learn of them, so she decided to tell Periandro and Arnaldo what had occurred.

At this same time it happened that while the younger Antonio was alone in his room a woman unexpectedly came in. She seemed about forty years old, though her energy and grace probably hid ten more. She wasn't dressed in the style of that country but rather after the Spanish fashion, and although Antonio didn't know anything about fashion except what he'd seen on the Barbarous Isle where he'd been born and raised, he could see very easily she was a stranger to Policarpo's land.

He got up to receive her courteously, for he wasn't such a barbarian as to be rude. They sat down and, after having gazed at Antonio's face, the young lady—if it makes sense to call her that at her age—said, "My coming to see you must seem really strange to you, young man, for you're probably not accustomed to being visited by women, since you were brought up, I've heard, on the Barbarous Isle, though not among barbarians but among rocks and crags. From them you've drawn your beauty and manly vigor, but if you also inherited their hardness of heart then I fear my soft one will do me no good. Don't turn away, calm yourself and don't be upset, for you aren't talking to some monster or anyone who'd try to tell or advise you to do anything against human nature. Notice I'm speaking Spanish to you, the language you understand, and that's a link that often promotes friendship among those who don't know each other. My name is Cenotia,[1] and I'm a native of Spain, born and raised in Alhama, a city in the kingdom of Granada.[2] I'm known by name in all the kingdoms of Spain and in many others also, for my talent won't allow my name to remain hidden, and my deeds made me famous. I left my homeland about four years ago fleeing the vigilance of the watchful guard dogs that keep the Catholic flock in that kingdom. I come from Mohammedan stock; my spiritual exercises are those of Zoroaster and I'm matchless in them. Do you see the sun shining on us? Well, if as a sign of what I can do you want me to take away its rays and cover it with clouds, just ask, and in a twinkling I'll make this brightness turn to darkest night; or if by chance you'd like to see the earth tremble, the winds quarrel with each other, the sea turn rough, the mountains clash together, wild beasts roar, or any other terrifying signs representing for us the confusion of original chaos, just ask, as I said, and you'll be satisfied and my claims substantiated.

"You should also know that in the city of Alhama there has always been some woman with my name, who along with the name Cenotia inherits the knowledge teaching us not to be witches, as some people call us, but enchantresses and sorcerers—words that describe us more accurately—since witches never do a lick of work that amounts to anything. They perform their tricks with things that sound like practical jokes, like jumping beans, needles without points, pins without heads, and hair cut in the waxing or waning of the moon. They use signs they don't understand and if perhaps they succeed somewhat in what they're trying to do, it's not by virtue of their simple-minded antics but rather because God allows the Devil to trick them for their greater damnation. But we who are known as sorcerers and enchantresses are people of distinction; we deal with the stars, we contemplate the motion of the heavens, we know the powers of herbs, of plants, or stones, of words, and by the joining of the active to the passive we seem to perform miracles. We dare things so wondrous they astonish people and give rise to our good or bad reputations—good if we do good with our skill, bad if we do evil. However, since nature seems to incline us more towards evil than good, often we aren't able to hold our desires sufficiently in check to keep them from slipping out of our hands to do harm to others. For who would prevent someone who feels angry and insulted from taking revenge? Or keep the scorned lover from wanting—if it's within his power—to force the one who now detests him to love him? The catch is that since changing people's minds and judgment violates the principle of free will, no science can do it nor are there herbs powerful enough to bring it about."

While the Spanish woman Cenotia was saying all this, Antonio was looking at her and feeling very anxious about what the sum total of such a long account would be. But Cenotia continued, saying, "In short, I'm telling you, my clever barbarian, that persecution in Spain by those known as Inquisitors tore me from my homeland, for when one is forced to leave it, one doesn't simply leave but feels torn away. I came to this island by strange roundabout ways, through countless dangers, and since I almost always felt as if they were nearby I kept turning my head around, thinking those dogs—which I fear to this day—were nipping at my skirts. I soon made myself known to the king who preceded Policarpo; I did some wondrous things that left all the people amazed and succeeded in making my skill so marketable and profitable that I've accumulated more than thirty thousand gold escudos. By carefully managing these earnings I've been able to live a pure life, not seeking any further pleasure, nor would I have sought any now had my fortune, good or bad, not brought you to this land, for it's in your hands to give me whatever fate you may wish. If I seem ugly to you, I'll arrange for you to find me beautiful; if the thirty thousand escudos I'm offering you seem too few, then increase your desires and stretch the sacks and pockets of your greed and get ready to count as much money as you could possibly want. To please you I'll make the sea shells give up their hidden pearls; I'll subdue the birds that split the air and bring them to your hands; I'll make the earth's plants offer up their fruits to you; I'll make the most precious hidden treasures spring forth from the depths; I'll make you invincible in all things, gentle in peace, feared in war; in short, I'll change your fate so you'll always be envied and never envious. And in exchange for all these good things I've described to you, I don't ask you to be my husband, but only to accept me as your slave. It's not necessary for you to be drawn to me enough to want to make me your wife, for provided I'm yours—whatever the arrangement— I'll be happy. Begin, then, noble youth, to show your wisdom by showing your gratitude; and before thanking me for my good wishes it would be only prudent for you to test my skills. Now to show that you want to do this, gladden my soul by giving me a sign of peace—by letting me touch your hand." And saying this, she rose to go over and embrace him.

On seeing this, Antonio, as full of confusion as though he were the most cloistered virgin in the world and enemies were assaulting the castle of his virtue, prepared to defend it; getting up, he went over to take up the bow he always carried with him or kept nearby and, fitting an arrow in it, took aim at Cenotia, about twenty paces away. The love-stricken woman wasn't very happy to see Antonio's menacing stance; she turned her body aside to avoid the shot and the arrow flew right by her throat. (With this act Antonio proved to be even more of a barbarian than his clothing made him appear.) The arrow's force wasn't wasted, however, for at that very instant the slanderer Clodio was entering the door to the room and became its target. It drove through his mouth and tongue, silencing his life forever—just punishment for his many faults.

Cenotia turned her head and saw the arrow's deadly blow. Fearing a second one, and taking no advantage of the many powers she claimed for her science but full of confusion and fear, she left the room stumbling here and falling there, resolved to take revenge on the cruel and cold-hearted youth.

Chapter Nine of the Second Book

A ntonio wasn't pleased with the blow his hand had struck, for although he hit a mark by mistake, since he didn't know Clodio's faults but had seen Cenotia's for himself, he wished he'd aimed better. Going over to Clodio to look for any signs of life left in him, he saw that death had taken them all. Realizing the seriousness of his mistake he felt he truly was a barbarian. His father came in at this point and seeing the blood and Clodio's dead body knew by the arrow that the blow had been struck by his son's hand. Putting the question to him he received an affirmative answer; he inquired the cause and it, too, was explained to him.

This astonished the father and full of indignation he said to him, "Look here, you barbarian, if you try to kill those who love and desire you, what will you do to those who hate you? If you're so concerned about being pure and modest, protect your purity and modesty with patient long-suffering; dangers like this can't be countered by arms or ambushes, but only by running away from them. It seems clear you don't know what happened to that young Hebrew fellow who left his cloak in the hands of the lascivious woman trying to seduce him.[1] If you weren't so ignorant you'd give up that primitive skin you're wearing and that bow, which induces to you to be braver than bravery itself; you shouldn't use it against the gentleness of a woman who's surrendered herself to you, for at a time like that she can find a way around any obstacle blocking the path to the fulfillment of her desires. If you continue like this throughout your whole life you'll be taken for a barbarian by everyone you meet. I'm not saying you should offend God by any means, but you should rebuke, not punish, any women who might want to disturb your pure thoughts. And prepare yourself for more than one battle, for the tenderness of your years and your body's vigorous manliness will threaten you with many battles. And you needn't think you'll always be the object of seduction, for some time you'll become the would-be seducer and may find death in the midst of your own unsatisfied desires."

Antonio had been listening to his father with downcast eyes, as ashamed as he was sorry, and this was his reply: "Try to overlook what I've done, sir, for I feel terrible about it. I'll strive to be better from now on, trying not to appear either barbarous by being severe or lustful by being passive. Give orders for Clodio to be buried and thus to receive the most appropriate recompense due his honor."

The rumor of Clodio's death had already flown through the palace, though not its cause, for the love-smitten Cenotia had concealed it, saying only that without her knowing why the barbaric youth had killed him. This news reached the ears of Auristela, who still had Clodio's note in her hands intending to show it to Periandro or Arnaldo so they would punish his audacity; but seeing that Heaven had taken charge of his punishment she tore up the note and kept the dead man's faults from being made public—a decision as prudent as it was Christian. Although Policarpo was disturbed about the matter and feeling offended that someone had avenged himself within his house, he chose not to investigate but to entrust the matter to Prince Arnaldo, who at Auristela and Transila's request, pardoned Antonio and ordered Clodio buried without determining who was at fault in his death. He believed Antonio had told him the truth, that he'd killed him by accident, for Antonio didn't reveal Cenotia's schemes so they wouldn't think him a total barbarian.

The rumors ceased, Clodio was buried, and Auristela avenged, as though her noble heart could harbor any sort of desire for revenge at all comparable to that which was in fact harbored in Cenotia's, who was thirsting for vengeance, as they say, and thinking how to take revenge on the cruel archer. Within two days he began to feel very ill and collapsed into bed in such a weakened condition that the doctors said his life was ebbing away, although they couldn't diagnose the disease. His mother Ricla wept continuously, while the heart of the older Antonio, his father, was being consumed by grief. Neither Auristela nor Mauricio could be cheered, and Ladislao and Transila shared their sadness.

Seeing this, Policarpo went to his advisor Cenotia and asked her to try to find some cure for Antonio's illness, for since the doctors didn't recognize the disease they couldn't begin to find a cure. She was encouraging, assuring him the disease wouldn't be fatal but recommending a delay in treatment for awhile, and Policarpo believed her as though her words had been spoken by an oracle.

All these events didn't bother Sinforosa very much for she realized they would delay Periandro's departure. The sight of him kept her heart at ease, and even though she wanted him to leave—since he couldn't return if he didn't go away—seeing him gave her so much pleasure she couldn't bring herself to encourage his departure.

A time and opportunity arose when Policarpo and his two daughters—with Arnaldo, Periandro and Auristela, Mauricio, Ladislao and Transila, and Rutilio (who after writing the note to Policarpa, even though he'd torn it up, was going around repentant, sad, and pensive, like the guilty man who thinks everyone looking at him knows about his guilt)—as I was saying, all the above company found themselves in the room of the sick Antonio. They were visiting him at Auristela's urging, for she respected and loved both him and his parents and was grateful for the good the barbarous youth had done them when he brought them out of the fire on the island and took them to his father's camp; what's more, shared misfortunes draw people closer together and establish firm friendships, and since she had gone through so many trials in the company of Ricla and Constanza and the two Antonios, it was now not only out of gratitude but also by choice and destiny that she loved them.

Therefore, being all together one day, as has been said, Sinforosa begged Periandro to tell them some of the events of his life.

She was especially eager to know from where he had been traveling the first time he'd arrived on the island, when he'd won the prizes in all the games and festivities held that day in honor of the anniversary of her father's election. To this Periandro replied that he would answer, providing he was allowed to begin his story not at the very beginning, for that was something he couldn't tell or reveal to anyone until he got to Rome with his sister Auristela. Everyone told him to do as he liked for they'd be happy to hear anything he might tell them. But the one who felt happiest was Arnaldo, who thought he'd be able to determine something from what Periandro might say which would reveal who he was. With this guarantee of safe passage Periandro spoke as follows.

Chapter Ten of the Second Book

Periandro Tells the Story of His Voyage

Since all of you want me to tell you my story, sirs, I want its opening and preamble to be this: imagine my sister and me, along with her old nursemaid, on board a ship whose owner doesn't look like a merchant, rather every inch a pirate. We were sweeping the shores of an island, that is, we were sailing so close to it we could clearly distinguish not only the trees, but the differences among them. My sister, tired of being at sea for several days, wanted to go ashore to relax. She asked the captain to allow this and, since her wishes always carry the force of a command, he consented to her request and sent me and my sister ashore in the ship's boat accompanied by just one sailor and Cloelia her nursemaid. As we neared shore the sailor saw that through a small mouth a tiny river was paying its tribute to the sea. It was shaded on both banks by a great number of green and leafy trees mirrored in its crystal clear waters.

"Beckoned by the pleasantness of the place we asked him to turn into the river. He did so and began to move upstream; when the ship was out of sight he dropped the oars, paused, and said, 'Consider carefully, sirs, what you should do about this voyage, and as you do, think of this small boat now carrying you as your ship, for you shouldn't go back to the one waiting for you at sea, that is, assuming this lady doesn't want to lose her honor and you, who say you're her brother, your life.'

"In short, he told me the ship's captain wanted to dishonor my sister and kill me, urging us to think of our safety and offering to follow and accompany us wherever we might go and no matter what might happen to us. Let anyone accustomed to receiving bad news where he expected good be the judge of whether or not this upset us. I thanked him for the warning and offered to reward him as soon as we might find ourselves in happier circumstances. 'At least,' said Cloelia, 'I brought my lady's jewels with me.'

"After the four of us talked together about what we should do; it was the sailor's feeling we ought to go farther upstream, as we might possibly find some place from which to defend ourselves in case those on board the ship should come looking for us.

"'But they probably won't come there,' he said. 'For all the people of these islands think everyone who sails along these shores is a pirate, and as soon as they see a ship, or ships, they immediately take up arms to defend themselves; so unless they use surprise night attacks the pirates never get anywhere.'

"His advice seemed good to me; I took up an oar and helped him get on with the work. We went upstream, and after going about two miles a sound coming from many different instruments reached our ears; then a forest of moving trees came into view, sprinting from one bank of the river to the other. We came closer and saw that what seemed to be trees were boats covered with branches, while the sound was being produced by instruments played by people in the boats.

"No sooner had they seen us when they came over and surrounded our boat. My sister stood up and, tossing her beautiful hair over her shoulders (though it was held in place around her forehead by a tawny band or ribbon her nursemaid had given her), she appeared like an unexpected and almost divine vision, which I later learned was the impression given everyone on board the boats. According to the sailor, who understood them, they began shouting, saying, 'What's happening? What Goddess has come to visit us and congratulate Carino the fisherman and the matchless Selviana on the most happy occasion of their wedding?'

"Then they threw a line to our boat and towed us to disembark at a place not far from where they'd found us. No sooner had we set foot on the bank than we were surrounded by a crew of fishermen (we could tell what they were by their clothing), and one by one, full of astonishment and reverence, they came forward to kiss the hem of Auristela's dress. Though terribly anxious about the frightening information she'd just received, she radiated such beauty at that moment that I can forgive the error of those who thought her divine.

"A short distance from the bank we saw a bridal pavilion supported by thick juniper trunks, covered with green sedge, and fragrant with various flowers strewn on the floor like a fine carpet. We also saw two young women and two attractive young men get up from their seats. One of the women was exceedingly beautiful, the other exceedingly ugly; one of the youths cut a fine and dashing figure, while the other wasn't quite so impressive. All four got down on their knees before Auristela and the more outstanding young man said, 'Oh you—whoever you may be—must be something from Heaven! With all the strength we can muster my brother and I would like to express our gratitude to you for the favor you've shown us by honoring our poor but—since your arrival—richer wedding. Come, my lady, and if here, in place of the crystal palaces you left in the depths of the sea where you dwell, you find our huts have walls of shells and roofs of willow, I mean, walls of willow and roofs of shells, here, at any rate, you'll find golden wishes and pearls of goodwill to serve you. I draw this comparison, which may seem inappropriate, because I know of nothing finer than gold or more beautiful than pearls.'

"Auristela leaned down to embrace him, confirming their good opinion of her with her composure, courteous manner, and beauty. The less-striking fisherman went over to tell the rest of the crowd to lift their voices in praise of the newly arrived stranger and to play all their instruments as a sign of rejoicing. Both the fishermen's fiancées, ugly and beautiful, kissed Auristela's hands in humble submission, and she embraced them in a courteous and friendly way.

"Delighted by this development the sailor informed the fishermen about the ship standing offshore; he told them it belonged to pirates and there was reason to fear they'd come for the highborn young lady, the daughter of kings. (He thought it necessary to bear this sort of witness to my sister in order to win their hearts for her defense.) As soon as they'd heard this they put down their instruments of rejoicing and took up those of war, sounding 'to arms! to arms!' up and down both sides of the river.

"Then night began to fall and we all gathered at the bridal couples' hut; they set sentries all the way down to the mouth of the river, baited their fish traps, spread out their nets, and adjusted their hooks, all for the purpose of providing for and serving us newcomers. To honor us even more, the two newly betrothed grooms chose

141

not to spend the night with their brides but to turn their huts over to the brides and Auristela and Cloelia, while they, along with their friends, myself, and the sailor, would be sentries and stand guard over them.

"Although a waxing moon provided more than enough light in the sky and on earth bonfires lit for the interrupted celebration were still burning, the grooms wanted us men to have supper outside and the women to eat in the relative safety of the hut. That's what we did, and the dinner was so abundant it seemed the land was trying to outdo the sea and the sea the land in offering up meat on the one hand and fish on the other. When supper was over Carino took me by the hand and strolled with me along the riverbank where, showing signs his spirit was full of strong emotions, he said to me between sobs and sighs, 'Because I believe your arrival at this particular time and juncture was miraculous—for you've delayed my wedding—I'm sure my misfortune will be set to rights by means of your counsel. So, even though you may think me crazy and a man of little sense and less taste, I want you to know that of those two women you've seen—the ugly and the fair—it's my luck to be taking the beautiful one (whose name is Selviana) as my wife. I don't know what to tell you or what excuse I can give for my fault in the matter or for the mistake I'm making, but I adore Leoncia, the ugly one, and can't make myself feel anything else. On top of that I want to tell you another truth I'm not mistaken in believing: with my inner eyes I see the virtues of her soul and find that Leoncia is the most beautiful woman in the world, and what's more, I have more than just a suspicion that Solercio, the other groom, is dying for Selviana.

"'So it turns out that our four wills are crossed, and this has come about because all four of us are trying to obey our parents and relatives, who've arranged these marriages. I can't think of any reason a man should agree to shoulder a load he'll carry his whole life to please not himself, but someone else. So even though this afternoon we were to have given our consent to and the "I do" for the imprisonment of our wills, it was prevented by your coming, and, as I see it, not by anyone's design but by order of Heaven. This means there's still time for us to change our fortune, and with this goal in mind I ask for your advice, since as an impartial stranger you'll know how to counsel me. What's more, I've decided, if no path can be found leading toward my salvation, to leave the banks of this river and never more be seen on them for as long as I live, whether or not my parents become angry, my relatives rebuke me, or my friends get mad at me.'

"As I listened to him carefully the solution for him came suddenly to my mind and these very words to my tongue: 'There's no reason for you to go away, friend. At least you shouldn't until I've talked with my sister Auristela, that extremely beautiful maiden you've seen. She's so wise she seems to have divine understanding, just as she's divinely beautiful.'

"After that we returned to the huts and I told my sister everything that had gone on with the fisherman. Then she in her wisdom found a way to make my words come true and to make everyone happy, which was to take Leoncia and Selviana aside and say to them, 'I want you to know, my friends, that after today you'll be even truer ones to me, for along with the good looks Heaven has given me it's also endowed me with a keen and perceptive mind, so by just seeing a person's face I can look into his soul and guess his thoughts. To put this truth to the test I'll present you yourselves as evidence; you, Leoncia, are dying for Carino, and you, Selviana, for Solercio. Maidenly modesty keeps you both silent, but thanks to my tongue your silence will be broken, and thanks to my advice, which you'll no doubt take, your desires will be correctly matched. Keep quiet and let me act, for either your longings will have a happy ending or I'm not as wise as I think.' Without saying a word, just kissing her hands countless times and embracing her tightly, they confirmed the truth of everything she'd said, especially concerning their crossed affections.

"Night came to an end and a very festive day dawned, for the fishermen's boats appeared adorned with fresh, green branches; their instruments resounded with new and happy sounds and the day's gladness increased as everyone raised their voices. The bridal couples came out to take their places in the bridal pavilion where they'd been the day before. Selviana and Leoncia had on fresh wedding clothes, but my sister had intentionally adorned and dressed herself in the same clothes she'd been wearing the day before and by putting a cross of diamonds on her beautiful forehead and pearls in her ears (jewels of such worth that up to now no one has been able to appraise them at their full value, as you'll see when I show them to you), she'd assumed the appearance of an image raised above the level of ordinary mortals.

"She was leading Selviana and Leoncia by the hands and, after mounting the platform where the bridal pavilion was, she called Carino and Solercio over to her. Carino came forward trembling and confused, not aware of what I'd arranged; then when the priest was about to join their hands and perform the sort of Catholic ceremonies they use, my sister signaled them to listen to her. A deep silence immediately spread over all the people; it was so hushed the air scarcely moved. Seeing, then, that she had everyone's rapt attention, she said in a loud and clear voice, 'This is what Heaven wants.' And taking Selviana by the hand she gave her to Solercio, and grasping Leoncia's gave her to Carino. 'This union, sirs,' continued my sister, 'as I've already said, is ordained by Heaven, not by any wishes forced on them by circumstances but by the true desires of these fortunate bridal couples, proven by the happiness on their faces and the "I do" on their tongues.'

"The four embraced each other, all present taking it as a sign they should approve the switch, and they were strengthened in their belief (mentioned before) that my sister's understanding and beauty were supernatural, since she'd changed the all but finalized marriages by simple command.

"The festivities began and four boats appeared, freshly cleaned and bright from being newly painted in many different colors. There were six oars on each side, no more and no less; the many pennants tied to the sides were also of various colors; the twelve oarsmen on each boat were dressed in fine, dazzling white linen in the same style I was wearing when I first came to this island. I soon realized they planned for the boats to race to a banner placed on the mast of another boat, which was about three times the length of a horserace from the first four. The banner was made of green taffeta, striped with gold, showy, and large enough to kiss the water and flutter over it.

"The noise of the crowd and the sounds of the instruments were so loud we couldn't hear the orders the race official gave as he came up in another painted craft. The boats decorated with branches moved to either side of the river, leaving an open space in the middle through which the four competing ones might race, and to avoid blocking the view of the multitude eagerly watching them from the pavilion and both banks. Having grasped the oars, their bare arms revealing thick sinews, wide veins, and taut muscles, the oarsmen were waiting for the starting signal, impatient with the delay and as spirited as a noble Irish setter when his master won't let him off the leash to get at the prey that has sprung up before his eyes. At last the awaited signal was given and all four boats leaped forward at the same time, seeming to fly through the air and not over the water. One of them, which bore as its insignia a blindfolded Cupid, moved into the lead by almost three of its own boatlengths, an advantage leading all the onlookers to expect it would succeed in winning the

coveted prize. The boat running behind it kept its hopes up by relying on the iron tenacity of its oarsmen, though on seeing that the
crew of the first boat didn't let up in any way they were on the verge
of dropping their oars.

"But conclusions and outcomes are often different from what
one imagines, and although it's a rule that in combat and contests
none of the spectators should favor any of the participants with hand
or voice signals or in any other way communicate with the combat-
ants, when the people on the bank saw the boat bearing Cupid's insignia pulling so far ahead of the others, believing the victory was
already theirs and heedless of any rules, many of them shouted,
'Cupid's winning! Love's invincible!" Hearing their shouts, Love's
oarsmen apparently slacked off a little. Taking advantage of this the
crew of the second boat, which was coming up behind Love and carrying Wealth represented by a small but very richly bedecked giant
as its insignia, pulled on its oars with such force that it drew even
with Love and, coming alongside it, splintered all the oars on Love's
right side, having first drawn in its own; it moved ahead, dashing
the hopes of those who'd first hailed Love's victory, and they began
to shout, "Wealth's winning! Wealth's winning!"

"The third boat's insignia was Diligence in the form of a naked
woman whose entire body was covered with wings, so if she'd carried a trumpet in her hands she'd have looked more like Fame than
Diligence. Seeing how well things were turning out for Wealth, Diligence's confidence grew and its oarsmen pushed themselves so they
drew even with Wealth, but because their helmsman steered poorly,
their boat became so entangled with the first two that none of its oars
on either side could be used. The last boat, whose insignia was Good
Fortune, was feeling discouraged and about ready to drop out of the
race, but seeing the intricate tangle of the others, it turned away from
them somewhat to avoid falling in the same trap, dug in its heels, as
the saying goes, and slipping by on one side moved into the lead.
The shouts of the spectators changed again and their voices inspired
the oarsmen who, intoxicated with the pleasure of seeing their standing improve, felt certain that even if those they'd left behind had been
holding the same lead as they, they still could have overtaken them
and won the prize; and win it they did, although more by luck than
by speed.

"In short, Good Fortune was the lucky one, but right now my
own luck won't be so good if I keep on with the story of my many
strange adventures. And so I beg you, sirs, let's put it aside for now
and tonight I'll bring it to an end, if it's possible for my misfortunes

to have one." At the very moment Periandro finished speaking the sick Antonio fainted dead away. His father, seeing this and almost as if he'd guessed its cause, left them all and, as we'll see later, went to look for Cenotia; what happened to him with her will be described in the following chapter.

Chapter Eleven of the Second Book

I t seems to me that if Arnaldo and Policarpo's patience hadn't been strengthened by the pleasure they derived from gazing at Auristela, just as Sinforosa's was from looking at Periandro, they would have lost it listening to his long tale, which Mauricio and Ladislao judged to have been somewhat lengthy and not very much to the point, for they felt there was no need for him to tell about the pleasures of others while relating his own misfortunes. But despite all this they enjoyed his story and stayed there with him hoping to hear the end, if for no other reason than his elegance and good style in relating it.

The elder Antonio found Cenotia, the person he was looking for, and in the king's chamber, no less; with a drawn dagger in his hands and full of Spanish fury and blind rage, he rushed at her, then started to speak, grabbing her by the left arm, raising the dagger, and saying to her, "You sorceress, give me back my son alive and well! If you don't, you can be sure the hour of your death has come! Beware if you have his life all wrapped up in some bundle of needles without eyes or pins without heads; beware, you traitor, if you've hidden it in some door hinge or any other place known only to you!"

Cenotia was terrified and trembling to find herself threatened by a drawn dagger in the hands of an enraged Spaniard so she promised to restore his son to life and health. In fact, fear so gripped her soul she'd even have promised to give him back the health of everyone in the world if he'd asked for it; then she said to him, "Let me go, Spaniard, and sheathe your steel, for it was your son's steely heart that got him into this present mess; and since you know we women are naturally vengeful (being scorned and slighted especially causes us to seek revenge), you shouldn't be surprised that your son's hardness of heart has hardened mine. Advise him to act in the future with more humane compassion for those who surrender to him, and not to show contempt for those who beg him for mercy; now go in peace, for tomorrow your son will get up feeling well and healthy."

"If that doesn't happen," replied Antonio, "I'll not be without means to find you or rage to take your life." He left her at this point, and she was so overcome by fear that, forgetting all her grievances, she removed from a door hinge all the spells she'd prepared to consume bit by bit the life of the cruel youth who had conquered her with the magic of his grace and charm.

No sooner had Cenotia removed her hellish concoctions from the door when Antonio's lost health again burst forth, his face taking on its original colors, his eyes a cheerful look, and his diminished strength a new vigor, making everyone who knew him happy.

When they were alone his father said to him, "In all I'm going to tell you now, my son, I want to stress that you should realize my words are intended to advise you not to offend God in any way, something you should've already figured out during the fifteen or sixteen years I've been teaching you the law my parents taught me, which is the Catholic and true one, and the one by which all those who have been saved in the past and shall be from this time forward will enter into the Kingdom of Heaven. This Holy Law teaches us we shouldn't punish those who offend us, rather counsel them to mend their ways, for punishment belongs to the judge while reprimands are everyone's province, provided they're given under the conditions I'll describe to you later. Whenever someone tempts you to commit offenses that may lead to the disservice of God, you'll have no reason to arm your bow, nor to shoot arrows, nor to use insults, for simply by not accepting the offer and escaping from the situation you'll turn out to be the winner in the struggle—free, and certain not to find yourself again in a danger like the one you've just been in. Cenotia has had you under a spell, a slow-acting one that little by little, in less than ten days, would have taken your life if God and my vigorous efforts hadn't prevented it. Now come with me so the sight of you can cheer up all your friends and let's listen to Periandro's adventures, for he's going to finish telling them tonight." Antonio promised his father that with God's help and despite whatever persuasions and traps might be used against his virtue, he'd follow all his advice.

Now Cenotia, ashamed, insulted, and offended by the son's cold-hearted haughtiness as well as the father's reckless anger,

147

wanted someone else to avenge the insult to her, but without depriving her of the company of her unrequiting barbarian. So, with her mind resolutely made up and this thought in it she went to King Policarpo and said to him, "You already know, my lord, that ever since I came into your house and your service I've made every effort to be faithful to it; you also know that, trusting in the truthfulness you've found in me, you've made me the archive of your secrets; finally, since you're a wise man you know, too, that in personal affairs—particularly if they involve love's desires—plans apparently right on the mark often miss it. For all these reasons I want to warn you that your decision to let Arnaldo and all his company freely go is foolish and beyond the bounds of reason. Tell me, if you can't win Auristela over when she's present, how are you going to win her over when she's absent? And why should she want to keep her word to return to take for her husband an old gentleman, which in fact you are (the truths one recognizes about himself cannot be used to deceive him), when close at hand she has Periandro (who just might not be her brother) and Arnaldo, too, a young prince who wants her to be nothing less than his wife? Don't let this occasion, my lord, slip away from you and turn its bald spot towards you rather than its forelock, which you should seize; take this opportunity to detain them by saying you want to punish the insolence and audacity this barbarian monster in their company showed by killing the man called Clodio in your very own house; if you do this you'll earn the reputation of harboring not favoritism but justice in your heart."

Policarpo was hanging on her every word; at each one spoken by the malicious Cenotia he felt his heart pierced by sharp nails and wanted to run instantly to carry out her advice. He already pictured Auristela in Periandro's arms, and not as her brother but as her lover; at other times he imagined her with the crown of the kingdom of Denmark on her head and Arnaldo mocking his amorous plans. In short, the fury of the hellish disease of jealousy so took control of his soul that he was on the verge of shouting and calling for revenge on someone who had never offended him. But Cenotia, seeing how ripe and ready he was to carry out whatever she might most want to advise him to do, told him to calm down for the moment, since they should wait for Periandro to finish telling his story that evening as a way of gaining time to decide what would be best for them to do. Policarpo thanked her while she, both cruel and in love, searched her thoughts to figure out how she might satisfy the king's desire and her own.

Night began to fall at this point, and as before they all gathered to chat. Periandro repeated some of the things he had said earlier so his story would make sense as he took up its thread, which he had broken off at the boat race.

Chapter Twelve of the Second Book

*Periandro Continues His Pleasant Story
and Auristela Is Kidnapped*

The person listening to Periandro with most delight was the beautiful Sinforosa, hanging on his words as though bound to him by the chains coming out of Hercules' mouth,[1] such was the grace and charm with which Periandro told his story.

At last, as has been said, he took up its thread again, continuing in the following way. "Good Fortune left Love, Wealth, and Diligence behind, for without it diligence is worth little, wealth is unprofitable, nor can love make use of its powers. The fishermen's festivities, as merry as they were poor, outshone those accompanying the Roman triumphs, for perhaps the finest pleasures may be found hidden away in unpretentious simplicity.

"But human happiness for the most part hangs by slender threads easily broken and destroyed by change and, as the threads of my fishermen's good luck broke, those of my own bad luck became twisted and strengthened. Attracted by the green and pleasant place, we all spent that night on a small island in the middle of the river. Not acting like newlyweds who wish to be alone, rather with all modesty and diligence the two bridal couples were made happy just trying to please those who'd earlier pleased them so much by bringing them to their long-awaited and present happy state of matrimony; and so they commanded the festivities to begin again on the island in the river and continue for three days.

"The time of year, which was early summer, the pleasantness of the place, the brilliance of the moon, the murmur of the springs, the fruits of the trees, the fragrance of the flowers, each of these individually and all of them together tempted us to agree to the idea of staying there for as long as the festivities lasted. But scarcely had we gathered on the island when out of a clump of woods there came about fifty assailants lightly armed like highwaymen, ready to rob and run away in the space of a moment; and since careless victims are usually defeated by their own carelessness, almost without defending ourselves and dazed by the surprise attack, we simply looked on as the thieves charged like hungry wolves into our flock of dumbfounded sheep and carried off—if not in their mouths then in their arms—my sister Auristela, her nursemaid Cloelia, Selviana, and Leoncia, as though they'd come to harm only them, for they left behind many other women also endowed by nature with exceptional beauty.

"I felt more angry than amazed at the strange event and threw myself after the raiders, keeping them within sight and sound of my voice, yelling insults at them—as if they were capable of feeling insult—and hoping my abuse would irritate them enough to make them want to turn back to avenge it; but they, intent only on getting what they were after, either didn't hear or didn't want revenge and so went on out of sight. Immediately the bridegrooms and I plus some of the more important fishermen huddled—as they say—to decide what we should do to correct our error and recover our beloved jewels.

"One of them said, 'It can only be that some ship full of robbers is off the coast where they can easily come ashore, possibly knowing about our gathering and our festivities. If that's the case, as I think it doubtless is, the best solution is for our boats to go out to them and offer as much ransom as they may want for their prey without haggling over the price, since when the stolen treasure is wives it deserves the very lives of their husbands as ransom.' 'I'll be the one,' I said then, 'to take care of this business, since to me my sister's life is a jewel worth as much as the lives of everyone in the world put together.' Carino and Solercio said the same, weeping in public while I was dying in secret.

"By the time we committed ourselves to this course of action it was beginning to get dark. Nevertheless the bridegrooms and I got into a boat along with six oarsmen, but by the time we reached the open sea night had completely fallen and we couldn't see any sign of a vessel through the darkness. We decided to wait for the coming day, to see if with daylight we could make out some ship, and as luck would have it we spotted two, one leaving the shelter of land and the other moving toward it. By both the flags and the sails, which had red crosses on them, I recognized the one leaving land as the same one we'd left to go ashore on the island. The ingoing one had green sails, but the men on board both ships were pirates.

"Since I thought the ship leaving the island belonged to the thieves who'd taken their prey from us, I had a white flag of truce put on the end of a lance; I came alongside the ship to arrange the ransom, being very careful not to be captured myself. The captain came over to the railing and just as I was about to raise my voice to speak to him, my words were—if I can put it this way—confused, interrupted, and cut short in the middle by a fearful thundering produced by the discharge of a round of artillery from the incoming ship signaling it was challenging the outgoing one to battle. It was immediately answered by another no-less-powerful round, and in an instant the two ships began to bombard each other as though they were two well-acquainted and angry enemies.

"Our boat steered clear of the middle of the fray and we watched the battle at a distance; having fired artillery for almost an hour, the two ships grappled with each other with unprecedented fury. Those on the ingoing ship, who were luckier or—to be more precise—braver, jumped aboard the other and in a moment had cleared the whole deck, taking the lives of their enemies and sparing no one. Then finding it free of defenders they set about looting the ship of all the most valuable things on board. Since it belonged to pirates there were few, although in my estimation they were the most precious things in the world, for the pirates carried off my sister and Selviana, Leoncia, and Cloelia to enrich themselves, thinking that for Auristela's beauty they'd gain a precious and unparalleled ransom.

"I tried to bring my boat alongside to talk to the victorious captain, but just as my luck was always being blown off course, a gust of wind blew out from land and carried the ship farther off. I couldn't catch up to it, let alone offer everything possible or impossible as ransom for the prisoners, and so we were forced to return with no hope of recovering our loss. Since the ship's only course seemed to be that permitted by the wind it was impossible to tell at that point what direction it might ultimately turn, nor did we have any clue to help us learn who the victors were, so we couldn't even begin to estimate, as we might have had we known their homeland, what our hopes for restitution were. In short, the ship moved swiftly out to sea while we, discouraged and sad, went back up the river where all the fishermen's boats were waiting for us.

"I don't know if I should tell you, sirs, what I have to tell you now; at that moment a certain feeling came over me which, without changing my nature, made me feel more than mortal, and so, standing up in the boat, I had all the others form a circle around me and listen carefully to these or other similar words I said to them: 'A turn of bad luck has never been improved by idleness or laziness; true happiness never dwells in spirits that shrink from challenge; we make our own luck, and no soul exists incapable of rising to the occasion. Cowards, even though they may be born rich, are always poor, like misers who continually beg for more. I say this to you, my friends, to stir your spirits and urge you to improve your luck, to get you to leave behind these poor possessions of yours—nets and a few narrow boats—and to seek instead the treasure found in noble work. I call noble the work of the person who takes on great enterprises. If the digger sweats as he breaks ground and earns scarcely enough to sustain him for more than a day without gaining any glory at all, why doesn't he take up a lance instead of a spade? And not fearing the sun's heat or any kind of inclement weather, why doesn't he try to earn not only his sustenance, but also glory to make him greater than other men? War, just as it's the stepmother of cowards, is the mother of the brave, and the rewards won in it can be said to come from beyond this world. Come on, then, my friends and brave young men; set your eyes on that ship carrying off your kinsmen's precious jewels, and let's get into the other one that I almost think Heaven commanded them to leave at the shore for us.

"'Let's go after it and become pirates, not to be greedy like all the others, but as agents of justice, which we'll be. We all know the art of seamanship; on board we'll find supplies and everything necessary for sailing, for their adversaries stripped it of nothing except the women; if the offense we've received is great, the opportunity to avenge it now being offered to us is even greater. Follow me, then, all you who will; I entreat you, and Carino and Solercio beg you to do it, for I know full well they won't leave my side in this brave undertaking.'

"I'd scarcely finished presenting these arguments when a murmur was heard throughout all the boats, for everyone was discussing among themselves what they should do, then with one voice they said, 'Set sail, noble guest, and be our captain and our guide, for all of us will follow you.' I took this unforeseen unanimous decision as a favorable omen and, fearing any delay in putting my good ideas into action might allow them the opportunity to give the matter more considered thought, I hurriedly took the lead in my boat, which was followed by about forty others. I reached the ship and

152

looked it over, went on board, examined everything closely, saw what was there and what was lacking, and found everything I could have wished for or that might be necessary for the voyage. I advised them no one should return to land, a measure designed to avoid the possibility that the weeping of the women and dearly loved children might make them abandon their noble resolve. Everyone took my advice, and right from where they were said goodbye in their hearts to their parents, children, and wives. A strange event, indeed, and one that requires a courteous listener to be believed!

"Not one went back to land, nor provided himself with any more clothes than those he was wearing on boarding the ship; there, without formally dividing up the duties, they all worked as sailors and pilots, with the exception of myself, named captain by common consent. Commending myself to God, I immediately began to carry out the duties of my post, and my first order was to remove the corpses left on the ship by the earlier skirmish and to clean up the blood that was all over it. I ordered them to bring me any offensive or defensive weapons found on board; on distributing them later I gave each one—in my judgment—the weapon best for him. I checked over the supplies and, taking into account the number of people, I estimated how many days, more or less, they would last.

"With this inspection completed and after a prayer was offered to Heaven, begging divine guidance for our voyage and favor for our most honorable intentions, I ordered the sails, still lashed to the masts, hoisted and spread to the wind, which, as I said before, was blowing from the land. Then, as happy as we were daring and as daring as we were confident, we began to sail on the same heading we believed the ship carrying the prisoners had taken.

"There I was, my fine listeners, first turned into a fisherman and matchmaker, now rich with the presence of my dear sister and then poor without her, robbed by raiders and then promoted to the rank of captain to oppose them; the turns of my wheel of fortune have no stopping place nor any limits."

"No more," said Arnaldo at this point, "no more, friend Periandro; for although you may not tire of telling your misfortunes, it tires us out just to hear about them, there are so many." To this Periandro replied, "My life, my lord Arnaldo, is similar to this thing called *place* in expressions such as: where everything fits and nothing is 'out of *place*,' and in me all things unfortunate 'have a place,' although since I've found my sister Auristela I think everything that takes place is fortunate, for any evil that ends without ending one's life isn't so bad."

Hearing this Transila said: "I for one, Periandro, don't understand that last concept; I only know it would be very bad, indeed, if you didn't satisfy the desire we all have to learn about the events in your story, for it seems to me its events are such that many tongues will seize the opportunity to tell them and many harmful pens[2] the chance to write them down. I'm astonished to hear of you turned into the captain of an outlaw band (I think your brave fishermen fit that description), and I'll be waiting in suspense to be further amazed to hear about your first heroic exploit and the first adventure you encountered." "Tonight, my lady," responded Periandro, "I'll bring the tale to its conclusion, if one is possible, for at this point it's really only getting started." Then, since everyone agreed they'd get back to the topic that evening, Periandro set it aside for the time being.

Chapter Thirteen of the Second Book

Periandro Tells of a Remarkable Event that Happened to Him at Sea

The lifting of the hex from Antonio entirely restored his health and good looks, but with them Cenotia's evil desires were also renewed; they in turn renewed her fears of finding herself far from him. But those desperate for a solution to their sufferings never manage to realize they're deceiving themselves, and instead continue to do so as long as they're in the presence of the cause of their ills. And so, making use of all the schemes her sharp mind could concoct, she tried to see to it that none of the guests left the city. Once again she advised Policarpo by no means to let the audacity of the homicidal barbarian go unpunished and, even if he didn't give Antonio punishment commensurate with his crime, at the very least he should arrest and intimidate him with threats; after that, justice could be tempered with mercy, as it often is even in the most serious cases.

Under the circumstances, however, Policarpo declined to carry out her advice, telling Cenotia it would be an insult to the authority of Prince Arnaldo, who had Antonio under his protection, and would anger his beloved Auristela, who treated him like a brother. In addition the crime had been accidental and unavoidable, more a case of bad luck than malice; not only that, there was nothing to hold him accountable for, since everyone who'd known Clodio insisted the punishment was what he deserved for his crime, for he'd been the worst slanderer anyone had ever heard of.

"How can it be, my lord," replied Cenotia, "that now you're so far from arresting him when just the other day the two of us had made up our minds to seize him and so give you the opportunity to detain Auristela? They'll get away from you, she won't come back, you'll weep over your confusion and hesitation at a time when tears will do you no good, and then you won't be able to undo what you're planning to do now in the name of mercy. The offenses committed by a man in love to satisfy his desires aren't really offenses, because the desires aren't his, nor is he the one who commits them, since it's love that really commands his will. You're a king, and injustice and cruelty on the part of kings are merely considered strict discipline. If you seize this youth you'll give justice its due, and by letting him go you'll be known for your compassion; both acts will strengthen your reputation as a good man." This is the sort of advice Cenotia was giving Policarpo, who both alone and in all his comings and goings among people was constantly thinking about the matter, not knowing how he could detain Auristela without offending Arnaldo, whose bravery and power he had reason to fear.

But in the midst of these thoughts—and of Sinforosa's, who, since she was neither as cunning nor as cruel as Cenotia and wanted Periandro to leave so she could begin hoping for his return—it came time for Periandro to resume his story, which he continued as follows: "My ship was flying swiftly wherever the wind wanted to take it, none of us on board opposing her course and everyone putting our voyage in the hands of fortune, when we saw a sailor fall from the topsail; before hitting the deck he was stopped short and left hanging by a rope he had tied around his neck. I went forward quickly and cut him free, thus preventing the long rope from shortening his life. He looked as though he were dead and remained unconscious for almost two hours, after which he came to; when asked the cause of his desperation he said, 'I have two children, one three and the other four years old, whose mother is no older than twenty-two and poorer than you can imagine since she was supported only by the work of these hands. And just now when I was up on that topsail I turned my eyes toward the place where I'd left them and, almost as if I could make them out, saw them on their knees with their hands raised to Heaven, praying to God for their father's life and calling out to me with tender words. I also saw their mother weeping and calling me the cruelest of men. This scene was so vivid in my mind I'm compelled to say I saw it, and for me there's no doubt it actually happened. Then seeing this ship flying away and taking me from them, not knowing where we're going and realizing I had little or no reason to board her in the first place, I was overwhelmed, desperation put this rope in my hands, and I put it around my neck to end in one moment those ages of pain I saw threatening me.'

"All of us listening to him were moved to pity and, having consoled him and more or less assured him we'd soon return happy and rich, we put two men on guard to prevent him from making another evil attempt on his own life and then we left him. So the event wouldn't awaken in anyone's mind the desire to imitate it I said to them, 'It's the worst cowardice in the world to kill yourself, for taking your own life is a sign you don't have the courage to endure the evils you fear. But what greater evil than death can happen to a man? And since this is so, there's nothing foolish about trying to delay it, for while there's life all sorts of bad luck can still be remedied and improved, but in the hopelessness of death not only does misfortune not come to an end or improve—it actually gets worse and begins anew.[1] I'm saying all this, my friends, so you won't be shaken by what you've seen this desperate man do, for even though we've just started sailing today I've a feeling countless happy events are waiting expectantly for us.'

"They let one of them be the spokesman for all and he responded, saying, 'Valiant Captain, many difficulties come to light whenever things are too much studied, and when it comes to understanding courageous deeds, some credit, indeed, must be given to reason, but much more to luck. Now that we've had the good luck to choose you for our captain we can press forward sure and confident of obtaining the good things you've mentioned. Let our wives be left behind, our children, too; let our aged parents weep and may poverty come to all of them; for Heaven, that sustains even the lowly water-worm, will take care to sustain the people on shore. Order the sails hoisted, my lord, and station lookouts on the topsails to see if they can spot opportunities to demonstrate that those of us here who have set forth to serve you are not fearful, but bold.'

"I thanked them for their reply and had all the sails spread to the wind. We sailed all that day, and at dawn on the following one the lookout on the main topsail yelled out loudly, 'Ship ahoy! Ship ahoy!' They asked him which way it was heading and what size it seemed to be. He answered that it was as large as ours and we had it off our bow.

"'Drop everything, friends,' I said, 'Seize your weapons and show these pirates—if that's what they are—the courage that's made you leave your fishnets.' I immediately had them lay on more canvas and in a little more than two hours we spotted and then overtook the ship, which we immediately attacked. Not encountering any defensive action, more than forty of my soldiers leaped aboard but found no one to bloody their swords on since it only held a few sailors and servants. As they were looking the ship over carefully, in one of the compartments and separated from each other by a space of almost two yards, they found a very handsome man and a more than moderately beautiful woman held in stocks by iron rings around their necks. Stretched out on an elegant bed in another chamber they found a venerable old man who radiated such authority that his mere presence obliged them all to respect him. He didn't move from the bed because he was unable, but raising himself a little he lifted his head and said, 'Sheathe your swords, sirs, for on this ship you'll find no enemies against whom to use them, and if necessity is making and forcing you to use this means to seek your fortune at the expense of others, then you've come to a place that will make you all happy indeed, not because there are riches and jewels on this ship to make you wealthy, but because I'm on it, and I am Leopoldio, king of the Daneans.'

"His calling himself a king aroused my curiosity to know what events had led to a king's being so alone and defenseless. I went up to him and asked if what he said were true, because even though his dignified appearance promised it was, the small entourage with which he traveled made it hard to believe him. 'Order these people, sir,' responded the old man, 'to quiet down and listen to me for a little while, for I'll tell you many important things in a few words.' My companions became quiet and we all prepared to listen carefully to what he wanted to say, which was this: 'Heaven made me king of Danea,[2] a title that I inherited from my parents, who were also kings and had inherited it from their ancestors and come to the throne without tyranny or any political manipulations. In my youth I married a woman who was my equal; she died leaving me without heirs. Time passed and for many years I kept myself within the bounds suitable for a respectable widower, but finally through my own fault (for no one should blame anyone but himself for the sins he commits), I repeat, through my own fault I tripped and fell in love with

157

one of my wife's ladies-in-waiting; had she turned out to be what she should have been, today she'd be queen and not tied up and placed in stocks, as you must have already seen. But feeling it wasn't inappropriate to prefer the curly locks of one of my servants to my own white hair, she became involved with him and was not only content to steal my honor but also tried to take my life, scheming against me with such strange plots, such tricks and subterfuge that if I hadn't been warned in time my head would now be off my shoulders and flying in the breeze on a meathook while theirs would be wearing the crowns of the kingdom of Danea. In short, I found out about their plan in time and at the same time they learned I knew about it.

"'One night, fleeing punishment for their crime and my furious indignation, they embarked in a small boat with its sails already set for departure. I learned of this, flew to the harbor on the wings of my anger, and found that they'd spread their own wings to the wind about twenty hours earlier. Blind with anger and driven by the desire for revenge, not thinking anything through in a sensible way, I then set sail on this ship and followed them, without all the grandeur and entourage of a king, but like any private citizen with a score to settle. I found them at the end of ten days at a place called the "Island of Fire"; I took them unawares, put them in the stocks you've seen, and have been taking them back to Danea to bring them to lightning-swift justice and the proper punishment for their crime. This is the truth, pure and simple, and in there are the culprits, testifying to it even though they might not want to. I am the king of Danea and promise you a hundred thousand gold coins, not because I have them here with me, but because I give you my word to send and deliver them to you wherever you may want, and as a guarantee, if my word isn't sufficient, take me with you on your ship and have one of my men go in mine—which is now yours—to Danea and afterwards deliver the money to wherever you choose. That's all I have to say to you.'

"My companions all looked at one another, then gave me leave to answer for them all although it wasn't necessary since I, as captain, could and should have done so. But even though they gave me permission I still wanted to confer with Carino and Solercio and someone from the rest of the band so they wouldn't think I was trying to put myself above them by means of the command they'd given me of their own free will. So in answer to the king I said, 'My Lord, neither necessity nor any desire akin to ambition put weapons in the hands of those of us who have come here, for our purpose is to search out thieves, punish raiders, and destroy pirates, and since you're far from being a person of that sort, your life is safe from our weapons; on the contrary, if you need us to put them to use in your service nothing will prevent us from doing so. And although we appreciate the generous promise of your ransom, we release you from it, for as a captive you aren't obliged to keep it. Go on your way in peace, and as our reward for your leaving this encounter better off than you might have thought, we beg you to pardon these offenders against you, for the grandeur of a king gleams much brighter when he's merciful than when he's merely just.'

"Leopoldio would have liked to humble himself at my feet, but neither my courtesy nor his illness would permit it. I asked him to give me some gunpowder, if he had any, and to share his provisions with us, which he did immediately. I also advised him that if he couldn't bring himself to pardon his two enemies, he should leave them on my ship and I'd take them someplace where they'd have no further occasion to offend him. He said he'd do that, knowing the offender's presence often reminds the one offended of the harm done him.

"I ordered our return to the ship at once with the gunpowder and supplies the king was sharing with us. Then as we were trying to transfer the two prisoners, now released and freed from the heavy stocks, the exchange was prevented by a strong wind that unexpectedly came up, separating the two ships and not allowing them to come together again. From the railing of my ship I shouted farewell to the king and he, supported in the arms of his men, got up from his bed and bid farewell to us. And I, too, bid farewell now, for I need to rest before getting into the second adventure."

Chapter Fourteen of the Second Book

Everyone shared in the pleasure of hearing the way Periandro was recounting his strange pilgrimage except perhaps Mauricio who, coming over to his daughter Transila and speaking in her ear, said, "It seems to me, Transila, that Periandro could have related the details of his life with fewer words and more succinct narration; there wasn't any reason for him to waste time telling us in such detail about the festival of the boats or even about the fishermen's weddings, since episodes included to adorn the story shouldn't be as long as the story itself; still, I'm sure what Periandro wants to do is show us the keenness of his wit and the elegance of his words." "That must be it," replied Transila, "but all I can say is, whether he goes into detail or makes what he says brief, it's all fine and enjoyable."

But no one enjoyed it more—as I believe has been said already—than Sinforosa, for every word Periandro spoke was a caress that left her beside herself with pleasure. Policarpo's scrambled thoughts kept him from paying very careful attention to Periandro's ideas, and he would have liked him to run out of things to say so he himself could get on with more of the things he wanted to do, for hopes close to being realized are more trying than those remote and out of reach.

But Sinforosa wanted so badly to hear the end of Periandro's story that she asked everyone to gather again the next day, when he continued his tale as follows: "Ladies and gentlemen, imagine my sailors, companions, and soldiers, richer in reputation than in gold, and me, with some suspicion that they didn't exactly approve of my generosity. Even though the matter of Leopoldio's freedom was as much their decision as mine, still, since all men don't think alike, I had reason to fear not everyone might be happy and it might seem to them it would be difficult to make up the loss of a hundred thousand gold coins—which was how much Leopoldio had offered to pay us for his ransom. This concern moved me to say to them, 'My friends, no one should be sad about the chance we've lost to possess the great treasure the king offered us, for I want you to know that an ounce of good reputation is worth more than a pound of pearls; and only someone beginning to experience the glory that comes with having a good name can know this. A poor man made wealthy by his virtue usually becomes famous, just as a rich man, if he's corrupt, can, and indeed does, become infamous. Generosity is one of the most winning virtues and builds a good reputation; this is made obvious by the fact that a generous man never looks bad, while a miser never looks good.'

"I was going to say more since it seemed to me they were all listening very willingly—judging by their cheerful faces—when the words were taken right out of my mouth by the sighting of a ship not far from our own that was crossing in front of us and sailing close to the wind. I ordered everyone to battle stations, gave chase with all sails spread, and after a short time came within cannon range; we fired an unloaded charge as signal to lower its sails, and it did just that, striking them from the top down.

160

"Coming closer, I saw one of the strangest sights in the world; I was astounded to see more than forty hanged men dangling from the lower spars and rigging. Then, as we came alongside the ship, my soldiers jumped aboard and met no resistance. They found the deck covered with blood and bodies of half-dead men, some with their heads split open and others with their hands cut off, some vomiting up blood and some their souls; one moaning quietly in pain and another screaming at the top of his lungs. This death and destruction seemed to have happened during a meal, for food was floating around in the blood, and the glasses mixed in with it still smelled of wine. In short, stepping on dead men and trampling the wounded, my men moved forward and in the sterncastle found about twelve extremely beautiful women drawn up in a squadron, with one in front who was clearly their captain. She had on a white breastplate, so smooth and clean it could have been used as a mirror had you wanted to look at yourself in it; she was also wearing armor to protect her throat, but none on her thighs or arms. However, she did have on a helmet made in the shape of a coiled serpent and adorned with countless different stones of various colors; in her hands she carried a javelin decorated from top to bottom with golden nails and a huge knife forged of sharp and shining steel; with all this she looked so spirited and bold that her glance was enough to stay the fury of my soldiers, who had begun to gaze at her in rapt astonishment.

"I'd been watching her from my ship, but to see her better I went over to her vessel just when she was saying, 'I'm sure, soldiers, this small squadron of women you see before you astonishes more than frightens you, but since we've already taken revenge for the wrongs done us there's nothing at all that could bring us to feel any fear whatsoever. Attack if you're thirsty for blood and spill ours while you take our lives; as long as you don't deprive us of our honor we'll feel we didn't die in vain. Sulpicia's my name; I'm the niece of Cratilo, the king of Bituania; my uncle married me to the great Lampidio, who was as famous for his family line as for the many good qualities with which nature endowed him and his worldly wealth. We were going together to visit my uncle the king, feeling all the security that comes with traveling among one's own vassals and servants, all of whom were obligated to us for the good things we'd always done for them; but beauty and wine, which often unsettle even the keenest minds, erased their obligations to us from their memories and replaced them with lustful urges. Last night they drank so much they were buried in a deep sleep; still, some who were half-awake laid hands on my husband and began to carry out their horrible plan

161

by taking his life. But since self-defense is natural, we women, thinking that at least we'd die avenged, prepared to defend ourselves; so,
taking advantage of the unsteadiness and drunkenness of our attackers, making use of some weapons we took from them, and, with the
help of four servants free of Bacchus' fumes, we did to them what
can be seen in those corpses on deck. Then pushing our vengeance
further, we made those spars and yardarms blossom with the fruit
you see hanging there. Forty's the number of those hanged, but if
there had been forty thousand they'd have died, too, because their
weak or nonexistent defense, coupled with our fury, led to all this
savagery—if that's what it really was. I bring riches I can share, although it would be more accurate to say, riches you can take; I can
only add that I'll give them to you very gladly. Take them, sirs, but
don't touch our honor, for that would make you infamous rather
than rich.'

"Sulpicia's arguments seemed so good to me that, even had I
been a real pirate, I'd have softened. One of my fishermen said at this
point, 'May I be struck dead if we aren't being offered here today
another King Leopoldio so our worthy captain can show his generous nature! Yes, sir, Lord Periandro, let Sulpicia go free; we want no
other glory than that of having overcome our animal instincts!' 'So
be it, my friends,' I responded, 'since you all want it, and you should
realize Heaven never leaves such deeds unrewarded, just as evil ones
never go unpunished. Strip those trees of their bad fruit and clean the
deck; then give those ladies, along with their freedom, your best
wishes to be of service to them.'

"My order was carried out and an amazed and wondering Sulpicia bowed before me, and since she couldn't quite comprehend
what had happened to her neither could she formulate a reply. What
she did do was order one of her ladies to have the chests with her
jewels and money brought out to her. The lady did so, and in a moment, as if they'd appeared or rained down from Heaven, four chests
full of jewels and money were set before me. Sulpicia opened them
and let my fishermen see samples of that treasure, the splendor of
which, perhaps (and conceivably without any perhaps), blinded some
of them to the intentions they had of being generous, for there's a
big difference between giving away what one possesses and has at
hand and giving away what one merely hopes to possess.

"Sulpicia took out a valuable gold necklace, gleaming with precious stones set in it, and said, 'Take this valuable token, brave captain, even though its real value lies only in the goodwill with which

it's offered you; it's the offering of a poor widow who yesterday, safe with her husband, found herself lifted to the heights of good fortune, but who today is subject to the discretion of these soldiers all around you; among them you can divide these treasures that—as they say—have the power to melt hearts of stone.'

"To this I replied, 'Offerings from such a great lady must be valued as though they were favors freely given.' And taking the necklace I turned to my soldiers and said to them, 'This jewel is mine now, my soldiers and friends, and thus I can dispose of it as my own property; but its value, which seems incalculable, is too great for it to be given to just one person; let whoever wants take it and keep it safe, and after a buyer is found the price we get will be divided among everyone. But don't touch the rest of what the matchless Sulpicia is offering you and your good name will be praised to the skies.'

"To this one of them replied, 'We'd rather, our good Captain, you hadn't jumped the gun on us with your advice, so you could have seen that our own free will is the same as yours in this matter. Return the necklace to Sulpicia; no necklace can encircle nor any boundary limit the good reputation you're promising us.' I was very pleased by my soldiers' answer, and Sulpicia was astonished at their lack of greed. Finally she asked me to give her twelve of my soldiers to act as her guards and sailors to take her ship to Bituania. That was done and all twelve I chose were extremely happy just to know they were going to do a good deed.

"Sulpicia supplied us with excellent wines and plenty of preserved food, which we were short on. The wind was blowing in a favorable direction for Sulpicia's voyage and for ours, which had no definite destination, so we said goodbye to her. She learned my name as well as Carino and Solercio's; then, after embracing the three of us, she embraced all the others with her eyes; she was weeping tears of joy and sadness, sadness for the death of her husband and joy to find herself free from the hands of men she'd thought were pirates. We parted company and went our separate ways. (I forgot to tell you how I returned the necklace to Sulpicia and she took it back, though only because I insisted so much, and how she felt practically insulted that I valued it so little as to give it back to her.)

"I consulted with my men about which heading we should choose and we decided to take whatever course the wind set for us, since that was the one all the other ships on the sea would also take, or at least, if the wind didn't suit the purposes of some of them, they'd just tack back and forth until it became more favorable. At this point a clear and serene night fell and, calling to one of the fisher-men—sailors who was serving as our skipper and pilot, I sat down on the quarter deck and began to gaze at the sky with searching eyes."

"I'll bet," said Mauricio to his daughter Transila at this point, "Periandro will now proceed to describe the whole celestial sphere for us, as if telling us about the movements of the stars were impor-tant to what he's relating. As for me, I wish he'd finish, for my desire to leave this land leaves me with no wish to entertain or occupy my-self with finding out which are the fixed and which the wandering stars. What's more, I know much more about their movements than he can ever tell me." While Mauricio and Transila were talking in low voices, Periandro caught his breath to continue his story this way.

Chapter Fifteen of the Second Book

Sleep and silence were beginning to take possession of my com-panions' senses, and I was getting ready to ask the man with me many things about what's necessary to know in order to practice the art of navigation, when suddenly it began to rain; not just drops, but whole clouds of water fell on the ship; it seemed exactly as though the entire sea had gone up into the sphere of the wind and from there was rushing down over the ship. We all became alarmed; standing up and looking all around, we were frightened and amazed to see clear skies in some directions with no signs of a squall.

"At this the fellow with me said, 'I'm sure this rain is part of the water that pours out of the holes below the eyes of those mon-strous fish called "shipwrecks,"[1] and if this is so, we're in great danger of losing our lives! We must fire off all the artillery; its noise frightens them.' At that moment I saw a neck like that of a horrible serpent rise up and come onto the ship, and snatching a sailor it gobbled him up and swallowed him down without having to chew. '"Shipwrecks" it is,' said the pilot, 'so fire away with cannon balls or without them for, as I said, it's the noise and not the impact that'll save us!'

"Fear had the sailors confused and cringing, for they didn't dare stand up lest they be carried off by those terrible monsters; still, de-spite everything they hurried to fire the artillery, some yelling and others manning the pumps to return the seawater back to the sea. We hoisted all the sails and, as if escaping from some huge fleet of enemy ships, fled the danger that was upon us, the worst we'd found ourselves in till then.

"At nightfall on the next day we found ourselves near the shore of an island not known to any of us; planning to take on water there, we decided to wait for morning, not moving away from shore. We lowered the sails and dropped the anchors, handing our worn-out bodies over to rest and sleep, which softly and gently took possession of them. Later, we all disembarked and set foot on a very pleasant beach whose sand, putting aside all exaggeration, was made of grains of gold and tiny pearls.

"Going farther inland we saw meadows whose grasses were green not because they were grass but because they were emeralds, and through whose greenness flowed not crystal-clear waters, as they say, but streams made of liquid diamonds that looked like crystal serpents crisscrossing the whole meadow. Then we came upon a forest of many different kinds of trees, so beautiful our minds were filled with amazement and our senses with gladness; hanging from some of them were branches of rubies that looked like cherries, or perhaps cherries that looked like fine rubies; from others hung pippin apples with one rosy cheek and the other of finest topaz; on another branch were pears with the fragrance of amber and the colors of the sky at sunset. In short, all the known fruits were there and in season, notwithstanding the fact that they usually ripen at different times of the year; there everything was spring, everything early summer, everything late summer without its discomforts, everything a pleasant and unbelievably exquisite autumn.

"What we saw satisfied all five of our senses. Our eyes were filled with beauty and loveliness; our ears, with the gentle murmur of the springs and streams and with the sound formed by the untutored voices of countless birds, and as they hopped from tree to tree and branch to branch, their freedom seemed to be held captive in that place though they neither tried nor wished to recover it. Our sense of smell was satisfied by the fragrances given off by the grasses, flowers and fruits; our taste by the samples we took of their savor, and our touch by holding them in our hands; they made us feel we held pearls from the South Seas, diamonds from the Indies, and Tiber gold."[2]

"I'm sorry Clodio is dead," Ladislao said to his father-in-law Mauricio at this point, "for I swear Periandro would have given him something to talk about with what he's saying now." "Be quiet, sir," said his wife Transila, "for, whatever you may say, you can't deny Periandro's telling his story well." Periandro, himself, as we've said, whenever he was interrupted by the comments of his listeners, would stop to catch his breath before continuing his story, for even good ones may cause more annoyance than pleasure if they go on too long.

"You haven't heard anything yet," continued Periandro, "for what remains to be said requires your intelligence to get a clear picture of it, not to mention your courtesy to believe it. Open your mind's eye once again, ladies and gentlemen, and imagine that out of the heart of a rocky cliff you see coming—just as we saw it and weren't deceived—I repeat, first coming out of a crack in the rock, a very soft, mellow sound produced by various musical instruments which struck our ears and compelled us to listen closely. Then a coach came out like a float made of I-don't-know-what kind of material, though I can describe its shape as that of a damaged ship escaping from a violent squall; it was pulled by twelve exceedingly powerful apes, very lustful animals. Riding on the float was a very beautiful lady wearing showy clothing decorated in several different colors and a crown of bitter-yellow oleander. She rode holding on to a black staff that had a sign or shield attached to it bearing these letters: *Sensuality*. After her came many other beautiful women with various kinds of instruments in their hands, making music that was alternately happy and sad, but they themselves were all exceedingly merry.

"All my companions and I were stunned, as if we were mute statues made of solid rock. Sensuality came up to me and said in a voice both angry and seductive, 'It's going to cost you dearly to be my enemy, noble young man; if not your life, then at least your pleasure.' Saying this she moved on and the musical young ladies snatched up—you might as well call it that—seven or eight of my sailors and carried them off with them; then following their mistress they reentered the cleft in the rock.

"I turned to my companions to ask them what they thought of what they'd seen, but was prevented by another voice or voices that reached our ears. These voices were quite different from the preceding ones, sweeter and more delicate, and were coming from a squadron of extraordinarily beautiful virgins, or so they seemed; but judging by their leader they doubtless were, for in the lead came my sister Auristela, and if the subject weren't so close to my heart I'd use some words here in praise of her more-than-human beauty. What could anyone have asked of me that I wouldn't have given as reward for the good news of such a precious discovery? Had I been asked to give up my life I wouldn't have refused, unless to keep from losing this treasure found so unexpectedly. My sister had a young woman on either side of her, and one said to me: 'We're Self-Control and Modesty, friends and companions always in attendance on Chastity, who today has decided to disguise herself in the form of Auristela, nor will we leave your beloved sister's side until she brings her trials and pilgrimages to a happy end in the nurturing city of Rome.'

"Attentive to such happy news, astonished at such a beautiful sight, and not certain whether to believe the grandeur and novelty of yet another new and strange event, I lifted up my voice to express with my tongue the glory I felt in my soul. Wishing to say, 'Oh, my soul's only consolation, oh, rich treasure come for my benefit, sweet and happy, I welcome you in this or any other season!'³ I said it with such vehemence that I woke myself up and the beautiful vision disappeared; then I found myself on my ship with all my men, not one of them missing."

At this Constanza said, "So, Sir Periandro, you were dreaming?" "Yes," he replied, "because all my treasures are only dreams." "To tell you the truth," added Constanza, "I was just about to ask my lady Auristela where she'd been during the time she hadn't appeared in the story." "My brother has related his dream so well," responded Auristela, "he was even making me wonder whether or not what he was saying was true." To this Mauricio added, "This shows the power of the imagination; often it can picture things so vividly that even if they're lies, they're absorbed by the memory and stay in it as if they were the truth."

During all this discussion Arnaldo was silent, thinking about the passion and persuasiveness with which Periandro told his story, but none of it brought him to a definite conclusion about the suspicions the dead slanderer Clodio had planted in his mind concerning whether Auristela and Periandro were really brother and sister. But in spite of this, he said, "Go on with your story, Periandro, but don't relate your dreams, for weary souls always have lots of confusing ones; the matchless Sinforosa is waiting for you to get to the part in which you tell about where you were coming from the first time you arrived on this island and were crowned the victor of the festivities held every year to celebrate her father's election." "My pleasure in what I dreamed," responded Periandro, "made me fail to notice how fruitless digressions are in any narration, which should always be succinct and not unnecessarily drawn out."

Policarpo was keeping quiet, occupying his eyes with gazing at Auristela and his thoughts with thinking of her, and so to him it mattered little or not at all whether Periandro talked or kept still. The latter, aware now that some of them were growing tired of his long story, decided that as he continued he'd shorten it and proceed with as few words as possible. And so he said,

Chapter Sixteen of the Second Book

Periandro Continues His Story

I awoke from the dream, as I've said. I consulted with my companions about which course we should set, and we decided to head wherever the wind might take us; that way, since we were looking for pirates, who never sail against the wind, we'd be sure to find them. I was still so befuddled from sleep that I asked Carino and Solercio if they'd seen their wives in the company of my sister Auristela, whom I'd seen in my dream. They laughed at my question and urged—even forced—me to tell them my dream.

"For two months we sailed without anything at all important happening to us except that we cleaned the sea of rubbish in the form of more than sixty pirate ships and, since they really were pirates, appropriated their stolen goods and took them over to our own ship, filling it up with countless items of booty. This made my companions happy and not sorry to have exchanged their fishermen's trade for piracy, but they weren't robbers except from robbers, nor did they steal anything not already stolen.

"It happened, then, that a persistent wind came up one night and, not giving us a chance to lower the sails or even trim them somewhat, it caught and stretched them out just as they were, unfurled, so, as I've said, we sailed on the same course for more than a month; so long that my pilot—who'd observed the height of the North Star above the horizon at the point where the wind grabbed hold of us—estimated the leagues per hour we were making and counted the days we'd sailed, and found we'd traveled more or less four hundred leagues. He measured our latitude again and found we were far north, in the vicinity of Norway; then in a loud voice filled with great sadness he said, 'Things look very bad for us; if the wind doesn't give us a chance to turn and go another way our lives will end on this course, for we're in the Glacial Sea, that is, the frozen sea, and if ice closes in on us here we'll be stuck fast in these waters.'

"No sooner had he said this than we felt the ship touch something like loose boulders along its sides and keel, which told us the sea was already beginning to freeze and its icebergs, forming under the water, were hindering the ship's movement. We lowered all the sails at once so the ship wouldn't be split open as it ran against them, and during that day and night the water froze so hard and squeezed so tightly, holding us caught in the middle, that the ship was left set in it and mounted like a precious stone in a ring. Almost instantaneously the ice began to numb our bodies and sadden our spirits, and since fear did its job as we contemplated our obvious danger, we didn't give ourselves any more days to live than those during which we'd be sustained by whatever provisions might be on board; they were soon rationed and doled out, but so miserly and scantily that we immediately began to die of hunger.

"We gazed in all directions and saw nothing to raise our hopes except a black shape, which seemed about six or eight miles away; but it soon occurred to us that it must be another ship held prisoner in the ice by the same misfortune. This peril went beyond and surpassed countless others in which I've found myself in danger of losing my life, for protracted fear and unrelenting dread weary the soul more than sudden death; getting it over with quickly spares one the fears and anxieties death brings with it, which are often as bad as death itself. This threat, then, of a death as ravenous as it was prolonged, led us to come to a decision that, if not desperate, was at the very least reckless. Since we felt that if our provisions ran out starvation would be the most maddening death conceivable to the human mind, we decided to leave our ship and walk over the ice to see if the other ship we could make out might have something on it of use to us, planning to obtain it either by consent or by force.

"We put our thoughts into action and immediately a squadron, which though small was made up of very brave soldiers with me as their leader, assembled into formation on the frozen water without getting their feet wet; repeatedly slipping, falling, and getting up, we reached the other ship, which it indeed turned out to be, and one almost as large as ours. There were people standing on deck, and guessing the purpose of our approach one of them began to shout at us, 'What have you come for, you reckless fools? What are you looking for? Are you here, by chance, to hasten our death and to die with us? Go back to your own ship, and if you're short on provisions, gnaw on the rigging and fill your stomachs with the tarred timbers if you can! And if you think we're going to take you in, forget that foolish notion, for it breaks the rules of charity, which should begin at home. They say this ice holding us usually lasts for two months; we have rations for fifteen days, so I'll let you decide whether or not it's wise for us to share it with you.'

"To this I replied, 'In times of unrelenting danger all reason's trampled under foot, due respect isn't observed, and nothing's kept within sensible limits. Take us on board willingly, we'll combine what's left of the provisions from our ship with yours, and let's all eat them as friends before harsh necessity drives us to take up arms and use force.' I responded in this way thinking they weren't telling the truth about the amount of provisions they claimed to have. But aware of their superior numbers and position of advantage, they weren't afraid of our threats and didn't heed our pleas, rather seized their weapons and got into position to defend themselves. Adding new spirit to their recklessness our men, whom desperation had changed from brave to utterly tenacious, attacked the ship and, receiving almost no wounds at all, boarded and took it; then a voice rose up from among our band saying we should kill them all, to cut down both on bullets and on stomachs that would use up whatever provisions we might find on board.

"I held a different opinion, and perhaps because it agreed Heaven helped us in this matter, as I'll explain later; but first I want to tell you that this ship was the one belonging to the pirates who'd stolen my sister and the two new brides of the fishermen. As soon as I recognized it I shouted, 'Where are you keeping our souls, you thieves? Where are the lives you stole from us? What have you done with my sister Auristela and with Selviana and Leoncia, who form part of, indeed are the better halves of, the hearts of my good friends Carino and Solercio?' To this one of them replied, 'Those fishermen's wives you're talking about were sold by our captain (who's dead now) to Arnaldo, the prince of Denmark.'"

"That's true," spoke up Arnaldo, "for I bought Auristela, her nursemaid Cloelia, and two other very beautiful young women from some pirates who sold them to me, and not at the price they were worth." "For God's sake!" said Rutilio at this. "What roundabout and far-fetched connections you've used to tie your wandering story together, Periandro!" "In satisfying the debt you owe to the desire we all have to serve you," added Sinforosa, "you should shorten your story, even though you're a storyteller as truthful as you are

170

delightful!" "Indeed, I will," replied Periandro, "provided it's possible for great things to be confined within narrow bounds."

Chapter Seventeen of the Second Book

All the delay caused by Periandro's story proved to be so contrary to Policarpo's liking that he could neither pay attention and listen to him nor think rationally about what he should do to keep Auristela. Without casting any aspersions on his reputation for generosity and sincerity we can admit he was thinking about the rank of each of his guests. Arnaldo who was prince of Denmark not by election but by birth came to his mind; he felt that Periandro's actions, refinement, and spirit revealed a person of great importance, and to him Auristela's beauty suggested a great lady. He truly would have liked to satisfy his desires in an open, straightforward manner, not using subterfuge or tricks but covering all difficulties and objections with the veil of matrimony. And even though his advanced age wouldn't really permit this fine solution he could still pretend it did, thinking that at any age it's better to marry than to burn.[1]

He was stimulated and driven by the same thoughts driving and distressing the deceitful Cenotia, with whom he agreed on a plan to be put into action before Periandro held another session. That plan was to sound a false alarm in the city two nights later and to set fire to the palace in three or four places so those staying there would be forced to come out in search of safety; during the confusion and disturbance bound to result he'd arranged for his people to kidnap the barbarian youth Antonio and the beautiful Auristela. His plan also called for him to see to it that his daughter Policarpa, moved by Christian compassion, would tell Arnaldo and Periandro about the danger threatening them. She wasn't to let anything slip out about the kidnapping but only show them the way to save themselves from the fire. They were to get down to the waterfront where they'd find a small sailing vessel waiting to pick them up.

Night fell and three hours into it the alarm sounded, producing confusion and chaos among all the townspeople. The fire began to blaze, and its flames fed those Policarpo felt in his heart. Meanwhile, unflustered, calm, and collected, his daughter went to warn Arnaldo and Periandro—but not only about the fire and escaping, for she also extended her warning to include all the information about her traitorous and infatuated father's plans, which called for holding on to Auristela and the barbarian youth while leaving no evidence to incriminate himself. Hearing this, Arnaldo and Periandro called Auristela, Mauricio, Transila, Ladislao, the barbarian father and son, Ricla, Constanza, and Rutilio; thanking Policarpa for her warning they all formed a compact group and then, with the men in front, they followed her advice and found the way to the harbor clear; they safely embarked in the sailboat whose pilot and sailors had been instructed and bribed by Policarpa to head out to sea as soon as those escaping had gotten on board, and not to stop until reaching England or some other place even farther from the island.

Amidst the confused cries and continual shouting of "To arms! To arms!," amidst the explosive crackling of the scorching fire, which seemed to know it had the permission of the owner of the palace's buildings to burn them, a cloaked Policarpo lurked about, spying to see whether Auristela's kidnapping was really being accomplished, while the sorceress Cenotia was anxious to see to Antonio's. But discovering, as his heart's misgivings predicted and the truth made plain, that they'd all embarked and no one was left behind, he hastened to order the cannons on all the ramparts and on all the vessels in the harbor fired at the ship carrying those escaping. This only added to the already fearful din and terror flowed through the hearts of all the city's inhabitants, who didn't know which enemies were attacking or what inopportune events had befallen them.

Not knowing anything about what had happened, the infatuated Sinforosa, her hopes wrapped in innocence, placed her trust in her feet and with stumbling and fearful steps went up into a high tower in the palace, a place she thought safe from the fire consuming the rest of the buildings. Her sister Policarpa managed to follow her there and, as if she'd witnessed it herself, told her about their guests' escape: this news caused Sinforosa to faint and Policarpa regretted bringing it to her.

The day that dawned at this point was a happy one for all who hoped to find out with its coming the reason or reasons for the present calamity, but in Policarpo's heart the saddest night one could ever imagine was falling. Cenotia was gnawing on her hands, cursing her deceitful science and the promises of her damned teachers. Sinforosa was still unconscious and alone, while her sister, also alone, was weeping for her misfortune, though not neglecting to do whatever she could to make her sister come to. Finally, she regained consciousness and looked out over the sea where she saw the vessel flying away with half her soul—or rather the best part of it. Like another deceived Dido grieving over another fleeing Aeneas,[2] sending sighs up to Heaven, tears down to earth, and cries out into the air, she said the following, or something similar.

"Oh, handsome guest, you came to these shores for my misfortune though certainly not as a deceiver, for I've not yet been so fortunate as to have you say loving words to deceive me! Lower those sails or at least trim them a little so my eyes can longer see that ship, for just seeing it and knowing you're aboard it consoles me. Remember, sir, you're fleeing the person who follows you, you're separating yourself from the person who seeks you, and you show signs of hating the person who adores you. I'm the daughter of a king, yet happy just to be your slave. And if I'm not beautiful enough to satisfy your eyes, I have enough passion to fill up all the empty spaces in love's greatest desires. Don't worry that the whole city is ablaze, for if you come back these flames will serve as festival lanterns celebrating the happiness of your return. I have wealth, my hasty fugitive, and it's put away in a place where the fire won't find it, search for it as it may, because Heaven is saving it for you alone."

Then she turned to speak to her sister, saying, "Doesn't it seem to you, dear sister, that it's lowered its sails a little? Doesn't it seem to you it's not traveling quite so fast? My God! Can he have changed his mind? My God, perhaps my will, like a remora,[3] is holding the ship back!" "Oh, sister!" responded Policarpa. "Don't deceive yourself, for longing and self-deception often go hand in hand. The vessel is flying away, not only unhindered by the remora of your will, as you call it but even pushed forward by your many sighs."

At this point they were taken by surprise by their father the king, who like his daughter wanted to see from the high tower, not just half, but his whole soul leaving him, even though it could no longer be seen. The men who'd taken charge of setting fire to the palace also took responsibility for putting it out. That very day, when the citizens learned the cause of the disturbance and thus found out about their King Policarpo's evil desires and about the sorceress Cenotia's fraud and bad advice, they deposed him and hanged her from a yardarm. Sinforosa and Policarpa were respected for who they were and their fate matched their merits, though not in any way to allow Sinforosa a happy ending for her desires, for Periandro's luck had better fortunes in store for him.

Those on the ship, finding themselves all together and free, tirelessly gave thanks to Heaven for the good turn of events. They learned about Policarpo's treacherous plans in greater detail from Arnaldo and Periandro, but those plans didn't seem so treacherous that they couldn't be excused somewhat; for they were forged in love, which excuses even the gravest mistakes. When love's passion fills a soul everything the lover says is off the mark and all reason is trampled underfoot.

They had clear weather and although the wind was brisk, the sea was calm, so they set their sights on reaching England; once there they intended to adopt whatever plan might seem most suitable, and they sailed along with such peace of mind that they felt no hint of anxiety or fear of adversity. The calm sea lasted for three days and during that time the wind blew favorably, until at sundown on the fourth day the wind kicked up and the sea turned rough; the threat of a heavy squall began to make the sailors uneasy, for the sea is a symbol of the inconstancy of our lives, neither one promising safety or stability for any length of time. But as good luck would have it, just when this fear was pressing in on them, they spotted an island nearby that the sailors immediately recognized, saying it was called The Hermitages; this made them very happy for they knew that along its shore there were two coves large enough to protect more than twenty ships from any wind, coves, in short, that could serve as a sheltering harbor.

They also said the hermit at one of the hermitages was an important French gentleman named Renato, the other a French lady called Eusebia, and that their story was the most remarkable ever heard. Their wish to hear the story and to take shelter from the storm, if it were coming, made them all decide to turn the ship's bow in that direction. This was done so skillfully that they promptly entered one of the coves, where no one interfered with their dropping anchor. Arnaldo—being advised the island was uninhabited except for the previously mentioned man and woman who were hermits, and in order to please Auristela and Transila who were tired of being at sea—with the approval of Mauricio, Ladislao, Rutilio, and Periandro, ordered the skiff put into the water so everyone could go ashore to spend the night in peace, free from the tossing of the waves. And although that's what was done, Antonio the barbarian felt he and his son, along with Ladislao and Rutilio, should stay on board guarding the vessel, for the sailors' loyalty was still untested and couldn't be trusted enough to be counted on. But as it turned out those staying aboard were the two Antonios, father and son, and all the sailors, for to seamen the tarred planks of a ship feel like the best land; pitch, tar, and the resin of their vessels smell better to them than roses, amaranths, and other flowers growing in gardens do to other people.

Those on shore took shelter from the wind in the lee of a boulder and protected themselves from the cold in the warm brightness of a bonfire that they quickly made of broken branches. Since they were accustomed to going through similar calamities all the time they survived the night painlessly, and it was made even easier by the comfort Periandro brought them in continuing his story at Transila's request. He declined to do so at first, but given the pleas of Arnaldo, Ladislao, and Mauricio—seconded by Auristela—together with the circumstances and the opportunity at hand, he felt obliged to continue in the following way.

Chapter Eighteen of the Second Book

If it's true, and it is, that it's very enjoyable to tell about a storm when everything's calm, to relate the dangers of a previous war in peacetime, and to talk in times of good health about the suffering of an earlier illness, then I'm really going to enjoy telling about my trials during this calm moment of rest; for although I can't say I'm free of them yet—they've been so dreadful and numerous—I can state that I feel at ease, for it's the nature of the human condition that when good things begin to add up they seem to call forth others that join them and go on increasing without end, just as bad things get worse and worse.

"I believe the trials I've suffered up to now have reached their limit of misery and bad fortune and will necessarily diminish, for when the most extreme trial doesn't lead to death—the ultimate one—then a change must follow, and not from bad to worse, but from bad to good and from good to better. Sharing this present trial with my sister, who is the true and effective cause of everything bad and good that happens to me, assures and promises me I'm going to reach the heights of all the happiness I could want. And so, with this happy thought, let me say I was still on my defeated opponents' vessel where, as I've already said, I found out they'd sold my sister plus the two brides of the fishermen and Cloelia to Prince Arnaldo here.

"My men were going around inspecting and making estimates of the supplies on board the icebound ship when, suddenly and without warning, we spotted a squadron made up of more than four thousand armed people coming across the ice from the direction of land. The sight left us more frozen than the sea itself and we readied our weapons, more to show we were men than thinking we could defend ourselves.

"They were all moving along on only one foot, pushing off with the right one while their weight was on their left heel, in this way impelling themselves and sliding a very long way over the sea; then pushing off again, they once more glided a long distance over their path;[1] in this manner they came up to us in no time and completely surrounded us. One of them, who I later learned was their captain, approached our ship to within a distance where he could be heard, guaranteeing us peace with a white cloth that fluttered from his arm; in a clear voice he said in Polish, 'Cratilo, king of Bituania and lord of these seas has the custom of sending armed men to search them and remove from them the ships held fast in the ice or at least any people and goods on board, taking the goods for himself as payment in exchange for the service rendered. If you all are willing to agree to this arrangement and offer no resistance, you will enjoy your lives and liberty, for we won't hold you captive in any way. Think it over carefully; but if the answer is no, prepare to defend yourselves against our weapons, which are always victorious.'

"I liked the brevity and decisiveness of the man speaking to us. I replied he should let us confer; what my fishermen then told me to say was that both the end of all evils and the worst of them is an end to life, which must be sustained by all possible means (except dishonorable ones), and as there was no dishonor involved in the arrangement they were offering us, and since as things stood we were just as certain to lose our lives as we were doubtful we could defend ourselves, the best thing would be to surrender and let the bad luck pursuing us do its duty, for it might possibly be saving us for better times.

"I gave the captain of the squadron this reply almost word for word. Immediately, looking more like they meant war than showing any signs of peace, they rushed aboard the ship; in a moment they'd stripped it of everything and bundled it all—even the artillery and rigging—into some ox hides they'd spread on the ice; then tying them up they made sure they could haul and pull them along with rope without losing anything. In exactly the same manner they stole everything they found on our other ship and, after placing us on some other skins, amidst an uproar of lighthearted shouts they pulled and hauled us to land, which must have been about twenty miles from the ship's location. It seems to me it must have been quite a sight, so many people walking dryshod over the water without Heaven using any of its miracles. In short, that night we reached the shore, which we didn't leave until the next morning, for it was crowned with countless crowds of people come to see the frozen booty.

"Among them on a beautiful horse came King Cratilo (we knew it must be he by the splendid royal insignia he was wearing); at his side, also on horseback, was a most beautiful woman, wearing white armor almost entirely covered by a black veil spread over it. I couldn't take my eyes off them, as much for her beauty as for King Cratilo's striking appearance; then looking at her carefully I realized it was the beautiful Sulpicia, to whom the courtesy of my companions a few days before had granted the freedom she was now enjoying.

"The king came forward to see the people who had given themselves up; leading me by the hand the captain said to him, 'In this youth alone, oh valiant King Cratilo, I feel I'm presenting you with the most valuable booty human eyes have ever seen.' 'God in Heaven!' said the beautiful Sulpicia at this point, throwing herself from her horse onto the ground. 'Either I've gone blind or this is Periandro, my liberator.' And no sooner had she said this than she wrapped her arms around my neck; these unusual demonstrations of affection also moved Cratilo to dismount from his horse and welcome me with the same signs of happiness.

"At that moment even a faint hope for anything good to happen had been far from my fishermen's minds; but taking courage from seeing me received with such expressions of happiness, their eyes began to brim over with contentment and their mouths with thanks to God for this unexpected good, which they already considered not just simple goodness but an unmistakable and singular blessing.

"Suplicia said to Cratilo, 'This youth is a person in whom the highest degree of courtesy has its home and generosity itself makes its dwelling; and although I personally have experienced this, I want you to verify it for yourself and using your sound judgment remove any doubt surrounding this truth I'm telling you simply by looking at his noble person.' (Here it can easily be seen that she was speaking like someone grateful and a little carried away.) 'This is the man who gave me liberty after the death of my husband; this is the man who didn't scorn my treasures, yet still refused to take them; this is the man who, after receiving my gifts, returned them to me in better condition, wishing, if only he could, to give me greater ones; in

short, this is the man who by making adjustments to his own situation (or, I should say adjusting the wishes of his soldiers to match
his own in giving me twelve of them to accompany me) made it possible for me to be here with you now.' With a red face, I imagine,
from the flattering and excessive praise I'd heard spoken about me, I
didn't know what else to do except kneel before Cratilo, asking to
take his hands, which he held out not for me to kiss but so he could
lift me up from the ground.

"Meanwhile the twelve fishermen who had come as Sulpicia's
guard were walking among the other people looking for their companions and, embracing one another relieved and full of happiness,
they told each other of their good and bad luck; those who had been
on the sea exaggerated their ice and those on land their riches. 'Sulpicia has given me,' one of them was saying, 'this golden chain.' 'She
gave me,' another was saying, 'this jewel worth two of those chains.'
'She gave me,' replied this one, 'a great deal of money,' and that one
echoed, 'She gave me more with this one diamond ring than to all
the rest of you put together.'

"All this chattering was silenced by a great murmur that ran
through the crowd, caused by the noise a very powerful wild horse
was making while two brave grooms who really couldn't handle him
were trying to lead him by the bridle. He was reddish black but spotted all over with white flakes that made him exceptionally beautiful;
his back was bare, for he would only allow the king himself to saddle
him; however he didn't show him that same respect whenever he got
on his back, for then he couldn't be restrained, not even by the endless mountains of obstacles they placed before him, and this bothered
the king so much he'd have given a city to anyone who could break
the horse of his bad habits. He told me all this quickly and succinctly,
but even more quickly I made up my mind to do what I'll describe
now."

Periandro had reached this point in his talk when to one side of
the boulder where those from the ship were gathered Arnaldo heard
a noise like the footsteps of someone walking toward them. He stood
up, put his hand on his sword, and waited with resolute courage to
see what would happen. Periandro also became quiet and they all
waited expectantly, the women with fear and the men—especially
Periandro—boldly, for whatever it might be. Then by the faint light
of the moon, which couldn't be seen through a covering of clouds,
they made out two shapes coming toward them; they wouldn't have
been able to figure out what they were if one of them hadn't said in
a clear voice, "Don't be alarmed, ladies and gentlemen, whoever you

178

may be, by our unforeseen arrival, for we've come only to be of service to you. This deserted and lonely shelter you have here can be improved by coming to ours, if you'd like; it's located at the top of this mountain, and there you'll find light and a warm fire along with dishes of food that, if not expensive delicacies, are at least basic and tasty."

❧ I answered,[2] "Are you, by chance, Renato and Eusebia, the pure and true lovers who keep fame busy telling of their goodness?" "If instead you'd said, 'unfortunate,'" replied the figure, "you'd have been more accurate; but, yes, we're the people you mentioned and with sincere goodwill offer you the most hospitable welcome our austere way of life can provide."

It seemed to Arnaldo they should take the advice being offered them, feeling they were obliged to do so by the threat of harsh weather. They all got up, and following Renato and Eusebia, who acted as their guides, they came to the top of a small mountain where they saw two hermitages, whose comforts were more appropriate for spending a life of poverty than for dazzling the eyes with rich furnishings. They went in, and in the one that looked somewhat larger found two lamps by whose light their eyes could distinguish what was inside, which was an altar with three holy images. One was the Author of Life, now dead and crucified; another, standing above the world, was the Queen of Heaven and Our Lady of Happiness, though she looked sad; the third was the beloved disciple who saw more while sleeping than was seen by all the starry eyes of Heaven.[3]

They kneeled down and, after saying the proper prayer with devout respect, Renato took them to a dwelling adjoining the hermitage, which they entered through a door made at the side of the altar. In short, since minor matters don't call for or bear up under long accounts, I won't dwell on the details of what took place there; there was a scant supper with modest fare, abundant only in the goodwill displayed by the hermits, both of whom were notable for their humble clothing and their advanced years—bordering on old age—while Eusebia was particularly remarkable for her beauty, which still shone with signs of having been extraordinary.

Auristela, Transila, and Constanza stayed in that dwelling, having as their beds dry rushes and other herbs chosen more for their pleasant aroma than to please any of the other senses. The men tried to make themselves comfortable around the hermitage in different spots, all of which were as cold as they were hard and as hard as they were cold. Time passed as it usually does, night sped by and the day dawned clear and serene; when the sea could be seen again it looked polite and well behaved, seeming to invite them to enjoy it by embarking once more. And doubtless they would have done so if the pilot of the ship hadn't come up to tell them not to trust the weather, for even though the signs promised peace and quiet the actual outcome might be very different. His opinion won out because everyone respected him, since when it comes to the art of seamanship the simplest sailor knows more than the most learned scholar in the world.

The ladies left their herbal beds and the men their hard stones, they all went out to view from the vantage point of the peak the delights of the small island for, even though its perimeter measured only about twelve miles, it was so full of fruit trees, so refreshed by abundant waters, so pleasant in its green grasses, so fragrant with flowers, that it could satisfy all five senses to the same degree and at the same time. The day was only a few hours old when the two venerable hermits called their guests and, spreading out on the floor inside the hermitage both green and dried rushes, made a pleasant carpet, one possibly more showy than those usually adorning the palaces of kings. Then on it they spread a variety of fruits, fresh as well as dried, and bread (though not fresh enough to avoid some resemblance to hardtack). The table was crowned with glasses skillfully wrought of cork and filled with crystal-cold liquids. The decoration, the fruit, the pure and clean water, which despite the dark color of the cork showed its clarity, together with everyone's need to eat, obliged them all and even forced them—to be more precise—to sit down around the table. They did just that and, after a meal as short as it was tasty, Arnaldo asked Renato to tell them his story and what had prompted him to lead such an austere life.

Renato, being a gentleman and therefore the soul of courtesy, without having to be asked a second time began to tell the tale of his true story as follows.

Chapter Nineteen of the Second Book

Renato Relates the Circumstances that Led Him to the Island of the Hermitages

U sually when past trials are related from the perspective of present prosperity, the pleasure in telling them is greater than the hardship endured in suffering them. I can't say this about my own trials, though, for I'm not telling them from somewhere outside the tempest, but from the midst of the storm. I was born in France, the offspring of noble, wealthy, and well-meaning parents. I was brought up and trained as a gentleman. I kept my thoughts within the bounds set by my station in life; nevertheless, I dared entertain hopes regarding the Lady Eusebia, a lady-in-waiting to the Queen of France; only my eyes let her know I adored her, but she, either because she failed to notice or failed to care, did nothing with either her eyes or her tongue to let me know she understood me. And although disregard and disdain usually kill love in its early stages by removing the support of hope to make it grow, they had just the opposite effect on me, for from Eusebia's silence my hope took wings to fly up to the Heaven of being worthy of her.

"But envy or the excessive curiosity of Libsomiro, also a French gentleman no less wealthy than noble, led him to discern my thoughts. Not putting them in the proper perspective he developed more envy than pity for me, though he should have felt just the opposite, for there are two misfortunes in love that go beyond all limits: one is to love and not be loved in return, the other to love and be despised in return, and neither separation nor jealousy is equal to these misfortunes.

"In short, without my having given any offense to Libsomiro, one day he went to the king and told him I was involved in an improper relationship with Eusebia and was thereby offending his royal majesty and breaking the law I must uphold as a gentleman. He was prepared to prove this truth with his weapons but didn't want it to come out in writing or from any other witnesses so it wouldn't ruin Eusebia's reputation, though he himself accused her a thousand times over of being shameless and loose.

"Upset by this information, the king had me called in and repeated what Libsomiro had told him about me; I pleaded my in-

181

nocence, defended Eusebia's honor, and in the most restrained terms
I could muster gave the lie to my enemy. It was decided to put the
question to a test of arms. The king refused to let us take the field
anywhere in his kingdom, so we wouldn't break the Catholic law
forbidding duels, but a place was given us by one of the free German
cities.[1] The day of the combat came and he showed up at the site with
the weapons that had been selected, which were sword and shield
without any other gear. The seconds and the judges performed the
ceremonies customary in such cases. They placed us in position so
the sun gave neither one of us the advantage, then stepped back.

"I entered the fight confident and encouraged by the thought
that beyond any doubt I was in the right and had truth on my side.
As for my opponent, I know full well he, too, came into it very sure
of himself, though feeling more proud and arrogant than secure in a
good conscience. Oh, Heaven's decrees! Oh, God's unfathomable
judgments! I did all I could, placing my trust in God and in the purity
of my unsatisfied desires; fear had no power over me, nor were my
arms weak or my movements sloppy. Yet despite all this—and I can't
explain how—I found myself stretched out on the ground with the
point of my enemy's sword pressed against my forehead, threatening
me with immediate and inevitable death.

"'Go ahead and make your thrust,' I said then; 'you've beaten
me more by luck than by courage! Take away my soul, since it's defended its body so poorly, but don't expect me to surrender, for my
tongue shall not confess a guilt not mine. Yes, I have sins that deserve severe punishment; but I don't want to add to them by bearing
false witness against myself, and so I wish to die with honor rather
than live dishonored.'

"'If you don't surrender, Renato,' responded my opponent,
'this point will go all the way to your brain and make you affirm and
sign with your blood my truth and your sin.' At this point the judges
came up, ruled me as good as dead, and gave the victor's laurels to
my enemy. He was carried off the field on his friends' shoulders
while I was left alone overcome by deep sorrow and confusion, more
sad than wounded, and clearly suffering from less pain than I thought
at the time, since it wasn't enough to take the life spared by my
enemy's sword. My servants came to my assistance. I returned to
my homeland. Neither on the road nor once there did I dare raise
my eyes to Heaven, for it seemed to me the burden of dishonor
and the heavy sorrow of infamy were weighing down my eyelids.
When friends talked to me I felt they were insulting me. For me the
clear sky was covered with gloomy darkness. No sooner did the

smallest group of townspeople gather in the streets than I thought my dishonor the subject of their conversation. Finally, I found myself so hemmed in by my melancholy feelings, thoughts, and confused imaginings that in order to escape them, or at least to relieve them somewhat (or perhaps to put an end to my life), I resolved to leave my homeland. So giving my estate to a younger brother of mine I set sail with some of my servants and sought to exile myself and come to these northern parts to look for a place where the disgrace of my infamous defeat couldn't reach me and where silence would bury my name.

"I found this island by chance; the place pleased me, and with the help of my servants I built this hermitage and shut myself away in it. Then I dismissed the servants, instructing them to come see me once a year so they could eventually bury my remains. The love they felt for me, the promises I made them, and the gifts I gave obliged them to grant my requests, which I prefer to call them, instead of orders.

"They went away and left me to my solitude where I found such good company in these trees, in these grasses and plants, in these clear springs, and in these cool bubbling streams that for the first time I felt sorry for myself for not having been defeated long before, for that trial would have brought me sooner to this rest and enjoyment. Oh, happy solitude, companion of the sorrowful! Oh, silence, such a pleasant voice to the ears; neither praise nor flattery accompanies you! Oh, what things I could say, ladies and gentlemen, in praise of holy solitude and delightful silence!

"But I'm prevented from doing so by telling you first that within a year my servants returned and brought my beloved Eusebia with them, she being the other hermit whom you see here. My servants had told her the situation I was in and she, grateful for my good intentions and sorry about my disgrace, chose to be my companion not in the guilt but to share the punishment. So embarking with them she left behind her homeland and parents, her luxury and riches, and above all she left behind her honor, for she left it to be judged in the frivolous and almost always inaccurate murmurings of the common people, since her flight seemed to confirm her error and mine.

"I welcomed her as she hoped I would, and the solitude and beauty that might have enflamed our already kindled desires had the opposite effect thanks to Heaven and to her purity. We gave each other our hands in lawful marriage, we buried fire in snow, and in peace and in love, like two mobile statues, we've lived in this place for almost ten years, during which not one year has gone by without my servants coming back to see me, supplying me with some of the things I need in this solitude. Sometimes they bring a priest with them to hear our confession, and in the hermitage we have sufficient vestments and vessels to celebrate the divine offices. We sleep apart, eat together, speak of Heaven, scorn life on this earth and, confident in God's mercy, await life eternal."

With this Renato came to the end of his story, and everyone present had the opportunity to express their amazement about what had happened to him, but not because it seemed new to them for Heaven to inflict punishment contrary to what human thinking expected, for everyone knows that punishments considered undeserved arise from one of two causes: those inflicted on bad people are indeed for punishment, but those suffered by the good are to make them better. And numbering Renato among the good, they gave him some words of consolation, then did just the same for Eusebia, whose expression of appreciation demonstrated her good judgment and showed she felt consoled.

"Oh for a life of solitude!" said Rutilio at this point, who deep in silence had been listening to Renato's story. "Oh, for the life of solitude," he said, "holy, free, and secure, granted by Heaven to favored spirits! Who wouldn't love you, who wouldn't embrace you, who wouldn't choose you, and who, finally, wouldn't find bliss in you?"

"Well said, friend Rutilio," interjected Mauricio. "But such considerations are applicable only to important people; we wouldn't be at all surprised to see a rustic shepherd withdraw into the solitude of the countryside, nor would we be amazed if someone poor who's starving to death in the city should seek solitary refuge where he won't lack for food. There are ways of living supported by idleness and sloth, and I'd be more than a little lazy if I were to leave the solution to my troubles in others' hands, even if they were kind ones.[2] If I were to see Hannibal the Carthaginian secluded in a hermitage as I saw Charles V shut up in a monastery[3] I'd be startled and amazed; but that a commoner should retire into seclusion, that a poor person should withdraw from the world, neither amazes nor startles me. That isn't Renato's story, however, for he was brought to this solitude not by poverty but on the strength of a wise decision. Here he enjoys abundance in the midst of scarcity and companionship in solitude, and his having nothing more to lose lets him live more securely."

To this Periandro added, "My fortunes have landed me in such dangers and crises that if I were as old as I am young, I'd, too, feel extremely happy to be accompanied by solitude and to have my name entombed in the silence of the sepulchre; but I can't look to my own wishes nor change my life now because I feel pressed to get back to Cratilo's horse, which is where I left off my story."

Everyone was happy to hear this, seeing that Periandro wanted to return to his often-begun and yet still-unfinished tale, which went as follows.

Chapter Twenty of the Second Book

Periandro Tells What Happened with Cratilo's Horse,
One as Highly Valued as It Was Famous

The magnificence, the wild spirit, and the beauty of the horse I've described to you had captivated Cratilo and made him want to see him tamed, just as I wanted to show how much I wished to be of service to Cratilo, for it seemed to me Heaven was giving me this chance to win favor in the eyes of the man I took to be my lord, and allowing me to confirm in some way the good things the beautiful Sulpicia had told the king about me.

"And so, not quite so mature as I was eager, I went over to where the horse was, got up on him without putting my foot in the stirrup (since there wasn't any), made him charge forward without reining in at all, came to the edge of a cliff overhanging the sea and, urging him on again with my legs (something as much to my liking as it wasn't to the horse's), I made him fly through the air so both of us would land in the depths of the sea; but in the middle of our flight I remembered the sea was frozen and the impact would smash me to pieces, so I felt certain we were both going to die. But it didn't turn out that way, because Heaven, which must be saving me for other things known only to it, made the front and rear legs of the powerful horse withstand the impact and no harm came to me other than being thrown off the horse and sent rolling and sliding for a long way. There was no one on shore who didn't expect and believe I'd been killed, but when they saw me stand up, even though they thought it a miracle, they condemned my daring as madness."

Mauricio found the horse's terrible leap without injury hard to

swallow; he'd have liked him at least to have broken three or four
legs, and then Periandro wouldn't have placed quite so much strain
on his listeners' courtesy to believe such an outrageous jump; but the
credibility Periandro had with everyone made them curb any doubts
about believing him; for just as the liar's punishment is not to be
believed when he tells the truth, so the truthful person's reward is to
be believed even when he may be telling a lie.

Meanwhile, since Mauricio's thoughts couldn't interfere with
Periandro's story, the latter continued it, saying, "I returned to shore
with the horse, got up on him again and, repeating the same steps as
the first time, urged him to jump a second time; but it wasn't to be,
for once he was at the edge of the high cliff he made such an effort
not to throw himself over that he sat back on his rump, broke the
reins, and stayed riveted to the ground. Then he broke out in a sweat
from head to foot and was so fearful he turned from a lion into a
lamb and from a wild beast into a noble steed; then the boys dared
pet him and the king's grooms saddled and bridled, mounted and
rode him in safety while he demonstrated his speed and quality, the
likes of which had never been seen before. The king was extremely
pleased and Sulpicia was happy to see my deeds had been equal to
her praise.

"There were three months of hard freeze left and it took just
that long to finish building a ship the king had begun, its purpose
to sail those seas in better weather to rid them of pirates while at
the same time enriching himself with their spoils. Meanwhile I performed some service for him in the hunt, where I proved myself
intelligent, skillful, and possessing the stamina to withstand hardships, for no other activity resembles war more than hunting, which
always involves fatigue, thirst, hunger, and sometimes even death.
The beautiful Sulpicia was extremely generous with me and my men,
and Cratilo's courtesy was equal to hers. The twelve fishermen Sulpicia had brought with her were already rich, while those who'd been
lost with me had also profited. When the ship was finished the king
ordered it outfitted and abundantly stocked with everything necessary, then made me its captain, free to act at will, with no obligation
to do anything except whatever I wished. Then, after having kissed
his hands in gratitude for such a great kindness, I asked his permission to go look for my sister Auristela, who I'd heard was in the
hands of the king of Denmark.

"Cratilo gave me leave to do anything I wanted, telling me my
conduct had obliged him to do that and more; he was speaking like

a king, which implies the granting of kind favors, a pleasant manner and, if one may say so, good breeding. Sulpicia possessed the latter to a high degree and combined it with generosity, the benefits of which allowed me and my men to embark rich and happy, and no one stayed behind.

"The first course we set was toward Denmark, where I believed I'd find my sister, but instead I learned that she and some other young ladies had been stolen from the seashore by pirates. My trials were renewed and my laments began again, accompanied by those of Carino and Solercio, who believed my sister's misfortune and imprisonment implied the same for their wives." "They guessed right," said Arnaldo at this point.

Then going on, Periandro said, "We swept all the seas, sailed around all or most of the islands in that area, always asking for news of my sister; for it seemed to me (with no offense intended to all the beautiful women in the world) that the light of her face couldn't be hidden no matter in how dark a place she might be, and her extraordinary intelligence would be the thread to lead her out of any labyrinth. We captured pirates, set prisoners free, restored property to its owners, and made off with the ill-gotten gains of others. Because of this, having filled our ship to overflowing with all sorts of worldly goods, my men wanted to return to their nets, their homes, and the arms of their children, and Carino and Solercio thought it might just be possible to find their wives in their own land, since they hadn't found them in any other.

"Before we arrived there, however, we reached an island that I believe is called Escinta where we learned about Policarpo's festival, and all of us felt like participating in it. Our ship couldn't maneuver there due to a contrary wind and so, dressed as oarsmen, we quickly got into the ship's boat, as has already been described. It was there I won the prizes, there I was crowned winner of all the competitions, and because of all that Sinforosa decided she wanted to learn my identity, as can be seen in the steps she took with that purpose in mind.

"After we'd returned to the ship my men were resolved to leave me; I asked them to let me have the boat as a reward for the trials I'd undergone with them. They left it for me and would have thrown in the ship, too, if I'd wanted it, telling me they were leaving me alone only because it seemed to them I had only one desire, and that one impossible to satisfy as our efforts to do so had shown. In short, I was accompanied by just six fishermen who, swayed by the reward

I gave them and another I promised, chose to follow me. Then after embracing my friends I set sail and headed toward the Barbarous Isle, whose inhabitants, I knew, were deceived by a custom and false prophesy I won't discuss with you now since I know you know all about it.

"I was wrecked on that island, captured, and taken where the living were buried alive; the next day they took me out to be sacrificed; the storm at sea came up; the timbers used as their raft broke apart; and I was washed out to the open sea on a piece of that raft with chains around my neck and manacles binding my hands. I then fell into the kind hands of Prince Arnaldo here, under whose command I went onto the island to be a spy and investigate whether my sister was there, although he didn't know I was Auristela's brother. The next day she was brought forth in men's clothing to be sacrificed. I recognized her, sympathized with her suffering, and prevented her death by saying she was a female, just as her nursemaid Cloelia, who was with her, had already done; but how the two of them came to be there is something she'll tell when she wishes to. You all know already what befell us on the island, and with this and what my sister still has left to say, you'll be satisfied regarding almost everything you could possibly want to know about the truth of what's happened to us."

Chapter Twenty-One of the Second Book

I don't know if I can accept as fact and dare state that Mauricio and some of the other listeners rejoiced that Periandro had put an end to his story, but most of the time long stories, even though they may be important, become tiresome. Auristela may have had this thought in mind for she declined to prove it true, as she would have if, at that moment, she had begun the story of what had happened to her. Even though there had been only a few events from the time she was stolen from Arnaldo until Periandro had found her on the Barbarous Isle, she chose not to add them until a more convenient time. But even had she wanted to do so she wouldn't have had a chance, because she'd have been prevented by a ship they saw heading under full sail toward the island from the open sea. It reached one of the island's coves in a short time and was immediately recognized by Renato, who said, "This, ladies and gentlemen, is the ship my servants and friends usually come on when they pay their occasional visits to me."

While the sailors sang a sea chantey the dinghy was launched into the water; it filled up with people and set out for shore where Renato and all those with him were waiting to greet it. Those disembarking must have numbered about twenty, among them one of noble bearing and clearly lord of all the rest; as soon as he saw Renato he came up to him with open arms, saying, "Embrace me, brother, as reward for my bringing you the best news you could possibly want." Renato embraced him, recognizing him as his brother Sinibaldo, to whom he said, "No news could be more agreeable to me, dear brother, than to see you here; even though I find myself in this dreadful state where no happiness can make me truly happy, seeing you takes precedence over and is an exception to the general rule of my misfortune."

Then Sinibaldo turned to embrace Eusebia, and said to her, "Give me your embrace, also, my lady, for you, too, are indebted to me for the news I bring, and so as not to prolong your pain, its telling shouldn't be delayed any longer. You should know, friends, that your enemy has died of an illness that made him unable to speak for six days before he died; but Heaven restored his voice for six hours before his soul departed and during that time, with signs of great repentance, he confessed the guilt he'd incurred by bearing false witness against you. He confessed his envy, declared his malice, and finally, gave enough evidence to prove his sin. He attributed to God's secret judgments the fact that his own evil had triumphed over your goodness; nor was he content just to tell about it, but chose to make public record of this truth. When the king learned of it, he made a proclamation restoring the honor of you both and declared you, my brother, victorious, and Eusebia chaste and pure; he further ordered you be looked for and, once found, brought into his presence so with his magnanimity and greatness he could make up for the hardships you both must have suffered. I leave it to you to decide if this news can truly make you happy."

"It's so good," Arnaldo said then, "that nothing could increase life's fulfillment more, nor any acquisition of unexpected wealth compare to it, for honor lost yet then recovered to its highest degree is a treasure none other on earth can equal. May you both enjoy it for many years, Lord Renato, and may the matchless Eusebia enjoy it in your company, for she's clung to you like a vine on a wall, been the elm to support your ivy, the mirror of your delights and an example of goodness and gratefulness." Although they used different words everyone gave them similar good wishes and then went on to ask Sinibaldo for news of what was happening in Europe and in other parts of the world, about which they'd heard very little due to their travels at sea.

Sinibaldo responded that what was being most discussed was the disastrous situation the old king of Denmark had been put into by Leopoldio, king of Danea, and his partisans. He also said it was rumored to be due to the absence of Arnaldo, prince and heir to the throne of Denmark, that his father was on the brink of losing everything; it was also reported this prince was flitting like a butterfly attracted by the light of the beautiful eyes of one of his prisoners, someone whose family line was so unknown that no one even knew who her parents were. Along with this he told about the wars of Transylvania's ruler and the movements of the Turks, the common enemy of the human race. He gave news of the glorious death of Charles V, king of Spain and Holy Roman Emperor, terror of the Church's enemies, and scourge of Mohammed's followers. He also related other less important things, some of which cheered while others astonished them; both kinds of information were gladly received by everyone except for a thoughtful Arnaldo, who from the moment he heard about the pressures on his father turned his eyes to the ground and put his hand on his cheek.

After staying like this for quite a while he lifted his eyes from the ground and turning them toward Heaven cried out in a loud voice, "Oh love, oh honor, oh compassion for my father, how you wrench my soul! Forgive me, love; my going away doesn't mean I'm leaving you; wait for me, honor, for my being in love won't keep me from following you; take comfort, father, for I'm returning; wait for me, vassals, for love never made anyone a coward, nor will I be one in defending you, for I love better and more truly than anyone else in the world. For the sake of the matchless Auristela I want to go win what is mine in order to merit, being a king, what I can't merit as a mere man in love; for unless good luck showers him with favors a poor man in love finds it practically impossible to satisfy his desires happily. As a king I want to court her, as a king I'll serve her, and as a man in love I'll adore her. Yet if despite all this I'm still not worthy of her I'll blame my luck more than her intelligence."

Everyone present hung in amazement on Arnaldo's words. But the one most amazed was Sinibaldo, to whom Mauricio had explained that the man speaking was the prince of Denmark, and the woman—here he pointed out Auristela—was the prisoner to whom it was said he'd given his heart. Sinibaldo looked at Auristela somewhat more carefully and immediately decided that what seemed to be madness in Arnaldo was in fact good judgment, for Auristela's beauty, as has been mentioned at other times, was so great it captured the hearts of all who looked at her and provided an excuse for all the errors in judgment that might be committed because of her.

What happened, then, is that on the same day it was agreed that Renato and Eusebia would return to France, taking Arnaldo in their ship in order to drop him off in his kingdom, and he in turn chose to take Mauricio and his daughter Transila and son-in-law Ladislao with him; likewise Periandro, the two Antonios, Auristela, Ricla, and the beautiful Constanza would take the ship in which they had escaped and continue their journey by going on to Spain.

Rutilio, seeing this division, was waiting to see which group they'd put him in; but before they could tell him he kneeled down before Renato and begged him to make him the heir to his possessions by leaving him on that island, if only so there'd be someone on it to light the lantern that guided lost sailors; he wanted to end his life well, for it had gone badly until then. Everyone seconded his Christian request and the good Renato, who was just as Christian as he was generous, granted him everything he'd asked for, telling him he wished the things he was leaving him were more valuable, although they were the basic items necessary for tilling the soil and living one's life. To this Arnaldo added that he promised, if peace should be established in his kingdom, to send him a vessel every year to assist him. Rutilio humbly offered to kiss everyone's feet, they all embraced him, and most of them wept to witness the new hermit's holy decision; for though our own lives may not improve, it's always a pleasure to see another's life on the mend, unless our perversity reaches the point where we'd like to be the abyss calling others down to it.[1]

It took two days to make arrangements and preparations to continue their separate journeys, and at the moment of departure there were kind and courteous words, especially among Arnaldo, Periandro, and Auristela; although they exchanged loving wishes, these were all expressed with a modesty and restraint that gave Periandro's heart no cause for alarm. Transila wept, Mauricio's eyes weren't dry either, nor were Ladislao's; Ricla sadly moaned, Constanza was moved, and her father and brother also showed tender

191

feelings. Rutilio went from one group to the next, already dressed in Renato's hermit's habit, bidding farewell to one and all, mingling sighs and tears at the same time. Finally, with calm weather inviting them and a wind that could be used for different destinations, they embarked and spread the sails while Rutilio sent them a thousand blessings from the heights of the hermitages.

Here the author brought to a close the second book of this singular story.

Book Three of The Trials of Persiles and Sigismunda, A Northern Story

First Chapter of the Third Book

Since our souls are in continual movement and can't stop or rest except at their center—which is God, for whom they were nurtured—it's no wonder our thoughts are changeable; we take this one up, drop that one, follow one, forget another. But the thought bringing us closest to inner peace will be the best, provided it's free from mistaken ideas. All this has been brought up to excuse the inconstancy demonstrated by Arnaldo's haste when he suddenly dropped the desire to serve Auristela he'd shown for so long; but it can't really be said he dropped it, he only postponed it during the time that desire for honor, which surpasses all other motives of human action, took control of his soul. Arnaldo, taking Periandro aside to talk, declared this desire to him on the Island of the Hermitages the night before their departure. There Arnaldo implored—for when asking for what one needs one doesn't request, but implores— him to watch over his sister Auristela and keep her safe so she might become queen of Denmark. And even though fortune might not favor him by allowing him to recover his kingdom, and if in making that most just claim he should lose his life, Auristela should be considered a prince's widow. As such she should choose an appropriate husband even though he knew and had said many times that in and of herself, without any other connections to high rank, she deserved to be queen of the greatest kingdom on earth, not just of Denmark. Periandro responded that he appreciated his good wishes and would be careful to watch out for her, as it was a concern very close to him and related to his own interests.

Periandro didn't pass on any of these words to Auristela, for praises someone in love gives to his sweetheart must be in his own words, not as though they came from another. The lover shouldn't try to win his love with someone else's pleasing words; he must present his very own to his lady. If he doesn't sing well, he shouldn't bring in someone else to serenade her; if he isn't very much of a gentleman, he shouldn't be seen with a Ganymede.[1] In short, my feeling is that no matter what one's shortcomings are, they shouldn't be patched up with someone else's surpluses. But this advice isn't for Periandro, who won the prize for natural gifts and was second to few in worldly possessions.

Now the ships were underway, with the same wind but in different directions, which is one of those things that seem so mysterious about the art of navigation. As I was saying, they were sailing along, not cutting through whitecaps but through crystal-clear blue waters; the sea looked like a bedspread since the wind, treating it with respect, didn't dare do any more than smooth its surface, and the ship gently kissed its lips and let itself slide over it so swiftly it scarcely seemed to touch it. In this manner and with the same tranquility and peace, they sailed for seventeen days without having to raise or lower the sails or even move a hand to trim them. This pleasure people feel while sailing in good weather would be unsurpassed were it not tempered by the fear of coming squalls.

At the end of these or a few more days, at dawn of one of them, a cabin boy reported he could see land from the main topsail. "Good news, ladies and gentlemen, and such good news that I want and deserve a reward! Land! Land! Although I should say 'Heaven! Heaven!,' for without a doubt we're in the vicinity of the famous Lisbon." This news brought tender and happy tears to everyone's eyes, especially to those of Ricla, the two Antonios, and their daughter Constanza, for it seemed to them they'd already arrived at the Promised Land they so longed for. Antonio threw his arms around Ricla's neck, saying to her, "Now, my dear barbarian, you'll learn how you must serve God, with a more complete explanation, though not different from the one I've given you; now you'll see the richly decorated churches in which He's worshiped; you'll also see the Catholic ceremonies in which He's served and observe Christian charity being administered as it should be. Here in this city you'll see how its many hospitals are the executioners of disease, and that he who does lose his life in one of them, wrapped in the efficacy of countless ecclesiastical indulgences,[2] will win life in Heaven. Here love and purity join hands and stroll along together, courtesy is never joined by arrogance, and bravery never lets cowardice come near it. All its residents are pleasant, courteous, generous, and in love—for they're bright and wise. It's Europe's leading and busiest trading city; here the riches of the Orient are unloaded, from here they're distributed throughout the whole world. Its harbor is spacious, with room not only for ships, which can be counted, but for whole movable forests of trees formed by ships' masts. The beauty of its women leaves one astonished and in love and its handsome men are stunning, as they say here. In short, this is a land that pays abundant holy tribute to Heaven.

"Say no more," said Periandro at this point. "Leave something for us to see for ourselves, Antonio. Praise shouldn't say everything; something must be left to be seen so we can be astonished afresh and thus our delight, growing by degrees, will turn out to be greater in the end."

Auristela was very happy, indeed, to see the time for her to set foot on dry land approaching, and that she'd no longer have to wander from port to port and from island to island, subject to the sea's inconstancy and the changeable will of the winds. And she was even happier when she learned she could get from there to Rome without wetting a foot or stepping on board a ship if she didn't want to.

It was around noon when they reached Sangián,[3] where the ship was inspected and where the commander of the fort and the men who went aboard with him were amazed by Auristela's beauty, Periandro's striking appearance, the two Antonios' barbarous clothing, Ricla's good looks, and Constanza's pleasing loveliness. They learned these were foreigners making a pilgrimage to Rome. Periandro made the sailors who had brought them happy by paying them magnificently with the gold Ricla had brought from the Barbarous Isle and turned into coin on Policarpo's island. The sailors were anxious to get to Lisbon and buy some profitable trading goods.

In the absence of the king, who wasn't in the city, the commander of Sangián sent a message to the governor of Lisbon, who was the archbishop of Braga at the time, telling him about the arrival of the foreigners and of Auristela's matchless beauty, also mentioning Constanza's, which not only wasn't hidden by her barbarian clothing but was actually enhanced by it. He also described Periandro's princely ways in the most favorable terms, as well as everyone's cultivated manner, for they seemed not barbarians but courtiers.

The ship reached the shores of the city and they disembarked at Belém because Auristela, feeling love and devotion for that famous and holy monastery,[4] wanted to visit it first and there worship the one true God, freely and not hindered by the warped rites of her land. Countless people had come down to the waterfront to see the strangers who'd come ashore at Belém, everyone hurrying to see something new, which always draws longing and curious eyes.

Soon, however, the newly arrived squadron of fresh beauty left Belém. The moderately beautiful Ricla was looking extremely so, dressed in the barbarian manner; Constanza was very beautiful and swathed in skins; the elder Antonio had bare arms and legs but wolf skins covered the rest of his body; the younger Antonio dressed the same way but with a bow in his hand and a quiver of arrows on his back; Periandro was wearing a green velvet coat and trousers to match, like a sailor, and on his head was a tight-fitting, pointed cap that still couldn't hide the golden ringlets of his hair; Auristela had all the elegance of the northlands in her dress, a most attractive grace in her body, and the world's greatest beauty in her face. Indeed, all of them together and each one separately produced startled wonder and admiration in everyone who looked at them, but the matchless Auristela and noble Periandro stood out above all the rest.

They went by land to Lisbon, surrounded by both commoners and courtiers; they were taken to the governor who, after his initial amazement on seeing them, never tired of asking who they were, where they came from, and where they were going. Periandro responded to all that, for he'd already thought through the answers to be given to such questions, knowing they'd be put to them often. When he wanted to, or whenever it seemed to his advantage, he told his story from beginning to end (always concealing who his parents were) and in such a way that he satisfied those asking by briefly outlining, if not all, then at least the major part of his tale.

The viceroy ordered that they be lodged at one of the best places in the city, which turned out to be the house of a magnificent Portuguese gentleman. Word had spread about Auristela, although, in fact, those good qualities they admired in her could be seen in all her traveling companions; nevertheless, so many people thronged there to see her that Periandro felt it best for them to change their barbarian clothes for those of pilgrims, for the novelty of the ones they were wearing was the principal cause of their being so hounded, and indeed, it seemed as though they were actually being pursued by the rabble; besides, no clothing would be more appropriate for the journey they were taking to Rome. So, they made just that change and in two days' time looked like perfect pilgrims.

It happened, then, that as they left the house one day a Portuguese man threw himself at Periandro's feet. Calling him by name and putting his arms around his legs, he said, "What good luck, Lord Periandro, makes you favor this land with your presence? Don't be surprised to hear me call you by your name, for I'm one of those twenty who recovered their freedom in the fire on the barbarous island where you had lost yours; I was present at the death of Manuel de Sousa Coitiño,[5] the Portuguese gentleman; I left you and your party at the lodge where Mauricio and Ladislao came looking for

Transila, wife of one of them and daughter of the other; good luck brought me to my homeland and here I told his relatives about his passionate death. They believed me, and even if I hadn't seen it myself they'd still have believed it, for among the Portuguese it's almost customary to die of love. A brother who inherited his estate conducted a memorial service for him, and on a white marble stone that he placed for him in a family chapel, as though he were buried beneath, there's an epitaph I want all of you to come and see, just as you are, because I think you're going to like its wit and charm."

By his words Periandro could easily see the man was telling the truth, though on looking at his face he didn't recall ever having seen him before in his life. Nevertheless, they went to the church he was talking about and saw the chapel and the stone on which the epitaph was written in Portuguese, though the elder Antonio read it mostly in Spanish, saying the following:

Here Lies the Living Memory
of the Quite Dead
Manuel De Sousa Coitiño,
a Portuguese Gentleman,
Who, Had He Not Been Portuguese, Would Still Be Alive.
He Died Not at the Hands
of any Spaniard,
but of Love, which Can Do All Things;
Learn of His Life,
and You Will Envy His Death,
Wayfarer.

Periandro saw the Portuguese fellow had good reason to praise the epitaph, and in general the Portuguese are very skilled in writing them.[6] Auristela asked the man what feelings the dead man's former lady—the girl who had chosen to be a nun—had shown on hearing of his death, and he replied that within a few days of finding out about it she went on to a better world, either due to the austerity of the life she'd been leading, or from the shock of the unexpected event.

From there they went off to the house of a famous painter, where Periandro directed him to paint on a large canvas all the major events in their story. On one side he painted the Barbarous Isle going up in flames and there, next to it, the prison island, and a little farther off, the raft or collection of logs on which Arnaldo found him and took him aboard his ship; in another part was the Snowy Isle, where

197

the passionate Portuguese lost his life; then came the ship in which Arnaldo's soldiers drilled holes; next to it he painted the separation of the dinghy and the ship's boat; in one place the duel of Taurisa's lovers, along with their death, was pictured; in another they were sawing through the keel of the ship that had been a tomb for Auristela and those traveling with her; the pleasant island where in his dreams Periandro saw the two bands of virtues and vices was in another spot; and there next to the vessel the giant fish caught the two sailors[7] and gave them burial in its stomach.

He didn't forget to have himself and his men painted like gems set in the frozen sea, the assault and combat on the ship, or the surrender to Cratilo. Likewise he had pictured his rash ride on the powerful horse, a lion turned into a lamb by fright (for such creatures are tamed by a shock). In a small space he had Policarpo's festivities sketched, and himself pictured with the winner's crown. He was careful and took pains to include and have painted into the story every important step along their way, down to putting in the city of Lisbon and their coming ashore wearing the same clothing in which they'd traveled; on the same canvas Policarpo's island could be seen burning, Clodio was pierced by Antonio's arrow, and Cenotia hanged from a yardarm; the Island of the Hermitages was painted, too, with Rutilio looking like a saint.

This canvas was used as a summary to save them from having to tell their story repeatedly in minute detail, for the younger Antonio would simply describe the pictures when people insisted he tell about the events.[8] But the famous painter was at his best in his portrait of Auristela, which led people to say he'd demonstrated his knowledge of how to paint a beautiful figure, although he didn't really do her justice; for unless the hand holding it were guided by divine thought, no human artist's brush could ever come close to expressing Auristela's beauty.

They were in Lisbon for ten days, all of which they spent visiting churches and setting their souls on the straight and narrow path of salvation. At the end of that time, with permission from the viceroy and with documents attesting to and authenticating who they were and where they were going, they said goodbye to the Portuguese gentleman who was their host and to the passionate gentleman's brother, Alberto, who showed warm feelings for them and gave them presents; then they set out on the road to Castile. It was necessary to make this departure at night for they feared if they left during the day the people following them would block their way, even though since their change of clothing the general astonishment had somewhat abated.

Second Chapter of the Third Book

The Pilgrims: Their Trip through Spain and the New and Strange Things that Happened to Them

Auristela's tender years and Constanza's even tenderer ones, along with Ricla's, which were somewhere between old and young, called for coaches and showy comforts for the long journey on which they were setting out. But the devotion of Auristela, who had promised to go to Rome on foot from the place where she reached dry land, stirred the devotion of the others, so everyone was of the same mind, men as well as women, and voted for a journey on foot, adding, if it should be necessary, that they would beg from house to house. Thanks to this Ricla closed the door on her giving and Periandro didn't have to make use of the diamond cross Auristela had with her, saving it, along with the priceless pearls, for a better occasion. All they bought was one pack animal to carry the loads they couldn't bear on their own backs; they provided themselves with pilgrims' staffs that served both for support and defense, as well as acting as sheathes for some sharp rapiers. Outfitted in this humble Christian manner they departed from Lisbon, leaving it deprived of their beauty and impoverished without the wealth of their wisdom, as evidenced by the countless gossiping groups of people gathered there talking of nothing but the extraordinary intelligence and good looks of the foreign pilgrims.

Having in this way readied themselves to endure the trial of covering two or three leagues of road every day, they arrived at Badajoz, where the Spanish magistrate[1] had already received news from Lisbon that the new pilgrims would pass by there. On entering the city they managed to find lodging at an inn where a company of famous actors was staying. That very night they were going to give a sample performance in the magistrate's house in order to obtain a license to perform in public. But scarcely had they seen Auristela's and Constanza's faces when they were overwhelmed by what usually overwhelmed everyone who saw them for the first time, namely, surprise and astonishment.

But no one made as much of his amazement as did a witty poet traveling along with the acting company for the purpose of adapting and patching up old plays as well as making them over completely, an exercise more clever than honest and involving just as much trial as error. But excellence in poetry is as clean as clear water, which improves everything unclean. It's like sunlight, which touches everything dirty without any dirt sticking to it; it's a skill as valuable as it is esteemed; it's a lightning bolt that leaps out from its hiding place, not to burn but to illuminate; it's a well-tuned instrument sweetly cheering the senses, bringing with it not only delight but purity and usefulness as well. In short, I say again that this poet whom necessity had obliged to exchange Mount Parnassus for roadhouses, and the springs of Castalia and Aganippes[2] for the puddles and streams of the roads and inns, was the one most astonished by Auristela's beauty. She immediately stuck in his mind and, not giving a thought to whether or not she knew the Spanish language, he felt she'd be more than good as an actress. He was pleased by her figure, he liked the way she carried herself, and in his mind's eye he dressed her in a flash in a man's short suit,[3] next he stripped her and dressed her again as a nymph, then almost in the same instant clothed her with the majesty of a queen. There wasn't any comic or tragic costume in which he didn't dress her, and in all of them he imagined how she'd look acting serious, carefree, wise, witty, and exceedingly modest, opposites not usually found in a beautiful entertainer.

Good Gracious! How easily a poet's wit runs away with him and tries to crash through a thousand roadblocks! How weak the foundations on which great fantasies are erected! Everything is seen as already accomplished, everything easy, and everything simple, with the result that there's a surplus of hope and a shortage of luck, as our modern poet demonstrated when he saw the canvas unrolled on which Periandro's trials were painted. He then confronted the greatest trial of his own life because his mind was filled with an immense desire to write a play based on them;[4] but he couldn't make up his mind what to call it—or whether he would call it a comedy, a tragedy, or tragicomedy—because while he did know the beginning, he didn't know its middle or end, for Periandro and Auristela's lives were still running their courses, and the ends to which they came would later determine what their story would be called.

But what bothered him most was wondering how in the midst of the sea and among so many islands, fires, and snows he could fit in a servant to act as confidant and comic relief.[5] Nevertheless, he didn't give up hope of writing the play and working in such a servant, despite all the rules of poetry and in defiance of those of dramatic art. While all this was running through his mind he had a chance to talk to Auristela and to propose what he wanted her to do, advising her how good it would be for her to become an actress. He told her that after a couple of stage appearances whole mines of gold coins would rain down on her, for the princes at that time acted as if money were made by alchemy and when they said gold, gold it was, and when they said copper, copper it was;[6] and they often surrendered their hearts to the nymphs they saw in the theaters, both to the full-fledged goddesses and the semigoddesses, to the studied queens and the pretend scullery maids. He told her that if some royal festival should take place while she was there she could count on being covered with golden petticoats, for all or most of the gentlemen would send their liveried servants to her house to show their respects and to kiss her feet. He described to her how pleasant her tours would be, accompanied by two or three gentlemen in disguise who would act both as servants and lovers; and above all, he extolled and praised to the skies the eminence and honor that would be hers when she took on the major roles. In short, he told her that if anything could verify the truth of the old Spanish saying it was beautiful actresses, for they could have their honor and eat up their profits, too.[7]

Auristela replied she hadn't understood a word of what he'd said to her, for it was perfectly clear she didn't know the Spanish language, and even had she known it her thoughts were on other matters and her mind was set on other activities perhaps not so pleasant but at least more appropriate. The poet was overcome with despair on hearing Auristela's resolute reply; he looked down at the feet of his ignorance, and the tail of his vanity and silly madness drooped low.[8]

That evening the players were going to give a performance in the house of the magistrate who, having learned the handsome band of pilgrims was in the city, had them sought out and invited to his house to see the play and to sample a small portion of his desire to serve them, for he'd already had a taste of their good qualities in the letter he'd received from Lisbon. Periandro accepted after conferring with both Auristela and the elder Antonio, whose advice they took out of respect for his years. Several of the city's ladies had gathered there with the mayor's wife when in came Auristela, Ricla, and Constanza, along with Periandro and the two Antonios, amazing, astonishing, and dazzling the eyes of those present. These feelings were produced by the matchless splendor of the new pilgrims, whose modesty and decorous manner increased the goodwill of those receiving them and made them decide to give them practically the most-honored place at the entertainment, which was a presentation of the fable of Cephalus and Procris in which the latter, more jealous than she should have been, and he with less thought than he should have given it, threw the javelin that simultaneously took away her life and all his happiness forever.[9]

The poetry reached the greatest possible limits of excellence since it was written, or so it was said, by Juan de Herrera de Gamboa,[10] who had the unflattering nickname of "Beanpole," but whose genius reached all the way up to the highest spheres of poetry. When the play was over the women took apart Auristela's beauty piece by piece and found that all together they made up a whole that could be called flawless Perfection, and the men said the same about Periandro's good looks, while in the same critique Constanza's good looks and her brother Antonio's striking appearance were also praised.

They were in the city for three days during which the magistrate proved to be a generous gentleman and his wife demonstrated her queenly nature by giving gifts and keepsakes to Auristela and the rest of the pilgrims, who showed their appreciation and gratitude by promising to keep her informed about what was happening to them, sending back word from wherever they might be. They left Badajoz, then, and set out for Our Lady of Guadalupe. Having walked for three days and covering five leagues in that time, night overtook them in the countryside at a place with countless oaks and other wild trees. The sky and the weather reflected the fact that the season of the year was hanging equally balanced between extremes, as it does at the two equinoxes; there was no tiring heat or any harsh cold, so that if necessary one could just as well spend the night out in the country as in a village. So for this reason, and since they were far from any town, Auristela chose to have them stay in some herdsmen's huts that looked hospitable.

They did what Auristela wanted. But scarcely had they gone two hundred steps into the woods when night fell with such darkness that it slowed them down and made them look hard for the herdsmen's fire, so its brightness could act as a North Star to keep them from straying off their path. Then the darkness of the night and a noise they heard brought them to a complete halt and caused the younger Antonio to ready his bow, his constant companion.

Just then a man arrived on horseback, his face hidden from

them, and said, "Are you from around here, good people?" "No indeed," answered Periandro, "but from somewhere very far away; we're foreign pilgrims going to Rome, though first to Guadalupe." "Can it be," said the horseman, "that charity and courtesy exist in foreign lands and compassionate souls are to be found everywhere?" "Why not?" responded Antonio. "Ask yourself, sir—whoever you may be—whether you need anything from us, and you'll find that what you've wondered about is true."

"Take this, señores," the horseman said then, "take this golden chain that must be worth two hundred escudos, and also take this precious and priceless jewel—at least *I* can't set a price on it—to the city of Trujillo where you must give it to one of two gentlemen well known there and in all the world; one is called Don Francisco Pizarro and the other Don Juan de Orellana.[11] Both are young, both wild, both rich, and both fit this description to the letter." And with this he put into Ricla's hands (being a compassionate woman she had stepped forward to take it) a tiny baby that had begun to cry and was wrapped in swaddling clothes that at the time couldn't be identified either as costly or cheap.

"And tell either one of them to take care of it, for they'll soon know who it is and what misfortunes have led it to the good fortune of having come to them. Now excuse me, for my enemies are following me, and if they should come here and ask if you've seen me, tell them 'no,' for saying that makes little difference to you. Or if you think it's better, tell them three or four men on horseback passed by saying as they went, 'To Portugal! To Portugal!' And God be with you, for I can't stay any longer; though fear spurs me on, those of honor are even sharper." And pressing hard against his horse with the ones he had on, he drew away from them as quick as lightning; but in almost the same instant he turned again and said, "It's not baptized," then started on his way once more.

Here you have our pilgrims: Ricla with the baby in her arms, Periandro with the chain around his neck, the younger Antonio with an arrow still set in his bow, his father poised as though to unsheath the rapier he was using as a pilgrim's staff, Auristela, confused and bewildered by the strange event, and the whole group astonished at the unusual happening. Its immediate outcome was that Auristela recommended they get to the herdsmen's camp as fast as they could, for there they might find some help to keep the newborn baby alive, since judging by its small size and weak cry it was only a few hours old. They did exactly that, and scarcely had they reached the herdsmen's camp—after much tripping and falling—when, even before they could ask the herdsmen if they would be so good as to give them lodging for the night, a woman arrived at the camp crying sadly but quietly, showing by her low moans that she was trying to stifle her voice. She was half-naked, but the clothes she did have on were those of a rich and important person. Despite her efforts to conceal it her face could be seen by the light of the campfire's flames, and they saw she was as beautiful as she was young, just as young as she was beautiful, and Ricla, who knew the most about judging ages, guessed she was around sixteen or seventeen years old.

The herdsmen asked her if anyone was following her, or if she had any other need that required immediate aid. To this the sorrowful girl replied, "The first thing, señores, you must do, is put me underground; I mean, hide me so anyone hunting for me can't find me. Secondly, you must give me something to eat, for I'm dying of exhaustion." "Our quick action," said an old shepherd, "will prove we're kind." Then hurrying over to a hollow in a sturdy live oak, he placed inside it some soft skins from sheep and goats raised among the larger animals; he made a sort of bed, good enough to meet her particular need at the moment, then took the woman in his arms and secured her in the hollow there, giving her what he could to eat, which was bread soaked in milk, and they would have given her wine had she wanted some to drink; then over the front of the hollow he hung some more skins, as if they were there to dry.

Seeing this and having guessed the girl must surely be the mother of the baby she was holding, Ricla went over to the kind shepherd and said to him, "Good sir, don't put an end to your charity now, but show it also to this baby I have in my arms before it starves to death." And she briefly told him how it had been given to her. The shepherd heeded her intentions if not her words, calling one of the other shepherds over and telling him to take the baby, carry it over to the goatshed, and find a way for one of the nanny goats to nurse it.

This was scarcely done—and so scarcely that the last echoes of the baby's cry could practically still be heard—when a troop of men on horseback arrived at the camp asking for the frail woman and the gentleman with the baby; but as they got no word or any news about what they were asking, they went on in a strange hurry, pleasing the rescuers more than a little. The pilgrims spent that night more comfortably than they had anticipated, and the shepherds with better cheer than usual, finding themselves in such good company.

The Third Chapter of the Third Book

*Which Reveals the Identity of
the Young Woman Hidden in the Tree*

The live oak was pregnant—let's put it that way—and so were the clouds, whose darkness closed in on those looking for the tree's prisoner, but nothing could keep the kind shepherd in charge of the flock from seeing to it that whatever might be necessary to make his guests feel welcome was provided. The baby took the nanny goat's udder, the hidden woman took the simple country nourishment, and the pilgrims took to their new and agreeable lodgings.

Everyone wanted to know right away what had brought the suffering, apparently fugitive woman and the helpless baby to that place, but Auristela felt they shouldn't ask her anything until the next day, for shocking surprises aren't usually conducive to loosening one's tongue, even to relate happy events, much less sad misfortunes. So even though the old shepherd frequently visited the tree, he didn't ask the person it contained about anything except her health; in reply he was told that even though there were many reasons for her not to be in good health, she would be very well, indeed, as soon as she were free from those looking for her, that is, her father and brothers.

The shepherd covered her up, hid her away, then left her and returned to the pilgrims who found more comforting brightness in the shepherds' blazing campfires than in any light the night alone could have provided. And before weariness obliged them to hand their senses over to sleep, it was agreed that the shepherd who'd taken the baby to have the goats be its wet-nurses should take it and give it to one of the old herdsman's sisters, who lived in a small village about two leagues away. They gave him the chain to take, along with instructions to have the baby nursed in that same village, and to say it came from another one some distance away.

All this was done to make them feel more secure and prepared to dissemble should the spies return or if others should come looking for the lost people, or, more precisely, for those who seemed to them to be lost. After arranging this and satisfying their hunger, and soon after the short time it took for sleep to take possession of their eyelids and for silence to hold their tongues, night's silence, too, passed and day came on at full speed; it was a happy day for everyone except the terrified girl, who was shut away in the tree and scarcely dared peek out at the sun's beautiful brightness.

Nevertheless, having first placed sentries at regular intervals near and far from the flock to give warning if anyone should approach, they took her out of the tree to give her some air and to learn from her what they wanted to know. By the light of day they saw that her face had a wonderful radiance, so much so they were in doubt as to whether she or Constanza should be placed second in beauty to Auristela (for wherever she was, Auristela always came in first, since nature hadn't chosen to make anyone her equal).

They all tried to get her to tell them her story, first begging, then asking her many questions; then out of sheer courtesy and gratitude, though wondering if she'd be strong enough and breathing with difficulty, she began in the following way, "Even though, señores, in what I want to tell you I'll have to reveal faults that will make me lose my virtuous reputation, still I prefer to seem respectful by obeying your request rather than ungrateful by not doing what I can to make you happy. My name is Feliciana of the Voice; my home is a town not far from here; my parents are much more noble than rich, and my beauty, because it hasn't always been as faded as now, has been valued and praised by some people. Close to the town that Heaven gave me for my home lives a very rich hidalgo[1] whose manners and many virtues make him a gentleman in peoples' opinion. This man has a son who already had shown himself to be as much the heir of his father's virtues, which are many, as of his estate, which is boundless. In the same town there also lives another gentleman with a son, but they're more noble than rich and live within such honorable but modest means that it neither humiliates them nor makes them grow vain. My father and my two brothers ordered me to marry this second youth from the noble family, turning a deaf ear to the pleas with which the rich hidalgo was asking for my hand; but Heaven—saving me for this misfortune in which I find myself now as well as for others in which I expect to find myself later—gave me the rich one for my husband and I gave myself to him, keeping it a secret from my father and my brothers, for to my great misfortune I have no mother. We often saw each other alone, for in such matters chance never turns its back but rather offers us its forelock[2] to grasp in the midst of impossibilities.

"Because of these meetings and this stolen love, my dress became shorter[3] and my dishonor grew—if it's disgraceful for betrothed lovers to have a relationship. At this time and without informing me, my father and brothers arranged for me to marry the young nobleman; they were so eager to bring it about that last night they brought him to the house accompanied by two of his close relatives so we could immediately become betrothed. I was shocked when I saw Luis Antonio come in—that's the name of the noble youth—and I was even more amazed when my father told me I should go to my room and dress myself for a special occasion because I was to be betrothed to Luis Antonio on the spot. My pregnancy had come to term two days before and the blow of the unexpected news left me practically lifeless; saying I was going to my room to get dressed, I threw myself into the arms of my maid, the confidante of my secrets, and bursting into tears said to her, 'Oh, dear Leonora, I really think my life has come to an end! Luis Antonio is in the other room waiting for me to come out and give him my hand in marriage. Isn't this the most terrible situation and the most desperate one in which an unfortunate woman could ever find herself? Stab me through the heart, dear sister, if you have anything to do it with. It would be better for my soul to leave this flesh than for my brazen shamelessness to be revealed! Oh, my friend, I'm dying! My life is over!'

"Saying this and heaving a deep sigh, I gave birth right there on the floor, something so unprecedented that it stunned my maid and so blinded my ability to think that, not knowing what to do, I waited for my father or my brothers to come in and take me not to get married, but to my grave."

Feliciana had gone this far with her story when they saw the sentries they'd set for security signaling that people were coming, and with rare alacrity the old shepherd was once again about to replace Feliciana in the tree, her safe refuge from misfortune. But then the sentries reported again announcing they could all feel safe now because the troop of people they'd seen was passing by on another path, and with everyone reassured, Feliciana of the Voice went back to her story, saying, "Just think, señores, of the pressing danger in which I found myself last night: my fiancé waiting for me in the hall, and the adulterer, if he can be called that, out in one of the house's gardens, waiting to speak to me and ignorant of the tight spot I was in, and of Luis Antonio's arrival. I was dazed from the unexpected event; my maid was in a state of confusion and with the baby in her arms; all the while my father and brothers were hurrying me along to come out for the wretched betrothal. This was a crisis that could have paralyzed more clever minds than my own and it interfered with any possibility for good reasoning and clear thinking. I don't know what else I can tell you except that while I was in a daze I heard my father come in, saying, 'That's enough, girl; come out just as you are, for your beauty will compensate for your lack of clothes and take the place of elegant finery.'

"At this point, I imagine, the sound of the baby's cries must have reached his ears, at least I assume so, for my maid must have gone to take it somewhere safe or to hand it over to Rosanio, the man I'd chosen for my husband. This sound upset my father, and holding up a candle in his hand he studied my face and realized I was in a state of shock and dismay. Again the echo of the baby's cries struck his ears, and laying hand to his sword he went out, following the voice to see where it led. The gleam of the blade penetrated my blurred vision and struck fear in the very midst of my soul. And since it's natural for each one of us to want to preserve his or her own life, the fear of losing mine gave me courage to save it. So, my father had scarcely turned his back when I, just as I was, went down a winding staircase to some first-story rooms in my house, and from them I easily got out into the street. From the street I got into the countryside, and from the countryside onto I don't know what road. Finally, driven by fear and urged on by terror, as if I had wings on my feet, I walked farther than my exhaustion should have been able to take me. A thousand times I was on the verge of throwing myself off the road down some bank to end my journey by taking my life, and just as often I felt like sitting or lying down on the ground to let myself be found by whoever might be looking for me. But encouraged by the light from your huts I managed to reach them to seek some rest for my weariness and, if not a solution to it, then at least some relief for my misfortune. In this manner I arrived in the condition you saw, and I find myself as I am now thanks to your charity and courtesy. This is, dear people, all I can tell you of my story. I leave its end to Heaven while entrusting it on earth to your good advice."

Here poor Feliciana of the Voice ended her talk, which filled her listeners equally with astonishment and sympathy. Periandro then told about finding the baby and the gift of the chain, along with everything that had happened with the gentleman who'd given it to him. "Oh!" said Feliciana. "Could that be my precious jewel? And could it have been Rosanio who brought it? If I were to see it perhaps the truth could be brought to light out of the darkness of my confusion and I could recognize it—if not by its face, for I've never seen that—then perhaps by the cloth in which it's wrapped. Since my maid was unprepared for this, what else could she wrap it in but cloths from my room, ones that would be familiar to me? And if that doesn't work, perhaps blood will tell and let me know by inner feelings what is mine."

To this the shepherd responded, "Right now the baby's in my village under the care of a sister and a niece of mine; I'll have them bring it to us here today where you'll be able, beautiful Feliciana, to make all the tests you want. Meanwhile, be calm, my lady, for my shepherds and this tree will act as covering clouds to shade you from any eyes that might be looking for you."

The Fourth Chapter of the Third Book

It seems to me, dear brother," said Auristela to Periandro, "that trials and dangers have jurisdiction not only over the sea but over all the land as well; misfortunes and accidents happen just as often to those who are set atop mountains as to those hidden away in their nooks and crannies. This woman they call 'Fortune,' whom I've sometimes heard talked about and who they say takes away and gives good things when, how, and to whomever she pleases, must certainly be blind and capricious, because it seems she raises up those who should be on the ground and brings low those who are on the mountains of the moon. I don't know, brother, what I'm saying, but I do know what I mean, which is that it shouldn't surprise us to encounter this lady who says her name is Feliciana of the Voice but who scarcely has enough of one to tell her troubles. I can see her just a few hours ago at home in the company of her father, brothers, and servants, hoping to think of some successful remedy for the problems resulting from her daring desires; but it's also a fact that now I see her hidden away in the hollow of a tree, having to fear the insects in the air and even the worms in the earth. While it's true hers is not a fall of princes,[1] it's still a case that can serve as an example for sheltered young women who'd like to set a good one in their own lives. All this moves me to beg of you, dear brother, to care for my honor, for ever since the moment I left the protection of my father[2] and your mother I've placed it in your hands! And even though experience has vouched for your goodness in the strongest possible terms, both in the solitude of exile and the society of cities, I still fear that with the passing of the hours some new thoughts, which come easily to everyone, might occur to you. It's up to you; my honor is yours; a single desire governs us and the same hope sustains us. The journey on which we've set out is long, but there is no road that doesn't come to an end provided it's not blocked by indolence and idleness. Heaven, which I heartily thank, has already brought us to Spain free of Arnaldo's dangerous company; we can now stride forward safe from shipwrecks, storms, and robbers, for Spain, judging by the fame it has as the most peaceful and holy region on earth, can certainly promise us a safe journey."

"My dear sister!" responded Periandro. "Your fine mind becomes increasingly obvious! I can clearly see you're afraid like a woman yet have courage like the person of intellect you are. I'd like to calm your latest uncertainties by looking for new opportunities to gain your trust. Even though past experience has already proven me capable of changing your fears into hopes and your hopes into a solid certainty that will eventually lead to the happy possession of what you long for—still, I'd like new circumstances also to vouch for me. There's nothing left for us to do here at the shepherds' camps, nor can we do anything more regarding Feliciana's affair than feel sorry for her; let's try to get this baby to Trujillo as we were instructed by the gentleman who gave us the chain, apparently as advance payment for doing so."

While they were discussing this the old shepherd arrived with his sister and the baby, for whom he had sent to town because Feliciana wanted to see if she could recognize it. They brought it to her; she looked it over and looked again, even took off the swaddling clothes; but there was nothing to make it possible for her to recognize it as the child she'd borne, nor did any natural affection—and this is even more important to consider—lead her to recognize the child, a baby boy.

"No," said Feliciana, "these aren't the swaddling clothes my maid had set aside to wrap up what I was going to give birth to, nor have I ever seen this chain (which they showed her) in Rosanio's possession. This precious little one must be someone else's, not mine; I couldn't be lucky enough to recover it after once losing it. Although . . . I've often heard Rosanio say he had friends in Trujillo, but I can't remember the names of any of them."

"In spite of all that," said the shepherd, "since the gentleman who handed over the baby to these pilgrims said specifically for it to be taken to Trujillo, I suspect he was Rosanio, and so it's my opinion, if I can be of any service to you, that my sister, with the baby and two of my other shepherds, should take the road to Trujillo to see if one of these two gentlemen to whom it's been directed will accept it."

Feliciana responded to this by sobbing and throwing herself at the shepherd's feet, then embracing him tightly, a sign she approved of his plan. All the pilgrims also agreed with it and made everything easier by handing over the chain. The shepherd's sister, who had recently given birth (as has been said),[3] made herself comfortable on one of the animals from the herd, it being understood she would go to her town and leave her own baby to be cared for, then depart with the other one for Trujillo, while the pilgrims, who were going to Guadalupe, would follow her later. Everything was done as planned, and immediately, because the urgency of the case would permit no delay.

Feliciana was quiet but with her silence showed her appreciation to those who were caring so sincerely for her concerns. To this was added the fact that Feliciana, having learned that the pilgrims were going to Rome and feeling inspired by Auristela's beauty and intelligence, Periandro's kind courtesy, Constanza and her mother Ricla's kindly conversation, the pleasant manner of the two Antonios, father and son (she'd observed, noted, and thought over all this in the short time she'd been in contact with them), and even more importantly, with a view to turning her back on the land where her honor lay buried, asked them to take her with them as a pilgrim to Rome; for she had previously wandered in error and wanted to try to walk in more holy paths, if Heaven would only grant her the favor of allowing them to take her with them.

No sooner had she voiced her thoughts than Auristela hurried to grant her wish, moved by compassion and wanting to remove Feliciana from the alarms and fears pursuing her. The only problem was her taking the road so soon after having given birth, and Auristela told her so. But the old shepherd said there was no difference between a woman and a cow giving birth, and since a cow, with no coddling at all after its delivery, is left outside exposed to the weather, so, too, could a woman go on about her business without being coddled, and it was only convention that had introduced comforts and all those precautions usually taken with women shortly after they've delivered. "I'm sure," he went on to say, "that when Eve gave birth to the first child she didn't go to bed or stay out of drafts or show such fastidiousness as is now connected with delivery. Take courage, Lady Feliciana, and hold firm to your intention, which I approve of here and now and call holy, for it's very Christian." To this Auristela added: "She won't stay here for lack of a pilgrim's habit, for I was careful to get two when I had this one made, and I'll give one to the lady Feliciana of the Voice on the condition she tell me the secret of why she's called 'of the Voice,' unless, of course, that's her last name."

"It isn't my family name," responded Feliciana, "but was given to me because it's the shared opinion of everyone who's heard me sing that I have the best voice in the world, so excellent that I'm commonly called Feliciana of the Voice: and if this weren't more a time to be moaning than singing, I'd easily prove the truth of this to you. But if things improve and my tears have a chance to dry, I'll sing, and while they may not be happy songs, at least they can be sad dirges that will cast their spell as they're sung and make you happy as you cry over them." Feliciana's words made everyone want to hear her sing as soon as possible, but they didn't dare plead with her to do it because, as she herself had said, the time wasn't right.

The next day Feliciana took off the unnecessary garments she was wearing and covered herself with the pilgrim's attire Auristela gave her; she removed a pearl necklace and two rings, and if personal adornment is a way of demonstrating social status, these pieces could have attested to the fact that she was rich and noble. As treasurer of everyone's goods Ricla took them, and Feliciana took her place as the second pilgrim woman of the band, just as Auristela was the first and Constanza the third, although this ranking was subject to different opinions, some people giving second place to Constanza; but no beauty in that age could have taken first place away from Auristela.

No sooner had Feliciana found herself dressed in this new habit than she felt new life and a longing to be on the road well up from within her. Auristela realized this and by common consent they bade farewell to the charitable shepherd and the others in the camp, then set out for Cáceres, eluding weariness by walking at their accustomed moderate pace. But occasionally when one of the women did feel tired they arranged for her to use the pack animal where the supplies were carried, or made her comfortable on the banks of some little stream or spring where they would sit down, or on the lush grass of some meadow inviting them to sweet rest. And so repose and weariness walked together with them, along with laziness and diligence: the laziness because they walked in short stretches, the diligence because they always kept on going. But since in most cases good desires never come to a happy end without obstacles blocking their way, it was Heaven's wish that the road taken by this beautiful band (made up of several individuals, but united in their common purpose) should be blocked by the obstacle that wil now be described.

They had found a place to sit on the green grass of a delightful little meadow; their faces were being cooled by the clear, sweet water of a small stream that flowed among the grass; a great number of brambles and thorn bushes surrounding them on almost all sides served as a protective wall, and it was a pleasant and much-needed place for their rest. Suddenly, forcing his way through the tangled underbrush, they saw a young man break out into the clearing; he was dressed for the road, but a sword was driven into his back with its point coming out his chest. He fell on his face and as he fell he said, "God be with me!"

With the last word his soul was torn from him and, although the strange spectacle had all the pilgrims on their feet with excitement, the first one to go over to help him was Periandro who, finding him already dead, dared pull out the sword. The two Antonios leaped through the brambles to see if they could find out who the cruel and treacherous murderer was, for the fact that the wound was in the back proved cowardly hands had made it; but they didn't see anyone so went back to the others. Seeing the dead man's youth, his attractive figure, and good looks made them feel even worse. They searched him and found that under a brown velvet jacket he was wearing over a vest there hung a chain made of four strands of small gold links, and a crucifix, also made of gold, was hanging from the chain as a sign of his piety; between his vest and shirt they also found a richly crafted ebony box and in it an exceedingly beautiful portrait of a woman painted on the smooth wood; around it in extremely small yet clear letters they saw these verses written:

> It freezes and burns, it gazes and speaks:
> Such are the miracles beauty performs!
> That your face on a piece of wood
> Should have such power!

These verses led Periandro, the first to read them, to suppose his death must have been caused by an affair of the heart. They turned out his pockets and searched all of them without finding anything to give them a clue as to who he was. While they were making this investigation four men armed with crossbows appeared from out of the blue and the elder Antonio immediately recognized them by their insignias as patrolmen of the Holy Brotherhood.[4] One of them shouted out, "Stop you thieves, murderers, and highwaymen! Don't finish him off by robbing him. The time has come for us to take you where you'll pay for your sin!"

"No you won't, you rogues!" replied the younger Antonio; "there are no thieves here, and we're all enemies of those who are!" "Everything certainly makes you look good," retorted the patrolman, "the dead man, his belongings in your possession, and his blood on your hands testifying to your evil. You're thieves, you're highwaymen and murderers; soon you'll pay for your crimes and the cover of Christian virtue you take on by dressing like pilgrims will do you no good!"

The younger Antonio replied to this by fitting an arrow to the string of his bow and shooting it through the man's arm, although he would have liked to shoot it right through his chest. The other patrolmen, either taking warning from the shot or in order to make the capture more certain, turned tail and then half running and half holding back called out very loudly, "Help over here for the Holy Brotherhood! Bring help for the Holy Brotherhood!"

And the brotherhood in whose name they were calling showed it was indeed holy, for in an instant, as though by miracle, more than twenty patrolmen assembled and, aiming their crossbows and arrows at people who weren't defending themselves, captured them and took them prisoners, not respecting Auristela's beauty or the rest of the pilgrim women. Then, along with the body of the dead man, they took them to Cáceres, whose mayor was a knight of the Order of Santiago[5] and who, seeing the dead man and the wounded patrolman, hearing the information given by the other patrolmen, noting the incriminating evidence of Periandro having blood on him, and following the advice of his deputy, immediately wanted to interrogate them under torture. Periandro defended himself with the truth, however, presenting in his favor the papers he'd obtained in Lisbon authorizing and guaranteeing the safety of their trip. He also showed him the canvas with the painting of the things that had happened to them and which were recounted and described very well by the younger Antonio. These proofs made it clear the pilgrims were entirely without fault in the matter, but Ricla the treasurer, who knew very little or nothing about the nature of clerks and solicitors, secretly offered one of them who was hanging around showing an interest in helping them I don't know how much money to take on their case. And she ruined everything, because when the foxy penpushers smelled that the pilgrims had money, they not only wanted to fleece them out of it but to put the bite on them right down to the bone, as is their usual crafty style; and certainly that's what they would have done if Heaven hadn't allowed the forces of innocence to vanquish those of malice.

It happened, then, that a host or innkeeper in the town, having seen the dead body brought in and having no doubts about who it was, went to the mayor and said to him, "Sir, the dead man the patrolmen have brought in left my house yesterday morning in the company of another man who seemed to be a gentleman. Shortly before departing he spoke privately with me in my room, telling me secretively, 'Good host, in the name of your Christian duty I beg you, if I don't return here within six days, to please open in the presence of a magistrate this paper I'm giving you.' After saying that he gave me the paper I'm handing over to you and which I imagine must contain something concerning this strange case."

The mayor took the paper and on opening it saw the following words written there:

> I, Don Diego de Parraces, left His Majesty's court on such and such a day [the date was written in there] in the company of Don Sebastián de Soranzo, a relative of mine who asked me to accompany him on a certain trip on which depended his honor and his life. Not wanting to seem to confirm certain false suspicions he had about me, and trusting in my innocence, I gave in to his malice and accompanied him. I think he's taking me out to kill me; if that should happen and my body be found, let it be known I was killed treacherously and died guiltless.

And he had signed: "D. Diego de Parraces."

This paper was promptly dispatched by the mayor to Madrid where the authorities did everything possible to find the killer. But he arrived at his house on the night they were there looking for him and, overhearing a few words that made the circumstances plain to him, reined his horse around without even dismounting and was never seen again. The crime went unpunished, the dead man went on being dead, the prisoners went free, and the chain that had been Ricla's was broken up link by link to pay legal costs. The portrait was left behind for the pleasure of the mayor's eyes, reparation was made for the patrolman's wound, and the younger Antonio again described the events painted on the canvas, leaving the whole town amazed. And speaking of the town, Feliciana of the Voice had been there in bed during the whole time of the investigation, pretending to be sick so she wouldn't be seen. They once again set out for Guadalupe, passing the time on the road by talking about the strange occurrence and wishing for an occasion when they could satisfy their desire to hear Feliciana sing—and sing she will, for all pain is either soothed by time or ended when life itself ends; but at this time and showing respect for her misfortune she limited her songs to weeping and her voice to moans. These subsided somewhat when on the road they encountered the compassionate shepherd's sister returning from Trujillo where she said she'd left the child in the care of Don Francisco Pizarro and Don Juan de Orellana, who surmised that the baby could belong to none other than their friend Rosanio, judging by the place where he had been encountered, since in that whole region they didn't know anyone else who'd take the chance of relying on them in that way.

"In any case," added the country woman, "they said they wouldn't disappoint the hopes of the man who trusted them. So, señores, the child's in Trujillo in the care of the people I've mentioned. If there's anything else I can do for you . . . I have the chain right here and haven't parted with it, for my being a good Christian places another chain on me that binds and obliges me more than this golden one." To this Feliciana replied she hoped she'd keep and enjoy it for many years without being confronted by the need to break it up since poor people usually don't hold on to their valuables for very long and they're either pawned, never to be redeemed, or sold, never to be bought again.

Here the country woman said goodbye, our pilgrims sent countless good wishes to her brother and the other shepherds, and slowly but surely they approached the most holy region surrounding Guadalupe.

The Fifth Chapter of the Third Book

No sooner had the devout pilgrims set foot on one of the two narrow passes that lead to the valley formed and surrounded by the high mountains of Guadalupe than with each step they took their hearts were filled with growing astonishment. But it reached its peak when they saw the large and magnificent monastery whose walls enclose the most holy image of the Empress of Heaven;[1] the most holy image, I repeat, that means freedom for captives, a file for their chains, and relief from their suffering; the holy image who provides health for the sick, consolation for the afflicted, a mother for orphans, and relief for the unfortunate.

216

They entered her church expecting to find on its walls purple cloth from Tyre,[2] damask from Syria, and brocade from Milan hanging for adornment; they found instead crutches left by the lame, wax eyes left by the blind, arms hung there by the maimed, and shrouds cast aside by the dead, things from all these people who, after having been bowed down by misery, are now alive, healthy, free, and happy, thanks to the generous compassion of the Mother of Compassion, who in that little place has her blessed Son take the field armed with her countless mercies.

These decorations commemorating miracles made such an impression on the hearts of the devout pilgrims that they gazed all around the church and imagined they could see captives come flying through the air with their chains wrapped around them, then go hang them on the holy walls, and the sick dragging their crutches, and the dead their shrouds, looking for a place to put them because there is no more room in the holy church, so great is the number that already cover the walls.

This was a first, something astonishing and never before seen by Periandro or Auristela, much less by Ricla. Constanza, or Antonio, and they didn't get tired of looking at what they were seeing or of reflecting with surprise on what they imagined. Then, showing their Christian devotion they kneeled down and began to worship God through the sacrament and to beseech his most Holy Mother—to the honor and credit of that image—to please to watch over them. But what is more remarkable is that the beautiful Feliciana of the Voice, having kneeled down and folded her hands over her chest, weeping tender tears with a peaceful face and without moving her lips or making any other sign or movement that would indicate she was a living creature, released her voice to the wind, lifted her heart to Heaven, and began to sing some verses she knew by heart and later wrote down; she dazzled the senses of everyone listening, justifying the praises she herself had given her voice and completely satisfying the pilgrims' desires to listen to her.

She had sung four stanzas when in through the church door came some strangers; devotion and custom made them kneel down at once, and the voice of Feliciana, who was still singing, also commanded their attention. One of them who seemed to be quite old turned to another next to him and said, "Either that voice belongs to one of the angels who's been confirmed in grace, or it's my daughter Feliciana of the Voice." "There's no doubt about it," replied the other, "She it is, but she soon won't be, if my arm doesn't miss when I strike this blow." And saying this he took hold of a dagger; then,

217

looking pale and dazed, he quickly strode over to where Feliciana was.

The dignified old man threw himself after him and clasped him from behind, saying, "Son, this isn't a theatre for violence or a place of punishment. Don't rush into this! The deceitful woman can't escape us, so don't be in such a hurry, for in thinking you'll punish someone else's crime you might just bring punishment for your own guilt down upon yourself." These words and the disturbance sealed Feliciana's lips and alarmed the pilgrims and everyone in the church, although the people didn't prevent Feliciana's father and brother from taking her out of the church and into the street—where in an instant almost all the townspeople and the authorities had gathered, the latter taking her away from the men who seemed more like executioners than a brother and father.

In the midst of this confusion—the father shouting for his daughter, the brother for his sister, while the authorities were defending her until they could find out what was going on—about six men on horseback came into the square from one side. Two of them were immediately recognized by everyone as Don Francisco Pizarro and Don Juan de Orellana; coming over into the uproar of the crowd along with another horseman whose face was covered by a black taffeta mask, they asked what the cause of all the shouting was. They were told that nothing was known except that the authorities were trying to defend a pilgrim woman whom two men claiming to be her brother and father wanted to kill.

While Don Francisco Pizarro and Don Juan de Orellana were listening to this, the masked horseman, leaping down from the horse he was riding, taking out his sword and uncovering his face, placed himself at Feliciana's side and shouted out, "On me, señores, it's on me the punishment for your daughter Feliciana's sin should fall, if a girl getting married against her parents' wishes is so great a sin as to deserve death. Feliciana is my wife and I am Rosanio, as you can see, and not of such a low station in life that I deserve to have dictated to me by others what my own experience has led me to choose. I'm a nobleman and can introduce witnesses to that nobility. I have enough wealth to maintain my position, so it's not right that what was gained by good luck should be taken away from me by Luis Antonio just to make you happy. If you feel I've offended you by marrying into your family without your knowledge, forgive me, for the powerful forces of love often confuse the most intelligent minds, and seeing you so favorably inclined toward Luis Antonio made me fail to show the proper respect I owed you, for which I again ask you to forgive me."

While Rosanio was saying this, Feliciana was clinging to him, having taken hold of his belt, trembling all over and overcome by fear, completely sad and completely beautiful at the same time. But before her father and brother could answer a word, Don Francisco Pizarro embraced her father and Don Juan de Orellana her brother, for they were good friends of theirs. Don Francisco said to the father, "What's happened to that good mind of yours, my lord Pedro Tenorio? How can this be? Is it possible you're trying to become the perpetrator of an offense against yourself? Don't you see that these injuries rather than punishment, deserve forgiveness? What's wrong with Rosanio to make him unworthy of Feliciana? And what will become of Feliciana now if she loses Rosanio?"

Don Juan de Orellana was making practically the same or similar arguments to her brother but adding others, saying, "My lord Sancho, anger never promises a happy ending for its impulses; it's a willful passion and when the will is overcome by passion it rarely achieves what it undertakes. Your sister has known how to choose a good husband; to take revenge on them because they didn't observe due ceremony and respect won't be wise, for you'll run the risk of knocking down and leveling the whole structure of your peace of mind. Look, my lord Sancho, I have a precious possession of yours at my house. I have a nephew of yours that you can't deny without denying yourself—he looks so much like you."

The reply the father gave to Don Francisco was to go over to his son Don Sancho and take the dagger out of his hand; then he went to embrace Rosanio who, letting himself fall at the feet of the man whom he now knew as his father-in-law, kissed them over and over again. Feliciana also kneeled before her father, shed tears, sighed, and was on the point of fainting. The happiness spread to everyone present; the father won a reputation for wisdom, the son, too, was called wise, the friends intelligent and eloquent. The mayor took them all to his house and the prior of the holy monastery treated them extremely generously. The pilgrims visited the relics, which were numerous, exceedingly holy and valuable. They confessed their sins, received the sacraments, and during this time, which lasted three days, Don Francisco sent for the baby the country woman had brought to him, it being the same one Rosanio had given Periandro the night he gave him the chain. The baby was so sweet that the grandfather, forgetting any offense against him, said when he saw him, "May the mother who bore you and the father who conceived you have all the happiness in the world!" And taking him in his arms he bathed his face in tears, then dried him with kisses and wiped them clean with his gray hair.

Auristela asked Feliciana to give her a copy of the verses she'd sung before the most holy image; she replied she'd sung only four stanzas from a total of twelve, all worthy of being learned by heart, so she wrote them down and they went like this:[3]

> Before the winged spirits had come forth
> from the eternal mind,
> before the swift or slow spheres
> had begun their assigned motions,
> and before that original darkness
> had seen the golden locks of the sun,[4]
> God built a house for Himself[5]
> of pure, clean, and most holy material.
>
> The lofty and strong foundations
> were built on deep humility;
> and the more mindful of humility they became,
> the higher they lifted the regal structure.
> It soared past the earth, it soared past the sea;
> the winds, on a lower plain, were left behind.
> It soars past the fire and with the same
> good fortune places the moon beneath its feet.[6]
>
> The pillars are made of faith and hope,
> and the walls of this blessed structure
> are clothed in charity, through which one gains,
> like God, a life everlasting.
> Its pleasure is increased by moderation,
> its prudence smoothes the way toward goodness,
> which it will enjoy through the majesty
> of its abundant justice and strength.
>
> This sovereign palace is adorned
> with deep wells, perpetual springs,
> and enclosed orchards whose wholesome fruit
> is the blessing and glory of all nations.
> At the left and the right hand are
> tall cypresses, lofty palms, tall cedars,
> and crystal-clear pools that reflect
> the light of grace both near and far.

The cinnamon and banana trees and the
Rose of Jericho are found in its gardens,
with the same colors, but even more beautiful
than the most brightly glowing cherubim.
The dark shadow of sin neither reaches
nor draws near its walls;
all is light, all is glory, and all is Heaven
in this edifice that now reveals itself on earth.

Solomon's temple shows itself to us today
in all the perfection possible to God alone,
where the sound of no blow was heard as
the skilled hand formed its pliant work of art;
today, gloriously revealing itself,
the light of the unreachable sun has shown forth;
today Mary's shining star[7]
has given new splendor to the day.

Today this star shines before the sun—
a marvelous sign—but one so fine that
the soul, putting aside the usual fear of omens,
is filled with delight and pleasure.
Today humility was raised to the heights;
today the chain of ancient iron[8] began to break
and into the world comes that other Ester,[9]
most wise and more beautiful than the sun.

Daughter of God, born for our sake;
tender, but so strong that you broke
Hell's serpent's forehead
that had been hardened by arrogant evil.
Sparkling jewel of God, life of our death,
you were the fitting instrument to bring
the mortal discord of God and man
to peaceful harmony.

Today justice and peace have been joined
in you, Blessed Virgin, and have gladly
given each other the sweet kiss of peace
in promise and sign of the coming harvest.[10]
You are the first rays of the clear dawning
of the holy sun; you are the glory
of the just, the sinner's firm hope;
and the fair weather after the ancient storm.

You are the dove[11] eternally chosen
by Heaven; you are the wife who gave
immaculate flesh to the sacred Word,
and who turned Adam's fall to good fortune;
you are the hand of God
that stayed Abraham's harsh blade
giving us the true sacrifice
of that most gentle Lamb.

Grow, beautiful plant, and bring forth the ripe
fruit for which the soul awaits, so she may soon
change from the mourning in which she was dressed
by the first great sin into festive garb.
The true and fitting payment[12]
for that immense and common debt
must be made through you: Be assured, Lady,
that you are the universal comforter.

Already in Heaven's most hallowed halls
the winged messenger makes himself ready
and begins to move his golden wings
to come on his virtuous mission;[13]
for the fragrance of virtue that surrounds you,
Blessed Virgin, both asks and compels
that very soon God's great power
will come to perfect fulfillment through you.

These were the verses Feliciana had begun to sing earlier plus
the ones she wrote down afterwards and gave to Auristela, who valued them more than she understood them.

In short, those who had been quarreling made their peace with
one another; Feliciana, her husband, father, and brother set out for
their home, leaving instructions for Don Francisco Pizarro and Don
Juan de Orellana to send them the baby. But Feliciana decided she
couldn't stand to wait and instead took him with her, making everyone happy.

The Sixth Chapter of the Third Book

The pilgrims were at Guadalupe for four days, during which time they began to see the marvels of that holy monastery. I say they began to, because it's impossible to ever finish seeing all of them. Then they went to Trujillo, where they were entertained by the two noble gentlemen, Don Francisco Pizarro and Don Juan de Orellana, and again they told Feliciana's story, praising not only her voice and her intelligence but the fact that her father and brother had finally made the correct decision. Auristela also emphasized the kind wishes Feliciana had expressed to her at the time they parted.

The trip to Trujillo was followed two days later by their return to Talavera, where they found preparations under way for the great Monda festival,[1] which had its origins many years before the birth of Christ, but has been brought within such proper limits and bounds by the Christians that while it was then celebrated by the pagans in honor of the goddess Venus it is now celebrated in honor and praise of the Virgin of Virgins. They would have liked to stay for the festival, but couldn't spare any more time on their journey and so went on, leaving their wish unsatisfied. They had traveled six leagues from Talavera when ahead of them they saw an odd-looking pilgrim woman walking alone, and it wasn't necessary to shout to her to wait up for them because being either attracted by the pleasant spot or obliged by fatigue, at that point she sat down on the green grass of a little meadow.

They came up to her and found her appearance such that we're obliged to describe her. As for her age, it seemed to be just leaving the outer boundaries of youth and approaching the borders of old age. One side of her face ran into the other, and even someone with the eyesight of a lynx couldn't manage to see her nose, which was so flat and snub you couldn't have picked up a sliver of it with a pair of tweezers; her eyes cast a shadow on it, because they stuck out farther from her face than it did. Her dress was a torn pilgrim's robe brushing her heels, and over it she wore a short cape, trimmed half-way up with leather so worn and desintegrating you couldn't tell whether it was cordovan or just sheepskin. She had on a belt made of esparto grass, so thick and strong it was more like galley cable than pilgrim's cord. Her wimple was made out of coarse cloth, but it was clean and white. Her head was covered by an old hat without a band or strap, and on her feet were some ragged sandals, while in her hand she held a pilgrim's staff in the shape of a shepherd's crook with a steel point. Hanging at her left side was a larger-than-average gourd, while her neck was weighed down by a rosary whose beads were bigger than the balls boys use to play croquet. In fact, she was totally worn out and looked every inch the penitent, and, as became apparent later, was generally in a bad way.

As they came up they greeted her, and she returned their greetings in the voice one would expect from the snubness of her nose, that is, more twangy than smooth. They asked her where she was going and what pilgrimage she was on. They kept busy while they talked and, attracted like her to the pleasant spot, put the pack animal acting as their wardrobe, pantry, and wine cellar out to graze, sat down around her, and happily invited her to join them in satisfying their hunger. Then she, responding to the questions they'd asked her, said, "Mine is a pilgrimage undertaken by a lot of pilgrims nowadays, by which I mean that they keep themselves busy in their idleness with whatever pilgrimage is closest and most convenient. And so, I might as well tell you that right now I'm going to the great city of Toledo to visit the holy image of the Sagrario, and from there I'm going to the Niño de la Guardia; then veering off like a Norwegian falcon, I'll entertain myself by going to see the Santa Verónica at Jaén, to spend time until the last Sunday in April rolls around, the day on which the festival of Nuestra Señora de la Cabeza[2] is celebrated in the heart of the Sierra Morena mountains three leagues from the city of Andújar. It's one of the festivals celebrated entirely in the out-of-doors, and from what I've heard, not even the earlier pagan festivals imitated by the Monda at Talavera could have outdone it. I wish I could, if only it were possible, pull it out of my imagination where it's imprinted on my mind's eye, paint it for you in words, and set it out for you to see, so taking it all in you might see just how very right I am to praise it to you; but that's a job for a less limited mind than mine.

"In one of the galleries in a richly decorated palace at Madrid— the king's residence—this festival is painted in every possible detail, including the mountain, or more accurately, the towering rock the monastery sits on. In the building is deposited a holy image called Nuestra Señora de la Cabeza, because it takes its name from the rock on which it stands, which used to be called "el Cabezo" or "summit" due to its location on a clear, open plain, alone and set apart from any of the other rocks or mountains surrounding it, with a height of perhaps a quarter of a league and a circumference of a little more than half that. It makes its home on this spacious, pleasant spot that's always green and peaceful thanks to the moisture reaching it from the waters of the Jándula river, which as though bowing in reverence kisses its skirts in passing. The place, the rock, the image, the miracles, the countless people who come from near and far, and the solemn day I told you about make it famous throughout the world and celebrated in Spain above all other places even the longest memories can recall."

The pilgrims were fascinated by the account given by this new, yet old, pilgrim, and they began to feel an almost overwhelming desire to go with her to see so many marvels, but their desire to finish their journey wouldn't allow new ones to interfere. "After going there," continued the pilgrim, "I don't know which trip I'll take next, but I'm sure I won't have any trouble finding somewhere to pass the time and keep my idleness entertained the way many pilgrims do nowadays, as I've already said."

To this the elder Antonio said, "It seems to me, pilgrim lady, you don't have the right idea about what a pilgrimage is." "Oh, yes I do," she replied, "I know well enough they're pious, holy, and praiseworthy, and have always existed in the world and always will. But what I object to are bad pilgrims, the ones who make a profit out of holiness and filthy gain from praiseworthy virtue; I mean the ones who rob alms from the truly poor.[3] And I'll say no more, although I could."

Just then they saw a man approaching on horseback along the king's highway, which was close by, and as he came up to them, just when he courteously took off his hat to greet them, his mount—it was discovered later—put a leg into a hole and took a bad fall that brought both it and its master to the ground. Everyone immediately hurried over to help the traveler, whom they expected to find injured. The younger Antonio tied up the horse, which was a powerful stallion, and they cared for its owner as best they could, coming to his aid with the most common remedy used in such cases, which was to have him drink some water. Finding that his injury wasn't as bad as they'd thought, they told him it would be all right to mount again and continue on his way, but the man said to them, "Perhaps, good pilgrims, luck has allowed me to fall down on this plain in order to raise me above the danger my soul has been placed in by my mind. Even though you may not be interested, I want you to know, señores, that I'm a foreigner of Polish nationality. As a boy I left my country and came to Spain, which is the center toward which foreigners are drawn and the motherland of all peoples. I was in the service of Spaniards, I learned the Spanish language to the extent you hear me speak it, and carried along by the common desire we all have to see other countries, I went to Portugal to see the great city of Lisbon. The very night I got there something happened to me that, if you can believe it, will be a lot to swallow, but if you can't, it doesn't matter at all, since truth always has a basis in fact, even though the fact of the truth can't always be verified.''

Periandro, Auristela, and their companions were surprised by the impromptu yet well-worded narration given by the fallen traveler and, wanting to hear him talk at greater length, Periandro told him to go ahead and say whatever he wanted and they'd all give it credence, since they were courteous and familiar with the ways of the world. Encouraged by this the traveler continued, "I was saying that on the first night after reaching Lisbon, while going down one of the main streets (or *rúas* as they call them) looking for better lodging—for the one where I'd first dismounted hadn't looked very good to me—as I passed through a narrow and not very clean place, a cloaked Portuguese bumped into me and pushed me out of his way with such force that I found myself on the ground. The insult awakened my anger, I turned my revenge over to my sword and took hold of it, while the Portuguese with daring spirit and skill did the same; blinded by the night and guided by a fortune still more blind to what would have been more in my self-interest, not knowing what I was doing I directed the point of my sword into the eye of my opponent who, falling backwards, collapsed on the ground and sent his soul to God-only-knows-where. Fear immediately made me aware of the consequences of what I'd done. I was terrified; sought safety in flight; wanted to flee but didn't know where to go. Then the sound of people who seemed to be coming to the scene put wings on my feet and with hurried and stumbling steps I turned back down the street, looking for a place to hide or somewhere to clean my sword, so if the law should take me they wouldn't find me with any obvious evidence of the crime. By now almost overcome with fear, as I went along I saw a light in a large house and entered it impulsively, not really knowing why. I found myself in a large, open, and well-furnished room; I continued forward and went into another room, also richly decorated. Then, following the light I could see coming from yet another room, I found there a lady lying in a richly appointed bed. She became alarmed and, sitting up, asked me who I was, what I was looking for, where I was going, and who had given me permission to come with such little respect so far into the house.

"I answered her, 'My Lady, I can only respond to your many questions by telling you I'm a man from a foreign country, and I believe I've just left another man dead in the street, though it came about more through his bad luck and arrogance than because of any fault on my part. I beg you for God's sake and for who you are to help me escape the harshness of the law, which I think is following me.' 'Are you a Spaniard?' she asked me in her native Portuguese. 'No, my lady,' I answered her, 'I'm a stranger from a country very far away from here.' 'Well, even though you were a Spaniard a thousand times over,' she replied, 'I'd save you if I could and will if I can. Climb up onto this bed and get behind the wall-hanging and into a niche you'll find there; then don't move, and if the authorities should come, they'll respect me and believe whatever I may choose to tell them.'

"I immediately did as she'd instructed. I raised the tapestry, found the niche, squeezed into it, recovered my breath, and began to entrust myself to God for all I was worth. In the midst of my confused anguish a household servant came in saying, indeed, almost shouting, 'My Lady, they've killed my lord Don Duarte; they're bringing him here run completely through by a sword thrust through his right eye. The killer is unknown, and the reason for the fight, too, in which scarcely even the clashing of the swords was heard. There's only a boy who says he saw a man running away enter this house.' 'That must surely be the killer,' replied the lady, 'and he won't be able to get away. So much pain! So many times have I feared I'd see them carry in my son's lifeless body, for from his arrogant manner what else could I hope for but grief!'

"At this point four other men carried the dead man in on their shoulders then laid him down on the floor in front of his anguished mother, who with grieving voice began to say, 'Oh revenge, how hard you're knocking at the doors of my soul! But I can't satisfy you because I must keep my word. Nevertheless, the pain is crushing me!' Just think, señores, what I must have felt as I heard the mother's desperate words, for it seemed to me the presence of her dead son would place in her hands a thousand different ways to kill me in revenge, for it was quite clear she'd guessed I was her son's killer. But what else could I do at that point except keep quiet and hope in the face of desperation? And I needed even more hope when into the bedroom came the officers of the law, one of them saying politely to the lady, 'We've taken the liberty of entering your home, following up on the story of a boy who says the gentleman's murderer came into this house.'

"Then I perked up my ears and listened carefully to hear what answers the grieving mother would give, and she replied with a soul full of generosity and Christian pity, 'If that man did enter this house, he hasn't come into this room; you're free to look around for him, although God grant you don't find him, for one death is very badly set right by another, particularly when the harm wasn't done out of malice.'

"The courage that had deserted me came back when the authorities left the room to search the house. The lady ordered the dead body of her son removed from her presence and shrouded, and arrangements immediately made for his burial. She also instructed them to leave her alone because she was in no state of mind to receive words of comfort and condolences of countless people, not only relatives but also friends and acquaintances, who would come to console her. Having done this, she called one of her maids, who apparently was the one she trusted most, and after saying something in her ear she sent her away, having her close the door behind her. When the maid had left, the lady, sitting up in the bed, began to move her hands over the tapestry and, I think, must have placed them over my heart, which was beating rapidly and so showed the fear that gripped it.

"Realizing this, she said to me in a soft and pained voice, 'Sir, whoever you may be, you can see you've taken the breath from my chest, the light from my eyes and, in short, the life that sustained me. But since I understand this has been through no fault of yours, I want my word to stand in the way of my desire for revenge. And so, keeping the promise to help you escape that I made when you entered here, I'll tell you now what you must do: cover your face with your hands so if I should unintentionally open my eyes I won't be forced to see what you look like. Then, leave the niche you're in and follow my maid, who'll be right back and will lead you to the street and give you a hundred gold escudos to help you save yourself. You've not been recognized nor is there anything that could point to you. And calm yourself, for showing great agitation often gives a guilty person away.'

"At this point the maid came back; I emerged from behind the cloth, covered my face with my hand and, as a sign of gratitude, got down on my knees and kissed the foot of the bed several times. Then I followed the maid's lead. She was as silent as I and took me by the arm in the darkness and let me out onto the street through a hidden door in the garden wall. The first thing I did on finding myself outside was clean my sword. Then at a calm, deliberate pace I walked out into what luckily turned out to be a main street where I recognized my lodging and went in as though nothing exceptional, either fortunate or adverse, had happened to me. The innkeeper told me about the unexpected misfortune of the late gentleman, dwelling on his family's high rank and the arrogance of his nature, which was believed to have won him some secret enemy who must have brought him to such an end.

"I spent that night giving thanks to God for the mercies I'd received and reflecting on the courageous and unprecedented Christian spirit and the admirable conduct of Doña Guiomar de Sosa, for I learned that was the name of my benefactress. In the morning I went down to the river, there coming across a boatload of people heading for Sangián to embark in a large vessel that was about to depart for the East Indies. I returned to my inn, sold my horse to the innkeeper and, keeping close-mouthed about my business, returned to the river and the boat, the following day finding myself on the large vessel and outside the port, on course and with sails spread to the wind.

"I've been in the Indies for fifteen years, during which I've served as a soldier with the very courageous Portuguese. An entertaining and true story could perhaps be told about the things that have happened to me, especially those having to do with the heroic deeds of the Portuguese who in that region are invincible, for their deeds are worthy of unending praise in this century and for those to come. After making a profit there of some gold and pearls and other things more valuable than bulky, I took the opportunity provided by my general's return to Lisbon to go back there myself. From there I set out on the road to my country, after having decided to see first all the best and most important Spanish cities. I turned my riches into cash and, in turn, some of that into what I thought were enough bank drafts necessary for my trip, my first destination being Madrid, where the court of the great Philip III had recently returned.[4] But then my luck, tired of sailing the ship of my fortune through the sea of human life on a prosperous wind, willed it to run aground on a shoal that would tear it completely apart, and so it arranged that on coming one night to Talavera, a place not too far from here, I dismounted at an inn, but one that didn't turn out to be an inn for me but rather a grave, for it was there my honor was buried.

"Love is so powerful! Love, that is, which is heedless, hasty, lustful, and moved by evil inclinations, and it tramples good plans, pure intentions, and wise purposes so easily! It happened by chance, then, that while I was at this inn, in came a girl about sixteen years old, or at least she didn't seem any older than that to me, although I later found out she was twenty-two. When she came in she was wearing short sleeves and had her hair in braids; her dress was of plain cloth but she had a fresh, clean look, and when she passed by me I thought she smelled like a meadow full of flowers in the month of May, making all my senses forget the perfumes of Arabia. She went up to one of the boys who worked at the inn and, saying something in his ear, broke out laughing; then turning around, she left the inn and went into a house across the street. Another young man from the inn ran after her and barely caught her, except with a kick on her backside that made her fall flat on her face into her house. Another girl from the same inn saw this and said furiously to the boy, 'Good Grief, Alonso, you're doing it all wrong! Luisa doesn't deserve for you to make the sign of the cross on her with a kick!' 'On my life, I'll give her more of the same,' replied Alonso. 'Be quiet, Martina my friend; these sassy little girls need to have not only hands laid on them but feet, too, and everything else.'

"And with that he left Martina and me alone; I asked her who Luisa was, and whether or not she was married. 'She's not married,' replied Martina, 'but she soon will be to that guy Alonso you've just seen. And because of the deal being made between her parents and his, Alonso considers her practically his wife and so dares kick her around any time he feels like it, though it's rare when she doesn't deserve it, for, to tell you the truth, my fine guest, that Luisa is pretty saucy and a little free and easy. I've warned her often enough, but she won't listen; she'll do what she wants even if they put out her eyes for it. But what's truer than true is that one of the best dowries a girl can have is her purity, and may the mother who bore me have the reward she deserves for being the kind of person who wouldn't even let me look at the street through a peephole, much less get as far out of the house as the doorway. She knew very well, as she used to say, that when it comes to women, "if you leave the barn door open . . ."'

"'Tell me, Mistress Martina,' I replied, 'how did it happen that after such a straight and narrow novitiate you took your vows in such a wide-open inn?' 'That's a long story,' said Martina. And I, too, would say more about these trifles if only the time were right or the pain in my heart would let me."

The Seventh Chapter of the Third Book

The pilgrims were listening attentively to the Polish traveler, wanting to find out from him what pain he was carrying in his soul, since they already knew how his body must hurt. Periandro said to him, "Tell us, sir, whatever you'd like, adding whatever little details you may want, for telling them often adds more substance to a story; on a banquet table it doesn't look at all bad to see, next to a well-prepared pheasant, a plate of fresh, green, and tasty salad. The sauce for a story is the use of appropriately chosen language to express whatever is said. Therefore, sir, continue your story, tell about Alonso and Martina, kick Luisa to your heart's content, marry her off or don't, and let her be free and easy as a falcon, for the key to storytelling success isn't in an easy delivery but in the events one describes, at least, according to how I divine things."

"I'll continue, then, señores," replied the Pole, "and taking advantage of your kind permission, I won't leave anything in my inkwell, taking everything out for you to pass judgment on. So, with every bit of judgment I had (which mustn't have been much), that night I went over and over in my mind the charm and free and easy grace of the, for me, matchless girl whom I don't know if I should call the girl-next-door or the friend of my hostess. I made a thousand plans, built a thousand castles in the air, got married, had children, and didn't give a damn about what people would say. At last, I decided to abandon the original purpose of my journey and stay in Talavera, married to the goddess Venus, which is how beautiful the girl seemed to me, even though she'd been kicked around by the innkeeper's boy. That night passed, I took the pulse of my desire and found it in such a state that unless I married her I was promptly going to lose—by losing my lust for it—my life as well, which I'd placed in the hands of this country girl of mine. And pushing aside all considerations of how inadvisable this was, I decided to speak to her father and ask for her as my wife. I showed him my pearls and let him see the amount of money I had. I sang the praises of my intelligence and hard work to him, with which I'd not only keep what I had, but also increase it. Convinced by these arguments and the show I'd made of my wealth, he became softer than a kid glove and ready to comply with my request, especially when he saw I didn't insist on a dowry, feeling myself paid off in full, and happy and satisfied with this agreement, even though the only thing I received was his daughter's beauty.

"This enraged Alonso, and my new wife Luisa was more than a little displeased, as was borne out by the events that happened two weeks later, to my pain and her shame. Those events were that my wife, helping herself to some of my jewels and money, with them and with Alonso's help—which put wings on her will and on her feet—disappeared from Talavera, leaving me cheated and full of regret, and giving the town a chance to gossip about her infidelity and lowdown ways. The offense obliged me to look for revenge, and since I couldn't find anyone else to take it out on, a thousand times I was on the point of hanging myself. But my luck, perhaps saving me to give me some satisfaction for the offenses it's done me, has arranged for my enemies to turn up as prisoners in the Madrid jail, which has informed me I should go and press charges against them and try to get justice done for myself. So, I'm heading there with my mind made up to blot out the stains on my honor with their blood, and by taking their lives to take off my shoulders the heavy burden of their crime, which has destroyed and consumed me. By God, they're going to die! By God, I'm going to get revenge! By God, the whole world will learn I won't cover up offenses against me, especially ones so painful they cut to the marrow of my soul! I'm recovered now from my fall and I'm off to Madrid. All I have to do is mount my horse and even the mosquitos should get out of my way! I don't want to hear friars pleading with me, or devout people weeping about it, or promises made by well-intentioned bleeding-hearts, or about presents from the rich, or offers of power and authority from the nobility, or from anybody else in the mobs that flock to such cases, for my honor will walk over their crime like oil floats on water."

And with these words he was about to quickly get up to remount and continue his journey. Periandro, seeing this, took him by the arm and stopped him, saying, "You, sir, are blinded by your anger and don't realize you're only going to prolong and spread your dishonor. Until now you're only dishonored in the eyes of the relatively few people who know you in Talavera, but you're heading for dishonor in the eyes of all those who'll come to know you in Madrid. You're trying to be like the farmer who raised a poisonous snake under his shirt next to his heart all winter. When summer came and the snake was grown and could have made use of its venom, he couldn't find it because through Heaven's mercy it had left; but he, instead of thanking Heaven for this mercy, chose to go out and look

232

for it to bring it back in his house to nest next to his heart, not stopping to think that it's not exactly the height of wisdom for a man to look for what's not good for him to find, or as the sayings often go, 'let the devil take the high road' and 'a man's worst enemy is his own wife.'

"But this must be true for religions other than Christianity; in them marriage is a question of agreement and convenience, just like renting a house or any other property. But in the Catholic religion marriage is a sacrament that can only be undone by death, or by other things more difficult than death itself which can exempt the married couple from living together but can't untie the knot with which they were joined. What do you think will happen to you when the authorities hand your enemies over to you bound and submissive on public display and in view of countless people, with you up on the scaffold brandishing your knife and threatening to cut off their heads as if their blood, as you put it, could cleanse your honor? What other result could you expect, I ask you, but that of making the offense against you more public? For revenge punishes but doesn't remove guilt, and guilt for crimes committed in such cases, unless there's a sincere change of heart on the part of the offender, is always there and, what's more, is always alive in people's memory, at least as long as the offended party is alive.

"So, sir, come to your senses, show some compassion and don't race headlong after justice. And this doesn't mean I'm advising you to pardon your wife to the extent of taking her back into your house, for no law would oblige you to do that. What I advise you to do is leave her, which is the most severe punishment you could give her. Live far from her and you'll surely live, something you wouldn't be able to do with her, for together you'd live a continual death. The divorce law was often put into practice by the Romans. So, even though it would be more charitable to forgive her, take her in, endure her, and guide her with good advice, you must take the pulse of your own patience and do everything possible to make use of all your good sense, something very few people can count on in this life, especially when they come up against so many weighty problems. And finally, I want you to consider that you're going to commit a mortal sin by taking their lives, something that shouldn't be done for all the gains in honor the world can offer."

The furious Pole listened closely to Periandro's arguments and looking at him squarely, replied: "You, sir, have spoken beyond your years. Your good judgment exceeds that to be expected in someone your age, and your maturity places you beyond the days of green youth. An angel has moved your tongue, with which you've softened my resolve, for now I'll do nothing except return to my homeland to give thanks to Heaven for the compassion you've shown me. Help me up, for since anger has restored my vigor, it wouldn't be right for restraint, now that I've thought better of this, to take it away from me."

"We'll all be very glad to do that," said the elder Antonio. They helped him get up on the stallion after he had first embraced them all. He said he wanted to return to Talavera to take care of some business regarding his estate and from Lisbon would return to his homeland by sea. He told them his name was Ortel Banedre, which in Spanish would be Martín Banedre. Then once again placing himself at their service, he turned his horse toward Talavera, leaving everyone astonished by the events of his life and the charming way he'd related them.

The pilgrims spent the night right where they were and two days later, accompanied by the old pilgrim woman, arrived at the Sagra gate into Toledo, where they came in sight of the celebrated Tagus River, famous for its sands and crystal-clear waters.

The Eighth Chapter of the Third Book

The fame of the Tagus River is too great to be limited by borders or to remain unknown even among the distant peoples of the world; its name reaches and is well-known to all of them, and they all long to go see it. Now, since it's customary among the northern nations for the most important people to be well-versed in the Latin language and the classical poets, Periandro, being one of the principal people in his country, certainly knew those things. Due to this and to the fact that during those days the radiance of their worldwide fame had brought the celebrated works of the never sufficiently praised poet Garcilaso de la Vega[1] to his attention, and because he had seen, read, studied, and admired them, as soon as he saw the clear river, he exclaimed, "We won't say, 'Here Salicio brought his song to an end,'[2] but, here Salicio began his song; here he outdid himself in his eclogues; here his shepherd's flute trilled, the waters of this river paused to hear it, the leaves of the trees ceased fluttering, and the winds grew calm to give news of his astonishing song a chance to go from tongue to tongue and from one nation to another through all the world. How fortunate you are, crystal-clear waters and golden sands! But did I say golden? Made, rather, of pure gold! Shelter this poor pilgrim who, just as he adored you from afar, is now ready to worship at your feet."

Then turning to look at the great city of Toledo, this is what he said. "Oh, massive rock, the glory of Spain and brightest of its cities, in whose heart for countless centuries the relics of the brave Goths[3] have been kept to bring their dead glory back to life and to be a shining example and safe treasure house of Catholic ritual! Hail, then, oh holy city, and grant that those of us who have come to see you may find a place there within!"

It was Periandro who said this, although the elder Antonio might more appropriately have done so, had he known all that. But lessons learned in books often teach us more about things than is known by people who have actually seen them, since a person who reads with care thinks over and over again about what he's reading, while a person who looks without paying attention observes nothing, and so reading can, indeed, surpass seeing.

At almost this exact moment the sound of countless cheerful instruments spreading through the valleys surrounding the city reached their ears and they saw coming toward the place where they were, not armed squadrons of infantry, but clusters of girls[4] more beautiful than the sun and dressed country style; their chests—where even coral and silver would have been appropriate—were covered with necklaces of beads and medallions more showy than pearls and gold, which in this instance avoided the fronts of their dresses but came to rest in their long hair, as blonde as gold itself; and although worn loose down their backs, it was gathered close to their temples with green garlands of fragrant flowers. On that day and worn by them the blue woolen cloth made at Cuenca looked finer than damask from Milan or Florentine satin. In short, their country finery outdid the most elegant court attire because while displaying a modest unpretentiousness, they also showed a fresh purity; they were all flowers, all roses, all charming, and, even though it was formed by different dances, all of them came together in one pure movement, a movement inspired by the sound of the different instruments already mentioned.

Around the perimeter of each band, dressed in pure white linen and wearing embroidered kerchiefs tied around their heads, walked many young shepherds who were their relatives or friends, or neighbors from their home towns. One was playing the finger drum and flute, another the psaltery, this one the tambourine and that one the reed pipes. These sounds flowed together as though they were all one and lifted everyone's spirits with their harmony, the goal of music.

As one of these squadrons or groups of dancing maidens passed in front of the pilgrims, a man, who it later turned out was the village mayor, grabbed one of the girls by the arm and, looking her over very closely from head to toe, said in an angry voice and with a scowl on his face, "Tozuelo, Tozuelo, this is shameful! Should these dances be profaned? Shouldn't the solemnity of these festivals be as untouchable as one's own eyes? I don't know how Heaven can allow such awful things to happen! If my daughter Clementa Cobeña knows anything about this, then, by God, the deaf will hear about it!"

The mayor had scarcely finished saying these last words when another mayor arrived and said to him, "Pedro Cobeño, if the deaf could hear you, it would be a miracle. Be happy we can hear each other, and let's find out how my son Tozuelo has offended you, because if he's guilty of something against you, I'm an officer of the law and will be ready, willing, and able to punish him."

To this Cobeño retorted, "What he's done wrong is obvious, since he's a man but going around dressed as a woman; and not as just any woman, but like one of Her Majesty's ladies-in-waiting at a royal festival. So you can see, Mayor Tozuelo, it's more than just a case of a runny nose needing to be wiped. I'm afraid my daughter Cobeña must be mixed up in this, because this dress your son has on looks to me like hers. I hope the devil hasn't pulled one of his stunts and gotten them together without our knowledge or the Church's blessings. You know very well that these secret hasty marriages usually turn out badly and just put groceries on the table of the ecclesiastical court, which charges through the nose."

At this a country girl, one of several young women who had stopped to listen to the conversation, spoke up on behalf of the younger Tozuelo. "If the truth be told, Mister Mayors, Mari Cobeña is Tozuelo's wife and he her husband just as much as my mother is my father's wife and my father, her husband. She's pregnant and in no condition to dance or perform. Marry them, to Hell with the devil, and may Saint Peter bless whom God has joined together."

"Jesus, girl!" replied Tozuelo, "you've said a mouthful. They're well-matched; neither family can claim purer or older Christian blood than the other,[5] and their wealth can be measured with the same yardstick."

"All right," answered Cobeño, "call my daughter here and she'll set this all straight, for she's no mute dummy." The Cobeña girl, who wasn't far away, came over, and the first thing she said was, "I haven't been the first, and I won't be the last to trip and roll in these gullies. Tozuelo's my husband and I'm his wife, and may God forgive us both if our parents won't." "That's just great, girl," said her father. "If you've any shame you must've sent it off to the Ubeda hills because I don't see any on your face! But what's done is done, and it's best Mayor Tozuelo proceed with this case, since you two have gotten ahead of yourselves."

"For God's sake," said the first girl, "doesn't Mayor Cobeño sound just like an old man! Let these young people give each other their hands in marriage—if they haven't done it yet—and let them be man and wife as Our Mother the Holy Church commands. Now let's go dance under the elm tree; our festival's not going to be broken up by this childish nonsense." The elder Tozuelo agreed with the girl's suggestion, the young couple gave each other their hands in marriage, the dispute came to an end, and the dance moved forward. If all disputes could be brought to such a reasonable solution, notaries' eager pens would be left high and dry.

Periandro, Auristela, and the other pilgrims were pleased to have witnessed the proceedings concerning the two lovers and were astonished at the beauty of the country girls, who when taken all together seemed to embody the beginning, middle, and end of human beauty. Periandro decided they wouldn't go into Toledo since they'd been asked not to by the elder Antonio, who was spurred on by his desire to see his home and his parents, which weren't far away, and had said that to see the marvels of that city it would be better to allow more time than the urgency of their journey would allow them. For this same reason they also decided not to go through Madrid, where the Court currently was, fearing some obstacle there might block their way. The old pilgrim woman was of the same opinion, saying that there were certain insignificant peacocks hanging around the Court, said to be the sons of great people, and even though they were just fledglings, whenever they saw the decoy of any beautiful woman they would swoop down on her regardless of her rank or personal qualities, for infatuation doesn't look for quality, only beauty.

To this the elder Antonio added, "In that case it will be necessary for us to practice the ingenuity shown by the cranes. In their migrations they pass by Mount Limabo, where birds of prey are lying in wait to have them for dinner; but they avoid the danger by flying over at night, each one carrying a pebble in its mouth to keep it from singing and to prevent its being heard.[6] So, the best solution for us will be to follow the bank of this famous river, keeping the city on our right and not going to see it until some other time. Let's go instead to Ocaña, and from there to Quintanar de la Orden, which is my home."

Seeing the itinerary Antonio had proposed for the trip, the pilgrim woman said she preferred to go her own way, one more convenient for her. Beautiful Ricla gave her two gold coins as alms and the pilgrim woman took leave of them with courtesy and gratitude.

Our pilgrims went through Aranjuez, the sight of which, since it was late springtime, filled them with surprise and happiness at the same time. They saw straight, uniformly laid-out streets lined and protected by countless green trees, so green they looked like the finest of emeralds. They saw the kisses and embraces two famous rivers, the Henares and the Tagus, give each other where they come together. They looked at the town's sawmills; they admired the plan of its gardens and the diversity of its flowers; they saw its pools, which have more fish than grains of sand, and its exquisite orchards, where fruit trees take the weight off their branches by bending them down to the ground. In short, Periandro found that the worldwide fame this spot enjoys is well deserved. From there they went on to the town of Ocaña, where Antonio learned his parents were still alive, also finding out other things that made him happy, as will soon be recounted.

The Ninth Chapter of the Third Book

The air of his homeland lifted Antonio's spirits and visiting Nuestra Señora de Esperanza[1] gladdened everyone's hearts. Ricla and her two children were excited to think whom they'd soon see, she her father and mother-in-law, and they their grandparents, for Antonio had learned they were still living despite the grief they'd felt at being separated from their son. He also learned that the man he'd quarreled with had inherited his father's estate and that he had also died, but not before making friends with Antonio's father. For on the basis of countless kinds of proofs generated within the tangled sect of those who duel, it had been shown that what Antonio did was not an affront, since the words exchanged in the quarrel had been spoken after he'd drawn his sword. A weapon's gleam takes the force away from words, so those uttered with drawn sword carry no affront with them even though they may be insulting. And so, if someone wants revenge for them he should understand that he isn't satisfying an affront but punishing an insult, as will be demonstrated in the following example.

Let's suppose I say a self-evident truth; some dimwit replies that I'm lying and will be lying as often as I might say it, and putting his hand on his sword maintains that he's given me the lie. I, who have been called a liar, am not obliged to defend the truth of what I said, since there's simply no way the truth can be given the lie; yet I do need to punish the lack of respect he's shown me. Therefore, a person who's been called a liar in this manner can certainly take the field of honor with someone else. If people object and say he's received an affront and so can't take the field with anyone else until this matter has first been resolved, he can ignore them because, as I've stated, there's a big difference between an insult and an affront.

As I was saying, the fact is that Antonio learned of the friendship between his father and the man he'd quarreled with and realized that without having carefully examined the circumstances of the quarrel they would never have become friends. Hearing this good news and feeling happier and more at peace, he set out on the road with his companions again the next day, telling them everything he knew about the state of his affairs, including the fact that a brother of the man he'd thought to be his enemy had inherited the dead man's estate and had entered into the same friendship with Antonio's father that his late brother had enjoyed. Antonio advised it would be best for everyone to do as he said, for realizing that sudden happiness can sometimes kill just as easily as unexpected sorrow, he was planning to make himself known to his father in a gradual way that wouldn't be such a shock, and so make him even more pleased to recognize his son.

At twilight three days later they reached his town and came to the house of his father, who was sitting with a woman who turned out to be Antonio's mother at the street entrance of his house, relaxing in the cool of the evening, as the saying goes, since it was the time of the year for hot summer weather. They all arrived together; the first to speak was Antonio and it was to his own father: "Is there, by chance, sir, a hostel for pilgrims in this town?

"The people who live here are good Christians," answered his father, "so all the houses are pilgrims' hostels, but if there weren't any other, mine, which is spacious, could take the place of all of them. I have some precious treasures out there in the wide world, and I don't know but that right now they might be looking for someone to take them in."

"By chance, sir," answered Antonio, "isn't this the town called

239

Quintanar de la Orden, and doesn't a line of hidalgos by the name of Villaseñor live here? I ask this because I met a certain Villaseñor far from this land, and if he were here in this one neither I nor my companions would go without lodging." "And what was his name, son," asked his mother, "this Villaseñor you're talking about?" "He was called Antonio," replied Antonio, "and he said his father, if I remember correctly, was called Diego de Villaseñor."

"Oh, sir," said his mother, getting up from where she was sitting, "that Antonio is my son and because of a certain misfortune he's been gone from this land for fully sixteen years. I've bought him with tears, sighed his weight in sighs, and earned him with my prayers. May it please God my eyes might see him before they're shrouded in the night of eternal shadow! Tell me," she said, "has it been long since you saw him? Has it been long since you left him? Is he well? Does he plan to return to his homeland? Does he remember his parents, whom he can now come to see, since there are no enemies to prevent it and those who caused his exile from his land are no longer anything but friends?"

Antonio's aged father listened to all these words and, calling loudly to his servants, directed them to light lights and take the honored pilgrims into the house. Then going up to his unrecognized son, he embraced him tightly and said, "For your sake alone, sir, even without any other information to justify my giving you a room here, I'd give you one in my house, for I make it a rule to host all pilgrims, no matter how many, who pass through the town; but now, hearing this wonderful news you've brought me, I'll open my heart even wider and outdo myself to be of service to you."

By now the servants had already lit the lights and, as they were leading the pilgrims into the house, Antonio's sisters, two beautiful and modest young women born during his absence, came out into the center of a large patio there. Seeing Auristela's beauty, their niece Constanza's charm, as well as the attractive appearance of their sister-in-law Ricla, they couldn't get their fill of kissing and blessing them. Then, while they were waiting for their parents to enter the house with the last guest, they saw that a confused mob of people was coming in with them carrying a man who looked dead seated in a chair on their shoulders. The man, the sisters soon learned, was the count who'd inherited the estate of Antonio's enemy, his late brother. The uproar among the people, their parents' distressed confusion, and their own concern to welcome the new guests, so upset them they didn't know whom to turn to or whom to ask about the cause of the disturbance.

Antonio's parents hurried over to the count. He'd been wounded in the back by a bullet during a fracas two companies of soldiers lodged in the town had gotten into with the townspeople. The bullet had passed all the way through his back and come out his chest. Seeing he was wounded, he'd ordered his servants to take him to the home of his friend Diego de Villaseñor, and their bringing him there coincided with Villaseñor's opening his home to his son, his daughter-in-law, and his two grandchildren, as well as Periandro and Auristela. The last mentioned, taking Antonio's sisters by the hands, asked them to lead her out of that hubbub and take her to some other room where no one would see her. They did just that, and again were astonished no end by Auristela's beauty.

Constanza, who was bubbling over with the excitement of meeting her blood kin, neither wanted to nor could separate herself from her aunts, for all the girls were the same age and almost equally pretty. The same thing happened to the younger Antonio, who, forgetting the proper respect that goes with good manners and his obligation to his hosts, dared, with pure and joyful intentions, embrace one of his aunts. Seeing this, one of the household servants said to him, "If you value your life, sir pilgrim, keep your hands to yourself, for the master of this house won't tolerate any playing around. And if you don't, I swear I'll *make* you keep them to yourself, despite your shameless daring!" "For God's sake, brother," replied Antonio, "what I've done is very little compared to what I'm planning to do if Heaven grants my wishes, which are none other than to be of service to these ladies and to everyone in this house!"

Meanwhile, they'd made the wounded count comfortable in a richly appointed bed and had called for two surgeons to bleed him and examine the wound. They pronounced it fatal, there being nothing humanly possible to do to save him.

The whole town was up in arms against the soldiers who'd fallen into formation, gone out into the countryside, and were waiting to see if they'd be attacked by the townspeople. Their captains' concern and moderation weren't enough to calm them down, nor were the Christian efforts put forth by the priests and members of religious orders among the townspeople, for in general they're easily stirred up by the most trivial of matters. Therefore, their excitement grew just as ocean waves grow when they're moved by a light breeze; and the gentle breath of that zephir, grasped by a northern gale, mixes with the gale's hurricane force and piles the waves all the way up to the sky. And speaking of the sky, since there were signs on the horizon that dawn was coming, the captains had the foresight to march their soldiers off to somewhere else and the townspeople stayed within their own boundaries despite the harsh and hateful feelings they harbored for the soldiers.

Little by little, and carefully spacing his revelations, Antonio gave his parents a series of emotional shocks that enabled him to tell at last who he was, introducing to them their grandchildren and their daughter-in-law, whose presence brought tears to the old people's eyes, just as Auristela's beauty and Periandro's good looks brought stunned amazement to their faces and astonishment to all their senses.

As intense as it was unforeseen, this pleasure at the completely unexpected arrival of their children was diluted, disturbed, and almost nullified by the accident to the count, who was getting steadily worse. Nevertheless, Villaseñor introduced his children to him and reassured him that his house and everything in it that might be of any help in his condition were his to command, for although the count would have liked to be moved and taken to his own house, it wasn't possible, there being so little hope held out for his recovery.

Auristela and Constanza, being naturally compassionate, didn't leave the count's bedside but showed all possible Christian concern by acting as his nurses even though this went against the orders of the doctors, who'd said he should be left alone or at least not be surrounded by women. But Heaven, prompted by causes kept secret from us, makes its own arrangements and issues orders for things on earth, and it ordered and chose that the count should come to the end of his life. One day before he bid farewell to it, certain now that he couldn't recover, he called for Diego de Villaseñor, and when he was alone with him said the following words.

"I left my house intending to go to Rome during this year when the Pope has opened the treasure chests of the Church to pass on to us the boundless grace that can be won in such years of jubilee. I was traveling light, more like a poor pilgrim than a rich gentleman. I entered this town and found a quarrel going on, as you, sir, have already seen, between the soldiers who were lodged here and the townspeople; I got myself mixed up in it, and in trying to set others' lives straight, have managed to lose my own, for this wound given me by treachery—if that's the right word—is taking my life minute by minute. I don't know who inflicted it on me, for the quarrels of a mob give rise to sheer confusion. I don't grieve for my own death, but for the others it will cost if for the sake of justice or revenge someone should want to exact punishment for it. With this in mind, in order to meet my responsibility and do whatever I can as a gentleman and a Christian, I state that I pardon my killer and everyone who shared in his guilt. It is also my wish to show I'm grateful for the kindness you've shown me in your house, and my show of gratitude won't be of any ordinary kind, but the greatest and highest imaginable. In those two trunks over there containing my possessions, I think there are as many as twenty thousand ducats in gold and jewels, which don't take up much space; that's just a small amount, but even if it were as large as the riches hidden in the depths of the earth at Potosí,[2] I'd do the same thing with it that I intend to do with this. Take it, sir, while I'm still alive, or have your granddaughter the lady Doña Constanza take it, for I give it to her as both a bridegroom's present and her dowry. And what's more, I plan to give away myself, to someone who will soon leave her a widow, but a very honored one, and at the same time an honored virgin. Call her in, and bring someone here to marry me to her, since for her worth, her Christian virtues, and her beauty she deserves to be the queen of the universe. Don't be startled, sir, by what you're hearing, believe what I'm telling you. It isn't a crazy or unprecedented idea for a titled gentleman to marry an hidalgo's daughter when all the virtuous qualities to make a woman famous come together in her. This is what Heaven wants and I choose it of my own free will; as a wise man, don't let yours oppose it. Go right now without answering a word to me and bring someone to draw up ironclad papers about my turning over the jewels and money as well as my giving her my hand in marriage, so no slander will be able to undo this."

Villaseñor was stunned by these words and thought the count had surely lost his mind and the hour of his death had come, since in that moment people generally speak either great truths or great nonsense. So what he said in reply was, "Sir, I hope to God you'll recover your health and then with clearer eyes and free of any pain that might confuse your senses you'll be able to see the riches you're giving away and the wife you're choosing. My granddaughter is not your equal—she doesn't even come close—and so is only very remotely worthy of being your wife. I'm not so greedy as to want to buy this honor you want to confer on me; it will lead the common people, who almost always take things in the worst light, to say—and I can almost hear them saying it now—I had you in my house, I worked on your mind and by means of grasping servility made you do this." "Let them say whatever they will," said the count, "the rabble is always mistaken and will surely be wrong about whatever it may think of you."

"Let's get on with it, then," said Villaseñor. "I don't want to be so ignorant as to refuse to open up to good luck when it knocks at the doors of my house." And with that he left the room and communicated what the count had told him to his wife, his grandchildren, and to Periandro and Auristela, who felt that without losing a moment they should seize the occasion and bring in someone to finish up the business.

Indeed, it was accomplished and in less than two hours Constanza was married to the count and had the money and jewels in her possession, with all due formalities and documentation possible. There was no music at the wedding, only weeping and moans, because the count's life was slipping away more each minute. And finally, on the day after the wedding and after having received all the sacraments, the count died in the arms of his wife, the Countess Constanza, who covered her face with a black veil, kneeled down, raised her eyes to Heaven, and began to say, "I vow . . ." But no sooner had she uttered these words when Auristela said to her, "What vow do you want to make, my lady?" "To be a nun," replied the countess. "Be one but don't make a vow," responded Auristela, "for actions taken in God's service must not be hasty, nor should it appear they were the result only of circumstances, and this circumstance of your husband's death may perhaps make you promise something you'll either be unwilling or unable to fulfill later. Leave your free will in God's hands and your own; that way your own intelligence and that of your parents and brother will be able to counsel and set you on the road to what's best for you. Now have your husband buried, and trust in God, for the One who made you a countess when you least expected it will want and know how to give you another title that will honor and elevate you for a longer time than the present one can."

The countess bowed to this opinion, and while she was making arrangements for the count's burial, a younger brother of his arrived who'd already received the news in Salamanca,[3] where he was a student. He wept for the death of his brother, but the pleasure of inheriting the estate soon dried his tears. Though he learned then what had happened, he embraced his sister-in-law and didn't object to a thing. He had his brother's body deposited in a vault so it could be taken later to his own town, then set out for the Court in Madrid to seek justice against the killers. There was a trial; the captains were beheaded and many of the townspeople punished. Constanza kept the bridegroom's gifts and the title of countess. Periandro prepared to continue his journey, but the elder Antonio and his wife Ricla chose not to accompany him, for so many pilgrimages had tired them both out; but they hadn't worn out the younger Antonio or the

new countess, who found it impossible to leave Auristela and Periandro's company.

During all this, Antonio had never shown his grandfather the
canvas on which their story was painted. One day he showed it to
him saying they still needed a picture of how Auristela had come to
be on the Barbarous Isle when she and Periandro had found themselves dressed in opposite clothing, she in a man's outfit and he in a
woman's, a very strange metamorphosis. To this Auristela replied
she'd tell about it in a few words.

It turned out that after the pirates had stolen her from the beach
in Denmark, along with Cloelia and the two fisherwomen, they
"came to an uninhabited island to divide the booty among them; unable to divide it equally, one of the chief pirates was glad to have me
as his share, and actually paid extra to even out the excess in his
favor. I came into his hands all alone, with no one to accompany me
in my misfortune, for companionship can bring some relief to suffering. This man dressed me in men's clothing, fearful that in women's
even the wind might desire me.[4] For many days I traveled with him,
wandering around from place to place and serving him in every way
that didn't compromise my purity. Finally one day we came to the
Barbarous Isle, where we were suddenly captured by the barbarians.
He was killed in the struggle over my capture and I was taken to the
prisoners' cave where I found my beloved Cloelia, who by a different
but no less unfortunate path had been brought there. She told me of
the nature of the barbarians, about the vain superstition they believed, and the ridiculous and false subject of their prophecy. She also
told me she suspected my brother Periandro had been in the same
dungeon, although she'd been unable to speak to him due to the fact
that the barbarians had been in such a hurry to take him out for sacrifice." Then Auristela had wanted to go where he'd been taken, hoping to find out the truth of the matter, for she was dressed in men's
clothing. And so, pushing aside the arguments with which Cloelia
tried to dissuade her, she succeeded in her attempt to hand herself
over willingly to be sacrificed by the barbarians, being convinced it
would be best to end her life once and for all instead of tasting death
over and over while in danger of losing it at any moment. After that
she had nothing more to say, for they knew what had happened to
her since that time.

Old Villaseñor would have liked to have all this added to the
canvas but everyone felt it shouldn't be; what's more they'd have
liked to see what was already painted there erased, because such great
and unheard-of things shouldn't be carried around on flimsy canvas

but rather written on bronze tablets and engraved on people's memories. Nonetheless, Villaseñor chose to keep the canvas, if for no other reason than to see the well-executed portraits of his grandchildren and the matchless beauty and charm of Auristela and Periandro.

They spent some days organizing their departure for Rome, anxious to see their promised vows fulfilled. The elder Antonio stayed behind, but his son Antonio didn't want to stay, and even less so the new countess who, as has been said, felt an affection for Auristela that would have taken her not only to Rome but all the way into the next world, if it were possible to travel there with a companion. The day of their departure came bringing tender tears, close embraces, and pained sighs, especially to Ricla who felt her heart break when she saw her children leave. Their grandfather gave them all his blessing, for blessings given by old people seem to have the power of making things go better. With them they took one of the household servants to wait on them during the trip. Once they'd set out on it they left loneliness behind in the house and in their parents' hearts; and feeling happy and sad at the same time, they continued their journey with their companions.

The Tenth Chapter of the Third Book

Long pilgrimages always bring with them a variety of events, and since variety consists of different things the situations encountered will all necessarily be different. This history is a good example, for the story lines of the various episodes get cut off, leaving us unsure as to where it will be best to tie them back together again. Not everything that happens makes good telling, and there are things one could let pass untold without diminishing the story; there are acts that precisely because of their great consequences ought to be passed over in silence, and others so insignificant they shouldn't be mentioned. The outstanding thing about history is that anything written in it is made palatable by the taste of truth it brings with it. Fiction doesn't have that advantage, and its action must be prepared with such accurate details and good taste, and with such an appearance of fact, so that notwithstanding and despite its untruth, which unavoidably generates some dissonance in the mind, its structure may be truly harmonious.

Taking advantage, then, of this truth, I repeat that continuing their journey, the beautiful band of pilgrims reached a place neither very small nor very large, whose name I don't recall, and in the midst of the town square, through which they had to pass, they saw a lot of people assembled, all attentively watching and listening to two young men who, dressed in the clothes of recently ransomed captives,[1] were explaining the pictures painted on a canvas they'd spread out on the ground. They'd apparently relieved themselves of the weight of two heavy chains they had next to them, which were like badges testifying to their burdensome misfortune. One of them, who must have been about twenty-four years old and had a clear voice and an extremely skilled tongue, was from time to time cracking a flog or, to be more precise, a whip, he held in his hand. He was snapping it so hard that the sound pierced everyone's ears and reverberated all the way up to the sky, the way a coachman does when he punishes or threatens his horses, making the whip resound through the air.

Among those listening to the lengthy discourse were the two mayors of the town, both of them very old, though one younger than the other. The freed captive began his speech saying, "Señores, you see painted here the city of Algiers, the most insatiable glutton on all the shores of the Mediterranean, a universal haven for pirates and the shelter and refuge for thieves who, from this little harbor painted here, set out in their ships to trouble the world, for they dare go beyond the *plus ultra* of the columns of Hercules[2] to attack and steal from the remote islands that, because surrounded by the immense Ocean Sea, had thought themselves safe, at least from Turkish vessels. This ship, which you see reduced in size here because the picture requires it, is a small galley with twenty-two benches whose master and captain is the Turk standing on the center runway between the two lines of oarsmen; he's holding in his hand an arm he's cut from the Christian you see over there in order to use it as a whip and lash for the other Christians tied to the benches. He's afraid he'll be overtaken by these four galleys you see here, which are chasing and closing in on him. That first captive on the first bench, whose face is stained by the blood that has stuck to it from the blows with the dead arm, is I myself, who acted as the stroke[3] on this galley, and the other man next to me is my companion here, who isn't so bloody because he'd been beaten less. Listen, señores, and pay close attention; perhaps focusing on this moving story will bring to your ears the threatening and insulting shouts of this dog Dragut,[4] for that was the name of the galley's captain, a pirate as famous as he was cruel and as cruel as the Sicilian tyrants Phalaris and Busiris.[5] I, for one, can still hear the *rospeni,* the *manahora,* and the *denimaniyoc* he was saying in a hellish rage, for these are all Turkish words and expressions used to dishonor and insult Christian captives; the Turks call them Jews, worthless cowards who profess a black religion and think vile thoughts, and to instill in them greater horror and fear they beat their living bodies with dead arms."

It seems one of the two mayors had been a captive in Algiers for a long time, and in a low voice he said to his companion, "Up until now this captive seems to be telling the truth and in general seems not to be counterfeit. But I'll give him some more rope and we'll see if he hangs himself, for I want you to know I was on that galley and don't remember his being the stroke, but rather a certain Alonso Moclín, a native of Vélez-Málaga." Then, turning to the captive, he said to him, "Tell me, friend, whose galleys were those chasing you, and thanks to them did you obtain the freedom you longed for?"

"The galleys," replied the captive, "belonged to Don Sancho de Leiva.[6] We didn't gain our liberty because they didn't overtake us; we got free later when we made off with a galley loaded with wheat going from Shershel[7] to Algiers. We brought it to Orán and from there to Málaga, where my companion and I set out on the road to Italy, intending to serve his Majesty—may God watch over him—through the discipline of war."

"Tell me, friends," replied the mayor, "were you taken captive together? Were you taken to Algiers right off, or to some other part of Barbary?" "We weren't captured together," replied the other captive, "because I was captured near Alicante, on a wool ship bound for Genoa; my friend was captured at Percheles outside of Málaga, where he was a fisherman. We met in Tetouan in a dungeon; we've been friends and have shared a common lot for a long time. And for the ten or twelve miserable cuartos they've placed as alms for us on this canvas his Honor the Mayor is pushing us pretty hard."

"Not so hard, my good sir," replied the mayor, "that there aren't still some more turns I can give to the rack. Listen and then tell me how many entrances are there to Algiers and how many freshwater fountains and wells?" "That's a dumb question," replied the first captive; "there are as many entrances as there are houses, so many fountains I don't know the number, so many wells that I haven't seen them all, and the trials I've undergone there have even taken my memory away. If his Honor the Mayor wants to interfere with Christian charity we'll pick up the cuartos and fold up our tent,

and goodbye to you, for the bread they make in France is just as good
as that made here."

Then the mayor called to one of the men among the spectators
who apparently acted as the town crier as well as hangman when that
opportunity arose, and said to him, "Gil Berrueco, go to the square
and bring me here right away the first two asses you come across,
for by the life of our lord, the king, these two gentlemen captives
are going to take a ride through the streets on them for having taken
the liberty of trying to cheat the truly poor out of their alms by telling us lies and fabrications when they're as healthy as horses and
strong enough to take up a spade in their hands rather than a whip
to crack for no good reason. I was a slave in Algiers for five years
and know full well that you haven't described it to me accurately in
any of the things you've said."

"Good grief!" replied the captive. "Can it really be that his
Honor the Mayor wants us to be rich in memory when we're so poor
in money, and for a little child's play that doesn't amount to a hill of
beans he wants to dishonor two such outstanding students as ourselves and at the same time deprive His Majesty of two brave soldiers? For we were going to Italy and Flanders to break, smash,
maim, and kill all the enemies of the holy Catholic faith we might
run into. Because to tell the truth, which after all is God's daughter,
I want his Honor the Mayor to know we aren't captives at all, but
students from Salamanca. And right in the midst and the meat of our
studies we got an urge to see the world and find out what life feels
like in war, since we already knew what it feels like in pleasant peacetime. To make it easy to satisfy this desire it happened that some
captives passed through there, though they, too, like us now, were
probably counterfeit. We bought this canvas from them and obtained
information about some things having to do with Algiers we thought
would be necessary and sufficient to lend credibility to our fraud. We
sold our books and personal belongings for practically nothing, and
bringing with us just this merchandise we've come this far. We plan
on moving on, unless his Honor the Mayor directs otherwise."

"What I'm planning to do," responded the mayor, "is give each
of you a hundred lashes and, instead of that pike you were going to
drag off to Flanders hoping to plant it there triumphantly, I'm going
to put an oar in your hands so in the galleys you can brandish it in
the water, whereby you'll perhaps be of more service to His Majesty
than you'd have been with the pike."

"Does his Honor the Mayor," replied the talkative youth,

"want to show now that he's an Athenian legislator, and is he hoping the severity with which he carries out his duties will reach the ears of the councilmen, where it'll be interpreted by them in his favor as a sign he's strict and tough so they'll entrust him with important affairs where he can show his severity and adherence to the law? Well, his Honor the Mayor should know that *summum jus summa injuria.*"[8] "Watch what you're saying, brother," replied the second mayor, "because the mayors around here never get juiced and injure people. In fact, all the mayors of this town have been, are, and will be as clean and pure as a hair pulled out of the baker's dough. And you'll talk less, if you know what's good for you."

The town crier returned at this point and said, "Your Honor, I didn't find any asses in the square, just the two councilmen Berrueco and Crespo taking a stroll there." "I sent you for asses, you dummy, not councilmen. But go back and bring them over here whether they like it or not, for I want them to be present when I pass this sentence, which is going to be carried out no matter what, and won't be suspended for lack of asses since, thank Heaven, there are plenty of them around here."

"But Your Grace the honorable mayor won't have a place in Heaven," responded the youth, "if you go ahead with this severe punishment. For God's sake, stop and think, Your Grace. We haven't stolen so much, not enough to start an estate or set one up for our heirs. We scarcely make enough to earn a miserable living by our wits, which takes as much work as the jobs of tradesmen or day-laborers. Our parents didn't teach us any trade, and so we're obliged to live by our wits rather than our hands, as we would if we'd learned a trade. Punish those who bribe, burglars, highwaymen, those who bear false witness for money, those in the nation who keep themselves busy doing wrong, and those who are idle and lazy, who are good for nothing except to swell the ranks of lost souls, and leave the poor people alone who are going straight to serve His Majesty with the strength of their arms and the keenness of their minds, because there are no better soldiers than those transplanted from the field of studies to the fields of war. Never did a student set out to be a soldier who didn't become one of the best, for when strength comes together and unites with a good mind, and a good mind with strength, they form a miraculous combination, one that makes Mars rejoice, keeps the peace, and enhances the nation."

Periandro and all the others were amazed not only by the young man's arguments but by the speed with which he spoke, and he continued, saying, "Frisk us, Mister Mayor, search and examine us;

scrutinize the seams of our clothing, and if among everything we have you should find even six reales,[9] don't order us given a hundred lashes, but six million. Then you'll see if having accumulated such a small amount of profit is worth punishing us with such degradation and making martyrs of us in the galleys. And so, I repeat, Mister Mayor, you should take another look at this and not leap rashly into doing something that, after you've done it, will perhaps cause you regret. Wise judges punish but do not take revenge for crimes; prudent and merciful ones consider fairness as well as strict justice, and by finding the happy medium between harshness and clemency show the brilliance of their intellect."

"Goodness," said the second mayor, "this young man has spoken well, even though he's said too much, and not only will I not allow their lashing but I'm going to take them to my house and give them some help for their trip, on the condition they go straight to their destination without plowing a trail all over the place, because if they did that they'd appear more motivated by vice than truly in need." Then right away the first mayor, mild and merciful, softhearted and compassionate, said, "I don't want them to go to your house, but to mine, where I'll give them a lesson on things about Algiers, so that from now on no one will catch them making mistakes in their Latin, I mean, in their made-up story."

The captives were very grateful for this, the spectators praised their honorable intentions, and the pilgrims were pleased by the good disposition of the case. The first mayor turned to Periandro and said, "Do you, too, my good pilgrims, have some canvas with you to show us? Did you also bring with you some story you'll want us to believe is true, even though it may have been made up by Falsehood itself?"

Periandro didn't respond because he saw Antonio was taking out the letters of authorization, permission, and safe-conduct for their journey. Antonio placed them in the mayor's hands, saying to him, "These papers will show Your Grace who we are and where we're going even though we weren't obliged to present them since we're neither begging nor do we have any need to. So as free travelers you could have let us pass by freely."

The mayor took the papers, but since he didn't know how to read he gave them to his companion, who didn't know how either, and so they ended up in the hands of the town clerk who, glancing at them briefly, returned them to Antonio, saying, "Your Honors, this shows there's as much goodness in these pilgrims as there is splendor in their good looks. If they should want to spend the night

251

here my house will serve as an inn for them, and my goodwill as a palace to offer them shelter." Periandro thanked him; they stayed there that night since it was rather late and were made comfortable with love, with abundance, and with cleanliness in the clerk's house.

Chapter Eleven of the Third Book

Morning came and with it their expressions of appreciation for the hospitality. As they were setting out on the road and leaving town they encountered the counterfeit captives who said they were moving on, having been so well coached by the mayor that from then on no one would be able to catch them in any lies about anything having to do with Algiers. "Sometimes," said one of them—I mean the one who talked more than the other—"sometimes," he said, "you can steal with the authority and permission of the law. I mean, sometimes shady officers of the law join forces with law breakers so everybody can eat."

They all arrived together at a place where the road forked; the captives took the one to Cartagena, and the pilgrims the one to Valencia. The next day when dawn came peeking over the balconies of the East, sweeping the sky of stars and preparing the road where the sun would make its usual run, Bartolomé—I believe that's what the pilgrims' baggage handler was called—seeing the sun come up rejoicing cheerfully while embroidering the clouds in the sky with various colors so it was the most uplifting and beautiful sight one could ever see, with simple country good sense said, "The preacher preaching in our town a few days ago must have been telling the truth when he said the heavens and the earth proclaim and declare the greatness of the Lord. Why, if I didn't know God by what my parents and the priests and old people in my town have taught me, I could track him down and come to know him just by observing the immense grandeur of these Heavens—which I'm told there are lots of, or at least eleven,[1]—and by the grandeur of the sun that shines on us, which, although it doesn't look any bigger than a shield, is many times bigger than the whole world. And not only that, along with its being so huge they claim it's so fast that in twenty-four hours it travels more than three hundred thousand leagues. But, however true that may be, I don't believe a word of it. Still, so many well-respected folks say it that even though it strains my understanding I have to believe it. But what astonishes me most is that underneath us there are other people they call antipodes,[2] and all of us who are walking around up here have our feet on top of their heads, something that seems impossible to me, because to carry such a heavy load as us they'd have to have heads made of bronze."

Periandro laughed at the youth's countrified astrology and said to him, "I'd like to find the right words, Bartolomé, to explain to you the mistake you're making and the true situation of the world. But in order to do that it would be necessary to go way back to basics. Instead, I'll adjust myself to your perspective by limiting mine somewhat and telling you just one thing, which is that I want you to understand that it's an indisputable truth that the earth is the center of the Heavens. By 'center' I mean an invisible point where all lines perpendicular to its circumference meet, but I don't think you'll understand that either. So, I'll put aside words of that sort, and you'll be happy to know that all the earth has sky above it, and in whatever part of it men may be, they'll have the sky above them. Just as the sky you see covers us, it also covers the antipodes, as they're called, and nothing whatsoever could prevent this because it was ordained by Nature, chief assistant to the true God, Creator of Heaven and Earth."

The boy wasn't unhappy to hear Periandro's arguments, which also pleased Auristela, the countess, and her brother Antonio. Periandro was passing the time on the road teaching this and other subjects when from behind they were overtaken by a wagon accompanied by six musketeers on foot and one on horseback who had a shotgun hanging from his saddle horn. Coming up to Periandro, he said, "If, by any chance, good pilgrims, you're carrying in your supplies any candied fruit—and I imagine you are, since your attractive appearance identifies you more as rich ladies and gentlemen than poor pilgrims—if you have some, give it to me so I can use it to help an exhausted boy in that wagon who's condemned to the galleys for two years, along with another twelve soldiers who were present at the death of a count some days ago and who are also sentenced to the oars. And their captains, who were more at fault than they, I think, are sentenced to be beheaded at court."

When she heard this, the beautiful Constanza couldn't hold back her tears, for it reminded her of the death of the man so briefly her husband. But since her Christian spirit was stronger than her desire for revenge, she went over to the baggage and took out a box of candied fruit; then going over to the wagon, she asked, "Who's feeling weak here?" To this one of the soldiers replied, "There he is lying over in that corner, his face smeared with grease from the wagon tongue 'cause he doesn't want death to look beautiful on him when he dies, and that'll be awfully soon since he refuses to eat a bite of food."

At these words the besmeared boy raised his head and to Constanza he appeared ugly and filthy as he pushed back a ragged hat he wore pulled down over his forehead. Stretching out his hand for the box, he said as he took it, "May God repay you, my lady!" He pulled his hat down again and went back to his melancholy and to huddling in the corner where he awaited death. The pilgrims discussed a few other things with the wagon guards but their conversation ended when the two different routes they were following diverged.

Some days later our handsome band reached a Morisco village[3] set back about a league from the coast in the kingdom of Valencia. There wasn't an inn to be found there in which to spend the night; instead, every house in the town was opened to them with hospitable invitations. Seeing this, Antonio said, "I don't know who'd say bad things about these people; they all seem like saints to me!"

"The people," said Periandro, "who welcomed the Lord into Jerusalem with palm branches were the same ones who a few days later put him on a cross. So, putting ourselves in the hands of God and luck, as the saying goes, let's accept the invitation this kindly old man is offering us to stay at his house." And it was true, for an aged Morisco was pulling on their pilgrim cloaks and took them almost by main force into his house where he gave every indication of giving them not Morisco but Christian hospitality.

A daughter of his came out to wait on them dressed in Morisco clothing and looking so beautiful in it the most striking Christian girls would be lucky to look like her, for the barbarian women of Scythia[4] are usually as fortunate as the women of Toledo when Nature bestows her favors. This beautiful Moorish girl, then, speaking in a Morisco dialect of Spanish, took Constanza and Auristela by the hands and shut herself into a downstairs room with them. When they were all alone, without letting go of their hands, she cautiously looked all around, fearful of being overheard. After she had reassured herself regarding the fear she obviously felt, she said to them, "Oh, my ladies, you've come like meek and simple-minded sheep to the slaughterhouse! Do you see how that old man, who I'm ashamed to admit is my father, is being so attentively hospitable to you? Well, you should know he doesn't intend to be anything less than your executioner. Tonight sixteen ships of Barbary pirates are going to whisk away, if you can call it that, all the people in this town and all their belongings, not leaving anything behind here worth coming back to look for. These poor devils think they'll find in Barbary pleasure for their bodies and salvation for their souls, heedless of the fact that of all the many towns that have gone over there practically whole, not one reports back anything except regret accompanied by complaints of the losses they've suffered. The Moors of Barbary advertise the glories of that land, the Moriscos of this one run over to savor them and wind up in misfortune's snares.

"If you want to prevent your own misfortune and preserve the state of freedom into which your parents gave you life, get out of this house right now and take refuge in the church, for there you'll find someone to help you—the priest—he and the clerk are the only old Christians[5] in this town. You'll also find there my uncle Jarife the sacristan, who's a Moor in name only and a Christian in his deeds. Tell them what's happening, and say Rafala told you about it; with that you'll be believed and aided. And don't take this as a joke unless you want truth to set you straight at your own expense, for there's nothing more disillusioning than realizing the truth about one's illusions too late."

Fright and the dramatic way in which Rafala said all this gripped the souls of Auristela and Constanza so they believed her, not giving her any reply except their thanks. They immediately called Periandro and Antonio, and after telling them what was going to happen, without making any excuses, they all left the house with everything they had with them. Bartolomé, who would rather have rested than change lodgings, was unhappy about the move but obeyed his masters. They got to the church, where they were received by the priest and the sacristan, to whom they reported what Rafala had told them. The priest said, "It's been several days now, señores, since we got the alarming news that these vessels are coming from Barbary, and even though they make a habit of these raids the delay this time had almost made me forget about them. Come in, children, for we have a good tower and the church has fine ironclad doors that can't be broken down or burned through without real effort."

"Oh, I hope," the sacristan said at this point, "that my eyes, before they're closed forever, may see this land free of the thorns and brambles choking it! Oh, when will the time come prophesied by my grandfather, a famous astrologer, when Spain will be wholly and firmly Christian everywhere? It's the only corner of the world where the real truth of Christ is protected and venerated! I'm a Morisco, señores, though I wish I could deny it, but that doesn't keep me from being a Christian. God bestows divine grace on whomever he chooses, it being His custom, as you all know better than I, to make His sun to shine on the good and on the bad and to make it rain on the just and on the unjust. I repeat, then, my grandfather left a prediction that at about this time a king of the royal house of Austria would rule over Spain, one who would have the courage to make the difficult decision to banish the Moriscos from the country,[6] much like the person who takes a serpent that's gnawing at his bowels and hurls it away from him, or again, like the person who separates the fennel from the wheat, or hoes or pulls up weeds out of the planted crops. Come now, oh child of fortune and prudent king, and put into practice this bold decree of banishment, not yielding to the fear that this land will be left deserted and uninhabited, or to the concern that those people left in it who are truly baptized won't do well. Although these may be fears to reckon with,[7] the end result of such an important measure will make them groundless, and within a short time experience will show that new old Christians will populate this land and it will once again become productive and even more fertile than now. Its lords will have their vassals, and even though they may not be as numerous or as humble as before, they'll be good Catholics, with whose help the roads here will be safe and Peace will be able to carry her wealth in her hands without highwaymen taking it from her."

When he had finished talking they closed the doors securely, reinforcing them with the pews. They went up into the tower, pulling the ladder up behind them. The priest took the Holy Sacrament with him in its reliquary, and they gathered together a supply of stones and loaded two shotguns. The boy Bartolomé stripped the pack animal bare and left it at the door of the church, shutting himself in with his masters. Then with watchful eyes, ready hands, and resolute courage everyone waited for the attack that the Morisco's daughter had warned them about.

The priest could tell by the stars that midnight had passed, and as he spread his gaze over all the sea visible from the tower there wasn't a cloud silhouetted in the moonlight that he didn't take for the Turkish ships. Running to the bells, he began to ring them so rapidly and loudly that all the valleys and shores reverberated with the sound, rousting out the men of that district's coastal patrol to go up and down the whole coastline: but their efforts didn't prevent the vessels from approaching the beach and putting people ashore.

The townspeople were waiting for them there, loaded down with their finest and most valuable possessions; they were received by the Turks with a great many shouts and hurrahs, to the tune of a number of flageolets and various other musical instruments making a cheerful though warlike sound. The raiders set fire to the town and also to the doors of the church, not really hoping to get in, but to do whatever harm they could. They left Bartolomé on foot by hamstringing his pack animal and knocked down a stone cross standing at the entrance to the town while shouting out Mohammed's name. Thus the townspeople handed themselves over to the Turks—those cordial thieves and brazen scoundrels—but once the water began to lap at their feet, as they say, they began to feel the threat of poverty brought on by this move and the dishonor they were bringing on their wives and children.

Many times, perhaps some of them not in vain, Antonio and Periandro fired their muskets. Bartolomé threw down a lot of stones—all aimed at the place where he'd left the pack animal—and the sacristan shot many arrows. But even more numerous were the tears shed by Auristela and Constanza asking God, to whom their thoughts were turned, to save them from such an obvious danger, and also not to let the fire harm His temple, which in fact didn't burn, though not by a miracle but rather because the doors were made of iron and the fire they set against them was a small one.

It was almost daylight when the ships laden with their booty made out to sea to the sound of exultant *lilíes*[8] and countless small kettledrums and flageolets. Then they saw two people come running toward the church, one from the direction of the shore and the other from the land, and when they got closer the sacristan recognized one of them as his niece Rafala who was approaching with a reed cross in her hands and shouting, "A Christian, a Christian and free by God's grace and mercy!" They recognized the other person as the clerk, who by chance had been out of town that night and hearing the alarm sounded by the bells had been coming to see what was happening. What had in fact happened made him cry, though not for the loss of his children and wife, for they hadn't been at home, but for the loss of his house, which he found had been robbed and burned.

They waited until it was light and the ships had gone off into the distance, and until the coastal patrol had time to secure the coast, then they descended from the tower and opened the church, which Rafala entered with her face bathed in happy tears and her beauty enhanced by her excitement. She prayed before the holy images and then embraced her uncle, first kissing the priest's hands. The clerk didn't worship nor did he kiss anyone's hands, for his soul was busy regretting the loss of his property.

257

The alarm passed, those who had sought refuge in the church collected themselves, and the sacristan, taking heart again and thinking once more about his grandfather's prophecy, almost as if he were full of the Heavenly Spirit, said, "Oh, noble youth! Oh, invincible king! Trample down, break through, and push aside every obstacle and leave us a pure Spain, cleaned and cleared of this evil caste of mine that so darkens and defames it! Oh counselor as wise as you are distinguished, a new Atlas supporting the weight of this monarchy, through your wise counsel help to bring about more easily this necessary migration! Let the seas be filled with your galleys loaded with the useless weight of the descendants of Hagar;[9] may these briars, brambles, and other weeds hindering the growth of Christian fertility and abundance be flung to the opposite shore! For if the few Hebrews that went over into Egypt multiplied so much that at the time of their exodus they numbered more than six hundred thousand families, what might we have to fear from these people, who are even more numerous and live more comfortably? The religious orders don't harvest them, the Indies don't thin them out, wars don't draft them. They all get married and all or most of them have children. From this it follows and can be inferred that the multiplications of and additions to them will unquestionably be incalculable. So I repeat, make them go; make them go, sir, leaving the tranquil surface of the fountain of your kingdom shining like the sun and as beautiful as the sky!"

The pilgrims stayed in the town for two days while they replaced what had been lost and Bartolomé provided himself with a pack animal. The pilgrims thanked the priest for his good care of them, praised the fine ideas of the sacristan, and after embracing Rafala said farewell to everyone and continued on their way.

Chapter Twelve of the Third Book

They passed the time on the road talking about the danger just passed, the sacristan's optimism, the priest's courage, and Rafala's fervent piety. They'd forgotten to ask her how she'd escaped from the hands of the Turks when they'd landed and attacked the town, although it seemed most likely to them that in the confusion she must have hidden in some place from which she was later able to come out and satisfy her heart's desire, which was to live and die a Christian.

They drew near Valencia but didn't want to go in for fear things would happen there to detain them. But there was no shortage of people to tell them about the magnificence of its setting, the excellence of its inhabitants, its pleasant ambience, and finally, everything that makes it rich and beautiful beyond all cities, not only of Spain but of all Europe. Above all they praised the beauty of its women and its fresh cleanliness and charming language,[1] which only Portuguese can compete with in being sweet and pleasant.

In order to get to Barcelona sooner they decided to increase the distance they covered each day even though it might cost them in terms of fatigue, for they understood some galleys were going to call there and thought they could embark in them and go to Genoa without making port in France.

As they were leaving the pretty and very pleasant village of Villareal, a Valencian lass or shepherdess came out to meet them from some dense trees off to the side of their path. She was dressed country-style and looked as pure as the sun and as beautiful as it and the moon put together. Without saying anything else to them first or standing on any ceremony whatsoever, she said in her charming language, "Señores, shall I ask for it or give it?"

To this Periandro replied, "Beautiful shepherdess, if it's jealousy, neither feel it nor provoke it, because if you feel jealousy you diminish your self-respect, and if you provoke it, your reputation. If the man who loves you is wise, knowing your worth he'll value you and love you well, and if he isn't, why would you want his love?" "You said a mouthful!" replied the village girl, and saying goodbye, she turned around and slipped back into the dense trees, leaving them astonished by her question, her quickness, and her beauty.

Some other things happened to them on the way to Barcelona, but none important enough to deserve being written up, unless it was their seeing from a distance the very holy mountains of Monserrate,[2] which they worshiped with Christian devotion from afar so they wouldn't be delayed by going there.

They reached Barcelona just at the moment when four Spanish galleys were approaching the beach. They fired off their heavy artillery to salute the city then launched four boats. As it turned out, riding in one decorated with rich oriental carpets and scarlet cushions was a very young, beautiful, and elegantly dressed woman, along with an elderly lady and two pretty and modestly dressed young women.

As is customary, countless people came out of the city to see both the galleys and the people disembarking from them, and our pilgrims' curiosity brought them so close to the boats they could almost have taken the hand of the lady as she was alighting. She, after stepping ashore and looking them all over—especially Constanza—said: "Come over here, beautiful pilgrim; I want to take you into the city with me where I plan to pay a debt I owe you, one about which I think you know very little. Have your comrades come along, too, because I'm sure there's nothing that could make you leave such good company." "Your company, it's plain to see," responded Constanza, "is so distinguished that anyone who didn't accept it would be feebleminded. Let's go wherever you may wish and my comrades will follow me, for they aren't used to being separated from me."

The lady took Constanza by the hand and, accompanied by many gentlemen who came out of the city to welcome her and by other important people from the galleys, they set out for the city; during the time they were on the road Constanza didn't take her eyes off her, but was still unable to remember ever having seen her before. They lodged not only the lady but the women who'd disembarked with her in one of the larger houses; neither would she hear of the pilgrims going anywhere else. Then as soon as she found a convenient moment she had the following talk with them.

"Señores, I want to clear up the surprise you must feel on seeing I'm making a particular effort to be of service to you, so let me tell you that they call me Ambrosia Agustina. I was born in a city in Aragón[3] and my brother is Don Bernardo Augustín, commander of those four galleys down at the beach. Contarino de Arbolanchez, a knight of the order of Alcántara,[4] in the absence of my brother and stealthily foiling my relatives' precautions, began to court me, while I, carried along by my destiny—or rather, by my weak character—seeing I wasn't going to lose anything by it and considering myself his wife, made him master of my body and soul. The same day I gave him my hand he received from His Majesty a letter commanding him to go immediately to lead an infantry regiment down from Lombardy to Genoa and then to the island of Malta, which they thought the Turks were going to attack. Contarino, obeying his orders very punctually and choosing not to pick the fruits of marriage in a rush, paid no heed to my tears, and his getting the letter and setting out occurred in one continuous motion. I felt as though the sky had fallen in on me and the earth had squeezed my heart and pinned my soul between them.

"A few days went by until, after piling fantasy upon fantasy and one desire upon another, I was able to put one into action; that act, which did indeed deprive me of my honor, could also have taken my life. I left my house without anyone's knowledge, and in men's clothing that I got from a little household page. I became the servant of a drummer in an infantry company that was at a town about eight leagues, I think, from my own. In a few days I learned to play the drum as well as my master and learned, too, to be a cutup like all those who ply that trade. Another company joined ours, and together they set out for Cartagena to embark in my brother's four galleys, in which I planned to get to Italy to search for my husband, whose noble nature wouldn't, I hoped, think badly of my daring or blame my desire, which had so blinded me that I overlooked the danger I would risk of being recognized if I took ship in my brother's galleys. But since a heart in love encounters no obstacles that can't be trampled under foot, no difficulties that can't be pushed out of the way or fears that can't be swept aside, I smoothed over all the rough spots on the road ahead, conquering my fears and hoping for the best out of sheer desperation. However, the way things turn out often makes one change one's original plans, and mine, as ill thought through as they were badly conceived, got me in the spot you'll now hear about.

"The soldiers in the companies commanded by those captains I've mentioned to you started a violent quarrel with the people of a town in La Mancha[5] regarding their lodging, and during it a gentleman, who they said was a count of I-don't-know-what rank, was mortally wounded. An investigator came from Court and arrested the captains; the soldiers were split up and some even arrested, including poor me, for I was totally guiltless. The investigator sentenced them to row for two years in the galleys and I, too, as though I were an afterthought, received the same fate. In vain I lamented my misfortune on seeing I'd made my plans to no avail. I'd have liked to kill myself but the fear of going to a worse life in the next world dulled the knife in my hand and took the rope from around my neck. What I did was smear my face with mud, making it as ugly as I could, and hole up in the wagon where they put us, intending to cry so much and eat so little that tears and hunger would do what rope and steel hadn't done. We reached Cartagena, where the galleys hadn't yet turned up; we were placed under secure guard in the royal buildings, and there we stayed, not just awaiting but really dreading our misfortune. I don't know, señores, if you remember a wagon you encountered next to an inn where this beautiful pilgrim"—she pointed out Constanza—"helped an exhausted criminal with a box of candied fruit."

"Yes, I remember," replied Constanza. "Well, I want you to

261

know," said the lady Ambrosia, "that I was the boy you helped. Through the matting on the wagon I peeked out at all of you and was astonished by you all, because your noble bearing can't help but astonish anyone who looks at you. It turned out, then, that the galleys arrived with a Moorish brigantine they'd taken as a prize on the way; that same day they shackled the soldiers into them, stripped them of the clothes they were wearing, and dressed them like oarsmen, a sad and painful, yet bearable transformation since becoming accustomed to suffering pain that doesn't end one's life makes enduring it easier.

"When it was my turn to be stripped the boatswain had them wash my face because I didn't have the strength to raise my arms. The barber who cleans up the galley crew took one look at me and said, "I won't wear out many blades on this beard; I don't know why they've sent us this here sugarpaste boy, as if our galleys were made of saltwater taffy and our oarsmen of sugar icing! And just what're you guilty of, young fellow, to deserve such a punishment? I'm sure it's the swollen current of other peoples' crimes that's carried you along to this end." Then directing his comments to the boatswain, he said, "To tell you the truth, boss, it seems to me it'd be best to put a chain on his ankle and let this boy serve our general astern, for he won't be worth two shakes on the oars."

"This conversation and my thinking back over what had happened to me, which at that moment seems to have particularly weighed down my spirits, so burdened my heart that I fainted dead away. They say I came to after four hours, during which they'd tried many methods to revive me; and what would have most pained me, had I been in a condition to feel pain at the time, was that they must have discovered I wasn't male, but female. When I recovered from my collapse the first things I laid eyes on were the faces of my brother and my husband, for they were holding me in their arms. I don't know why death's shadow didn't fall over my eyes at that point. I don't know why my tongue didn't stick to the roof of my mouth. I only know I didn't know what I was trying to say when I heard my brother ask me, 'Why these clothes, my sister?' and my husband ask, 'What kind of change is this in my soul's other half? If your goodness weren't so inseparable from your honor, I'd soon make you exchange these clothes for a shroud!'

"'This is your wife?' said my brother to my husband. 'That's just as surprising to me as seeing her in this clothing; but that fact, if what you say is true, would do a lot to counteract the pain it causes me to see my sister like this.'

"At this point, when I'd recovered part of my lost strength, I remember saying, 'My brother, I'm Ambrosia Agustina, your sister, and I'm also the wife of Lord Contarino de Arbolanchez. Love and your absence, dear brother, gave him to me as my husband, though he left me before enjoying the pleasures of marriage. With headlong daring and ill-considered plans, I came to look for him dressed in these clothes you see.'

"And with this I told them the whole story you've heard from me, and my luck, which was improving as time went by, made them believe me and feel sorry for me. They told me my husband had been captured by Moors along with one of the two sloops in which he'd embarked to go to Genoa, and that he'd recovered his freedom only the day before at sundown. This circumstance hadn't given him time to see my brother until the moment when he found me fainted away—a coincidence so novel it might seem less than credible, nevertheless everything happened just as I've told you. On these galleys I met the lady traveling with me and her two granddaughters. They're going to Italy where her son is in charge of the royal estate in Sicily. They dressed me in the clothes I'm wearing, which are theirs, and my husband and my brother, cheerful and content, have brought us ashore today for a little recreation and a pleasant get-together with the many friends they have in this city. If you, señores, are going to Rome, I'll have my brother take you to the port closest to it. I'll repay you for the box of candied fruit by sticking with you for as long as you think best. And even if I shouldn't go over to Italy, my brother will honor my request and take you there. Such, my friends, is my story; I wouldn't be surprised if you found it hard to believe, but even though the truth can certainly fall sick, still, it can't die completely. And since it's commonly said that believing is a sign of courtesy, I entrust my credibility to yours, for you're sure to show it in abundance."

At this point the beautiful Augustina brought her exposé to an end, and the amazement of her listeners began to intensify to a climax of amazed curiosity. They began going over the details of the case with a fine-toothed comb, but no finer or more insistent than the embraces Constanza and Auristela gave the beautiful Ambrosia who, because it was her husband's wish, was going to return home, for no matter how beautiful a woman may be, her companionship is a hindrance in the midst of war.

That night the sea turned rough and it was necessary for the galleys to stand off the beach, which is unsafe in those parts. The courteous Catalans, a people who can become terribly angry and yet are mild and peaceful, a people who will gladly give their lives for their honor and outdo themselves in defending both (which is the same thing as outdoing every other nation on earth), entertained and showered attentions on the lady Ambrosia Agustina, and her brother and her husband thanked them when they returned.

Auristela, taking warning from the many experiences she'd had with storms at sea, chose not to embark on the galleys, rather to go through France, since it was at peace. Ambrosia went back to Aragón. The galleys continued their journey and the pilgrims theirs, entering France through Perpiñán.[6]

Chapter Thirteen of the Third Book

Our band chose to enter France through the region of Perpiñán and what had happened to Ambrosia gave them something to talk about for several days. Her many faults could be excused by her youth, and the love she had for her husband further pardoned her reckless daring. But in short, as has been said, she had returned to her home, the galleys had continued their journey, and our pilgrims, theirs. On arriving at Perpiñán they stopped at an inn near whose large front door a table was placed. Many people were standing around it watching two men throw dice, but only those two were playing.

The pilgrims thought it unusual for so many people to be watching and so few playing. Periandro asked the reason and was told that of the two playing the one who lost would lose his liberty and be taken into royal custody to row in the galleys for six months; the man who won would win the twenty ducats the king's ministers had offered to induce them to try their luck in the game and so guarantee themselves a loser. One of the two put his luck to the test; it didn't pass because he lost. They immediately put him in irons and then from the winner took off the irons they'd placed on him to make sure he wouldn't run away if he should lose. What a miserable game and miserable luck—where neither winning nor losing are given an even break!

At this point they saw a large crowd of people arrive at the inn. Among them, and with a genteel air although in shirt sleeves, was a man surrounded by five or six children ranging in age from four to seven. Accompanying him and crying bitterly was a woman with a canvas bag of money in her hand; in a pitiful voice she was saying, "Take your money, señores, and give me back my husband, for it wasn't vice but need that made him take this money. He didn't gamble, but rather *sold* himself, because at the cost of this hardship he chooses to support me and his children. What bitter support and bitter sustenance for me and for them!" "Be quiet, dear wife," said the man, "and spend the money, for I'll win it back again with the strength of my arms, which will sooner become used to handling an oar than a hoe. I chose not to gamble away the use of my arms because had I lost I'd have lost not only my liberty but also the money for your support."

The crying of the children almost drowned out this painful conversation between the husband and wife. The officers holding him told them to dry their tears, for although they might cry enough tears to fill an ocean, it wouldn't be enough to give him back the freedom he'd lost. But the children cried all the louder, saying to their father, "Sir, please don't leave us, because we'll all die if you go." This strange new event touched the pilgrims' hearts (especially Constanza's who was treasurer of the group), and they were all moved to beg the officials charged with that duty to agree to take back their money, to pretend the man didn't exist, and to be compassionate and not make the woman a widow or so many children orphans. In the end, they were such great talkers and kept on begging so long that the money went back into the possession of its original owners and the woman recovered her husband and the children their father.

The beautiful Constanza, wealthy since becoming a countess and more a Christian than a barbarian, after consulting with her brother Antonio gave the poor hopeless people fifty gold escudos, which saved them. They went back home as happy as they were free, giving thanks to Heaven and to the pilgrims for the alms, as extraordinary as they were unexpected.

The next day they stepped onto French soil and passing through Languedoc entered Provence, where at another inn they found three French ladies of such extreme beauty that if Auristela hadn't been in the world they could have hoped to win the palm branch for beauty. They appeared to be noblewomen, judging by the retinue serving them. On seeing the pilgrims they were struck by Periandro and Antonio's good looks, as well as by Auristela and Constanza's beauty. They came over and spoke to them with happy faces and polite graciousness, asking them in Spanish who they were, for they recognized the pilgrim women as Spaniards and in France there isn't a man or woman who doesn't learn the Spanish language.[1]

Since their questions had been directed to Auristela, and while the ladies were waiting for her answer, Periandro turned aside to talk with a servant he guessed belonged to the distinguished French-women. He asked him who they were and where they were going, and the servant answered him, saying, "The Duke of Nemurs, one of those known in this kingdom as blue bloods, is a dashing and very intelligent gentleman, but also one true to his own tastes. He's just recently inherited his estate and has decided not to marry in accordance with the wishes of anyone but himself, even though by obeying he might be offered an increase in rank and property, and by not obeying might go against his king's command; for he says a king can certainly give a woman to whichever of his vassals he chooses, but can't make him happy to get her. With this fantasy, madness, good sense, or whatever's best to call it, he's sent some of his servants out to various parts of France to look for a woman who, in addition to being noble, must also be beautiful, and whom he'll marry regardless of her wealth; he'll be content to let her rank and her beauty be her dowry.

"He heard that these three ladies are of quality and sent me, his servant, to look them over and have their portraits painted by a famous painter he sent along with me. All three of them are single and they're all young, as you've seen. The eldest, called Deleasir, is extremely bright, but poor; the middle one, called Belarminia, is strikingly good-looking and graceful, and moderately wealthy; the youngest, whose name is Feliz Flora, has the great advantage of being wealthier than the other two. They've also learned of the duke's wish and each of them would like to be the lucky one—as near as I can tell—to win him for her husband. So, taking advantage of the fact that this year one can go to Rome to reap the benefits of the jubilee (which is only about a hundredth as good as it used to be), they've left their home provinces and intend to go through Paris to meet the duke, trusting in that "maybe" that keeps our hopes up.

"But now that you're here, good pilgrims, I've decided to take my master a present that'll erase each and every one of the hopes these ladies may have framed in their minds, for I plan to take him a portrait of this pilgrim of yours, this one and only queen of human beauty. And if she's as highborn as she is beautiful, my master's servants won't have anything more to do, nor the duke anything more to desire. Tell me, I beg of you, sir, whether this pilgrim is married, what her name is, and who her parents are."

To this a trembling Periandro replied, "Her name is Auristela, she's going to Rome, and she never mentions her parents' name; I can assure you she's single, for I know beyond any shadow of a doubt that she is. But there's something else about her; she's so much her own person and so much the mistress of her own will that she won't surrender it to any prince on earth, for she says she's surrendered it to the one who reigns in Heaven. And just so you'll be sure everything I've told you is the truth, you should know I'm her brother and the one who knows her most private thoughts. This all means you won't gain anything from painting her portrait except an upset master, unless he can push aside the inconvenient obstacle of my parents' low rank."

"In spite of all that," responded the other, "I'll take her portrait with me, if only as a curiosity and to spread this new miracle of beauty throughout France." At this they said goodbye and Periandro decided to leave the place right away so the painter wouldn't have a chance to paint Auristela. Bartolomé immediately began to reload the pack animal and was annoyed with Periandro for being in such a big hurry to leave. The duke's servant, seeing that Periandro wanted to leave right away, came up to him and said, "Sir, I'd really like to ask you to stay here for a little while—at least until nightfall—to give my painter adequate time and make it more convenient for him to do the portrait of your sister's face. But on second thought, you can go ahead; go, and God be with you, for the painter's told me he has her so clearly pictured in his mind after having seen her just this once that he'll do just as good a job of painting her on his own as he could if he had her constantly in front of him."

To himself Periandro cursed the painter's unique talent, but it didn't keep him from departing, immediately saying goodbye to the three attractive Frenchwomen who embraced Auristela and Constanza tightly, offering to take them to Rome in their company, if they'd like. Auristela expressed her gratitude in the most courteous words she knew, but told them neither she nor Constanza could remain behind since her will obeyed that of her brother Periandro, and both he and Constanza's brother Antonio were leaving. With this they left, and six days later reached a place in Provence. What happened to them there will be related in the next chapter.

Chapter Fourteen of the Third Book

History, poetry, and painting resemble each other and indeed are so much alike that when you write history you're painting, and when you paint you're composing poetry. History doesn't always deal with weighty matters just as painting doesn't always portray great and magnificent things and poetry doesn't always have its head in the clouds. History accepts the trivial, painting allows weeds and brush in its pictures, and poetry sometimes does best when it sings about modest affairs.

This truth is nicely demonstrated to us by Bartolomé, the baggage handler for the pilgrim band who sometimes talks and is listened to in our story. Going over in his mind the story of the man who sold his liberty to support his children, at one point he said while talking with Periandro, "The force, sir, that makes parents feel compelled to support their children must be very strong; for if it's not, it certainly can't be disproved by that man who chose not to gamble so as not to run the risk of being lost to his family, preferring instead to pawn himself to support them. Freedom, judging by what I've heard, shouldn't be sold for any amount of money, and he sold his for so little that his wife was carrying it around in her hand. I also remember having heard my elders say that when an old man was being taken out to the gallows and the priests were helping him to die a good death, he said to them, 'Relax, Your Graces, and give me room to die, for although this is a terrible step I must take, I've often found myself faced by worse ones.' They asked him what they were and he replied to wake up in the morning surrounded by six small children asking him for bread and not having any to give them. 'So need put a picklock in my hand and soft shoes on my feet; they smoothed the way for my thefts, which weren't wicked but necessary.' These words reached the ears of the judge who'd sentenced him to die, and the result was that strict justice became compassion and guilt received a merciful pardon."

To this Periandro replied, "What a father does for his child he does for himself, because his child is another version of himself and in him his being continues. And so, it's just as natural and unavoidable for everyone to take care of their children as it is to take care of themselves. What's not so natural or unavoidable is for children to take care of their parents. The love a father has descends on his child and descent is an effortless movement, but the love of the child for his father ascends and rises, which means it has to go uphill, and from that comes the following expression: 'One father can have a hundred children more easily than a hundred children can have one father.'"

With this and other conversations they passed the time on the road through France, which is so populous, open, and peaceful, that at every step they came across country estates whose owners spend almost the whole year there not minding it a bit or wanting to be back in the towns or cities. Our travelers came to one of these houses located just off the royal highway. It was noontime, the sun's rays were beating straight down on the earth, the heat was already intense, and a huge tower on the house cast a shadow inviting them there to wait out the hours of the siesta which were threatening to be dreadfully hot.

Since by now hunger was beginning to gnaw at them, the obliging Bartolomé unloaded the pack animal and, after spreading a carpet on the ground, they all sat down around it to satisfy themselves with the food he was careful to keep in stock. But no sooner had they picked up the food and were about to put it in their mouths when Bartolomé looked up and shouted, "Get out of the way, señores, for someone, I don't know who, is flying down out of the sky, and it's going to be a mess if he lands on top of you!"

They all looked up and saw a shape coming down through the air, but before they could distinguish what it was, it was already on the ground almost at Periandro's feet. The shape turned out to be an exceptionally beautiful woman who had been thrown off the top of the tower, but her petticoats spread themselves out in the shape of a bell and acted as wings so that she landed feet-first on the ground completely unharmed, something possible and not at all miraculous. The event left her stunned and frightened, as were all those who'd seen her fly. Then from the tower they heard another woman screaming while she struggled in the arms of a man, the two apparently trying to throw each other off. "Help! Help!" the woman was shouting. "Help, señores; this madman wants to throw me down from here!"

The flying woman, having somewhat recovered her composure, said, "If there's anyone who dares go through that door"—she pointed to one at the base of the tower—"he can save my children and some other defenseless people up there from certain danger." Urged on by his generous spirit, Periandro went through the door and a short time later they saw him at the top of the tower struggling with an obviously crazy man from whom he took a knife and was then trying to defend himself. But luck, which wanted to bring down the curtain on the tragedy of his life, had it that both of them should fall to the ground and land at the base of the tower. The knife Periandro was holding had run through the madman's chest and Periandro was losing a lot of blood from his eyes, nose, and mouth; since he wasn't wearing clothing that could open out wide to break his fall, he'd felt its full effect and been left almost lifeless.

Auristela, seeing him like that and believing he must be unquestionably dead, threw herself on him and without any concern for decorum placed her mouth on his, trying to gather into herself some small part that might be left of his soul; but even had there been something left, she couldn't have taken it in, for his clenched teeth wouldn't let her. Constanza, overcome by emotion, was unable to take a single step to go over to help her and so stayed in the same spot where the fall had taken her by surprise, as if her feet were rooted to the ground or she were a statue made of solid marble. Her brother Antonio, however, hurried over to pick out those who were half alive and set them apart from those he judged were dead. Only Bartolomé, crying bitterly, showed in his eyes the great pain he felt in his soul.

While everyone was suffering the bitter affliction I've described, though no one had yet expressed his grief in words, they saw coming toward them a large troop of people who, having observed from the vantage point of the royal highway the flight of the fallen, were coming over to see what had happened. It was the party in which the beautiful French ladies Deleasir, Belarminia, and Feliz Flora were traveling. As soon as they arrived they recognized Auristela and Periandro, whose extraordinary beauty always made a lasting impression on all who saw them. But scarcely had compassion led them to dismount to render aid—if that were possible in the disaster they were observing—when they were assaulted by six or eight armed men who came upon them from behind.

This assault led Antonio to take up his bow and arrows, for he always had them ready either for offense or defense. With a brusque movement one of the armed men grabbed Feliz Flora by the arm and put her up in front of him on the saddle, then turned around and said to his companions, "That's it. She's enough for me. Let's go." Antonio, who never tolerated discourtesy, laid aside all fear and put an arrow to his bow; extending his left arm fully with his right he pulled the bowstring back to his right ear so the two ends of the bow almost touched. Taking dead aim on Feliz Flora's kidnapper, he shot the arrow so accurately that except for touching a piece of the veil covering Feliz Flora's head it missed her and went right through the at-

270

tacker's chest. One of the raider's companions rushed to avenge him and, not giving Antonio time to ready his bow again, wounded him on the head with a blow that knocked him to the ground more dead than alive. On seeing this Constanza stopped being a statue and ran to help her brother—for kinship often warms blood that may freeze for the best of friends—though both reactions can also be signs and indications of excessive love.

By now armed people had come out of the house and the servants of the three ladies provided themselves with stones—I mean those who didn't have weapons—and began to defend their mistresses. The attackers, seeing their captain dead and believing that since defenders were now at hand they could gain little in the affair—especially in light of the fact that it would be madness to risk their lives for someone no longer able to reward them—they turned their backs and deserted the field.

So far we've heard the sound of very few swords in this battle and few martial instruments have sounded their music. The grief the living typically feel for the dead hasn't broken the quiet; their tongues have wrapped their laments in bitter silence. Only a few "oh's" amid muffled moans have been heard, especially coming from deep within the grieving Auristela and Constanza, each of whom was embracing her brother and unable to take advantage of laments that usually bring relief to injured hearts.

But at last, resolving not to let them die so quickly and without laments, Heaven loosened the tongues stuck to the roofs of their mouths, and Auristela broke forth in words similar to the following: "I don't know why, having been struck by such a misfortune, I'm looking for breath in a dead man, since even if he had any I couldn't feel it, being so lost without him I don't even know if I myself am speaking or breathing. Oh, dear brother, what a fall this has been! It has felled my hopes, for the greatness of your lineage couldn't stand up to your misfortunes! But how could your misfortunes be so great, unless you were, too? Lightning strikes the highest mountains, and where it meets with the greatest resistance it does the most damage. You were a mountain, but a humble mountain hiding itself from peoples' eyes under the shadow of your discretion and wisdom. You went out to search for a fortune linked to mine, but death has blocked your path and turned mine toward the grave. The queen, your mother, will be certain to die when she learns of your unexpected death! Oh, and what will become of me, once again alone in a foreign land? I'm like the green ivy with nothing left to twine on!"

These words about a queen, about mountains and greatness,

held the attention of those present and listening, and their astonishment increased when they heard the words Constanza was saying as she held her badly wounded brother on her lap while the compassionate Feliz Flora, feeling obliged to the wounded young man for having saved her from dishonor, applied pressure to his wound and cleaned the blood away by gently wiping it with a piece of linen she had with her. "Oh, my refuge, my refuge!" Constanza was saying over and over. "What good did it do for Fortune to elevate my title to 'lady' if she were then just going to throw me down and call me 'miserable'? Come to, dear brother, if you want me to come alive again, and if not, oh, merciful Heaven, let a single fate close our eyes and a single grave cover our bodies; for the good so suddenly bestowed on me must have held hidden within it the flaw of being temporary." At this she fainted and Auristela did exactly the same, so they looked just as dead, indeed even more so than the two wounded men.

The woman who fell from the tower and who was the main cause of Periandro's fall, instructed her servants—for many of them had by now come out of the house—to take him to their lord Count Domicio's bed. She also ordered them to carry away her husband Domicio and to prepare for his burial. Bartolomé carried his lord Antonio in his arms; Feliz Flora embraced Constanza in hers, and Belarminia and Deleasir took Auristela in theirs. Then with bitter steps the companions in sadness set out for the house, which was practically a palace.

Chapter Fifteen of the Third Book

The wise words of advice the three French ladies were offering the grieving Constanza and Auristela did little good, for consoling arguments are out of place when misfortune is fresh in the mind. When pain and disaster occur suddenly people won't accept any consolation—no matter how wise it may be—before some time has passed. An abscess hurts until it ripens, but time is required for it to soften and finally break open. So, while someone is crying, while someone is moaning, and when you see someone whose laments and sighs fill you with compassion, it's not wise to hurry to their aid with strong remedies. So let Auristela weep a little longer, let Constanza moan a little more, and may they both close their ears to all consolation while the beautiful Claricia tells us the reason for her husband Domicio's madness, which was—according to what she told the French ladies—that before he was betrothed to her he was in love with a relative of his who had high hopes of marrying him.

"But, as luck would have it," said Claricia, "hers turned out badly where he was concerned. And concealing her anger, Lorena—that's the name of Domicio's relative—began giving him many different kinds of presents, though they were more showy and attractive than truly costly. Among them she once sent him, much as the treacherous Deianira sent the shirt to Hercules[1]—I repeat—she sent him some shirts made of fine linen and beautifully embroidered. No sooner had he put one of them on when he lost consciousness and for two days seemed dead even though they immediately took it off him, supposing one of Lorena's slaves who had the reputation of being a sorceress must have put a spell on it. "My husband came back to life, but his mind was so disoriented and altered there was nothing he did that wasn't insane; and he wasn't a gentle madman, but a violent, furious, and wild one, so much so that it was necessary to keep him in chains."

And she said that while she was in the tower that day the madman had gotten loose from his restraints; coming there, he'd thrown her down out of the windows, but Heaven had helped her by spreading her clothing wide, or more accurately, through God's usual compassion in watching over the innocent. She described how the pilgrim had gone up into the tower to free a young woman whom the madman wanted to throw down to the ground, and how after that he was also going to toss two little children out of the tower. But things turned out so badly that the count and the pilgrim crashed to the hard ground, the pilgrim still grasping the knife he'd apparently taken away from Domicio, and the count mortally wounded though the wound didn't contribute to his death since the fall itself was enough.

Meanwhile Periandro was unconscious in bed, where experts came to cure him and put his dislocated bones back into place. They had him drink things indicated for his condition, took his pulse, and found he could somewhat recognize the people around him, especially Auristela, to whom he said in a feeble voice that could scarcely be understood, "Sister, I'm dying in the Catholic Christian faith and in true love for you." And then he didn't, and couldn't, say another word for awhile.

The surgeons bled Antonio and after examining his wound asked his sister to reward them for the good news they were going to tell her—that his injury was substantial but not fatal and with Heaven's help he'd soon be well again. Feliz Flora gave them a reward before Constanza could get around to it, even though she was planning to give them one and later did. The surgeons accepted both their rewards, since there wasn't anything very ethical about them.

It took a month or a little more for the invalids to get well, and during that time the French ladies didn't wish to leave them, as they'd become good friends of theirs and greatly enjoyed the intelligent conversation of Auristela, Constanza, and their two brothers. This went especially for Feliz Flora, who couldn't bring herself to leave Antonio's bedside, though loving him with such a proper love that it didn't go beyond warm wishes and gratitude for the kindness she'd received from him when his arrow freed her from Rubertino's hands. As Feliz Flora told it, the latter was a knight, the lord of a castle located near one of hers, and moved not by a perfect love but by one growing out of vice, he'd persisted in following and pursuing her, begging her to give him her hand in marriage. But she'd realized, because of countless experiences and his public reputation—something that seldom lies—that Rubertino possessed a sharp and violent disposition along with a changeable and capricious will, and so had refused to give in to his demands. And she imagined that frustrated by her scorn he must have set out on the road to kidnap her, to do to her by force what her free will wouldn't consent to. But Antonio's arrow had put a stop to all his violent and ill-conceived plans, and this moved her to show her gratitude.

Everything Feliz Flora talked about had happened just that way, with no inaccuracies on her part. When the invalids reached the point of feeling better and their strength began to show signs of getting back to normal, they felt renewed desire, at least to be back on the road, and so took steps to satisfy it by gathering all the necessary supplies. The French ladies, as has been mentioned, didn't want to leave the pilgrims, whom they now treated with awe and respect because the words of Auristela's lament had given them the idea they must be great lords and ladies, for sometimes majesty wears burlap and greatness dresses itself in humility. In fact, they viewed them with some perplexity, for their modest retinue made them seem to be of only moderate rank, but their liveliness and good looks seemed to elevate their station in life all the way up to the skies. So they were uncertain what to think and found themselves wavering between a definite yes or no.

The French ladies arranged for everyone to travel on horseback since Periandro's fall wouldn't allow him to trust his feet. Feliz Flora, grateful for the blow struck on her behalf by Antonio the barbarian, wouldn't leave his side. While discussing the audacity of Rubertino whom they'd left behind dead and buried, the strange story of Count Domicio—whose cousin's gifts had deprived him of both his sanity and his life—and of his wife's miraculous flight, more amazing than believable, they came to a river that could only be forded with some difficulty. Periandro thought they should look for a bridge, but none of the rest agreed with him; then just as when a flock of meek sheep is bottled up in a narrow spot and one of them finds a way out and all the others immediately go along after her, Belarminia ventured out into the water and everyone followed, Periandro not leaving Auristela's side or Antonio Feliz Flora's, though he also kept his sister Constanza near him.

As luck would have it, Feliz Flora's wasn't too good, for the rush of the water made her dizzy and she lost her balance and fell into the middle of the current. The attentive Antonio shot after her with unbelievable speed and carrying her on his shoulders as if she were a new Europa[2] he set her down on the dry sand of the opposite bank. Seeing how promptly he'd come to her aid, she said to him, "You're very gallant, Spaniard." Antonio replied, "If my gallant deeds hadn't come about because of dangers to you, I could feel somewhat good about them, but since they have they make me more sad than glad."

The beautiful band, as I've called it before, went on, toward nightfall coming to a large farmhouse that at the same time was also an inn, where they were very glad to spend the night. But what happened to them there calls for a new style and a new chapter.

Chapter Sixteen of the Third Book

If, before some matters and situations happen, we were to turn them over in our imagination, it would be impossible to visualize them turning out as they do. Many cases, because of the unusual circumstances under which they occur, are judged to be apocryphal and not held to be as true as they really are, so one has to reinforce them with oaths, or at least consider the good reputation of the person telling them. But I still feel it would be better not to tell them, for as those old Spanish verses say:

275

You'd better hesitate
When you've astonishing things to relate,
For those not so very wise
Can't always distinguish *your* truth from others' lies.

The first person Constanza encountered was an attractive young woman, about twenty-two years old, dressed cleanly and neatly in the Spanish style. Coming up to Constanza she said to her in Spanish, "Praise the Lord, for though they may not be from my home town I see people who are at least from my country—Spain! Praise the Lord, I repeat, for now I'll finally be addressed as 'you' and not 'your grace'—even the kitchen boys get called that here!"

"Then that means you, Ma'm, are Spanish?" responded Constanza. "That's right!" she replied. "And from the best part of Castile." "Which part is that?" asked Constanza. "From Talavera de la Reina," she replied. No sooner had she said this than Constanza began to suspect she must be the Pole Ortel Banedre's wife, who'd been in jail in Madrid for adultery and whose husband had been persuaded by Periandro to leave her in custody there and go back to his own country. Then in a flash ideas came crowding into Constanza's mind and she came up with a plan that subsequently turned out almost exactly the way she'd imagined it would. She took her by the hand and went over where Auristela was; then taking the two aside with Periandro she said, "Señores, you question whether my skill as a mind reader is counterfeit or authentic, a skill that can't be demonstrated by foretelling the future since only God knows what's going to happen—even though some human may get it right by pure chance or by some clues observed in previous cases. But if I should tell you things already past of which I have no knowledge, nor indeed could have, what would you say then? Would you like to see that?

"This fine woman we have before us is from Talavera de la Reina. She married a foreigner, a Pole, whose name, if I remember correctly, was Ortel Banedre, whom she offended by being free and easy with a young man working at an inn and living across the street from her house. She let herself be swept away in the arms of her rash thoughts and inexperienced youth, and so left her parents' house with the young man I've mentioned and was later jailed with him in Madrid for adultery. She must have suffered many hardships both in prison there and then while coming here, and so I want her to tell us all about them, for even though I might be able to guess them, she'll tell us in greater detail and with more style."

"Oh, God above!" said the girl. "Who's this lady who's read my thoughts? Who's this fortune teller who knows all the shameless story of my life? My lady, I'm that adulteress, I'm that prisoner, I'm the woman sentenced to only ten years in exile because no one prosecuted me, and I'm the woman who's in the clutches of a Spanish soldier heading for Italy, buttering my bread with pain and just barely getting through life—at times desiring death. My first lover died in jail. This one—I don't know how many I've had in all—helped me there, got me out and, as I've said, is dragging me around with him through the wide world for his pleasure and my sorrow, 'cause I'm not so dumb I don't know the danger threatening my soul by my being such a tramp. For God's sake, señores, since you're Spanish, since you're Christians, and since you're nobles—judging by your appearance and manner—please get me out of the clutches of this Spaniard, and it'll be like saving me from lion's claws."

Periandro and Auristela were astonished by Constanza's insightful intelligence, and not only did they accept as true what she claimed to know but they verified her information with more of their own. They even felt moved to make every effort to help out the hopeless girl who said the Spanish soldier didn't always travel with her, but that to confuse the authorities he'd often be a day's journey either ahead or behind. "That's perfect," said Periandro, "and we'll plan a way to help you right now, for the woman who knew how to guess your past life will know how to arrange things for you in the times ahead. Try to be good, for without the foundation of virtue you can't build anything even resembling goodness. Stay close to us now, for your age and your face are the two worst enemies you could have in foreign lands."

The girl began to cry, Constanza felt sorry for her, and Auristela showed signs of having the same feelings, thereby obliging Periandro to look hard for a solution to the girl's problems. They were in the midst of this when Bartolomé came up and said, "Señores, come see the strangest sight you'll ever see in your lives!" He said this in such a frightened and terrified way that, thinking they were going to see some wonder, they followed him. In a suite somewhat separated from where the pilgrims and ladies were lodged, they could see between some screens into a room all draped in mourning, but its gloomy darkness prevented them from making out in detail what was in it.

While they were there looking in, a very old man, likewise draped in mourning, came up and said to them, "Ladies and gentlemen, two hours from now, when it's one o'clock in the morning, if you'd like to observe the lady Ruperta without her seeing you, I'll arrange for you to see her, and the sight of her condition and her beauty will give you cause for amazement." "Sir," responded Periandro, "this servant of ours right here invited us to come and see something wonderful, but so far we haven't seen anything except this bedroom draped in mourning—and that's certainly no wonder."

"If you come back at the time I've said," answered the man in mourning, "you'll really have something to marvel at, for you should know that lodged in this room is the lady Ruperta, wife of the late Count Lamberto of Scotland who died scarcely a year ago. His marriage cost him his life and put her in danger of losing hers at every turn. This was due to the fact that one of the most important Scottish knights, Claudino Rubicón, made arrogant by his wealth and family line and being by nature amorous, fell deeply in love with my lady when she was a young woman; but she demonstrated if not downright hatred at least her rejection of him by marrying my lord the count. Rubicón called my lady's swift decision dishonor and contempt for him, as if the beautiful Ruperta didn't have parents who commanded her and unavoidable obligations that had compelled her to make it—plus the fact that it's better to have a balance in the ages of couples who marry; when possible, the husband should always be ten years older than the wife, or even a few more, so old age will overtake them at the same time. Rubicón was a respectable widower with a son almost twenty-one years old, very much a gentleman and much more attractive than his father; so attractive in fact, that if he'd entered the competition for my lady, today my lord the count would be alive and she'd be happier. It happened, then, that while my lady Ruperta and her husband were on their way to enjoy themselves at a country house of theirs, by chance and completely unexpectedly while on a deserted stretch of road we came upon Rubicón, accompanied by many of his servants. He saw my lady and the sight of her awakened in his mind the insult he felt had been given him, and so instead of love, wrath was born, and from wrath the desire to cause my lady grief. Now since revenge taken by people who've loved each other is usually more serious than the original offenses committed, the spiteful, rash, and bold Rubicón took out his sword and ran over to my lord the count. (He wasn't to blame in any part of the matter, of course, and didn't have time to defend himself from this unexpected attack.) As he sheathed the sword in his chest Rubicón said, 'Now you'll pay up even though you don't owe me! And if you think this is cruelty, your wife was crueler yet to me, since her scorn has taken my life not just once, but a hundred thousand times.'

278

"I was present at all of this; I heard the words, then saw with my own eyes and touched the wound with my own hands; I heard my lady's screams rising up to Heaven. We turned back to bury the count and, at the time he was buried, my lady ordered his head cut off; within a few days, due to some things put on it, the flesh fell off leaving only the bones. My lady had it put in a silver box, on which she placed her hands and swore this oath. . . . But I'm forgetting to say how the violent Rubicón, perhaps out of contempt or to be even more cruel, or perhaps just careless in his confusion, left his sword sheathed in my lord's chest, and his blood even now looks almost fresh on it. . . . I was saying, then, that she pronounced the following words:

> I, Ruperta the miserable—whom Heaven has only called "the beautiful"[1]—with my hands placed upon these pitiful relics do swear an oath to Heaven to avenge the death of my husband using my power and all my concerted efforts, even if I have to risk my worthless life a thousand and one times to do it; nor will I be frightened by trials or fail to beg help from anyone who might assist me. And until such time as this my just—if not Christian—desire be satisfied, I swear that my dress shall be black, my rooms gloomy, I will set a sad table, and my only companion shall be solitude itself. These relics shall be placed on my table to torment my soul, this tongueless head shall tell me to avenge this insult to his honor, and this sword, whose undried blood I feel troubling mine, shall not let me rest until I take my revenge.

"This said, she seems to have moderated her continual tears and contained her painful sighs. She has now set out on the road to Rome to ask the princes of Italy for their favor and help against her husband's killer who, perhaps out of fear, is still threatening her; but often the harm a mosquito can do is more than the assistance an eagle can lend. All this, ladies and gentlemen, you'll see two hours from now, as I've said, and if it doesn't astonish you, either I haven't known how to tell it very well or you must have hearts made of marble."

Here the squire in mourning brought his talk to an end, and even without having seen Ruperta the pilgrims naturally began to be amazed by her story.

279

Chapter Seventeen of the Third Book

Anger, it is said, is a violent disturbance of the blood flowing near the heart, stirring in the chest at the sight of the offending object or sometimes merely at its memory. Its ultimate purpose and final goal is to lead the offended person to take revenge, and its feels pacified whenever he does so, whether rightfully or not. This is something the beautiful Ruperta will teach us, for she was offended and angry and had such a strong desire to take revenge on her enemy that even though she didn't know he was already dead, she extended her wrath to include all his descendants. Had it been in her power, she wouldn't have wanted to leave any of them alive, for a woman's anger knows no limits.

The hour came for the pilgrims to go observe her unseen, and they saw she was extremely beautiful and dressed in a pure white wimple that reached from her head almost to her feet. She was seated at a table where she had her husband's head in the silver box, the sword with which his life was taken, and a shirt on which she imagined her husband's blood had still not dried. All these emblems of her pain awakened her wrath, though nothing was needed to wake it up since it never slept. She stood up and placing her right hand on her husband's head began to make and reaffirm the vow and oath the squire in mourning had described. Enough tears rained down from her eyes to wet the relics of her suffering, and such sighs broke loose from her chest that the air near and far was thick with them. To her usual oath she added further words to make it even more binding, and sometimes it seemed that not tears, but fire, was pouring out of her eyes, and from her mouth, not sighs, but smoke, so tightly was she gripped by her emotions and her desire for revenge.

Can't you see her weeping? Can't you see her sighing? Can't you see her beside herself with rage? Can't you see her brandishing the murderous sword? Can't you see her kissing the bloody shirt, her sobs interrupting the words? Well, just wait until morning and you'll see things to give you something to talk about for a thousand centuries, should you live so long.

Ruperta was in the midst of her flight from pain and had almost reached the threshold of pleasure (for making threats brings a measure of relief), when one of her servants came up to her (though it seemed only a black shadow had arrived as he was entirely covered up by mourning attire) and said in a whisper, "My lady, the young gentleman Croriano, the son of your enemy, has just now dismounted with some servants. Decide whether you want to keep yourself hidden or whether you want him to recognize you, or whatever it is you think would be best to do, since you've some time to think it over." "I don't want him to recognize me," responded Ruperta, "and warn all my servants not to carelessly mention my name or give me away while trying to be helpful." And saying this she gathered up her keepsakes and ordered the room shut up and that no one should come in to speak to her.

The pilgrims went back to their room and she was left alone and pensive. Later it was learned, though I don't know how, that while alone she'd spoken the following words, or ones very much like them. "Just think, oh Ruperta, that merciful Heaven delivered your enemy's soul into your hands like a simple-minded victim to the sacrifice; for children, especially when it's an only child, are pieces of their parents' souls. Oh, Ruperta! Forget you're a woman, or if you don't want to forget it, remember you're a woman but one who's been offended. Your husband's blood is crying out to you and from that head without a tongue he's saying to you, 'Revenge, my dear sweet wife, for I was an innocent victim of murder!' That's right, Holofernes' ferocity didn't frighten the humble Judith.[1] It's true her cause was quite different from mine; she punished an enemy of God, while I want to punish an enemy I don't even know is mine; love of her homeland put the blade in her hands, while love for my husband puts it in mine. But why am I making such foolish comparisons? What more do I have to do except close my eyes and sheathe the steel in this young man's chest, for the less his guilt the greater my revenge? Let me be renowned as an avenger and the Devil take the hindmost! Desires wanting fulfillment pay no heed to obstacles, even though they may be fatal; let me fulfill mine even though it may end in my own death!"

This said, she planned and arranged to be shut that evening into Croriano's bedroom, to which she was given easy access by a servant of his turned traitor to him for a bribe—though he didn't think he was doing his master anything but a great service by bringing such a beautiful woman as Ruperta to his bed. Hiding herself in a place where she couldn't be seen or heard and then putting her fate in Heaven's hands, she sunk into a stunned silence and awaited the appointed hour of her happiness, which she'd set as that of Croriano's death. As the instrument of that bloody sacrifice she'd taken with her a sharp knife, which because it was easy to use and compact seemed to her the most appropriate weapon. She'd also brought a completely darkened lantern in which a wax candle was burning. Her breathing

281

was so well controlled that she scarcely let out a breath. What won't an angry woman do? What heaps of difficulties won't she trample underfoot with her scheming? What enormous violence doesn't seem gentle and peaceful to her? (But no more, for there's so much one could say about this matter and it's better to leave well enough alone since words can't be found to express it fully.) At last the hour came. Croriano went to bed; being tired from the journey he fell asleep and surrendered himself to rest with no thought of death.

Ruperta was listening carefully to determine if Croriano showed any signs of being asleep, and she felt sure he was, both by the time elapsed since he went to bed and by his long drawn-out breaths, which only sleeping people take. Seeing this, without crossing herself or invoking any deity to help her, she opened the lantern, lighting up the room, and looked to see where she needed to step so she could get over to his bed without tripping.

Beautiful assassin; sweet, angry, and attractive executioner, act out your rage, satisfy your anger, erase and obliterate from the world the offense against you, for you have before you someone who'll make it possible! But remember if you will, beautiful Ruperta, not to look at this handsome Cupid you're going to uncover, or all your schemes will go up in smoke.

At last she got there and with trembling hand illuminated Croriano's face. She saw he was sleeping soundly, and found he had the same effect on her as Medusa's shield,[2] for he turned her to marble. She found him so handsome that she dropped the knife from her hand and had time to think about the enormity of what she was about to do. She saw that Croriano's good looks, just as the sun does to the fog, chased away the shadows of the death she was planning to inflict on him, and in an instant she chose him, not as the victim of a bloody sacrifice, but rather as a sacred burnt offering on the altar of her pleasure.

"Oh, noble youth," she said to herself, "how much better you'd be as my husband than as the object of my revenge! How can you be guilty of something your father did? What punishment do the guiltless deserve? Enjoy life, enjoy yourself, noble youth, and may my revenge stay in my heart and my violence be locked away, for when this becomes known, I'll gain a better reputation by having been compassionate than vengeful."

Saying this, and by now very upset and repentant, she dropped the lantern on Croriano's chest. He woke up when he felt the heat of the candle and found himself in the dark. Ruperta tried to get out of the room but couldn't. This led Croriano to shout out; then he took his sword and jumped out of bed, and while walking around the room bumped into Ruperta who, trembling all over, said to him, "Don't kill me, oh Croriano, for I'm a woman who less than an hour ago wanted to and could have taken your life, and now I find myself in the position of begging you not to take mine."

Hearing the noise, his servants came in at this point bringing lights, and Croriano saw and recognized the very beautiful widow as one sees the shining moon surrounded by white clouds. "What's this, Lady Ruperta?" he asked her. "Does the path that brought you in here lead to revenge? Can it be you want me to pay for the outrages committed against you by my father? And this knife I see here, what else can it mean except you've come to be my executioner? My father's already dead and the dead can't give satisfaction for the offences they've left behind. The living can indeed make compensation for them and so I, who now represent the person of my father, want to compensate you as best I can and know how for the offense he committed against you. But first let me modestly touch you, for I want to see whether you're a ghost come here to kill or trick me, or perhaps to improve my fortunes."

"May mine get worse," responded Ruperta, "—assuming Heaven can find any way to make my fortunes worse—if I came to this inn yesterday with any thought of you. You arrived here, too. I didn't see you when you came in but was told your name, which awakened my anger and moved me to revenge. I arranged for one of your servants to shut me into this room tonight, silencing him and sealing his lips with a bribe. I came in, got this knife ready, and fueled my desire to take your life. I heard you were asleep, came out from where I was hiding, and by the light of a lantern I'd brought with me looked at you and saw your face, which moved me to feel such respect and awe that the knife blade turned dull and my desire for revenge crumbled. When the candle fell from my hands the flame awakened you, you cried out, I was confused, and then what you've seen happened. I want no more revenge or memories of offenses. May you live in peace, for I want to be the first woman to give mercy in exchange for injury, if that's what pardoning you for guilt not yours can be called."

"My lady," replied Croriano, "my father wanted to marry you, but you refused. He killed your husband out of spite but then died, taking the affront with him to the next life. I've remained behind like a part of him and can now smoothe the path for his soul. If you want me to surrender mine to you, take me as your husband, if, as I've said, you aren't a ghost deceiving me—for great good fortune coming unexpectedly is always somewhat suspect." "Take me in your arms," responded Ruperta, "and you'll see, sir, that there's nothing ghostly about my body, and that the soul within it that I surrender to you is simple, pure, and true."

The witnesses to these embraces and these hands given in marriage were Croriano's servants, who'd come in with lights. That night gentle peace triumphed over cruel war, and the battlefield became a bridal bed. Peace was born from anger, life from death, and happiness from sorrow. Day dawned and found the newlyweds in each other's arms.

The pilgrims got up wondering what the grieving Ruperta had done about the arrival of her enemy's son, whose story was already well known to them. The rumor of the recent marriage got out, and like perfect ladies and gentlemen they went in to congratulate the bridal couple. As they were going into the suite they saw coming out of Ruperta's the old squire who'd told them her story. He was carrying the box containing her first husband's skull, along with the shirt and sword that so often had caused Ruperta's tears to flow, and he said he was taking it where it would never again bring to mind past misfortunes in the midst of present glories. He muttered something about Ruperta's easy virtue and that of women in general, and the least abusive thing he said was that they were fickle.

The bride and groom got up before the pilgrims came in, the servants rejoiced, Ruperta's as well as Croriano's, and the inn became like a royal palace worthy of such a distinguished match. Finally, Periandro and Auristela, Constanza and her brother Antonio, spoke to the newlyweds and told them something of their lives, at least the part that could be appropriately told at that time.

Chapter Eighteen of the Third Book

They were in the midst of this when in through the door of the inn came a man whose long white beard showed he was more than eighty years old. He was dressed neither as a pilgrim nor as a member of a religious order, even though he looked as though he could have been either one. His head was bare with a bald spot on top, while long pure-white hair hung down the sides. He leaned his bent body on the twisted shepherd's crook serving as his cane. In short, each and all of the parts together formed the very picture of a venerable old man worthy of every respect. No sooner had the mistress of the inn laid eyes on him when she knelt down before him and said, "I'll number this day, Father Soldino, among the most fortunate ones in my life, since today I've been worthy of having you visit my house, for you never come but what it doesn't do me some good." Then turning to those present she continued, "This snowy mountain, this white marble statue you see moving before you, ladies and gentlemen, is the famous Soldino, whose fame reaches not only throughout France, but to all regions on earth."

"Don't praise me, good woman," responded the old man, "for rarely does a good reputation come out of a bad lie. It's not the coming in but the going out that shows whether people are fortunate. When virtue has vice as its goal, it's not virtue at all but simply vice. But nevertheless, I want to try to live up to the good opinion you have of me. Mind your house well today, for this wedding and the merry feast being prepared here are going to start a fire that will consume almost all of it."

At this Croriano, speaking to his wife Ruperta, said, "This man must unquestionably be a mind reader or a fortune teller, for he's predicting the future." The old man overheard the words and responded, "I'm neither a mind reader nor a fortune teller, but a judicial astrologer, and that's a science, if one masters it, that practically teaches one to predict the future. Believe me, señores, at least this once; leave this place and come to mine, for in a nearby woods I'll give you safer lodging even though it may not be as spacious."

No sooner had he said this when in came Antonio's servant Bartolomé and shouted out, "Señores, the kitchens are on fire! Such a big fire has started in the huge pile of firewood stacked near them that it looks like all the water in the sea couldn't put it out!" His cries were urgently seconded by those of other servants, and the crackling of the fire itself began to show they were right. This obviously proved the truth of Soldino's words, so Periandro, putting his arms around Auristela without choosing to go see first whether or not the fire could be checked, said to Soldino, "Sir, lead us to your lodging, for the danger here is clear." Antonio did the same thing with his sister Constanza, and Feliz Flora with the French lady, whom Deleasir and Belarminia followed; the repentant girl from Talavera grasped Bartolomé's belt, while he in turn clung to the halter of his pack animal, and everyone together, along with the bridal couple and the mistress of the inn, who was familiar with Soldino's predictions, followed after him, even though he led them with very slow steps.

The other people at the inn who hadn't been present at Soldino's prediction, stayed there busily trying to put out the fire, but its furor soon made them realize their work would be in vain. The house burned the whole day, and had it surprised them at night it would have been a miracle for anyone to have escaped to tell of its violence.

They finally reached the forest where they found a small hermitage; inside it they saw a door apparently leading into a dark cave. Before going into the hermitage Soldino said to all those who'd followed him, "These trees with their peaceful shade will be golden roofs for you, and the grass in this exceedingly pleasant meadow will be your very soft—if not very white—bed sheets. I'll take the ladies and gentlemen with me to my cave, not in order to better their accommodations but because it's more appropriate. Then he called Periandro, Auristela, Constanza, and the three French ladies, Ruperta, Antonio, and Croriano, and leaving a lot of other people outside, shut himself into the cave with those named, closing behind him the doors to both the hermitage and the cave.

Bartolomé and the woman from Talavera, seeing they weren't among those chosen or called by Soldino, felt, either from spite or carried away by their weak natures, that they were just made for each other, and reached an agreement that Bartolomé would leave his masters and the girl her ideas of repentance. So they lightened the baggage by two pilgrims' habits and, the girl giving the slip to her compassionate ladies and the boy to his honored masters, she on horseback and he on foot, they, too, planned to go to Rome, as everyone else was.

It has been said before that things not very true to life or probable, even though they really happen, shouldn't be told in stories, because if they aren't believed they lose their value; a historian, on the other hand, ought to tell nothing but the truth, whether or not it seems really true. Keeping this principle in mind, then, the writer of this story says that Soldino, along with the whole band of ladies and gentlemen, went down the steps inside the dark cave, but within eighty steps the bright shining sky came into view and they could see some broad pleasant meadows that delighted their eyes and raised their spirits. Arranging those who'd come down with him in a circle, Soldino then said to them, "Señores, this is no magic spell. The cave through which we've come is just a shortcut to get from up there down to this valley, which as you can see has another easier, smoother, and less-obstructed entrance a league away from here. I built the hermitage with my own hands and constant effort, dug this cave, and made this valley mine; its water and its fruit abundantly sustain me. Here, fleeing from war I found peace. The hunger I felt in that world up there, if you can call it that, found satisfaction here. Here, instead of the princes and monarchs who rule in the world and whom I served, I've found these silent trees, and even though tall and magnificent they're still humble. Here, neither the contempt of emperors nor the annoyance of their ministers sounds in my ears. Here I have no lady rejecting me, no servant serving me badly. Here I'm lord of myself; here I have my spirit in the palm of my hand, and from here I send my thoughts and my wishes straight to Heaven.

"Here I've completed the study of mathematics and have contemplated the course of the stars and the movements of the sun and the moon. Here I've found reasons to be happy and reasons to be sad, reasons still in the future but so sure to happen, as I see it, that they're on a par with truth itself. Now, right now, as though it were in the present, I see a valiant youth from the royal house of Austria cutting off the head of a brave pirate.[1] Oh, if you could only see him as I do, dragging banners through the water, bathing their crescent moons[2] with contempt, ripping out their long hair, burning ships, dismembering bodies, and taking lives! But sad to tell, I'm grieved to see another crowned young man[3] stretched out on the dry sand, run through by a thousand Moorish lances. One of these men is the grandson and the other the son of that awesome lightning bolt of war, the never sufficiently praised Carlos V, whom I served for many years and would have served until the end of my life if it hadn't been prevented by a desire to exchange human armies for those of God.

"Here I am, without any books, grounding myself only in the experience I've acquired during the time I've been alone. I tell you, Croriano—and the fact that I know your name without ever having seen you before should vouch for me—you shall enjoy your Ruperta for many long years. And to you, Periandro, I give the assurance that your pilgrimage shall turn out well; your sister Auristela shall not be that for long—and not because she's soon going to lose her life. I can tell that you, Constanza, shall rise from countess to duchess, and your brother Antonio to the rank his valor merits. These French ladies, although they may not satisfy the wishes they have now, shall achieve others to honor and make them happy. My having predicted the fire, my knowing your names without ever having seen you before, the deaths I've described seeing before they've happened, all should convince you, if you're so inclined, that you can believe me. And you'll be even more persuaded when you find out it's true your boy Bartolomé, along with the pack animal and the girl from Castile, has gone off and left you on foot. Don't try to follow him for you won't overtake him; the girl belongs more to earth than to Heaven and wants to follow her natural bent in spite of and in the face of your advice.

"I'm a Spaniard and that obliges me to be courteous and true; out of good will I offer you all that these meadows offer me, and your experience with everything I've told you speaks for my truthfulness. If you should wonder about seeing a Spaniard in this distant land, remember there are places and towns in the world healthier than others, and the one where we are now is better than anywhere else for me. Catholic and devout people inhabit the farm houses, lodges, and villages in this area, and at the appropriate times I receive the sacraments and obtain whatever's necessary to sustain human life that's not provided by these fields. This is the life I lead and from which I expect to pass over to the one everlasting. And for the moment I've nothing more to say, except let's go back up. There we'll give nourishment to our bodies, just as down here we've given it to our souls."

Chapter Nineteen of the Third Book

The meal was prepared and though quite meager it was very clean and wholesome, nothing really new for the four pilgrims who remembered the Barbarous Isle, and the Hermits' Island, too, where Rutilio had stayed and where from straight off the trees they'd eaten fruit however they found it, sometimes ripe and sometimes not. They also remembered the false prophecy of the islanders and the many projections made by Mauricio, as well as the Moorish ones of the sacristan and most recently those of the Spaniard Soldino. It seemed to them they were surrounded by predictions and up to their souls in judicial astrology, something that, if it hadn't been verified by experience, would be difficult to believe in.

The brief meal ended, Soldino went out to the road to say goodbye to everyone, and there they found the Castilian girl and Bartolomé the baggage handler missing. Their disappearance worried the other four more than a little because they needed their money and the portable pantry. It was obvious Antonio was very worried and wanted to go on ahead to look for the boy, since he supposed either the girl was carrying him off or he her, or to be more precise, that they'd run off together. But Soldino told him not to let it bother him and not to lift a finger to look for them, because the next day their servant would return, sorry for the theft, and give back everything he'd taken. They believed this, and so Antonio didn't try to look for him, especially since Feliz Flora offered to lend him whatever he and his companions might need to make their trip pleasant from there to Rome. Antonio expressed as much gratitude as he possibly could for her generous offer, in turn even offering to give her some collateral that would fit in her fist but whose value exceeded fifty thousand ducados. (He said this planning to give her one of Auristela's two pearls, which she always carried hidden with her along with the diamond cross.) Feliz Flora couldn't bring herself to believe the figure set on the value of the pledge but didn't hesitate to renew the offer she'd made.

While this was going on they saw coming down the road and moving past them perhaps as many as eight people on horseback, and among them riding on a mule was a woman seated on an expensive saddle. She was dressed for the road and all in green, even to her hat, whose elegant and varied feathers fluttered in the air, and a mask,[1] also green, covered her face. The riders didn't say a word but greeted them by nodding their heads as they passed by and went on; those on foot didn't say anything either, greeting them in the same manner. However, one man from the group of riders stayed behind and, coming up to them, asked for the courtesy of a little water. They gave it to him and inquired who the people were who'd gone on ahead and who the lady in green was.

To this the traveler replied: "The man up front is Sir Alejandro Castrucho, a gentleman from Capua, and one of the richest men, not only in Capua, but in the whole kingdom of Naples. The lady is his niece, the lady Isabel Castrucho, born in Spain, where she's left her father buried; as a result of his death her uncle is taking her to be married in Capua, but I don't think she's very happy about it."

"That's probably not because she's going there to get married," commented Ruperta's squire in mourning, "but because it's a long trip; the way I see it, there isn't any woman who doesn't want to couple up with her missing half—her husband." "I'm not familiar with that philosophy," responded the traveler. "I only know she's sad and only she knows why. Now, God be with you, since my masters are getting 'way ahead of me." Then he spurred quickly on out of their sight.

Then they said goodbye to Soldino, embraced him, and left him behind . . . but I forgot to tell how Soldino had advised the French ladies that it would be better for them to take the road straight to Rome and not detour to Paris. They took this advice as if it had been spoken by an oracle and, since the pilgrims concurred, they decided to leave France through Dauphiné, then cross the states of Piedmont and Milan to see Florence, and finally go on to Rome. Ready to give this route a try, then, and planning to extend somewhat the length of each day's journeys they'd been covering up to that point, the next morning at the crack of dawn they saw coming toward them the person they'd taken for a thief—Bartolomé the baggage handler—following his pack animal and dressed like a pilgrim.

They all shouted when they recognized him and most of them asked why he'd fled, why he was wearing those clothes, and why he'd come back. At this, kneeling down in front of Constanza and almost crying, he replied to them all, "I don't know why I ran away. My clothes, as you can see, are a pilgrim's. My coming back has been to return what perhaps—and even with no 'perhaps' to it—has confirmed in your minds that I'm a thief. Lady Constanza, here's the pack animal with everything that was on it except for two pilgrims' habits, one of which is the one I'm wearing while the other is still making a pilgrim out of the whore from Talavera. To hell with love and with the devil who got me into this! And the worst of it is that I know him for who he is but have decided nonetheless to be a soldier marching under his flag! I just don't have enough strength to resist the pressures pleasure puts on ignorant people. Give me your blessing, Your Grace, and let me go back, for Luisa is waiting for me—but you should know I'm going back to her without a blanca[2] to my name, trusting more in my girl's charms than in the nimbleness of my fingers; they were never thieves and never will be, if God keeps me in my right mind—not even if I lived a thousand centuries."

Periandro used many arguments to try to convince him not to carry out his terrible plan. Auristela also offered him several, and Constanza and Antonio many more, but it was all, as they say, like shouting in the wind and preaching in the desert. Bartolomé dried his tears, left his pack animal, turned his back, and went off like a shot, leaving everyone amazed at his love and his simplemindedness.

Seeing him go racing away, Antonio put an arrow to his bow (with which he never missed his mark) intending to send it right through him and so remove the love and madness from his heart. But Feliz Flora, who rarely left his side, took hold of the bow and said to him: "Let him go, Antonio; his luck is already bad enough since

he's going to be in the power and under the yoke of a crazy woman."
"You're right, my lady," Antonio responded, "and with you giving
him life, who'd have the nerve to try and take it away from him?"

After that they walked for many days without anything happening to them worth telling. They entered Milan, were struck by
the city's greatness, its countless wealth, its golds—for there's not
only gold there, but great amounts of it. They were also amazed by
its forges of war—making it seem that Vulcan himself has installed
his own there[3]—the endless abundance of its fruits, the grandeur of
its churches, and finally, the clever genius of its inhabitants.

They heard one of their hosts say that the best thing to see in
that city was the Academy of the Elite,[4] adorned by the most emi-
nent academicians, whose subtle minds kept fame busy day and night
all over the world. He also said the academy was in season that day
and there was going to be a debate on whether or not love can exist without jealousy. "It most certainly can," said Periandro; "and it
wouldn't take long to prove the truth of that."

"I don't know what love is," countered Auristela, "but I do
know what liking is." To this Belarminia responded, "I don't understand this way of talking, or the difference between loving and liking
something or someone." "It's this," replied Auristela. "You can like
something or someone without there being an intense influence on
your will. Therefore, you can like a servant who serves you well or
a statue or painting that looks good to you and delights you; these
things don't cause jealousy, nor can they. But the thing they call love
is an intense passion in the soul, people say, and even if it doesn't
cause jealousy it can produce fears strong enough to take a person's
life. And it seems to me love can never ever be free from such fears."

"You've said a lot, my lady," responded Periandro. "There's no
one in love who, possessing what he loves, isn't afraid of losing it.
There's no good fortune so solid it can't sway from side to side.
There's no nail so strong it can stop the spin of the wheel of fortune.
And if the desire that moves us to come quickly to the end of our
journey didn't prevent it, perhaps today in the Academy I'd show
there can be love without jealousy, but not without fears."

The conversation came to an end. They spent four days in
Milan and only began to see its marvels because four years wouldn't
be enough time to see them all. They left there and came to Lucca,
a small but pretty city. Proud and free, it stands tall in the shadow
of the imperial eagle and of Spain, and from its position of freedom
observes the cities controlled by princes that would like to control it,
too.[5] There, more than anywhere else, are Spaniards welcomed and

accepted, for they don't issue commands there, rather make requests, and since they don't stay over for more than one day, they don't have a chance to reveal their character, which is generally considered arrogant. Here our travelers experienced one of the strangest adventures of all those related during the course of this entire book.

Chapter Twenty of the Third Book

The inns at Lucca are large enough to lodge whole companies of soldiers and our band took rooms in one of them, having been shown the way there by guards posted at the city gates who handed them over to the innkeeper on account. ("On account" because the next morning, or whenever the travelers might leave, he'd have to pay the guards for showing them to his inn.) As she was going in the lady Ruperta saw a doctor leaving—at least judging by his clothes she took him for one. He was saying to the mistress of the inn—whose identity she also guessed by her looks—"I, mistress, can't quite make up my mind whether this young woman is mad or possessed by an evil spirit, so to avoid any mistake I'm going to say she's both possessed by an evil spirit and mad as well; nevertheless I'm optimistic regarding her recovery, providing her uncle isn't in a hurry to leave."

"Oh, my goodness!" said Ruperta. "Now we're going to stop at a house where there are mad people possessed by spirits? Really and truly, if you take my advice, we won't set foot inside!" To this the mistress of the inn replied, "You can stop here with no qualms, your ladyship" (this is the flattering term they use in Italy), "because people would come from a hundred leagues 'round about to see what's at this inn." They all dismounted and Auristela and Constanza, who had heard the mistress' words, asked her what there was in the inn so worth seeing. "Come with me," responded the mistress of the inn, "and you'll see what you'll see; then you'll say, too, what I'm saying."

She led them in and they followed her to a place where they saw a very beautiful girl who seemed to be about sixteen or seventeen years old stretched out on a gilded bed. Her arms were fully extended and tied with some bandages to the rungs of the bedstead, apparently to prevent her from moving them at all. Two women who must have been acting as her nurses were trying to get hold of her legs to tie them down, also, and this led the sick girl to say, "It's enough to tie my hands; everything else is securely bound by my modesty."

Then turning to the pilgrim women she raised her voice and said, "Images from Heaven! Flesh and blood angels! I firmly believe you've come to restore my health because such beautiful looks and such a Christian visit can't mean anything else. As great and good ladies please order them to untie me, and after four or five mouthfuls that I'll take out of my arm, I'll be satisfied and won't do myself any more harm—but truly I'm not as crazy as I seem, nor is the one tormenting me so cruel that he'll allow me to bite myself."

"My poor little niece," said an old man who'd come into the room, "how you're suffering at the hands of the one you say won't let you bite yourself! Put yourself in God's hands, Isabela, and try to eat, but not your beautiful flesh, rather whatever this uncle of yours may provide, for he's truly fond of you. Anything the air produces, the waters sustain, or the earth nourishes, I'll bring to you; your great wealth and my heartfelt wishes offer you it all."

The suffering girl replied, "Leave me alone with these angels; perhaps my enemy the devil will flee from me so he won't have to be near them." By nods of her head she indicated that Auristela, Constanza, Ruperta, and Feliz Flora should stay with her, then said the others should go out, and they did so because her old and suffering uncle wanted it and begged them to. He informed them she was the noble lady in green they'd seen go by on the road as they were leaving the wise Spaniard's cave—the lady the servant who stayed behind had told them was called Isabela Castrucha[1] and who was going to the kingdom of Naples to be married.

The sick woman no sooner saw she was alone with them than she looked all around and said they should search to see if there was anyone else in the room besides those she'd said should stay. Ruperta looked everywhere, inspected everything, and made sure there was no one there except them. With this reassurance Isabela sat up in bed as best she could and showing signs of very much wanting to talk about something, heaved such a great sigh that it seemed as though her soul were being ripped out of her. The end result was that she lay back down on the bed and fainted, looking so much as though she were dying that those with her had to call out for a little water to bathe her face, as she seemed to be rapidly heading for the next world.

In came the miserable uncle carrying a cross in one hand and an aspergill with holy water in the other. Along with him came two priests who believed it was the devil harassing her and so were rarely far away. The mistress of the inn came in, too, bringing the water. They sprinkled her face and she came to, saying, "All these measures are useless for the time being. I'll come out soon, but it won't be whenever all of you may wish, rather when I'm good and ready, and that'll be when Andrea Marulo, the son of Juan Bautista Marulo, a gentleman of this city, shows up. Right now he's studying in Salamanca and unaware of these developments."

All these ideas strengthened the conviction held by her listeners that Isabela must be possessed by an evil spirit, because they couldn't imagine how she could know who Juan Bautista Marulo might be, much less his son Andrea. Of course someone immediately went to tell Juan Bautista Marulo what the possessed beauty had said about him and his son. Once again she requested to be left alone with the people she'd chosen earlier. The priests quoted the Gospels to her then did as she wished, all thinking about the sign she'd said would signal the devil's departure from her, and there was no doubt in their minds that she was possessed.

Feliz Flora once again searched the room and closing its door said to the sick girl, "We're all alone; now, my lady, what is it you want?" "What I want," replied Isabela, "is for you to take off my fetters, for even though they're soft they're tiring me out by keeping me from moving."

They took them off with all due haste and then Isabela sat up in bed, took hold of Auristela by one hand and Ruperta by the other, and had Constanza and Feliz Flora sit down next to her right there on the bed. And so, with all of them crowded together in a beautiful heap, with tears in her eyes she said softly, "I, my ladies, am the unfortunate Isabela Castrucha. My parents gave me breeding, my good fortune wealth, and Heaven a little beauty. My parents were natives of Capua, but they conceived me in Spain, where I was born and then raised in the home of my uncle, who's here now but previously lived at the emperor's court. (Oh, for goodness' sake! . . . why am I going so far back up the current of my misfortunes?) While I was living in my uncle's house, then, having been left an orphan by my parents (who'd left me in his charge and under his tutelage), a young man came to court. I first saw him in church, and looked at him so hard . . . you shouldn't think that immodest, ladies, and you won't if you remember I'm a grown woman . . . but as I was saying . . . I looked at him in church so hard I couldn't stop seeing him when I was at home, for his looks made such an impression on my mind that I couldn't get him out of it.

"Eventually I found ways to learn who he was, his place in society, what he was doing at court, and where he was going. The facts I came up with were that his name was Andrea Marulo, he was the son of Juan Bautista Marulo, a gentleman from this city more noble than wealthy, and that he was on his way to study at Salamanca. In the six days he was there I arranged to write him telling who I was and all about the large amount of property I had, adding that he could verify my beauty for himself by observing me in church. I also informed him in writing that I was aware my uncle wanted to marry me to one of my cousins in order to keep the estate in the family, and that the cousin was a man not at all to my liking and completely unsuited to me—no doubt about that! I also told him opportunity was knocking; by taking me he'd open the door to it, and so shouldn't let second thoughts stand in his way but should still value me even though I was easy to get.

"He replied, having seen me in church I don't know how many times, that simply for myself alone, without the adornments of nobility and wealth, he'd make me the ruler of the world if he could. Then he begged me to remain firm for a while in my resolve to love him, at least until he'd left a friend in Salamanca with whom he'd set out from this city to become a student. I replied I would, as my love was not impatiently insistent, nor an indiscreet one quickly born and soon dead. He left me then because he was honorable and wouldn't let his friend down. He went down my street the day he left with tears of a man in love in his eyes—tears I myself saw him shed—and so I knew that in his heart he didn't leave me behind, but that I went with him without ever leaving home.

"The next day . . . who could believe it? . . . what roundabout ways misfortune has to sooner overtake the misfortunate! . . . the next day, as I was saying, my uncle arranged for us to return to Italy, and I wasn't able to find any excuses or successfully pretend to be ill; since my pulse and color showed me to be healthy my uncle refused to believe I was ill, concluding I was unhappy about the marriage and looking for a pretext not to leave. I did have time to write to Andrea about what had happened to me, telling him I was compelled to leave but would try to go through this city, where I was planning to pretend to be possessed by evil spirits, using that scheme to give him time to leave Salamanca and come to Lucca where in spite of my uncle—or even the whole world—he'd become my husband. So my happiness as well as his own was in his hands, and it was up to him to show his gratitude. If the letters were delivered directly into his hands—as they must have been, because the carriers guarantee their

295

delivery—he should be here within three days. For my part, I've done all I can. I've put a legion of demons in my body and that's the same as adding an ounce of love to my soul—at least it's enough for hope to flirt with from a distance.

"This, ladies, is my story, this my madness, this my disease. Thoughts of love are the demons that torment me. I suffer hunger but only because I'm expecting complete satisfaction. Anxiety pursues me despite this hope, for as they say in Castile, 'Even the crumbs a poor man has slip through his fingers.' Find a way, ladies, to lend credibility to my lie and strengthen my arguments, convincing my uncle that since I'm not getting well, he shouldn't put me back on the road for several days. Perhaps Heaven will allow the day of my happiness to come with Andrea's arrival."

There's no need to ask whether or not the listeners were astonished by Isabela's story, for stories are designed to be astonishing and to bring amazement to their listeners' minds. Ruperta, Auristela, Constanza, and Feliz Flora offered to lend support to her plans and not to leave there until they saw how they turned out, something that clearly wouldn't take long.

Chapter Twenty-One of the Third Book

The beautiful Isabela Castrucha was in a hurry to reactivate her devil, and the four women, now her friends, hurried to corroborate her illness, affirming with all the arguments they could think of that it really was the devil speaking through her body. So we see what love is; it makes those in love seem possessed by demons.

While this was going on, and by now it must have been almost twilight, the doctor came back to make a second call. He happened to bring with him Juan Bautista Marulo, the father of the love-stricken Andrea. On entering the sick woman's bedroom the doctor said, "Just look at the pitiful state this girl is in, Sir Juan Bautista Marulo, and see whether she deserves to have the devil romping around in her angel's body. But one hope comforts us; it's told us it will soon leave her, and the sign of its departure will be the arrival of Sir Andrea, your son, whom it expects momentarily." "So they've told me," responded Sir Juan Bautista, "and I'd be most pleased if something related to me could be what brings such good tidings."

"Thanks to God and to my efforts it will be," said Isabela, "for if it weren't for me, right now he'd be stuck in Salamanca doing God knows what. Sir Juan Bautista here should believe me when I say he has a son who's more handsome than holy, and less a student than a playboy. A curse on young men's fancy clothes and their slick grooming that do so much harm in the nation! And a curse also on spurs without rowels, and ones that should be sharp and aren't, and on rented mules that don't go any faster than the mail!"

To this string of ideas she added other ambiguous ones, that is, ideas that could be taken two ways, one by the ladies who were her confidantes and the other by the rest of the listeners. The ladies interpreted them in their true sense, while the others thought they were confused nonsense.

"My lady, where did you see my son Andrea?" said Marulo. "Was it in Madrid or in Salamanca?" "It was in Illescas, no less," said Isabela, "when he was picking cherries on Midsummer's morning just as the sun came up.[1] But to tell the truth, even though it's a miracle for me to tell it, I see him constantly and always have him in my soul." "Well, at least," countered Marulo, "my son was picking cherries and not picking lice and fleas off himself, which is what students usually do."

"Gentlemen students," retorted Isabela, "imagining they're immune, rarely delouse themselves, but they scratch a lot, for those little bugs so common throughout the world are so daring they get into princes' pants as well as poorhouse blankets." "You know everything, evil one," said the doctor, "it's obvious you've been around a long time." This last remark was directed to the devil he thought Isabela had in her body.

While this was happening, seemingly orchestrated by Satan himself, Isabela's uncle came in looking extremely happy and saying, "Good news, my dear niece; good news, daughter of my soul. Sir Andrea Marulo, son of Sir Juan Bautista here, has just arrived! Oh, my sweet hope, now fulfill ours of seeing you free as soon as you see him! You, damn devil, *vade retro, exi foras,*[2] and don't even think of ever coming back to this house, no matter how well-swept and clean you may find it!"[3]

"Then come, come to me!" exclaimed Isabela, "You duplicate Ganymede, you likeness of Adonis, now free, healthy, and with no mental reservations, give me your hand in marriage. I've been here waiting for you, more solid than a rock set amidst the waves of the sea, struck, but not moved."

In off the road came Andrea Marulo, having been told in his father's house about the foreigner Isabela's illness, and how she was waiting for him to be the signal of the devil's departure. The young man, who was clever and had been forewarned by the letters Isabela had sent to him in Salamanca about what he must do if he caught up with her in Lucca, had hurried over to Isabela's inn without even removing his spurs and now entered her room acting confused and crazed, shouting, "Out, out, out! Leave, leave, leave! Here comes the brave Andrea, best platoon leader in all Hell, as if more than one squad would be necessary to take care of this business!" In all the uproar and shouting even the ones who knew the truth of the matter were almost at a loss, and the ruse was so effective the doctor and even his own father said, "He's just as much of a devil as the one in Isabela!"

Then her uncle commented, "We were waiting for this youth to come and help us, but I think he's come to do us harm instead." "Calm down, son, calm down," said his father, "you're acting crazy!" "And why wouldn't he be," said Isabela, "seeing me? Don't I just happen to be the center point at which all his thoughts come to rest? Am I not the target at which all his desires are aimed?"

"That's right," said Andrea; "you're very much the mistress of my will, the resting place after my trials, and the life that saves me from death. Give me your hand as my promised wife, my lady, and take me out of this slavery in which I find myself into the freedom of being under your yoke. I repeat, give me your hand, my love, and raise me from the humility of being Andrea Marulo to the heights of being the husband of Isabela Castrucho. Let any devils who might want to prevent the tying of such a delicious knot get out of here and may no man try to put asunder what God is joining together." "Well said, Sir Andrea," responded Isabela, "and freed from ruses, schemes, and frauds, give me your hand as my husband and take me as your wife."

Then as Andrea held out his hand Auristela raised her voice and said, "It's right for him to give it to her, for now they are one." Shocked and stunned, Isabela's uncle also stretched out his hand, and grabbing hold of Andrea's, asked, "What's going on, ladies and gentlemen? Is it the custom of this country for one devil to marry another?"

"Of course not," replied the doctor, "this must all be a trick to get the devil to go away; it's not possible that what's going on here could have been deliberately planned by a human mind." "Nevertheless," said Isabela's uncle, "I want to hear directly from both their mouths how we should classify this marriage—as authentic or as a trick."

"It's the real thing," responded Isabela, "because neither is Andrea Marulo crazy nor am I possessed by a devil. I love him and choose him for my husband, providing he loves me and chooses me for his wife." "I'm neither crazy nor possessed by a devil, but of the sound mind God has been pleased to give me," said Andrea taking Isabela's hand and she his, and after their two "I do's" they were unquestionably married.

"What *is* this?" exclaimed Castrucho. "Again? God help me! How could you so dishonor an old man's white hairs?" "Nothing relating to me can dishonor you," said Andrea's father. "I'm noble, and if not terribly wealthy, at least not so poor I need depend on anyone. I didn't have a thing to do with this business; these young people have gotten married without my knowledge. In matters of the heart lovers' wisdom exceeds their years and, while in most things young people miss the mark in what they do, at certain other times they're right on target; when they are, even though it's by sheer chance, things often come out much better than if they'd been thought through. But nevertheless, check to see if what's happened here is permanently valid for if it can be annulled, I won't use Isabela's wealth to improve my son's position." Two priests who were present said the marriage was valid. Even though they had begun it with them thinking like crazy people, they had later affirmed it when they were clearly of sound mind. "And we reaffirm it," added Andrea. And Isabela said the same.

Her uncle was utterly dismayed on hearing this. His head fell forward onto his chest and, heaving a deep sigh, with his eyes rolled back into his head, he suffered what seemed to be a fatal attack. His servants carried him to bed, Isabela got up from hers, and Andrea took her to his father's house as his wife. Two days later his family went in the church door to baptize Andrea Marulo's baby brother and to bury the body of Isabela's uncle, while she and Andrea went in to get married. Here you see how strange life's moments are—at the same time some people can be baptized, others married, and still others buried.

So, Isabela dressed in mourning for her wedding, since this thing called death mixes bridal beds with graves and gala finery with tokens of grief. Our pilgrims and our band of travelers stayed in Lucca four days more, where they were entertained by the newly-weds and the noble Juan Bautista Marulo.

Here our author brought the third book of this true story to an end.

The Fourth Book of
The Trials of Persiles and Sigismunda
A Northern Story

The First Chapter of the Fourth Book

Not once but many times our pilgrim band argued whether Isabela Castrucha's wedding, made possible by so many tricks, could be valid. Periandro kept on insisting it was, and that more importantly it wasn't up to them to pass judgment on the case. But what bothered him was the lumping together of the baptism, the wedding, and the burial, plus the ignorance of the doctor who hadn't properly diagnosed Isabela's strategy or the danger to her uncle. At times they discussed this and at others they talked about the dangers they'd been through.

With great interest Croriano and his wife Ruperta kept inquiring who Periandro and Auristela, Constanza and Antonio might be, questions they weren't asking about the three French ladies, for from the first time they saw them they'd known exactly who they were. Engaged in these conversations and traveling farther than usual each day, they arrived at Acuapendente, a village near Rome. As they approached the town gate Periandro and Auristela went on a little ahead of the others so they wouldn't have to be afraid someone might eavesdrop or overhear; then Periandro spoke to Auristela as follows.

"You'll well aware, dear lady, that the causes leading us to leave our homeland and give up our comfortable life were as morally correct as they were necessary. Now the breezes of Rome are blowing in our faces, now the hopes that have sustained us are stirring in our hearts, and right now I'm already imagining myself in sweet possession of what I've longed for. Ask yourself, my lady, whether you wouldn't do well to reconsider your thoughts and scrutinize your intentions to see if you're as firm in them now as in the beginning, and if you'll remain so after having carried out your vow. I have no doubt you will . . . your noble blood wasn't bred among lying promises or deceitful schemes. As for myself, my beautiful Sigismunda, I can tell you that this Periandro you see here is the Persiles you saw in the house of my father the king—that same one, I repeat, who while in his father's palaces gave you his word to be your husband, and who'll keep it even in the deserts of Libya, should adverse fortune take us there."

Auristela was looking at him very intently, amazed that Periandro should question her loyalty, and so she said to him, "I've been steadfast in my resolve during my whole life, my dear Persiles, and I surrendered it to you almost two years ago not because I was forced to do so, but of my own free will. It's just as unchanged and strong right now as the first day I made you its lord. And if it's possible, my resolve has actually increased and grown amidst the many trials we've gone through together. Just as soon as I've completed my vow I'll show just how grateful I am to you for keeping your word, and make your hopes of possessing me a reality. But tell me, what'll we do after we're both tied by the same halter and both our necks are under the same yoke? We're far from our own lands, known by no one in these foreign ones, with no support to which we can cling like ivy amidst our hardships. I'm not saying this for lack of courage to suffer all the hardships in the world—provided I'm with you—rather I'm saying it because seeing you in dire need will end my life, too. Until now, or at least until a little while ago, my soul suffered for itself alone, but from this point forward I'll suffer both for its pains and yours—although I've been wrong to speak of our two souls as separate, for they're really only one."

"Look, my lady," replied Periandro, "just as it isn't possible for anyone to devise his own fortune (even though some people say everyone is the author of his own from beginning to end), I'm unable to answer you now about what we'll do after good fortune has brought us together. But for the present let the barrier separating us be broken down, for after we're wed, there'll be fields on earth to sustain us, huts to take us in, and [caves] to shelter us.[1] There's no happiness to match the pleasure shared by two souls made one, nor could golden roofs provide us better shelter. We'll find a way to let my mother the queen know where we are and she'll find some means of helping us. In the meantime, the diamond cross and those priceless pearls you have with you will be a start toward helping us out; the only thing that worries me is if we part with them our disguise will fall apart at the same time, for how's anyone going to believe jewels of such value would be hidden under the cloak of a simple pilgrim?"

At this point the rest of the company was catching up to them so he ended the conversation, the first in which they'd spoken of things close to their hearts, for Auristela's great modesty never gave

302

Periandro the chance to speak to her in private, and by means of this remarkable ruse and security measure they'd passed as brother and sister with everyone who'd met them thus far. Only the late Clodio was so heartless and malicious that he'd suspected the truth. That night they came to within a day's journey of Rome, and at an inn—wondrous things were always happening to them at inns— the following happened to them, and you may or may not call it wondrous.

While they were all seated at a table that the innkeeper's desire to please and his servants' diligence kept abundantly supplied, out from one of the inn's rooms came an attractive pilgrim with some writing cases over his left arm and a notebook in his hand. After greeting everyone with all due courtesy, he said in Spanish, "This pilgrim's habit I'm wearing, which puts its wearer under the obligation to beg alms, obliges me to ask you for some, but ones so remarkable and unusual that without giving me any jewels whatsoever or any equivalent treasures you'll unquestionably make me rich. I, señores, am a strange man. Mars is the predominant influence over half my soul while Mercury and Apollo rule over the other half. For some years I was dedicated to the practice of war, and now for others, the more mature ones, I've been a man of letters. In the war years I earned something of a good reputation, while in my years as a writer I've been more or less respected. I've published some books that weren't condemned by the ignorant as bad and didn't fail to win the approval of the wise."

"Now since necessity, as they say, is the mother of invention, my inventive mind, which has a certain indefinable whimsical creativeness to it, has come up with a somewhat unusual and novel idea, which is to bring out a book at someone else's expense, with the work involved (as I've said) being someone else's while the profits will be mine. The book shall be called *The Flower of Unusual Aphorisms,*[2] which means it will contain maxims quoted from reality itself in the following manner. Whenever I run into anyone on the road or anywhere else who seems by my observation to be a person of intellect and talent, I ask him to write some clever saying for me in this notebook, if he knows one, or if not, some maxim that seems like one. In this way I've collected more than three hundred aphorisms, all of which deserve to be made known and printed, and not under my name but under that of their authors themselves, who after having said them have signed their names for me. These are the alms I ask for and the ones I'll value above all the gold in the world."

"Give us an example, Sir Spaniard," replied Periandro, "of what you're asking for so we can model ours on it, and as for complying with your request, our wits will do everything they possibly can for you." "This morning," responded the Spaniard, "a man and a woman, pilgrims from Spain, arrived here but then traveled on. Since they were Spaniards I told them what I'd like. Because she didn't know how to write, the woman told me to put the following idea down in my own hand: 'I'd rather be bad with some hope of becoming good, than good hoping to get to be bad.' And she told me to sign, 'The pilgrim woman from Talavera.' The male pilgrim didn't know how to write either, and told me to put down, 'There's no burden harder to bear than an easy woman.' And I signed for him, 'Bartolomé of La Mancha.' This is the kind of aphorism I'm asking for, and the ones I expect from this handsome group will certainly make the others look better still, for they'll surely adorn and embellish them even further."

"We get the idea," replied Croriano; "and for my part" (taking the pen and the notebook from the pilgrim) "I want to satisfy this obligation immediately, and so I'll write: 'A dead soldier on the battlefield looks better than a healthy one running away.'" And he signed, "Croriano." Then Periandro took the pen and wrote, "Happy is the soldier who knows his prince is watching him while he's in combat." Then he signed. He was followed by Antonio the barbarian who wrote, "Honor achieved through war, since it's engraved by steel points on bronze tablets, is more lasting than other honors." And he signed, "Antonio the Barbarian."

Then since there were no other men present, the pilgrim also asked the ladies to write, and the first who did was Ruperta, who said, "Beauty, when accompanied by purity, is true beauty, but when it's not it's merely good looks." And she signed. Auristela came second and wrote, "The best dowry a noble woman can have is her purity, for beauty and wealth are consumed by time or destroyed by ill fortune." And she signed. She was followed by Constanza, who wrote: "A woman shall not choose her husband by herself alone, but with the advice of others." Then she signed. Feliz Flora also wrote, saying, "Laws that enforce obedience are compelling, but much more so is the strength of one's own likes and dislikes." Then she signed.

Following her, Belarminia said, "A woman should be like the ermine,[3] which prefers to let itself be caught rather than get muddy." And she signed. The last to write was the beautiful Deleasir, who said, "Good or bad luck rules over all that happens in this life, but especially over marriage."

This was what our ladies and pilgrims wrote, leaving the Spaniard grateful and happy, and when Periandro asked him whether he knew by heart any of the other aphorisms he'd written down, and if so, if he'd tell them some, he replied he'd repeat only one, which he'd thoroughly enjoyed due to the signature of the man who'd written it. It said, "Don't desire anything and you'll be the richest man in the world." The signature read, "Diego de Ratos, hunchback, shoemaker of old at Tordesillas, a town in Old Castile near Valladolid."[4] "Good God!" exclaimed Antonio. "That surely is a long drawn-out signature, while the aphorism is the shortest and most condensed one imaginable! It's obvious that one always wants what he lacks and he who doesn't want doesn't lack for anything—so he must be the richest man in the world!"

The Spanish pilgrim repeated some other aphorisms that flavored their conversation and their dinner; he sat down with them and during the dinner conversation said, "I won't give the rights to this book of mine to any publisher in Madrid, even if he gives me two thousand ducados for it. There's not one of them who doesn't want the rights for nothing, or at least at such a small price there's nothing in it for the author of the book. While it's true that many times they buy the rights and print a book thinking they'll get rich but then lose their time and money, still, this book of aphorisms of mine has the promise of excellence and profits written all over it.

The Second Chapter of the Fourth Book

The Spanish pilgrim's book could just as well have been called "A Strange Story Taken from Several Authors," for that would have been the truth, considering who'd been writing it. They had a good laugh over the signature of Diego de Ratos, "the shoemaker of old," and there was food for thought in the saying of Bartolomé of La Mancha, who had said "there's no burden harder to bear than an easy woman"—a sign that the burden of the girl from Talavera already must have been weighing heavy on him.

They continued talking about this the next day when they took leave of the Spaniard—a modern and innovative author of novel and delightful books—and that same day they caught sight of Rome, which cheered their spirits, bringing a happiness that overflowed into glowing physical vigor and health. Periandro and Auristela were exhilarated to find themselves so close to the fulfillment of their hearts' desire. Croriano, Ruperta, and the three French ladies, too, were in the same state of happy excitement thinking of the good things that would come with the happy ending of their journey, and Constanza and Antonio also shared their glad feelings.

The noonday sun was beating down on them from the zenith, a circumstance that causes it to beat down then with a more intense heat, even though it's farther from the earth than at any other time of day. Attracted by a nearby woods that could be seen off to their right, they decided to spend there the heat of the siesta hours—which promised to be severe—and perhaps even the night, too, since there would be more than enough time to enter Rome the next day.

That's exactly what they did, and the farther they went into the woods the more they were convinced they were right to plan to spend the night there, so pleasant was the grassy place, with springs bubbling up and brooks running through it. They went in so far that when they turned around they saw they were now hidden from people passing by on the king's highway. And as the variety of good and pleasant spots was making them think first one and then another would be best, by chance Auristela looked up and saw a portrait hanging from a branch of a green willow. The picture was about the size of a sheet of paper but was painted instead on a board and showed the face of a most beautiful woman. Looking at it a little more closely she saw that the portrait was of her own face and, astonished and perplexed, she showed it to Periandro. At that exact same moment Croriano reported that the grass was bleeding, and in fact showed them his feet all covered with warm blood.

The portrait, which Periandro immediately took down, and the blood Croriano pointed out, had them all confused and trying to find out to whom the portrait and the blood belonged. Auristela couldn't think by whom, where, or when her face could have been sketched, nor did Periandro recollect that the servant of the Duke of Nemurs had told him the painter sketching the three French ladies would also do a portrait of Auristela by memory. Had he remembered this Periandro would have easily understood what he just couldn't grasp at the time.

Croriano and Antonio followed the trail of blood into a dense stand of trees nearby, where at the foot of one of them they saw a handsome pilgrim seated on the ground. His hands were folded close to his heart and he was completely covered with blood. The sight shocked them very much, and even more so when Croriano went up to him and raised his face—which had fallen down on his chest and was also covered with blood—and cleaned it with a linen cloth, for he recognized that without any doubt the wounded man was the Duke of Nemurs. Their friendship was so close that even the strange clothes he was wearing weren't enough to keep Croriano from recognizing him.

Without opening his eyes, which were sealed shut with dried blood, the wounded duke—or at least the man who seemed to be the duke—slurring his words managed to say, "Whoever you may be, you'd have done well, mortal enemy of my rest, if you'd raised your hand a little higher and struck me in the center of my heart, for there you'll unquestionably find a more vivid and true portrait than the one you made me take from my shirt and hang on the tree so it shouldn't help me as a sacred relic and shield during our combat." Constanza was present at this discovery and being naturally kind-hearted and compassionate, she hurried over, not to listen more closely to his painful words but to examine his wound and stop the bleeding.

Something similar was happening to Periandro and Auristela. That same blood led them on farther to look for its source, and among some tall green reeds they found another pilgrim stretched out. He was almost completely covered with blood except for his face, which was bare and clean. So, without having to clean it or take other steps to discover who he was, they recognized him as Prince Arnaldo, who was more stunned than dead. The first sign of life he gave was an attempt to get up, saying, "You won't take it away, traitor, because the portrait is mine, part of my soul! You've stolen it, and though I haven't offended you in any way you want to take my life!"

Auristela was trembling at the unexpected sight of Arnaldo, and although her obligations to him urged her to go over to him, she was restrained by the presence of Periandro. He, just as courteous as he was indebted to the prince, took his hands and, in a voice soft enough not to reveal to others something the prince might want to keep secret, said to him, "Come to, Sir Arnaldo, and you'll see you're in the care of your best friends, and that Heaven hasn't so abandoned you that you can't hope to see your luck improve. Open your eyes, I say again, and you'll see your friend Periandro and your dutiful Auristela, just as eager to serve you as ever. Tell us about your misfortune and all that's happened to you, and you can count on us for everything our efforts and strength can possibly do. Tell us if you're wounded, who wounded you and where, so we may immediately try to help you."

At this Arnaldo opened his eyes and recognized the two people before him. Then, as best he could—which was with great difficulty—he threw himself down on Auristela's feet but embraced instead those of Periandro, for even in a moment like this he showed respect for Auristela's modesty. Gazing at her he said, "It's not possible, my lady, that you're her image and not the true Auristela, because no spirit could have divine sanction or courage enough to hide behind such a beautiful form. You are unquestionably Auristela, just as I'm unquestionably the Arnaldo who's always wanted to serve you. I've come in search of you, for my soul will find no rest until it comes to rest in you, the center of my being."

During the time this was going on they'd told Croriano and the others about the discovery of the second pilgrim and that he also showed signs of being badly wounded. On hearing this, Constanza, who'd already stopped the duke's bleeding, hurried to see what the second wounded man needed. When she realized he was Arnaldo she was stunned and confused, but her quick mind overcame her alarm and, avoiding any discussion, she told him to show her his wounds. To this Arnaldo responded by pointing to his left arm with his right hand, a sign his wound was there. Constanza immediately took off his shirt and found his upper arm had been completely run through. She stopped the blood, which was still flowing, and told Periandro that the other wounded man was the Duke of Nemurs, and it would be best to take them both to the nearest town for treatment, since the greatest danger to them was from loss of blood.

On hearing the duke's name Arnaldo trembled all over and let cold jealousy enter all the way to his heart through his warm veins almost empty of blood. So he spoke, without considering what he was saying, "There's some difference between a duke and a king, but the high rank of both, and even of all the monarchs in the world, still cannot merit Auristela." Then he added, "Don't take me wherever you're going to take the duke, for the presence of the offender does nothing to help the illness of the offended." Arnaldo had two servants with him, the duke another two. Following the orders of their masters, they had left them there alone prior to the struggle and gone on ahead to a village nearby to arrange separate lodging for each of them, since at the time they hadn't made each other's acquaintance.

"Also look to see," said Arnaldo, "if hanging in one of these trees around here there isn't a portrait of Auristela, because the battle the duke and I have fought has been over it. Take it down and give it to me; it's cost me a lot of blood and by all rights it's mine." The duke was saying practically the same thing to Ruperta and Croriano and the others with him. But Periandro satisfied everyone, saying he had the portrait in his custody for safe keeping, and that at the appropriate time he'd return it to its rightful owner.

"How can there be any doubt," asked Arnaldo, "that the portrait is truly mine? Doesn't Heaven already know that since the instant I saw the original I made a copy of it in my soul? But let my brother Periandro keep it, for while it's in his care there'll be nothing to provoke the jealousy, anger, or arrogance of those who claim it. Now take me away from here; I'm slipping away." They immediately improvised something in which the two wounded men could be carried, for, more than the depth of their wounds, their spilled blood was taking their lives drop by drop. They took them to where their servants had arranged the best accommodations they could for them; and the duke still hadn't realized his adversary was the prince Arnaldo.

The Third Chapter of the Fourth Book

The three French ladies were envious and dismayed to hear that the portrait of Auristela stood much higher in the duke's opinion than any of theirs, for the servant whom he'd sent to paint their portraits, as has been said, told them the duke did indeed have theirs with him, among some other highly valued treasures, but that he not only valued but actually worshiped Auristela's. These words of bitter truth wounded them to their souls, for beautiful women are never pleased, rather mortally wounded to hear that other women's beauty is equal to their own—or can be compared to it in any way. It's often said—and it's true—that all comparisons are odious, but when they involve beauty they're exceedingly so; not even friendship, family ties, social rank, and quality can oppose the cruel strength of accursed envy—for that's what you might as well call the feelings kindled when beauties are compared.

He also said his lord the duke, traveling from Paris to seek Auristela on her pilgrimage and being in love with her portrait, had sat down at the foot of a tree that morning with the portrait in his hands. While he was talking to the lifeless thing as if he were speaking to the living original, the other pilgrim had come up behind him so quietly he could easily hear what the duke was saying to the portrait, "so neither I nor a companion of mine could keep him from it, as we were somewhat off to one side. In short, we ran over to warn the duke someone was listening to him. He turned his head and saw the pilgrim, whose first act, without saying a word, was to snatch the portrait out of the hands of the duke, who being caught offguard, didn't have a chance to defend it as he'd have liked, and what he said was—at least what I could make out—'You thief of heavenly treasures, don't profane it by holding it in your sacriligious hands. Put down that board on which Heaven's beauty is painted and do it both because you don't deserve it and because it's mine.'

"'I won't,' responded the other pilgrim, 'and though I can't provide witnesses to prove my action is justified, I'll make up for them with the blade of my rapier, which I have hidden in this pilgrim's staff. I am in fact the rightful possessor of this incomparable beauty, for in lands far distant from the one we're in now I bought it with my wealth and worshiped it with my soul, and I've served the person it portrays with loving concern through many trials.'

"Then the duke, turning to us, issued orders in unmistakable terms to leave them alone and come to this village to wait for him here, forbidding us to so much as turn our heads to look at them. The other pilgrim gave the same order to the two men who'd come with him and are apparently his servants. But in spite of that I was a little slack in my obedience to his order and satisfied my curiosity by looking back, whereupon I saw the other pilgrim hanging the portrait on a tree. I didn't actually see all that followed, but I did see him pull a rapier or at least some weapon that looked like one out of the pilgrim's staff he was holding; I guess he then moved to attack my lord, who in turn must have stepped forward to meet him with another rapier, since I know he, too, had one in his pilgrim's staff.

"We—I mean the servants of both of them—wanted to go back and put a stop to the fight, but I decided against it, telling the others that since the two men were equally matched and alone and we had no reason to fear or suspect they'd be helped by anyone else, we should leave them and continue on our way; for we'd never be making a mistake by obeying them, while if we returned we might be. Whether or not I was right about that then, I don't know now whether it was good advice or cowardice that put lead in our feet and tied our hands, or whether the gleam of the rapiers, unbloodied up to that point, blinded us so we couldn't make out the road that would take us from where we were back to the place where the fight was, but could only see the one leading forward to where we are now. We arrived here, hurriedly took rooms, then made the more courageous decision to return to see how luck had treated our masters.

We found them just as you've seen, and if they hadn't been helped by your arrival, ours would've been worthless."

The servant said this and the ladies listened, and they were grieved by it just as much as if they had been the duke's own true loves. In each one of their imaginations the fancied plans and castles in the air they might have made or constructed in hopes of marrying the duke were dashed in a moment, for nothing eliminates and erases love more quickly from the mind than feeling that new love scorned just as it's being born. Scorn at the beginning of love has the same effect as hunger on human life; courage capitulates to hunger and sleep, and the most enticing desires to rejection. Still, it's true while that's how it often is in the beginning stages, after love has had complete possession of the soul for some time, scorn and disillusionment only serve to spur it on and make it hasten all the faster to put its thoughts into action.

Physicians came out from Rome to see them, the wounds healed, and within a week the travelers were ready to set out on the road to enter the city. During this time the duke found out that his rival was the crown prince of the kingdom of Denmark, learning, too, of his intention to choose Auristela for his wife. His own thoughts, which were identical to Arnaldo's, strengthened the plausibility of this information, and it seemed to him a woman who was sufficiently esteemed to be a queen could certainly merit being a duchess. But mixed in with these thoughts, arguments, and imaginings was a jealousy so severe it soured his pleasure and disturbed his peace of mind. At last the day of their departure came, and the duke and Arnaldo entered Rome separately without making themselves known to anyone.

When the other pilgrims in our band caught sight of Rome and viewed it from a high hill, they kneeled down as though before something sacred and began to worship it. Then out from their midst came the voice of a pilgrim they didn't know. With tears in his eyes he began to say the following:

> Oh great, oh strong, oh sacred soul of Rome!
> This lowly pilgrim bows before your might.
> Devout and humble now I kneel to you
> And view, astonished, all your beauty grand.
>
> With tender reverence and unshod feet
> I've come to gaze on you and worship you.
> My mind, though made to hope for the divine,
> Is stunned to see that you transcend your fame.

311

The soil of this fair land that I survey,
So tilled and mixed with all your martyrs' blood,
Is everywhere esteemed a relic dear.

There is no part of you that does not serve
To show example of His holiness;
For God's own City was your model fair.[1]

When he finished reciting this sonnet the pilgrim turned to those present and said, "A few years ago a Spanish poet came to this holy city. His own worst enemy and a dishonor to his nation, he framed and composed a sonnet full of abuse for this illustrious city and its equally illustrious inhabitants,[2] and his neck will pay for his tongue's guilt, if they ever catch him. Not as a poet but as a Christian, almost as though to atone for his crime, I composed the one you've heard.

Periandro asked him to kindly repeat it, he did so, and they praised him highly for it. They descended the hill, passed through the lawns of Madama,[3] then entered Rome by the Pópolo Gate,[4] but not until they'd first kissed over and over again the thresholds and the exterior of the entrance to the holy city. While they were there before the gate two Jews came up to one of Croriano's servants and asked him if the whole band of people had made advance preparations and knew where they were going to stay; if not, they'd provide them with accommodations fit for princes.

"You should know, sir," they said, "that we're Jews. My name is Zabulón, and my associate is Abiud. Our business is furnishing houses with everything necessary and in accordance with the status of the person who wants to live there. The decorating goes as far as the price they want to pay for it." To this the servant replied, "Since yesterday another fellow in my master's service has been in Rome for the purpose of arranging lodging appropriate to his station and that of all the people arriving with him."

"Well, I'll be damned," said Abiud, "that must be the Frenchman who yesterday took a liking to our associate Manasés' house, which he's fixed up like a palace." "Let's go on, then," said Croriano's servant, for my own associate must be around here waiting to guide us, and if the house he's picked out doesn't measure up, we'll put ourselves in Mr. Zabulón's hands and in whatever house he may have for us."

With this they went on, and at the entrance to the city the Jews spotted their colleague Manasés and with him Croriano's servant, from whom they learned the lodging the Jews had described was in fact the elegant one belonging to Manasés and located near the Portuguese Arch,[5] so they led our cheerful and contented pilgrims there.

No sooner had the French ladies entered the city than they attracted the attention of almost everyone, for since this was a day of special devotion at the church of Our Lady of Pópolo, the street they were on was filled with countless people. Amazement began to work its way little by little into the people looking at the French ladies, but it grew by leaps and bounds in the hearts of those who saw the matchless Auristela with the charming Constanza at her side, for together they were much like two shining stars traveling parallel to each other through the sky.

They looked so beautiful that a Roman, who it's thought must have been a poet, exclaimed, "I'll wager the goddess Venus is returning to this city as of old to see the remains of her beloved Aeneas![6] By God, the governor is lax in not ordering the face of this moving idol covered. Does he, by chance, want the wise to be dumbfounded, the tenderhearted undone, and the fools to fall into idolatry?" With these words of praise, as extravagant as they were uncalled for, the attractive band moved on and reached Manasés' lodgings, which were spacious enough to house a powerful prince and a medium-sized army.

The Fourth Chapter of the Fourth Book

That same day news of the arrival of the French ladies and the attractive band of pilgrims spread through the whole city. They especially spoke of Auristela's extraordinary beauty, describing it in the most complimentary terms, which, while still not doing her justice, were at least the best that the most talented intellects could put into words. The house where our band was staying was immediately surrounded by people who'd heard the talk and were brought there by curiosity and the desire to see so many beauties together in one place. It got to such a point that the people in the street were yelling for the ladies and pilgrim women to come to the windows, but they were resting and didn't want to let themselves be seen. The people especially clamored for Auristela, but it was out of the question for any of the women to show themselves.

Among the other people who came to the door were Arnaldo

and the duke in their pilgrims' habits, and no sooner had they seen each other than their legs began to shake and their hearts to pound. Periandro recognized them from the window, told Croriano, and the two of them went down together to the street to prevent as best they could the disaster two such jealous suitors could be expected to produce.

Periandro took Arnaldo aside and Croriano spoke to the duke. What Arnaldo said to Periandro was this: "One of the greatest burdens Auristela has imposed on me is the pain I endure in consenting to this French gentleman, who they say is the Duke of Nemurs, being in a sense in possession of Auristela's portrait, for even though it's in your hands it appears he's agreeable to that simply because I don't have it in mine. Friend Periandro, think about the disease those in love call jealousy, and which could more accurately be called raging desperation. It's partner to envy and scorn, and once it takes control of a love-stricken soul, there's no thought that can calm him, or any remedy that can help. Even though the causes leading to it are small, the effects it produces are great, depriving him, at the least, of his judgment, and at the most, of his life, for a jealous suitor finds it better to die in desperation than live with jealousy. Now, he who loves perfectly mustn't be suspicious of his beloved; still, even though he might be so perfect as not to suspect her, he can't avoid suspecting himself, by which I mean his luck, for no one can be sure of that. Things that are costly and valuable keep their possessors or those who love them in constant fear of losing them; so this emotion is never absent from the soul of those in love and is a condition inherent in them.

"You'll be well advised, my dear friend Periandro (if someone can give advice who has none for himself) to remember that I'm a king and passionately in love, and on a thousand occasions you've seen and come to know that my actions fulfill all the promises I make in words. My promise now is to accept the matchless Auristela, your sister, with no other dowry than her most impressive virtues and beauty, nor do I want to investigate the nobility of her family line, for it's clear Nature wouldn't deny worldly goods to someone she'd endowed so bountifully with her own natural gifts. Never, or very rarely, do high virtues find a place in lowborn people, and the beauty of the body is often an indication of the beauty of the soul. . . . But to get down to the point, I shall only tell you what I've said to you before, that is, I adore Auristela, whether her family tree has its roots in Heaven itself or in the lowest of the low on earth. And now that she's in Rome, the place for which she told me to save my hopes, do your part, my dear brother, to see she fulfills them for me, and from this moment I shall divide my crown and my kingdom with you. Don't let me die ridiculed by this duke or scorned by the woman I adore."

Periandro responded to all these arguments, offers, and promises, saying, "If my sister bore any responsibility for the actions of the duke that anger you, while perhaps I wouldn't actually punish, I'd at least reprimand her, and for her that would be a severe punishment. But since I know she holds no guilt in the matter, there's nothing I can say to you. As for her having had you set your hopes on her being yours after reaching this city, I don't know how much hope she's given you, so I don't know what to tell you. Regarding the offers you're making and have made me, I appreciate them every bit as much as I should considering it's you who makes them and I to whom they're made. But in all humility let me say, valiant Arnaldo, perhaps my short pilgrim's cloak may turn out to be like a cloud, which though small can often overshadow the sun. And for now, calm down; we reached Rome only yesterday, and it's not possible that in such a short space of time things can be thought through, plans made, and disputes settled to bring our actions to the happy ending we want. As much as you can, avoid contact with the duke, because a suitor who feels himself scorned and short on encouragement will seize any occasion to invent some hope out of spite, even though in fact that invention may cause him to lose what he truly wants." Arnaldo promised him to do just that and offered him money and things of value to help him keep up appearances and cover his expenses, as well as those of the French ladies.

Croriano's conversation with the duke was different, for it all came down to the duke's having to recover Auristela's portrait, or Arnaldo's having to renounce any right to it. He also asked Croriano to intercede with Auristela in asking her to accept him as her husband, for his rank was not a bit beneath Arnaldo's, nor could any other of Europe's most illustrious noblemen claim bluer blood. In short, he acted with arrogance and jealousy, indeed, like someone very much in love. Croriano said he'd do as requested and agreed to bring him whatever answer Auristela might give to his proposal of marriage, which promised to bring her great good fortune.

315

The Fifth Chapter of the Fourth Book

With their hopes founded on thin air the two jealous and enamored rivals parted company, one of them from Periandro and the other from Croriano, having agreed above all to suppress their impulses and overlook the offenses committed against them—at least until Auristela had made her decision known. Each man thought it would go in his favor, since the offer of a kingdom and of a rank as lucrative as the duke's could well be expected to make any woman waver in her resolve and think seriously about choosing some other life. And while it's very natural for anyone to love greatness and to hunger after improving one's station in life, this desire is often particularly strong in women.

But Auristela was totally unconcerned about all of this, since for the time being none of her thoughts went beyond learning the truths necessary for the salvation of her soul; she'd been born in very remote regions and lands where the true Catholic faith isn't as perfectly understood as it ought to be, and she needed to purify it in the crucible at its original forge.

After Periandro had finished speaking with Arnaldo a Spaniard came up to him and said, "Judging by the description I was given and if you're Spanish, then this letter's for you." He placed in his hands a sealed letter, on the outside of which was written: "To the illustrious gentleman Antonio de Villaseñor, otherwise known as 'The Barbarian.'" Periandro asked who had given him the letter. The messenger replied it was a Spaniard, a prisoner in the jail called "The Tower of Nona."[1] Both he and a girlfriend of his—a beautiful woman called "The girl from Talavera"—were sentenced, at the very least, to be hung for homicide.

Periandro, who by their names recognized who they must be and could almost guess their crimes, answered, "This letter isn't for me but for that pilgrim coming this way." He said this because at that very moment Antonio was approaching. He gave him the letter and after the two of them moved to one side he opened it and read the following:

> If you're up to no good, you'll come to a bad end, for even if you have two feet and one of them is healthy, with the other one lame, you're likely to start limping. You know, you can't learn good habits from bad companions. The company I've kept (and shouldn't have) with the girl from Talavera has me and her sen-

tenced to be finished off on the gallows. The man who brought
her with him out of Spain found her here in my company in
Rome; that got to him and he hit her right in front of me. Now,
I won't put up with any fooling around and don't take anything
from anybody—instead I do the giving—so I defended the girl
and simply beat her attacker to death with a stick. While I was
making a getaway from this quarrel another pilgrim came up
and began to beat me about the head and shoulders, as I'd just
done to the first fellow. The girl says she recognized the man
beating me as her husband, a Pole she'd married in Talavera.
Fearing that after finishing with me he'd start in on her—since
she was the one who'd wronged him—what did she do but grab
a knife, one of two she always carried with her in sheaths, and
coming up to him jabbed it neatly into his kidneys, wounding
him so badly that he didn't need a doctor. To state it flatly, the
boyfriend got it with a stick and the husband with a knife, and
they finished their earthly race in nothing flat.

They arrested both of us at the same time and brought us to
this jail where we still remain—much against our will, of course.
They've taken down our confession; we confessed our crime because we couldn't deny it, and besides, that way we avoided
being tortured, which here they call *tortura*. The trial went forward, moving more quickly than we'd have liked. It's finished
now, and we've been sentenced to exile, except that it's from
this life to the next. What I'm saying, Sir, is that we're sentenced
to hang, something so grievous the girl from Talavera can't
stand the thought of it. She kisses Your Grace's hands as well
as my Lady Constanza's and my Lord Periandro's and my Lady
Auristela's, and says she'd feel ever so happy if she were free to
come to your homes and kiss Your Grace's hands. She also says
that if the matchless Auristela would put her mind to it and take
charge of obtaining our freedom, it would be a snap for her, for
what couldn't her great beauty accomplish, even if she made her
request to cruelty itself? And she says further that if Your Graces
can't manage to get us a pardon, at least try to arrange where
we'll die, and instead of it being in Rome, have it be in Spain.
The girl has found out that here people who are to be hanged
aren't taken through the streets with proper ceremony; instead
they have to walk and hardly anybody comes out to see them
so there's practically nobody to pray a Hail Mary for them—
much less if those being hung are Spaniards. And she'd like, if
it were possible, to die in her own land and among her own
people where there'd be sure to be some relative to take pity on
her and close her eyes in death. The same thing goes for me, for
I'll go along with anything that makes sense, 'cause I'm so mis-

erable in this jail that in exchange for getting out of the agony the bedbugs are putting me through here, I'd consider it a good deal if they took me out and hung me tomorrow.

And I want to point out to Your Grace, my Lord, that the judges in this land don't differ at all from those in Spain. They're all quite gracious and like to give and receive their just dues, for when there's no one paying for strict justice to be done, they're not above showing mercy. Now, if that same mercy reigns in all Your Graces' brave hearts—as I'm sure it must—it'll treat us as its most needful subjects, for we're in a foreign land, prisoners in jail, and eaten by bedbugs and other filthy vermin that may be tiny but are so numerous they vex us as though they were huge. And worst of all, we've been stripped down to the hide and raised to the nth degree of need by solicitors, attorneys, and clerks, from whom may our Lord God through His infinite goodness deliver us! Amen.

We await your reply longing for good news as much as baby storks up in the tower long for their mother to bring them food.

And he signed, "The miserable Bartolomé of La Mancha."

The two men who'd read the letter enjoyed it immensely, though they were also immensely concerned about the couple's dire situation, and immediately told the man who'd brought the letter to tell the prisoner to take heart and hope to be freed because Auristela and all of them would do everything in their power, including giving gifts and making promises, to arrange it. Then they immediately set about planning what steps would have to be taken. The first was for Croriano to ask the French ambassador, a friend and relative of his, to prevent the punishment from being carried out so soon, in order to allow time for the requests and petitions to be made. Antonio also got the idea of writing Bartolomé a letter of reply, for writing it would be just as much fun as reading his had been; but when he shared this idea with Auristela and Constanza they both thought he shouldn't do it, for one shouldn't heap more afflictions on the af- flicted, who might take the jokes seriously and feel even worse. What they did do was put the responsibility for the whole business on the shoulders and in the care of Croriano and his wife Ruperta, who pleaded earnestly for Bartolomé and the girl from Talavera. So, after only six days the two of them were back out on the street, for where well-placed gifts and special favors intervene, rough spots can be smoothed over and difficulties dissolved.

Meanwhile Auristela had taken some time to learn everything she felt she needed to know about the Catholic faith, at least those doctrines that in her country were practiced but only dimly understood. She found certain individuals she could communicate this desire to, namely the penitentiaries,[2] to whom she made her full, true, and frank confession. They taught her and answered all her questions as accurately as they could, explaining to her all the most important and essential mysteries of our faith.

They began with Lucifer's envy and pride, and his fall into the abyss with a third of the stars,[3] a fall that left the seats of Heaven vacant and empty, lost to the evil angels through their stubborn guilt. They explained to her the way God chose to fill these seats—by creating man, whose soul is capable of the glory the evil angels had lost. They went into the truth of the creation of man and the world, and the holy and love-filled mystery of the Incarnation. Then reasoning beyond reason itself, they outlined the most profound mystery of the Holy Trinity. They told why the second person of the Three— the Son—was made man, so he might pay man's debt both as a man and also as God, and why only this essential union was great enough to satisfy God for the infinite sins committed, for God had to be infinitely satisfied and man, by nature finite, could not do so by himself; God by himself was incapable of suffering, but the two of them together formed an infinite treasure sufficient for the payment.

They explained Christ's death to her and his life's trials from the moment he appeared in the manger until he put himself on the cross. They stressed the strength and efficacy of the sacraments, and pointed out the second timber of our shipwrecked lives—penance— without which there's no way to open the pathway to Heaven, usually closed by sin. They also explained to her Jesus Christ the Living God, seated at the right hand of the Father, just as living and whole when He enters the sacrament on earth as He is in Heaven, and whose most holy presence cannot be separated or removed from us by any absence whatsoever, for one of God's greatest attributes— though they're all equal—is that through his power, essence, and presence, he is everywhere. They assured her that without fail this Lord will come in a cloud from Heaven to judge the world, and likewise that the gates of Hell, or rather its armies, can do little against the constancy and firmness of His Church. They dealt with the power of the pope, God's viceroy on earth and keeper of the keys to Heaven. Finally, there was nothing left for them to say that they considered necessary to make themselves understood either in general or by Auristela and Periandro in particular. These lessons so gladdened their souls that they were taken out of themselves and carried up to Heaven, for all their thoughts were there.

The Sixth Chapter of the Fourth Book

From this time forward Auristela and Periandro looked at each other with different eyes, at least Periandro looked at Auristela differently, for it seemed to him that now she'd fulfilled the vow that had brought her to Rome and could freely and without impediment take him as her husband. But if Auristela while still half pagan loved her chastity, after being confirmed in her Christianity she adored it, not because she felt there was anything wrong in marrying, but she just didn't want to show any sign of tender thoughts without first being compelled to, either by some obligation or by impassioned pleading. She was also searching to see if Heaven was showing her some light in any direction to indicate what she should do after marrying, for she thought that returning to her homeland would be a reckless mistake since Periandro's brother, who'd been the first to choose her for his wife, on seeing his hopes disappointed might take revenge on her and on his brother Periandro for their offense against him. These thoughts and fears were making her somewhat wan and pensive.

The French ladies visited the churches and made the rounds with pomp and grandeur, for Croriano, as has been said, was a relative of the French ambassador, who supplied them with everything necessary to keep up distinguished appearances. They always took Auristela and Constanza with them, so whenever they left the house they were invariably followed by almost half of Rome. One day while going along a street called Banchi,[1] they happened to see on a wall there a full-length portrait (that is, from head to toe) of a woman wearing a crown on her head—though the crown was split in half—whose feet were set on a globe of the world. No sooner had they seen it than they recognized the face as Auristela's, drawn so true to life there was no question about it.

Astonished, Auristela asked whose portrait it was, and whether by chance it was for sale. The owner (who, it was later learned, was a famous painter) replied he was selling the portrait, but didn't know who the subject was. All he knew was that after having copied it for him in France, another painter—a friend of his—had told him it was of a young foreign woman dressed as a pilgrim and traveling to Rome.

"What does it mean," countered Auristela, "that she's painted with a crown on her head and her feet on that globe? And what's more, why is the crown split in two?" "Those, lady," said the owner, "are the fantasies of painters, or caprices, as they're called. Perhaps it's trying to say this maiden deserves to wear the crown of beauty and is trampling the world under foot. But I feel it means that you, my lady, are its original and deserve a whole crown, and not just a painted world, but one that's real and true."

"What are you asking for the portrait?" asked Constanza. To this the owner replied, "There are two pilgrims here, and one has offered me a thousand gold escudos, while the other says he won't let it get away at any price. I haven't closed the deal yet because it seems to me they must be joking; their exorbitant offers make me suspicious." "Well, you needn't be," countered Constanza, "for those two pilgrims, if they're the ones I think they are, can easily double the price and pay you to your complete satisfaction."

The French ladies, Ruperta, Croriano, and Periandro were dumbfounded when they saw the picture's accurate likeness of Auristela's face. The other people looking at the portrait discovered that it looked like Auristela, and little by little the word began to spread, to first one person here and then another there, until finally everyone all together confirmed the truth of it: "The portrait that's for sale is of the pilgrim woman who's riding in this carriage. Why should we want to see the copy when we can see the original!" Then they began to crowd around on all sides of the coach, preventing the horses from either going forward or turning back, and leading Periandro to say, "Sister Auristela, cover your face with a veil, for the light shining from it is blinding and we can't see where we're going." Auristela did as he requested and they moved on, but that didn't keep several people from following them, hoping she'd eventually remove the veil so they could see her.

As soon as the carriage had left that spot, Arnaldo, dressed in his pilgrim's habit, came up to the owner of the portrait and said, "I'm the one who offered you the thousand escudos for this portrait. If you want to get rid of it, bring it and come with me, and I'll pay you in pure gold right away." At this the other pilgrim, who was the Duke of Nemurs, said, "Don't worry about the price, brother, just come with me, think of any figure you might like to get for it, and I'll give it to you in cash on the spot." "Señores," replied the painter, "you two must get together on which one is going to have it—I won't worry about the price, since in any case I think you're more likely to pay me in wishes than in fact."

Several people were listening to this conversation, waiting to see how the sale would turn out, because the sight of two apparently poor pilgrims offering several thousands of ducados seemed like some kind of trick to them. At this point the owner said, "Whichever one of you wants it, show me something up front and lead on, because I'm taking it down to deliver it." Hearing this, Arnaldo reached into his vest and took out a gold chain with a diamond pendant hanging from it, saying, "Take this chain—it and the pendant are worth more than two thousand escudos—and bring me the portrait." "This is worth ten thousand—" said the duke, giving the owner of the portrait a diamond chain, "—and bring it to my house."

"My God!" exclaimed one of the onlookers. "Whose portrait is this anyway? Who are these men and what kind of jewels are these? This whole thing looks like enchantment to me, and for that reason, brother painter, I advise you to set a touchstone[2] to the chain and put the quality of the stones to the test before you part with your property, because the exaggerated value placed on them makes me suspect the chain and gems might be counterfeit."

Both the princes became angry, but to avoid any further baring of their feelings in the street, they agreed to let the owner of the portrait determine the true value of the jewels. All the people on Banchi Street were in an uproar, some looking in wonder at the portrait, others asking who the pilgrims might be, others staring at the jewels, and all very intent on finding out who was going to end up with the painting, for it seemed to them each of the two pilgrims was resolved not to let it get away at any price, even though the owner would part with it for much less than they were offering him if they'd just stop badgering him and let him sell it to one of them.

In the midst of all this, who was going down Banchi Street but the governor of Rome! He heard the noise of the crowd, asked the reason, saw the portrait, and glimpsed the jewels. Then, since it seemed to him these were the possessions of more than just ordinary pilgrims, he hoped to find out what the mystery was but in the meantime had the jewels taken into safekeeping, the portrait carried to his house, and the pilgrims arrested. The painter was distraught, seeing his hopes depleted and his property in the hands of the law, for nothing that fell into them ever got out with the original shine still on it—if, indeed, it got out at all. He hurried to look for Periandro to tell him what had happened concerning the sale and to express his fears that the governor would keep the painting. He told him he'd bought it in France from a painter who'd copied it from the original in Portugal, and Periandro thought that quite plausible since several had been painted during the time Auristela was in Lisbon. Despite all this, Periandro offered him a hundred escudos for it, assuming the risk of recovering it himself. This pleased the painter, and even though the drop from a thousand to a hundred was rather abrupt, he considered the painting well sold and better paid for.

That afternoon Periandro joined some other Spanish pilgrims in taking the walking tour of the seven churches,[3] and among the pilgrims he happened to encounter the poet who'd recited the sonnet on catching sight of Rome. They recognized and embraced each other, then asked each other about what had been happening in their lives. The pilgrim poet told him something so astonishing had happened to him the day before that it was worth relating—namely, that he'd learned of a rather strange and rich monsignor on the pope's cabinet who had the most unusual museum in the world, unusual because there were no figures in it of people who in fact had lived or did exist, but rather some blank spaces prepared so the distinguished people of the future could be painted on them, especially those who'd be famous poets in centuries to come. Among these empty places he'd especially noticed two; at the top of one of them was written Torcuato Tasso,[4] and a little farther down it said, *Jerusalem Delivered,* while on the other was written Zárate,[5] and below that, *The Cross and Constantine.*

"I asked the man showing them to me what those names meant. He replied it was hoped that soon the light of a poet who'd be called Torcuato Tasso would be discovered on earth. He would sing of Jerusalem retaken with more heroic and pleasing inspiration than any poet before him had ever done, and that almost immediately he'd be followed by a Spaniard called Francisco López Duarte,[6] whose voice would fill the four corners of the earth and whose harmony would fill peoples' hearts with rapture as it sang about the discovery of Christ's Cross and the wars of the emperor Constantine, a work truly heroic, devout, and worthy of being called an epic poem."

To this Periandro replied, "It's hard for me to believe trouble is being taken so far in advance to prepare blank spaces on which to paint people who'll appear in the future, but the fact of the matter is that this city, the capital of the world, contains other marvels even more astonishing. Are there places prepared for more future poets?" "Yes," replied the pilgrim, "but I didn't want to stop and read the titles, being satisfied with seeing just the first two. However, I saw so many just at a glance that I gather the age when these shall live (which, according to my guide, can't be far off) will yield an immense harvest of all kinds of poets. May God direct it according to His holy purposes."

"One thing we do know," responded Periandro, "is that in a year when poetry flourishes, hunger usually abounds, too. Give me a poet and I'll give you a poor man (provided nature doesn't strain itself and perform some miracles), for there's a logical series of consequences: there are many poets, therefore there are many poor men; there are many poor men, therefore it's a lean year."

The pilgrim and Periandro were discussing this when Zabulón the Jew came up to them and told Periandro he wanted to take him that afternoon to see Hipólita from Ferrara,[7] one of the most beautiful women in Rome, indeed, even in all Italy. Periandro replied he'd be glad to go, a reply he wouldn't have given if he'd been told as much about her character as he was about her beauty, for Periandro's high standards were such that he didn't hurry toward and stoop to things in the gutter, no matter how beautiful they might be. In this respect nature had made him and Auristela identical, forming them in the same mold. He did, however, conceal from her the fact that he was going to see Hipólita, and the Jew managed to take him to see her much more by trickery than through any real desire on Periandro's part; sometimes curiosity makes even the most circumspect virtue trip and fall on its face.

The Seventh Chapter of the Fourth Book

Many defects can be covered up by having good manners, using costly personal adornments, and displaying elegant furnishings and splendor in one's house; it's not possible for good manners to offend, costly adornment to annoy, or rich furnishings to displease.

Hipólita had all these things and was a lady of the Court who in her wealth could compete with Flora of old,[1] and in courtesy with good manners personified. It was impossible for anyone who knew her to think badly of her, for with her beauty she made herself enchanting, with her wealth she made herself respected, and with her courtliness—if that's the right word—she made herself adored. When love dresses in these three qualities, it breaks hearts of bronze, opens ironclad purses, and subdues wills as immovable as marble; and even more so if in addition deceit and flattery are employed, since they're convenient tactics women use when they want to display their charms openly.

Is there, by chance, a mind in the world so keen that while gazing on one of the beautiful women I'm describing it can set aside thoughts of her beauty to focus instead on whether or not she's well behaved? Beauty partly blinds and partly illuminates; pleasure runs after it blindly, but only afterwards is the mind illuminated by thoughts of reform.

So Periandro had none of this in mind when he went into Hipólita's house. Love often builds its schemes on careless foundations, and this one was devised with no thought whatsoever for Periandro's desires, rather only Hipólita's. One doesn't have to put forth much effort to get together with the ladies usually labeled as being of easy virtue, for they may have many regrets but feel no remorse. Hipólita had already seen Periandro in the street and his attractive and gentlemanly looks had already set her heart astir. But above all, she liked the idea that he was a Spaniard, for from their reputation she could hope for impossibly rich gifts and cleverly devised pleasures. She had communicated her thoughts to Zabulón, begging him to bring Periandro to the house, which was so beautifully decorated, so clean, and so neat that it looked more prepared to be a bridal chamber than a place to receive pilgrims.

The Lady Hipólita—that's how she was addressed in Rome, even though she was no lady—had a boyfriend called Pirro the Calabrian,[2] a short-tempered, wicked bully, whose living depended on the edge of his sword, the quickness of his hands and Hipólita's tricks, for with them she often succeeded in getting what she wanted without having to give herself to anyone. But above all Pirro improved his lot by the use of his feet, which stood him in better stead than his hands, and what he was most proud of was the fact that he always had Hipólita in awe of him, regardless of whether he was in a loving or an angry mood; tame doves like her always have birds of prey that pursue them and tear them to pieces, for such is the sad way these worldly and foolish people treat each other!

As I was saying, then, this gentleman, who was one only in name, happened to be in Hipólita's house when the Jew and Periandro came in. She took him aside and said, "Go with God, my friend, and take with you for the road the gold chain this pilgrim sent me with Zabulón this morning. "Watch what you're doing, Hipólita," replied Pirro, "because from what I can deduce this pilgrim is a Spaniard, and for him to let this chain worth at least a hundred escudos out of his hands without touching you, looks to me like a big complication, and I can think of a thousand different possibilities to worry about."

"Go ahead and take the chain, dear Pirro, and leave it to me to take care of things so I don't have to return it, no matter how Spanish he may be." So Pirro took the chain Hipólita gave him, one she'd had bought for just that purpose that morning—in other words, to seal his lips and get him out of the house in a hurry. Then having thrown off her fetters, free and no longer hindered by this shackle, the first thing Hipólita did was go up to Periandro and in a very easy and charming manner throw her arms around his neck, saying to him, "I really must see if Spaniards are as brave as their reputation."

When Periandro saw her shameful boldness he felt as if the whole house had fallen in on him. Putting out his hand between them, he held her off and pushed her away, saying, "The habit I'm wearing, Lady Hipólita, cannot be profaned, or at least I certainly won't allow it to be. Pilgrims, even though they may be Spaniards, aren't required to be brave when there's nothing important involved. So think again, my lady, how you might like me to show my valor in some way that won't harm either one of us, then I'll obey without contradicting a word you say."

"It seems to me, sir pilgrim," replied Hipólita, "you're just as brave in spirit as you are in body. But since you tell me you'll do whatever I say provided it doesn't harm either one of us, come into the next room with me; I want to show you my art gallery and living room." To this Periandro replied, "Although I'm a Spaniard, I'm somewhat cowardly and more afraid of you by yourself than a whole army of enemies. But have someone else come as our guide and you can take me wherever you wish."

Hipólita called the Jew Zabulón, who'd been there the whole time, and two of her maids, instructing them to lead them to the gallery. They opened the room, and as Periandro later said, it was as well decorated as any a rich, worldly, and fastidious prince might have. The most perfect creations of the brushes of Parrhasius, Polygnotus, Apelles, Zeuxis, and Timanthes[3] were there, bought with Hipólita's treasures, along with the best of the devout Raphael of Urbino and of the divine Michaelangelo, treasures with which a great prince should and could show off his wealth. Royal buildings, proud palaces, splendid churches, and valuable paintings are true and proper signs of the greatness and wealth of princes; they are treasures, indeed, that compete with time, which flutters its wings and speeds its flight in vain, for both like it and in spite of it they demonstrate the magnificence of the past.

Oh, Hipólita, you're good only in this! If among all the many portraits you have, you'd possessed just one showing you being good, you'd have left Periandro alone to behave himself. He, meanwhile, was walking around dazed, stunned, and bewildered, absorbed in seeing just how far the opulence of the gallery would go, when he saw a sparkling clean table spread from one end to the other with the confused but pleasingly harmonious music made by several different kinds of birds in richly decorated cages.

In short, it seemed to him that of everything he'd heard told about the gardens of the Hesperides,[4] those of the sorceress Falerina,[5] the celebrated hanging ones of Babylon, and all the others whose fame had spread throughout the world, none could match the decoration of that room and that gallery. But since he was going around with his heart in turmoil—for to his virtue's credit he felt it was being crushed in a vise—things didn't appear to him as they really were. Then, tired of too many objects of delight and irritated to see they were all planned to have an effect contrary to his wishes, he turned his back on courtesy and tried to leave the gallery; indeed, he would have left if Hipólita hadn't stepped in his way, forcing him to use his hands to communicate what would have been some rather discourteous and harsh words.

Hipólita grabbed Periandro's cloak and, pulling open his jacket, she saw the diamond cross that until then had escaped so many dangers. It dazzled her eyes as well as her thoughts, so, seeing he was getting away from her despite her smooth efforts to prevent it, she thought of a plan that, had she known just a little better how to carry it out and implement it, would have made things go much worse for Periandro. Meanwhile, leaving his pilgrim's cloak in the hands of this new Egyptian temptress[6] and, minus his hat, minus his staff, and minus the cloak's belt, he got out into the street—for winning that kind of battle depends more on running away than on waiting around. As for her, she went to the window and began to call out loudly to the people in the street, shouting, "Stop that thief! He came into my house as nice as anyone, then robbed me of a heavenly jewel that's worth a city!"

Two of the pope's guards just happened to be in the street—the ones they say can arrest people caught in the act—and since the shouting was about a thief they made use of their questionable authority and arrested Periandro. They reached into his jacket and took out the cross, slapping him around in the bargain; such is the payment the law makes to those just arrested, not even bothering to find out if they've committed a crime.

Periandro, then, seeing himself crucified but without his cross, spoke to the Swiss guards in their own language and told them he was no thief, rather a nobleman, that the cross was his, that they'd see he couldn't have gotten his riches from Hipólita, and that would they please take him before the governor, as he hoped to make short work of proving the truth of the matter. He offered them money, too, as well as speaking to them in their own language—something that makes peace even among strangers—and after that the Swiss guards paid no attention to Hipólita and took Periandro before the governor.

Seeing this, Hipólita left the window and almost scratching her own face in rage said to her maids, "Oh, sisters, what a fool I've been! I've harmed the man I hoped to give my favors to! I've given offense to the man I'd thought to serve! The man who's stolen my heart has been arrested as a thief! What kind of tender words and flattery was it, do you think, to have a free and honorable man arrested and defamed?"

Then she told them two of the pope's guards were taking the pilgrim away under arrest. She also ordered them to prepare the coach immediately, as she wanted to follow after him and clear him, for her heart couldn't stand to see its most dearly beloved wounded, and to prevent it she'd rather be taken for a false witness than a cruel woman. There's no excuse for cruelty, while there is for false witness when the blame can be attached to love, for it reveals and makes its desires known through a thousand different foolish blunders, and does harm to the person it loves the most.

When she arrived at the governor's house she found him holding the cross in his hands and questioning Periandro about the matter. On seeing her, Periandro told the governor, "The lady now entering has stated I stole from her the cross Your Grace is holding, and I'll agree she's telling the truth if she can say what the cross is made of, what it's worth, and how many diamonds it contains, for unless angels or some other kind of well-informed spirit has told her, she can't possibly know these facts, having only seen it on my chest, and only once at that." "What does Lady Hipólita have to say to that?" queried the governor, covering up the cross so she couldn't see what it looked like.

She replied, "When I tell you I'm blindly and madly in love, this pilgrim will be cleared and I'll await whatever punishment his honor the governor might want to give me for my crime of passion." Then she told him step by step what had happened between her and Periandro; the governor was flabbergasted, but more by her boldness than her love, for to people like her lascivious folly comes naturally. He rebuked her, asked Periandro to forgive her, set him free and gave him back the cross (and he was more than a little lucky in that nothing was written down about the case).

The governor wanted to know who the pilgrims were who'd put their jewels down as deposits on Auristela's portrait, and also who he and Auristela were. To this Periandro responded, "The portrait is of Auristela, my sister. Those pilgrims probably have jewels much more valuable than these. This cross is mine, and when I have enough time and am forced to do so by necessity, I'll say who I am; but whether or not I reveal it now isn't in my hands, but in those of my sister. I've already bought the portrait Your Grace is holding from the painter at a reasonable price, and the purchase involved no exaggerated offers such as those others that were based more on ill will and fantasies than on what's fair."

The governor said he'd like to keep the painting and would pay the same price, thereby enriching Rome with a work to outshine those of the most excellent painters that had already made it famous. "I give it to Your Grace," responded Periandro, "for it seems to me that in giving it to such an owner, I'll be doing it the greatest possible honor." The governor thanked him and the same day set Arnaldo and the duke free. He gave them back their jewels but kept the portrait, for after all, it was only fair he should get something.

The Eighth Chapter of the Fourth Book

Hipólita was on her way home more confused than contrite. She was pensive, too, and what's more, in love, for although it's true that in the beginning of love rejection usually puts an end to it, the rejection she'd suffered at the hands of Periandro had only fanned her kindled desires. It seemed to her a pilgrim couldn't be so made of bronze that he wouldn't soften up after the gifts she was planning to give him.

But in talking over the matter with herself, she said, "If this pilgrim were poor he wouldn't have such a valuable cross with him, for its many costly diamonds are a clear indication of his wealth. So the strength of this rock won't be broken by seige and hunger; other skills and maneuvers will be needed to bring about its surrender. Isn't it possible this young man has his heart set on someone else? Isn't it possible this Auristela isn't his sister? And isn't it possible, too, that the other side of the coin of all this scorn for me is kind favors he'd like to do for Auristela? Hold it! As God is my witness, I think I've just found the solution to my problem! Kill Auristela! Let's get the mystery out into the open, or at least let's see what kind of feelings the boy's untamed heart is capable of. Let's at least try this plan. . . . We'll have Auristela get sick, and that'll take the sun out of Periandro's eyes. . . . We'll see whether or not when we take away beauty—the principal cause of love—love itself will also disappear. It's possible that if I then supply what I'm depriving him of by removing Auristela, he might be persuaded to have more tender thoughts towards me . . . at least I have to give it a try, because as they say, 'there's no harm in trying . . . you might just get lucky!'"

Somewhat consoled by these thoughts, she reached home and found Zabulón, to whom she outlined her whole plan, counting on the fact that his wife was the most famous sorceress in Rome. After having first given him some gifts and promises of more to come, she asked him to persuade his wife not to change Periandro's mind—for she knew that was impossible—but to make Auristela fall ill, and within a certain length of time, if it should be necessary, to take her life. Zabulón assured her that was something easily within the scope of his wife's power and knowledge. He received I don't know how much as a down payment and promised that on the following day Auristela's health would begin to fail. And not only did Hipólita pay Zabulón well, she also threatened him; gifts and threats will make a Jew promise and even perform the impossible.

Periandro told Croriano, Ruperta, Auristela, the three French ladies, Antonio, and Constanza about his arrest, Hipólita's love, and the fact that he'd given Auristela's portrait to the governor. Auristela wasn't at all happy to hear about the courtesan's love for him because she'd already heard it said she was one of the most beautiful women in Rome, one of the most free and easy, as well as one of the most wealthy and intelligent; imaginary causes of jealousy, even if there's just one smaller than a gnat, are magnified in the mind of a person in love until they look bigger than Mount Olympus. When modesty ties your tongue so you can't complain and torments your soul in bonds of silence, then with every step you take your spirit looks for some way to get out of your body. As has been observed before, the only help for jealousy is to hear reassurances. But if a person won't allow herself that relief, you can just write off her life, and Auristela would have lost hers a thousand times over rather than voice any complaint about Periandro's faithfulness.

That night was the first time Bartolomé and the girl from Talavera went to visit their lords. They weren't free, even though they were out of jail, rather they were tied with stronger bonds—those of marriage—for they'd united in wedlock. The Pole's death when fate brought him to Rome had given Luisa her liberty; before reaching his own country he'd encountered in Rome the very person he had no intention of looking for. He'd remembered the advice Periandro had given him in Spain but couldn't avoid his destiny, since it wasn't something made by his own hands.

That same evening Arnaldo, too, visited all the ladies and informed them about what had happened to him when he set out to look for them, after having made peace in his homeland. He told them he'd come to the Island of the Hermitages and hadn't found Rutilio there. But another hermit who'd taken his place said Rutilio was in Rome. Arnaldo also reported he'd gone ashore on the fishermen's island and had found all the wives back there—free, healthy, and happy—as well as all the fellows who, he was told, had sailed with Periandro. He told them he'd learned indirectly that Policarpo was dead and Sinforosa had refused to marry. He said the Barbarous Isle was being resettled, the inhabitants carrying on their belief in its false prophecy. He reported that Mauricio and his son-in-law Ladislao, along with his daughter Transila, had left their country and gone to live more peacefully in England. He added that after bringing the war to an end he'd stayed with Leopoldio, king of Danea, who'd married to insure succession to his throne; furthermore, he'd pardoned the two traitors he was holding prisoner when Periandro and his fishermen had encountered him, and sent his gratitude to them for the kind and courteous treatment they'd given him. Among the names that necessarily came up in his account he sometimes mentioned Periandro's parents and sometimes Auristela's, making their two hearts stand still and bringing memories both of grandeur and misfortune to their minds.

He told them that in Portugal, and especially in Lisbon, their portraits were highly valued; he also reported the fame Constanza's beauty and that of the three French ladies had left all along their route through France. He said Croriano had earned the reputation of being noble and wise by having chosen the matchless Ruperta as his wife. He recounted, too, that in Lucca everyone was talking about Isabela Castrucho's cleverness and about Andrea Marulo's brief courtship, and that by means of a feigned devil Heaven had given him a life fit for an angel. He also said Periandro's fall was considered a miracle, and that he'd left a poet behind on the road—a young man on a pilgrimage—who chose not to come along with him because he was traveling slowly while writing a play about the events that had happened to Periandro and Auristela, events he knew by heart from having seen them represented on a canvas in Portugal where they'd been painted, and who was totally committed to marrying Auristela if she'd have him. Auristela thanked the poet for his good wishes and even at that distance offered to give him money for a new suit of clothes, in case he should arrive tattered, for even one good wish from a good poet deserves to be well rewarded.

Arnaldo said, too, that he'd been at Lady Constanza's and Antonio's home, that their parents and grandparents were well and only distressed by the worry they felt because they didn't know how their children were. They were hoping Lady Constanza would return to marry the count, her brother-in-law, who wanted to emulate his brother's wise choice, either so he wouldn't lose the twenty thousand ducados, or because he was moved by Constanza's merits—the latter being much more likely. This was news that made everyone more than a little happy, especially Periandro and Auristela, who loved them like a brother and sister. Arnaldo's account again led the listeners to suspect that Periandro and Auristela must be important people, because arrangements involving the weddings of counts and thousands of ducados couldn't fail to transmit intimations of great and glorious things.

He also related that in France he'd encountered Renato, the French gentleman wrongly defeated in combat, but now free and victorious thanks to his enemy's conscience. In fact, there were very few events of the many in which he was involved and which have been recounted during the course of this elegant true story that he didn't call to mind again at that point. He even included the question of who'd keep Auristela's little portrait on wood, which Periandro was holding against the duke's and his own wishes, even though he said that in order not to vex Periandro he'd overlook the offense.

"I'd have already undone the offense, Sir Arnaldo," responded Periandro, "by returning the portrait to you, had I believed it yours. The duke's luck and his own efforts gave it to him; you took it from him by force and so have no basis for complaint. Lovers must not judge their suits according to the measure of their own desires, for it's very likely to be impossible to satisfy them; rather they'll have to adapt themselves reasonably to the demands of other considerations. So I'm going to do something that, while not leaving you content, Lord Arnaldo, won't give the duke satisfaction either, and that is to have my sister Auristela keep the portrait, because it's more hers than anyone else's." Arnaldo found Periandro's idea satisfactory, and Auristela felt exactly the same. With this the conversation came to an end.

332

By morning of the next day the spells, poisons, enchantments, and malice of the Jewess, Zabulón's wife, had begun to take effect on Auristela.

The Ninth Chapter of the Fourth Book

The illness didn't dare take on Auristela's good looks face to face, being afraid her beauty would scare its ugliness away. Instead, at dawn it attacked her from behind, giving her chills up her back so she couldn't get out of bed all that day. Immediately it took away her appetite, the sparkle in her eyes began to fade, and the growing signs of her weakness, something that usually comes over the sick only after they've been ill for some time, sowed the seeds of dismay in all of Constanza's senses; it had the same effect indirectly on Periandro, too, and at once they both became apprehensive, fearing the worst, especially the eventuality unfortunate people fear most.

Auristela hadn't been ill for two hours when the healthy roses in her cheeks suddenly became livid; the scarlet of her lips seemed to have turned green and her pearly white teeth to topaz yellow; even her hair appeared to have changed color. Her hands became emaciated, as did her face, which seemed changed almost in its very structure and frame. But even all this made her seem no less beautiful to Periandro, for he was looking at her not as she was—lying there in bed—but as she looked where he kept her pictured in his heart. Not until two days later did he hear some words from her, but they were very weak, confused, and uttered by a stumbling tongue. The French ladies became exceedingly frightened and went so far with their wish to care for Auristela's health that they needed to be careful of their own.

The best doctors were selected and called in, or at least those with the best reputation. A good name indicates a successful practice, though there can be lucky doctors just as there are lucky soldiers; good luck and happiness are one and the same and, what's more, can arrive at a miserable person's door in a homespun bag just as well as in a silver box. But none came to Auristela's door, either in silver or wool, and that drove the brother and sister Antonio and Constanza to quiet despair.

The duke's reaction was quite the opposite. Since the love in his heart had been inspired by Auristela's beauty, as soon as that beauty began to fade away, love also began to fade in him, for love must put out many roots into the soul to draw sufficient strength to go to the edge of the grave with the beloved. Death is horribly ugly, and pain is what most often accompanies it all the way to the end; to love ugly things seems supernatural and is rightly considered a miracle. Auristela, in short, was wasting away by the minute and everyone who knew her was losing all hope for her recovery. Periandro was the only one—the only one who remained firm, the only one who kept his love alive, the only one who with courageous heart held out against misfortune and death itself, which was threatening him through Auristela.

The Duke of Nemurs waited for two weeks to see if Auristela would get better, and not a day went by that he didn't consult with the doctors about Auristela's health, though not one gave him any reassurance, for they didn't really know the cause of her suffering. Seeing this, seeing, too, that the French ladies were paying no attention to him whatsoever, and seeing finally that Auristela, his angel of light, had turned into one of darkness,[1] he invented some reasons that excused his change of heart, if not entirely, at least in part. One day he came up to Auristela in her sickbed and said to her in Periandro's presence, "Luck has been so against me, beautiful lady, that it hasn't seen fit to let me fulfill the desire I had to take you as my lawful wife. So before desperation can bring me to the point of losing my soul, as it has brought me to the point of losing my life, I want to try my fortune down some other road, though you can be sure nothing good will come to me, even though I may strive for it. In the end, since bad things I don't want to find will find me, I'll eventually lose myself and die a miserable, if not a desperate, death. My mother summons me and has arranged for me to marry; I wish to obey her and so kill some time on the road of life until death overtakes me. But still, it will find in my heart memories of your beauty and of your illness, though—and God forbid I should have to say it—none of your death." And he managed to look a little teary-eyed.

Auristela couldn't reply to him, or perhaps she didn't want to, in order not to say the wrong thing in front of Periandro. What she did was put her hand under her pillow, take out her little portrait, and return it to the duke, who kissed her hands in gratitude for such a great favor. But Periandro stretched out his own hand and took it from him, saying, "If you don't mind, great lord, in the name of what you love best, I beg you to loan it to me so I may keep a promise I've made, a matter which, while it won't be to your detriment, will be greatly to mine if I don't honor it."

The duke returned it to him, at the same time making extravagant offers to risk all his possessions for him, even his life and his honor and more, if that were possible; then he left the brother and sister, planning not to see them again in Rome. He was a prudent suitor, and perhaps among the best in knowing how to seize the occasion when opportunity knocks.

All these things probably awakened Arnaldo to just how low his hopes had sunk, and just how close the whole scheme of his pilgrimage was to going under, since, as has been said, death was practically stepping on Auristela's skirts. He'd made up his mind to accompany the duke,[2] if not on the same road then at least following up his same intention, though in his case he'd return to Denmark. But love and his noble heart wouldn't allow him to leave Periandro with no friendly consolation or desert his friend's sister Auristela at the very brink of her life's end. So he visited them, and once again offered to help, finally deciding to wait and see if time would improve things, despite his feeling beset by numerous anxieties.

Chapter Ten of the Fourth Book

Hipólita was ecstatically happy to see that the skills of the cruel Julia were proving so damaging to Auristela's health, for in a week they transformed her into someone so different from who she was before that she could no longer be recognized except by the sound of her voice, something that stumped the doctors and astonished everyone who knew her. The French ladies watched over her health with as much concern as if they'd been her own dear sisters, particularly Feliz Flora, who felt a special affection and fondness for her.

Auristela's illness reached such a point that, not being satisfied with the boundaries of its own jurisdiction, it crossed over into that of her neighbors, and as Auristela had none closer than Periandro, the first one it encountered was he, not because the poison and spells of the evil Jewess worked directly and especially on him as they did on Auristela, for whom they'd been made, but rather because the suffering he felt on seeing Auristela's illness was so great it had the same effect on him as it did on her. So he, too, was wasting away and everyone began to be just as concerned for his life as they were for Auristela's.

When Hipólita saw this and realized she was killing herself with the edge of her own sword, she diagnosed the source of Periandro's illness and sought to cure him and Auristela at the same time, the latter being by now wasted away and ghastly pale, her life reaching out for the knocker on death's door. Since Auristela believed that at any moment that door would certainly be opened up for her, she chose to unlock and open the way out for her soul via the sacraments, having now been taught the truths of the Catholic faith. So doing all things necessary as devoutly as she could, she bore witness to her good intentions, demonstrated the depth of her morality, and showed signs of having learned well what they'd taught her in Rome. Then with resignation calming her spirit and placing it in the hands of God, she gave up all thoughts of kingdoms, pleasures, and nobility.

As has already been said, Hipólita saw Periandro was dying along with Auristela, and so went to the Jewess to ask her to moderate the violence of the spells destroying Auristela, or to remove them completely, as she didn't want to be responsible for taking three lives with a single blow. For if Auristela died, Periandro would, too, and if Periandro died, Hipólita's life would also come to an end. The Jewess did as she asked, as though the health or sickness of others were in her hands, or as though all suffering as punishment for our sins didn't depend on God's will, just as all suffering we cause others is *not* God's will; but God, being compelled—if you can put it that way—by our own sins to punish them, allows this thing called witchcraft to steal away other peoples' health, and lets sorceresses do just that. There's no question He permits them to use potions and poisons that within a short time can take the life of whomever they wish, while the person afflicted is powerless to escape this danger because he's unaware of it and ignorant of the cause from which such a deadly effect proceeds; and to heal such diseases God's great mercy must be the physician giving the medicine.

Then Auristela suddenly stopped getting worse, in itself a sign of improvement. The sun of her beauty began to show hints and glimmers of dawning again in her heavenly face; the roses in her cheeks began to bud anew, and happiness returned to her eyes; the shadows of her melancholy slunk away; the sweetly timbered organ of her voice was restored; the red of her lips resumed its splendor, and the ivory of her teeth its pearly whiteness. In short, in a brief space of time she once again became all beautiful, wholly pleasing, and completely happy, while these same effects spilled over to Periandro, the French ladies, and to all the others, Croriano and Ruperta, Antonio, and especially to his sister Constanza, whose happiness or sadness changed along with Auristela's. Meanwhile, Auristela gave thanks to Heaven for the mercies and kindnesses it granted her in sickness and in health.

Then one day she called for Periandro; when they'd carefully arranged to be alone, she spoke to him as follows, "Dear brother of mine—Heaven has led me to call you by that sweet and pure name during these two years without allowing any delight or forgetfulness to tempt me to call you by any other one not as pure and pleasing— I'd like this happiness to continue and only the ending of life to put an end to it, for fortune is only good to the extent it's lastingly good, and it's only as lasting as it is pure. Our souls, as you well know and they've taught me here, are always in constant movement and can come to rest only in God, their center. The desires of this life are countless and linked together in an endless chain, a chain that sometimes reaches all the way up to Heaven and at others sinks into Hell. If you will, brother—though this language isn't mine and goes beyond what I've been able to learn during my few years and in the remote place of my upbringing—observe that on the blank slate of my soul experience has drawn and written important things.

"Primarily, it has written that knowing and seeing God is the highest glory, and all the means directed toward that end, such as charity, purity, and virginity, are good, holy, and pleasing. At least, I see it that way, and together with that understanding I also understand that the love you feel for me is so great you'll want whatever I may want. I'm the heiress to a kingdom, and you already know that the reason my dear mother sent me to the house of your parents the king and queen was to keep me safe from the great war then feared. You know, too, that going there was the cause of my coming with you here, so entirely subject to your will that I haven't strayed from it in the slightest. You've been my father and you've been my brother, you, my shadow, my help, and finally, my guardian angel. You've been my instructor and my teacher, bringing me to this city where I've become a Christian, as I ought.

"I'd like now, if possible, to go to Heaven with no delays, no unpleasant surprises and no worries, but that won't be possible if you won't give me back what I myself have given you, which is my promise and desire to be your wife. Let me have, sir, my promise back, and I'll try to give up my desire, even if I have to force myself; for to achieve a happiness as great as going to Heaven everything on earth should be left behind and given up, even parents and husbands or wives.[1] I don't want to leave you for another. I'm leaving you for God, who will give Himself to you, and the rewards of that are infinitely greater than your loss in letting me go. I have a little sister just as beautiful as I, if mortal beauty is, in fact, truly beautiful. You can marry her and obtain the kingdom that falls to me; in that you'll be doing what makes me happy, while your own desires won't be entirely cheated. . . . Why do you bow your head, brother? Why are you looking down at the floor? Are my words distasteful to you? Do my wishes seem misguided to you? Tell me, answer me! At least let me know what your wishes are; perhaps I'll be able to temper mine somewhat and find a way for your pleasure and mine to coincide."

Periandro had been listening to Auristela from the depths of a profound silence, and in next to no time thousands of ideas rushed into his mind. But they all brought him to the worst possible conclusion, that is, he imagined Auristela despised him and that the change she contemplated in her life was planned solely to bring his to an end, since he felt she must have known full well that if she'd no longer agree to be his wife he'd have nothing left to live for in the world. He went over and over this so intently in his mind that without answering a word to Auristela he got up from where he was seated and, on the pretext of welcoming Feliz Flora and the Lady Constanza into the room, he left it. I don't know if I should say Auristela was left feeling remorseful, but I do know she was pensive and confused.

Chapter Eleven of the Fourth Book

When water is bottled up in a small-mouthed jar, the more it hurries to escape, the slower it pours out. The liquid at the mouth is pushed forward by the drops behind, which block each other's way and slow the forward motion of the current until at last it breaks through and the contents all empty out. The same thing happens with ideas conceived in the mind of a wounded lover; sometimes all of them rush together toward the tongue and block each other's way, and he doesn't know which one to express first to get his thoughts out. Thus, by keeping silent he often says more than he'd like.

This fact was demonstrated by the minimal courtesy with which Periandro treated the people coming in to see Auristela. Although he was full of things to say, pregnant with ideas and filled to the brim with thoughts, he left Auristela's room feeling rejected and disillusioned, not knowing how, or wanting, or being able to answer a single word to all she'd said to him. Antonio and his sister went up to Auristela and she seemed to them like a person just awakened from a deep sleep; she was talking to herself in clear and understandable words: "I've done the wrong thing; but, does it matter? Isn't it better for my brother to know my intentions? Isn't it better for me to leave the crooked roads and uncertain paths before it's too late and turn my steps toward the easy, clear paths leading us by an unquestionably better way toward our journey's happy destination? I realize Periandro's company won't keep me from going to Heaven, but I feel, too, that I'll get there sooner without it. I certainly owe more to myself than to anyone else, and the attraction of Heaven and its glory has to take precedent over kinship, and even more so in this case, since I'm not even related to Periandro."

"Stop, sister Auristela!" Constanza said then. "You're revealing things that may clear up some of our confused suspicions, but may leave you dismayed. If, on the one hand, Periandro isn't your brother, you've certainly been on familiar terms with him. On the other hand, if he is, there's no reason for you to be upset by his company." At this point Auristela came back to her senses. Hearing what Constanza was saying to her, she tried to smooth over her carelessness but couldn't manage it. When you try to patch up a lie the threads get tangled up in a lot of others, leaving the truth in doubt and suspicions stronger than ever.

"I don't know what I've been saying to myself, sister," said Auristela, "or if Periandro is my brother or not. What I can tell you is that he is, at the very least, my soul. In him I live, in him I breathe and move, and by him I'm sustained. Nevertheless, I've held myself within the bounds of reason, not indulging in any improper thoughts, or failing to observe modest behavior, just as a noblewoman having such a noble brother should behave."

"I don't understand you, Lady Auristela," Antonio said to her then; "from what you say it sounds just as much like Periandro is your brother as that he isn't. Tell us who he is and who you are, if you can reveal it, for whether he's your brother or not at least you can't deny now you're both noble, and we, I mean my sister Constanza and I, are not so naively inexperienced that we'll be astonished by any situation you might describe. Even though we left the Barbarous Isle what seems like only yesterday, the trials through which you've seen us pass have been our teachers in many subjects. No matter how slight the information available to us, we can follow a thread until we get to the heart of the most complicated matters, especially those related to love, since it seems they practically unravel themselves. Would it matter if Periandro weren't your brother and instead you were his lawful wife? Would it matter, I repeat, since until now your modesty and restraint have kept you wholly pure in the eyes of Heaven and completely correct in the eyes of everyone who's seen you? Not all loves are rash and foolhardy, nor does every lover set his pleasure's sights solely on physical enjoyment, ignoring his beloved's fine mind.[1] Now since all of this is so, my lady, again I beg you to tell us who you are, and who Periandro is, too, for judging by the way he went out of here, there's a volcano burning behind his eyes but a gag on his mouth."

"Oh, I'm so miserable!" replied Auristela. "I'd have been so much better off if I'd remained locked in eternal silence, because had I kept quiet I wouldn't have been the cause of this gag you say he has on his mouth! We women are imprudent, impatient, and worse at keeping our mouths shut. While I kept quiet, my soul was at peace; then I spoke up and was at rest no more. Now to finish off my peace of mind once and for all, and at the same time to bring the tragedy of my life to a close, I want you both to know—since Heaven has made you really and truly brother and sister—that Periandro isn't mine—much less is he my husband or my suitor, at least not one of those who while racing after his own pleasure, tries to end up at the finish line in possession of his beloved's honor. He's the son of a king; I'm the daughter and heiress of a kingdom, and we're equal in blood. I hold some small advantage over him in estate and wealth, though we're equally matched in goodwill. As a matter of fact, we share the same intentions, and our desires gaze at each other thinking only of the most pure consummation. It's only bad fortune that disturbs and thwarts our wishes, forcing us to place all our hopes on its improvement. Now because the knot Periandro has around his throat is choking mine, too, I don't want to say any more to you for the moment, friends, except to beg you to help me look for him. Since he took leave without excusing himself, he won't want to return unless someone goes to find him."

"Get up, then," said Constanza, "and let's go look for him, for love binds lovers so tightly it doesn't let them stray very far from their beloved. Come, we'll soon find him, you'll soon see him, and find your happiness sooner than you think. Why not ignore the scruples enveloping you and give them the back of your hand by offering it to Periandro as his wife? By making him your mate you'll be able to silence any gossip." Auristela got up and in the company of Feliz Flora, Constanza, and Antonio, went out to look for Periandro. All three of them saw her now as a queen, so they looked at her differently and served her with more respect.

While they were all searching, Periandro was deliberately trying to evade anyone looking for him. He left Rome on foot and alone, unless bitter solitude, sad sighs, and continual sobs can be counted as companionship, for these and all sorts of ideas racing around in his mind wouldn't let him alone for a minute. "Oh most beautiful Sigismunda, you're a queen by your very nature, exceedingly fair by special favor and grace from nature herself, extremely wise, and extraordinarily delightful!" he was saying to himself. "How little it was costing you, my lady, to think of me as your brother, for my behavior and thoughts never betrayed the truth of the matter, even though malice itself might have wanted to get to the bottom of it and had stayed awake all night trying to figure it out! If you want to be taken up to Heaven single and all alone, with your actions not controlled by anyone except God and yourself, so be it. But I'll have you know you won't set out totally blameless on the road you wish to take. Though not exactly my murderer, my lady, you'll have been guilty of wrapping your thoughts in silence and deceit by not revealing to me sooner that you were going to pull my soul out by the roots of my love, a soul so much belonging to you that I leave it entirely in your hands, banishing all will of my own. Peace, my love, and know that the best thing I can do for you is leave you."

Night had fallen by this time and, moving a little off the road to Naples, he heard the sound of a stream flowing through some trees. He threw himself down roughly on its bank and silenced his tongue, though his sighs knew no rest.

Chapter Twelve of the Fourth Book

Which Tells Who Periandro and Auristela Were

It seems good and bad fortune are separated from each other by so little space that they're like two convergent lines; even though they begin at different and distant points, they come together at the same one. Periandro was weeping in the company of the gentle brook and the clear light of the night. The trees were his companions and a soft, fresh breeze was drying his tears. He was carried away with thoughts of Auristela, while the wind promised hope of finding a solution for his problems. Then to his ears came the sound of someone speaking in a foreign language, and on listening to it attentively he could tell it was that of his homeland, even though he couldn't make out whether the person was talking under his breath or singing, and curiosity led him to go closer. When he was nearer, he could hear two people neither singing nor whispering, but rather carrying on a normal conversation. What amazed him most was that they were speaking in the language of Norway, though so far from there.

He hid himself behind a tree in such a way that the tree's shadow and his own were the same, then he quieted his breathing, and the first words to reach his ears were, "Sir, you don't have to convince me that Norway's one long day is divided into two halves. I was taken there for some time by my misfortunes, so I'm aware night takes up half the year and day the other. I know that's true; I just don't know *why* it's that way."

The reply was, "If we reach Rome, I'll have you put your finger on the cause of this wondrous effect on a globe. It's an effect as natural in that latitude[1] as it is for day and night together to last twenty-four hours in this one. I've also told you that approaching the North Pole in the most distant part of Norway is the island held to be the last one on earth—at least in that direction. Its name is Thyle, which Virgil called Thule[2] in those verses in the first book of the *Georgics* which say: ' . . . Ac tua nautae/Numina sola colant: tibi serviat ultima Thule,'[3] for *Thule,* in Greek, is the same as *Thyle* in Latin.

"This island is just as large or only slightly smaller than England, and is rich and abundant in everything necessary for human life. Farther on, practically at the North Pole itself, is the island called Frisland,[4] which was discovered and made known about four hundred years ago; it's so large it's known as a kingdom, and not a small one. The king and lord of Thyle is Magsimino, the son of Queen Eustoquia. His father passed from this life to a better one not many months ago leaving two sons; one is Magsimino, the heir to the kingdom whom I've mentioned, and the other is a splendid youth called Persiles, richly endowed beyond all telling with nature's gifts and loved by his mother more than I can tell you. In fact, I don't know how I could sufficiently heap praises on the virtues of this Persiles, so I'll not even try because I wouldn't want my limited ingenuity to fall short. I'm the tutor who raised him and the love I feel for him should lead me to go on and on, but I'd rather keep quiet than not do him justice."

Periandro was listening to all this and immediately realized the person praising him could be none other than his tutor Seráfido, and that likewise the one listening to him was Rutilio, judging by the voice and the words with which he was responding from time to time. I'll leave it up to you whether he was astonished or not, and he was even more so when he heard Seráfido, indeed the very person Periandro thought him to be, say, "Eusebia, the Queen of Frisland, had two extraordinarily beautiful daughters, especially the elder one, Sigismunda, while the younger was called Eusebia, after her mother. In the elder daughter nature had gathered together all the pieces of beauty it had strewn around the world. Her mother, with I don't know what plan in mind but taking as a pretext the fact that some enemies were going to make war against her, sent Sigismunda to Thule to be in the care of Eustoquia so she could be raised safely in her house without the disturbing experience of war. Now, I personally feel this was not the main reason for sending her, but rather to lead Prince Magsimino to fall in love with her and take her as his wife, for exceptional beauty can be expected to turn hearts of marble into wax and pull together the most widely divergent opposites.

"At any rate, what I've seen so far doesn't disprove the truth of what I suspect, because I know Prince Magsimino is dying for Sigismunda. At the time she arrived at Thyle he wasn't on the island, so his mother the queen sent him her portrait along with a delegation from the girl's mother. He answered saying they should shower her with attention and care for her, because she was going to be his wife.

"This response, like an arrow, pierced the heart of my son Persiles (I call him my son because I brought him up), and once he'd heard Magsimino's reply he wouldn't stand for hearing about anything he enjoyed; he lost his youthful spirits and, in short, wrapped in dutiful silence all the deeds that usually made everyone notice and love him. Worst of all he lost his health over her, sinking into the arms of desperation.

"Doctors examined him, but since they didn't know the cause of his illness they couldn't find a cure for it; since heartaches don't have pulses to be taken, it's difficult and almost impossible to diagnose the diseases that spring from them. His mother, seeing her son dying and not knowing who was killing him, asked him over and over again to reveal to her the source of his suffering, for it wasn't possible that he himself didn't know the cause, since he was feeling the effects. So powerful was her persuasion, so many the entreaties of this grieving mother, that Persiles' stubbornness or resolve was overcome and he went to tell her he was dying for Sigismunda, and that he'd decided to let himself die rather than betray the respect he owed his brother. This confession brought the queen's dead happiness back to life. She gave Persiles hope, saying she'd help him even though it would mean pushing aside Magsimino's wishes, for when it comes to saving a life there are more important things to consider than a brother's anger.

"Finally Eustoquia spoke to Sigismunda, stressing to her what she'd lose if Persiles lost his life, for he was a person in whom all the graces in the world made their home—just the opposite of Magsimino, whose rough habits were somewhat repugnant. She bragged about him a little more than she should and used all the exaggeration she could, praising Persiles' virtues to the skies. Sigismunda, a girl all alone and subject to this influence, replied that she had no will of her own, nor any counselor except her own modesty, and provided that was respected they should make whatever arrangements for her they might want. The queen embraced her, told Persiles her answer, and together the mother and son planned for the couple to leave the island before his brother should come back. When he didn't find her there, they'd give him the excuse that she'd made a vow to go to Rome to learn more about the Catholic faith, which in those northern regions is somewhat in need of repair. Persiles first swore to Sigismunda that in no way, either by word or deed, would he act contrary to her modesty. And so, loading them down with jewels and advice, the queen sent them off, she herself later telling me everything I've told you so far.

"Two years or a little more after these events, Prince Magsimino returned to his kingdom, for during that time he'd been occupied with the war he always had at hand against his enemies. He asked for Sigismunda, and not finding her there became uneasy. Learning of her journey he set out to look for her without a moment's delay, for although he trusted his brother's goodness he still suffered from the misgivings that seldom leave lovers in peace.

"As soon as his mother learned of his decision, she called me aside and entrusted me with the health, life, and honor of her younger son, instructing me to go on ahead, find, and warn him that his brother was looking for him. Prince Magsimino departed in two great ships. Passing through the Straits of Hercules[5] and encountering a variety of weather and storms, he reached the island of Tinacria,[6] from there traveled to the great city of Parthénope,[7] and now isn't far from here in a village called Terrachina,[8] the last of those belonging to Naples and the first of the Roman ones. He's ill, having contracted the disease that comes with the stifling weather here,[9] and is at the point of death. From Lisbon, where I disembarked, I bring news of Persiles and Sigismunda, or at least of a man and a woman on a pilgrimage whose fame for beauty is being loudly proclaimed and who must be, if not Persiles and Sigismunda, angels in human form."

"If instead of calling them Persiles and Sigismunda," responded the person who was listening to Seráfido, "you called them Periandro and Auristela, I could give you very accurate news about them; I met them many days ago and have suffered many trials in their company." Then he began to recount the ones that happened to them on the Barbarous Isle, along with others. He was still going on at daybreak, indeed, at such length that Periandro left them alone so they wouldn't find him there and went back to look for Auristela to tell her about his brother's coming and to discuss with her what they should do to flee his wrath, for he thought it a miracle to have learned about the situation in such an out-of-the-way place. And so, full of fresh thoughts, he returned to the presence of his contrite Auristela and recovered his nearly lost hopes of achieving his desire.

Chapter Thirteen of the Fourth Book

The pain and sensation of recently inflicted wounds are allayed by anger and hot blood, but after they cool off become so grievous they wear out the patience of the person suffering from them. The same thing happens with passions of the spirit; when there's been some time and opportunity to think about them, they can become trying enough to take a person's life.

Auristela revealed her wishes to Periandro, thereby satisfying her desire; happy to have made it known to him, she then expected him to comply, since she was confident he'd bend his will to suit hers. But as has been said, when he left Rome his only response was silence, and what happened to him has already been related. He came upon Rutilio telling his tutor Seráfido the whole story of the Barbarous Isle, along with his suspicions that Auristela and Periandro might be Sigismunda and Persiles. He'd also told Seráfido that he'd surely find them in Rome, for ever since he'd come across them they'd been headed there under the guise and ruse of being brother and sister. Then he asked Seráfido at length about the nature of the people in those remote islands where Magsimino was king and the matchless Auristela queen.

Seráfido again told Rutilio that the island of Thyle or Thule, which is now commonly called Iceland, was the most remote in those northern seas, even though "a little farther on there's another island, as I've said, called Frisland, which was previously ignored by the ancients and discovered by Nicholas Temo the Venetian,[1] in the year 1380. It's as large as Sicily and its queen is Eusebia, the mother of Sigismunda, for whom I'm searching. There's also another major island almost always covered with snow. It's named Greenland and on one of its headlands there's a monastery called Saint Thomas where there are monks from four nations: Spaniards, French, Tuscans, and Latins;[2] they teach their languages to the noblemen on the island so when they leave they can make themselves understood wherever they may go.

"This island, as I've said, is buried in snow, and at the top of a low mountain there's a spring, marvelous and worth knowing about. From it spills and pours forth a great abundance of water so hot that when it flows into the sea it not only thaws a large part of it, but heats it as well, so that incredible numbers of different kinds of fish congregate in those waters. The monastery and the whole island support themselves by fishing, the source of all their income and earnings. This spring also produces some viscous material from which a sticky cement is made and used to build houses similar to those constructed of solid marble. I could tell you other strange and seemingly inaccurate facts about these islands," continued Seráfido to Rutilio, "but they're all actually true." Periandro didn't overhear the entire discussion, rather it was related by Rutilio later, and after being strengthened by what Periandro added, many people were led to give this information about the islands the exact degree of credibility it deserved.

By now day had dawned and Periandro found himself near the church and basilica of Saint Paul, which is magnificent and almost the largest in Europe. He saw coming toward him a crowd of people, some mounted and some on foot, and as they drew closer he recognized those approaching as Auristela, Feliz Flora, Constanza, and her brother Antonio, and also Hipólita, who having learned of Periandro's absence, didn't want any other woman to have the joy of reporting him found—so, acting just like the woman whose friend was no one's friend, she was guided by information provided her by the wife of Zabulón the Jew and followed Auristela's every move.

At last Periandro approached the beautiful band, greeted Auristela, observed the look on her face, and found her earlier harshness now more gentle and her eyes softer. Then in front of everyone he related what had happened the night before when he'd overheard his tutor Seráfido and Rutilio. He told them how his brother Prince Magsimino was ill from the stifling weather and staying at Terrachina, but that he planned to come to Rome to be cured and then would disguise his rank, change his name, and start looking for them. He asked Auristela and the others for advice about what he should do, for judging by his brother the prince's character, he couldn't expect any sort of pleasant reunion. Auristela was stunned by the unexpected news; all her hopes of maintaining her purity and her noble intentions, as well as those of being able to take the more open road to companionship with her beloved Periandro, evaporated instantly.

All the rest of the people present mulled over in their minds what advice they'd give Periandro, and the first one who came up with something, even though they didn't ask her for it, was the wealthy and love-smitten Hipólita, who offered to take him, along with his sister Auristela, to Naples, and to spend on them the hundred thousand and more ducados that her estate was worth. Pirro the Calabrian was there and heard her offer, considering it the same as hearing an irrevocable death sentence passed on him. Among thugs it's not rejection that produces jealousy but self-interest; since his interests were being lost to Hipólita's new concerns, with each passing minute desperation was taking a stronger hold on his soul, where he was storing up deadly hatred for Periandro, whose nobility and good looks, although they were impressive—as has been said—seemed even more impressive to him, for it's the nature of a jealous man to see his rival's qualities as magnificent and grand.

Periandro thanked Hipólita but didn't accept her generous offer. The others didn't have a chance to give him any advice because at that moment Rutilio and Seráfido arrived. Scarcely had they spied Periandro when both of them at once ran over to throw themselves at his feet, for his changed clothes couldn't change his nobility. Rutilio embraced him around the waist and Seráfido around the neck, Rutilio weeping with delight and Seráfido with happiness.

Everyone present was absorbed in watching this strange and joyful reunion. Only in Pirro's heart was melancholy stirring, and it gripped him with burning tongs hotter than fire itself. The pain he felt on seeing Periandro praised and honored was so intense that not knowing what he was doing—or perhaps knowing all too well—he took his sword in hand and plunged it between Seráfido's arms and into Periandro's right shoulder with such fury and force that the point of it came out his left shoulder, running him through almost diagonally, from one side to the other.

The first to see the blow was Hipólita, and hers was the first voice to cry out, saying, "Oh, you traitor! My mortal enemy! How could you have taken the life of someone who deserved to live forever?" Seráfido opened his arms and Rutilio let go, both of them warm with Periandro's spilled blood, and so he fell into the arms of Auristela, whose voice was caught in her throat; finding no breath for her sighs, nor tears for her eyes, her head fell forward on her chest and her arms to her sides.

This blow, more deadly in appearance than in fact, shocked everyone present and stole the color from their faces, sketching death in its place, for now, because of his loss of blood, death was coursing through Periandro's veins, and the fear of losing him threatened to bring everyone's days to an end. Certainly Auristela's life was hanging by a thread, one she was about to bite in two. Seráfido and Antonio rushed Pirro and, despite his ferocity and strength, subdued him. With the help of some people who came up they sent him off to prison, and four days later the governor sent him to the gallows as a hardened criminal and murderer. His death brought life to Hipólita, who began to truly live from that time forward.

Chapter Fourteen of the Fourth Book

So flimsy is the security with which man enjoys his pleasures that no one can promise himself even a minimal degree of certainty in them.

Auristela, who regretted telling her thoughts to Periandro, had happily set out to look for him, thinking it was in her hands and up to her change of heart to direct Periandro's will wherever she liked, for she imagined herself to be the peg on the wheel of his fortune and the sphere within which all his desires moved. Nor was she mistaken, for Periandro had already decided not to let his desires stray from hers.

But just look how unstable fortune deceives us! As has been seen, in the wink of an eye Auristela finds herself someone different from before. She'd thought she'd laugh, and she's crying; she'd thought she'd live, and is already dying; she'd thought she was going to enjoy seeing Periandro, and instead what her eyes beheld was his brother Prince Magsimino, who with several carriages and a large retinue was entering Rome on the road from Terrachina.

His eye was caught by the band of people surrounding the wounded Periandro. He came closer in his coach to see what was happening, and Seráfido stepped forward to welcome him, saying, "Oh, Prince Magsimino, punishment is the only reward I can expect for the bad news I have to give you! This wounded man whom you see in the arms of this beautiful young woman is your brother Persiles, and she is the matchless Sigismunda, both of them found through your efforts at such a cruel moment and at such a harsh time that you'll not have the opportunity to lavish attention on them but will be obliged instead to carry them to their graves."

"They won't go alone," replied Magsimino, "for I shall keep them company, judging by the condition I'm in." Then leaning his head out of the carriage he recognized his brother, even though he was all covered and stained with blood from his wound. Despite the fact that her face had gone pale, he also recognized Sigismunda, for the alarm had altered her color but couldn't make her features ugly. Sigismunda was beautiful before this misfortune befell her, but after it she was extremely so; often one of the side effects of pain is that it increases beauty.

He dropped from the carriage into the arms of Sigismunda, who no longer was Auristela but the queen of Frisland and, in his imagination, also the queen of Thule. These strange reverses fall within the power commonly called Fortune, but which is nothing less than Heaven's unwavering plan. Magsimino had set out with the intention of reaching Rome to be healed there by better doctors than those in Terrachina, who'd predicted that before he entered Rome he'd be waylaid by death, and in this diagnosis they turned out to be more accurate and experienced than in knowing how to treat him. The truth is that the disease prevalent there during the extreme weather is one very few know how to cure.

In fact, out in the open in front of Saint Paul's Basilica ugly death came forth to meet the handsome Persiles. It dashed him to the ground, but it buried Magsimino, who on finding himself at the point of death, with his right hand took hold of his brother's left and brought it up to his own eyes, while with his left he grasped Periandro's right hand and placed it in Sigismunda's. Then in a voice racked by exhaustion he said with his dying breath, "I believe you're prepared for this, my true children and brother and sister. Dear brother, touch these eyelids and close these eyes of mine in eternal sleep, while with this other hand, clasp Sigismunda's and in so doing seal the promise I want you to give her to become her husband, and let the witnesses of this marriage be the blood you're losing and the friends

349

who surround you. Your parents' kingdom awaits you and you'll also inherit Sigismunda's. Strive for good health and you'll enjoy them for countless years to come." These words, so tender, so happy, and so sad, revived Persiles' spirits; obeying the command of his brother who was in death's grip, he closed his brother's eyes with his hand; then not knowing whether to feel happy or sad, with his tongue he pronounced the "I do" that gave him to Sigismunda as her husband.

The shock of the unexpected and painful death took its toll on the emotions of those present; sighs began to fill the air and tears to water the ground. They picked up Magsimino's body and carried it to Saint Paul's. They took the half-dead Persiles in the dead man's carriage back into Rome to recover, but when they got there they didn't find either Belarminia or Deleasir, because they'd gone off to France with the duke. Arnaldo was very upset by Sigismunda's strange and novel wedding. It hurt him deeply that nothing had come of so many years of service and so many years of good deeds performed in order to gain the peaceful enjoyment of her matchless beauty; but what gnawed at him most were the slanderous Clodio's unheeded words, for now, in spite of himself, he'd thoroughly vindicated their truth. Confused, dazed, and stunned, he almost departed without saying a word to Persiles and Sigismunda. But considering that they were royalty and what their excuse had been, and that this alone was his destiny, he decided to go see them, and so he did.

He was very well received and, so he wouldn't be able to complain about losing everything, they offered him Sigismunda's sister the princess Eusebia as his wife, and he gladly accepted her. He would have gone back with them right then if he hadn't wanted to ask his father's permission. In marriages between important people, and indeed in all marriages, it's only right for children to bend their wills to that of their parents. He accompanied his future brother-in-law during the recovery from his wound, and when he was well went to see his father and to prepare the festivities of his wife's arrival.

Feliz Flora decided to marry Antonio the barbarian, not daring to return to live among the relatives of the man Antonio had killed. Croriano and Ruperta, having finished their pilgrimage, went back to France with much to tell about all that had happened to the woman who pretended to be Auristela. Bartolomé of La Mancha and Luisa from Castile went off to Naples, where it's said they came to a bad end because they never quite could be good.

Persiles deposited his brother's body in a crypt in Saint Paul's, gathered together all his servants, visited the churches of Rome again, and took care of Constanza (to whom Sigismunda gave her diamond cross), accompanying her until leaving her married to her brother-in-law the count.

After having kissed the pontiff's feet, Sigismunda's spirit was at peace knowing she'd fulfilled her vow. The course of her life was spent in companionship with her husband Persiles, and her days were increased by the enjoyment of living to see great-grandchildren in their long and happy line of descendants.

THE END OF
THE TRIALS OF PERSILES AND SIGISMUNDA
A NORTHERN STORY

Appendix

Certificate of Price

I, Jerónimo Núñez de León, clerk of Our Lord the King's Chamber and on behalf of those who hold a seat in his Council, do hereby certify that the book entitled *The Story of Persiles and Sigismunda,* composed by Miguel de Cervantes Saavedra, having been seen by those lords, was published with the permission of the said lords who set the value of each quarto at four maravedís.[1] Since it appears to have fifty-eight quartos, which would come to two hundred thirty-two *maravedís,* they have commanded that it be sold for this price, and for no more, and that this certificate of price be placed in the front of each and every copy printed.

In witness whereof, and by command of the said lords of the Council, and on petition of the said Miguel de Cervantes, I hereby issue this certificate.

In Madrid, the twenty-third day of December in the year one thousand six hundred and sixteen.

Jerónimo Núñez de León

It has fifty-eight quartos, which at four maravedís each comes to six reales and twenty-eight maravedís.

Errata to Edition of 1616

This book entitled *The Story of the Trials of Persiles and Sigis-munda* is identical to the original copy.

Issued in Madrid, the fifteenth day of the month of December of the year one thousand six hundred and sixteen.

Dr. Murcia de la Llana

The King

In so much as you, doña Catalina de Salazar,[2] the widow of Miguel de Cervantes Saavedra, provided us information that the said Miguel de Cervantes on his death left a book he had written entitled *The Trials of Persiles,* to which he had dedicated much study and work, and since you requested that we command a license be given you so you might print it with a copyright for twenty years or for whatever period it might be our pleasure to grant, and in as much as the matter was examined by the members of our Council, and by their command the measures were taken as required by our decree recently issued about the printing of books, it was agreed that we should command this letter patent of ours be granted you, and we have seen fit to do so.

We therefore give you or whomever you may empower, and no one else, license and permission for the period of the next ten years, beginning and being counted from the date here shown, to print and sell said book mentioned above, copying from the original examined by our Council, and which is signed and endorsed by Jerónimo Núñez de León, the clerk of our Chamber, acting for those who have a seat there, provided that before it is sold you bring it before them along with said original so that it can be determined whether said printing is identical to it, and you must bring a sworn certificate to the effect that a proofreader appointed by us has examined and corrected said printing against the original.

And we do hereby command whichever printer may print said book not to print the beginning nor first quarto, nor to deliver more than a single copy of the book along with the original to the author or to whichever person at whose expense it may be printed and to no one else, until such time as said book has been proofread and its price fixed by the members of our Council. And when this has been done, and not until then, may said book be printed with the beginning and first quarto, and on the first pages must appear this license and privilege, together with the approval, certificate of price and errata, under pain of incurring those penalties provided in the laws and regulations of our kingdoms regarding such matters.

And we do hereby command that during said period of ten years, no person may without your permission print or sell it, under penalty that the person who may print it will and shall lose each and every printing of it, along with the type and forms used in the printing, and shall in addition be assessed a fine of fifty thousand maravedís; of the said fine a third shall be for our Chamber, another third for the judge passing sentence, and the other third for the person making the accusation.

And we hereby command the members of our Council, presidents and judges of our high courts of justice, mayors and constables of our palace and court and of the Chancery courts, and all the magistrates, chief judges, governors, high mayors and ordinary mayors, and all other judges and law officers whatsoever, in all the cities, towns, and villages of our kingdoms and domains to keep and comply with this our patent to you, and not to act in violation of its spirit or letter or infringe on it in any manner whatsoever.

Set down at San Lorenzo,[3] the twenty-fourth day of the month of September in the year one thousand six hundred and sixteen.

I, the King
By command of our lord the king,
Pedro de Contreras.

Approval

By command of His Majesty I have examined the book *The Trials of Persiles* by Miguel de Cervantes Saavedra, illustrious son of our nation, and illustrious father of so many good children[4] with which he has happily ennobled it; and I find nothing in it against our holy Catholic faith and good morals; on the contrary, it contains much decent and pleasant amusement, and one can say the same thing about it that Saint Jerome did about Origen's commentary[5] on the *Song of Solomon*: *cum in omnibus omnes, in hoc seipsum superavit Origenes,*[6] for of all the writings he left us, none is more brilliantly inventive, more cultured, or more entertaining. In short, like a swan in his saintly old age and almost in the very grip of death, he sang this creation of his venerable intelligence. This is my view. Unless, etc.[7]

At Madrid, the ninth of September in the year one thousand six hundred and sixteen.

Master José de Valdivieso[8]

From Don Francisco de Urbina[9]

TO MIGUEL DE CERVANTES, ILLUSTRIOUS AND CHRISTIAN GENIUS
OF OUR TIMES, WHOM THE BROTHERS OF THE THIRD ORDER
OF SAINT FRANCIS[10] CARRIED FOR BURIAL WITH HIS FACE UNCOVERED,
HE HIMSELF BEING A BROTHER OF THE THIRD ORDER

EPITAPH[11]

Look Traveler; here within lies
The pilgrim Cervantes;
The earth covers his body, but not his name,
Which is divine.
In short, he walked his road;
But his fame is not dead,
Nor his good works;
They are sure proof that he could depart
From this life to the next
With his head held high.

On the Tomb of Miguel de Cervantes Saavedra,

A CHRISTIAN MAN OF GENIUS,
BY LUIS FRANCISCO CALDERON[12]

Sonnet[13]

In this small monument, oh traveler dear,
If not a lofty pyre, a mournful urn,
Behold the holy ashes of a man
Whose genius dares scorn time's forgetfulness.

The grains of sand that wash along the banks
Of the glorious river Tagus[14] number less
Than the tongues astonished here today by his;
A grateful Spain aspires to praise his name.

We greet the shining virtues of his books
With wonder sweet: his style has moral weight
And is as pure devout invention known.

We Spaniards to his genius have bestowed
Abundant tribute known to all the world,
And for his body, offer endless tears.

To Don Pedro Fernández de Castro[15]

COUNT OF LEMOS, OF ANDRADE, OF VILLALVA;
MARQUIS OF SARRIA, GENTLEMAN OF HIS MAJESTY'S CHAMBER,
PRESIDENT OF THE SUPREME COUNCIL OF ITALY,
KNIGHT COMMANDER OF THE *ENCOMIENDA* OF LA ZARZA
AND OF THE ORDER OF ALCANTARA[16]

I wish those old verses, which were so famous in their time and which begin

"With my foot already in the stirrup,"

weren't so made to order for this epistle of mine, for with almost the same words[17] I can begin it saying

With my foot already in the stirrup,
In the agony of death,
Great Lord, I write you this.

Yesterday they gave me Extreme Unction and today I'm writing this. Time is short, my agony waxes while hope wanes, and yet despite all this, my desire to live keeps me alive, and I would like not to bring my life to an end until I have kissed Your Excellency's feet; perhaps the happiness of seeing Your Excellency safely back in Spain might give me life again. But if it's decreed that I must lose it, let Heaven's will be done, and at least Your Excellency will know of my desire and that in me You had a servant so fond of serving you that he chose to show his good intentions even as he passed into death. Still, as though with the gift of prophecy, I already share in the joy of your Excellency's return; and while I rejoice to see you singled out for recognition, I rejoice even more that my hopes came true and were even exceeded by the fame of Your Excellency's good deeds.

There are still some fragments and traces in my mind of the "Weeks in a Garden," and the famous "Bernardo,"[18] and if happily by good luck—though it wouldn't be luck now but rather a miracle—Heaven should give me life, you will see them, and along with them the conclusion of the *Galatea*,[19] of which I know Your Excellency is fond. And with these works I wish Your Excellency the best, as always, and hope God will keep Your Excellency as only He can.

361

From Madrid, the nineteenth of April of the year one thousand six hundred and sixteen.

Your Excellency's Servant,
Miguel de Cervantes

Cervantes' Far North

One of the many differences between the first and second half of the *Persiles and Sigismunda* is the part of the world traversed by the heroic pair and their companions. Once on the European continent the journey on foot follows a clearly recognizable route over civilized Portuguese, Spanish, French, and Italian roads leading to Rome (see map following). In contrast, the northern shipboard wanderings of the first half strike one as confusing, not to say almost chaotic. The effect is not unintentional and matches the jumbled profusion of characters, many of whose stories begin in the middle and are suddenly cut short and resumed only after interruption by others as the band hops from island to island, from celebrations to shipwrecks to capture by pirates and rescue by kings. While our quintessentially Baroque author probably wanted order strikingly to emerge from confusion, modern readers may easily find themselves uncomfortably and unfairly disoriented if they do not have some idea of what Renaissance Spaniards' mental map of the North Atlantic looked like.

Cervantes had certainly seen Olaf Magnusson's mid-sixteenth-century map of Scandinavia included in his *History of the Northern Peoples* (Rome, 1555), while other cartographers as well as Magnusson in his *Carta marina* also showed the islands as far west as Greenland. The map drawn for this translation represents a simplified composite picture of maps from the period. Names are shown as they appear in the *Persiles and Sigismunda,* with Iceland and Ireland indicated in parentheses and our speculations regarding some identifications of place are followed by question marks because they are considerably less than certain. Still, the general shape of a plausible setting for Books I and II can be conceived of without doing major violence to either the plot or contemporary maps, and simply having a defined space where one can picture that Cervantes imagined the action taking place may well make the reading more enjoyable and seem less plunged into perpetual arctic twilight.

The couple's journey begins at Persiles' home in Ultimate Thule, in classical antiquity considered the farthest point from the center of civilization, the end of the earth. Renaissance geographers identified it with Iceland, even after the discovery of Greenland. At the end of the northern adventures, both spatially and with respect to plot, is the small, gardenlike island that Cervantes has the sailors

363

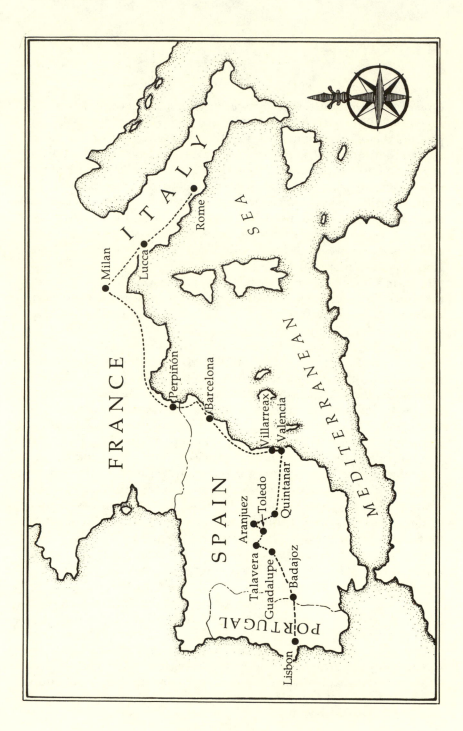

refer to as the hermitages. Located at a distance from Lisbon commensurate with seventeen days sailing, easily accessible by ship from France, it is tempting to identify it with Iona, which lies close to the northwestern coast of Scotland. Small, hilly, fertile and the country's most famous Christian community since St. Columba founded a monastery there in 563, part, moreover, of the austere Celtic monastic tradition, it seems different from Cervantes' fictional place of retreat from the world and into Christian asceticism only in its larger number of hermitlike inhabitants. And for good measure, the Island of the Hermitages is described as located three and a half days sailing from Policarpo's Island on a course set from there to England, a position that would make sense for Iona if Policarpo were thought of as a king on one of the Shetland or Orkney islands. Another of these could easily be the smaller, adjoining island of Scinta at which Periandro and his fishermen/pirates left their ship to row over to Policarpo's athletic festival.

If we take Iceland and Iona, then, as the beginning and end of the northern trials, and look again at maps like that of Olaf Magnusson, it is easier to visualize a misfortune-plagued, sometimes wrongway movement that still, on balance, progresses toward the south running parallel to the length of Norway, and the many islands shown off its coast as a plausible geographic niche for those symbolic Cervantine places called only the Snowy, Fruitful, Desolate, and Barbarous Islands. In Book II, Chapter 16, Periandro tells those listening to the tale of his adventures as a pirate captain that a storm drove his ship to the far northern coast of Norway, where it became frozen in the ice and was attacked by a force of soldiers skiing out from the mainland.

The only major objection to this view is Cervantes' island of Golandia; on the basis of the name and its similarity to the description in Olaf Magnusson's *History* as a busy center of international maritime trade, it has logically been assumed to correspond to Gotlandia, which is in the Baltic off the southeastern corner of Sweden. Still, all things considered, it seems more satisfying to suppose Cervantes needed just such a well-known meeting place for those sailing the northern seas—in fact, it is the place where Mauricio manages to find his daughter Transila after she has sailed off alone over the horizon from Hibernia—and chose to move it rather than his travelers, to the other side of the Scandinavian peninsula. Finally, it may be worth noting that this whole island-dotted area of the North Atlantic had been in the minds of Spaniards since 1588 when the defeated Invincible Armada had strayed up the eastern coast of Britain, through the northern islands and then southward past Scotland and Ireland, suffering many of the same trials as did Persiles and Sigismunda and their friends.

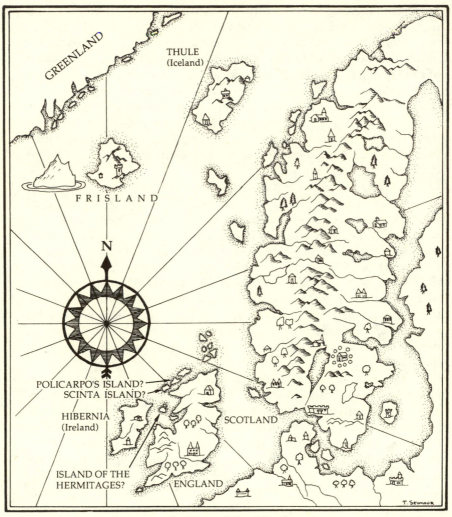

Cervantes' Far North

Notes

PROLOGUE

1. *Esquivias*: located in the province of Toledo in Central Spain, it was the hometown of Cervantes' wife, Catalina de Salazar y Palacios. They were married there in 1584.
2. Our translation of this sentence imitates Cervantes' pun on the words *pardo* and *pardal*. Several of their meanings could come into play: rustic; a flat, dull, brownish grey; sparrow or sparrow-colored; drab; leopard-like—in color and/or temperament; cunning; and clever.
3. *Leggings*: *antiparras*, high gaiters or chaps covering the front part of the leg and foot.
4. *Chaped scabbard*: a *contera* has metal trim and a metal plate covering the end where the point of the sword rests.
5. *Lace collar*: a *valona*, a collar starched in the simple shape of a "W" or later a more complicated series of "W" shapes. It was often held on by and later decorated with braided pieces of muslin or lace hanging down from it. If there were enough of these they also formed the "W" shape.
6. *His Most Illustrious Grace* refers to the title accorded to bishops who controlled appointments to the ecclesiastical hierarchy for their dioceses.
7. These phrases in praise of the author reflect his very real fame in Spain following the publication of *Don Quixote*. The novel's humor and the fact that he had lost the use of an arm in the famous naval battle of Lepanto explain the specific tongue-in-cheek epithets used here by Cervantes to describe himself.
8. *Ocean Sea*: the term *el mar Océano* properly referred to all the oceans of the world taken as a whole, but was often applied to just the Atlantic.
9. Cervantes actually died not on Sunday, but on *Saturday*, April 23, 1616.

BOOK I, CHAPTER 2

1. *Casting out*: '*arrojar*' is the verb that Cervantes uses three times in his text. Some other possible meanings which could also come into play here are: to throw out, to launch, to drive out, to dismiss angrily, and to drop a litter. Cervantes seems to intend at least a partially humorous meaning, but one tempered by the fact that the person speaking is truly in a dangerous situation.
2. *Slave*: *esclava*; it is evident only at this point in the Spanish text that the unidentified speaker is a woman.
3. *Taurisa*: the name of the woman captive may have the humorous connotation of 'taurine' or 'bovine.'
4. *Flageolets*, a high-pitched oboe common in the Spain of Cervantes' time.

BOOK I, CHAPTER 4

1. *Castilian*: by Cervantes' time this was the official and literary language of Spain, based on the dialect of the central Spanish provinces of Old and New Castile.

BOOK I, CHAPTER 5

1. *Fine china*: *de Pisa*, literally, "[dishes] from Pisa," which were considered to be made of high-quality ceramic.
2. *Candía*: a region of Crete well-known for its wines.
3. *Grammar*: *la gramática*, the first of the seven liberal arts studied during the Middle Ages and the Renaissance. *Las demás ciencias*, the "other branches of knowledge" that Cervantes then refers to, were rhetoric and logic, completing the *trivium*, the "threefold way"; with geometry, arithmetic, music, and astronomy, which formed the *quadrivium*, the "fourfold way."
4. *Arms*: *las armas*, the question of the relative value of scholarly attainment and military prowess was a long-standing topic of debate of particular importance during the Renaissance and is an important theme in *Don Quixote*.
5. *Ceres, Bacchus, Venus*: a phrase from the Roman writer Terence in his *Eunuchus* (*The Eunuch*): "Sine Ceres et Bacco, friget Venus" ("Without bread and wine, love grows cold"). It was the source of a similar popular Spanish saying.
6. *Germany*: during the sixteenth century, Charles, who ruled both as Charles V of the Holy Roman Empire and Charles I of Spain, fought a series of wars against the Protestant rulers in Germany who wished to free themselves from Hapsburg control.
7. *Hidalgos*: a title created by Ferdinand and Isabel at the end of the fifteenth century to reward those of the middle class who helped them unify Spain in opposition to many of the older titled nobility. These *hijos de algo*, "sons of something," had no right to property but could use the title *Don* or *Doña* and had the right to be addressed as *Vuestra Merced*. (See the following note regarding titles of address.)
8. *You're looking gallant*: *bravo estáis*, an ambiguous phrase that could be taken as a veiled insult on the nobleman's part since *bravo* could have many possible meanings. Some of the more positive ones were: brave, hardy, fearless, and gallant; while in more colloquial usage it could mean, among other things: wild, rude, or savage. The use of the verb *estar*, "you're looking,"—rather than *ser*, "you are," which would describe a more permanent or undoubted characteristic—could also imply that Antonio only appears to be or has recently become as he is de-

scribed. The condescending tone is reinforced by the *vos* or familiar form of the verb, often used to address underlings.

9. *He looks very fine: está bizarro*, like *bravo, bizarro* can have a variety of meanings ranging from "gallant" and "brave" to "strange" and even "funny-looking." Again, the verb *estar* is important to hint that this quality is of a temporary or recent nature and Antonio only "seems" to be as he is described. Moreover, the change of verb form and pronoun creates a certain deprecating ambiguity about whether the son of the titled nobleman is talking to Antonio or about him, but it seems that the man has turned to the onlookers and begun to speak to them about Antonio as if he were not there.

10. *Your Lordship: vuesa señoría*; in Cervantes' Spain, this title was used with the highest-ranking members of nobility. A form of address used with those of the lesser nobility was "your Grace," *vuestra merced,* which eventually evolved to the *usted* or more polite form of "you." The common people were simply called *vos.* The question here, obviously involving the honor of both, is which form of address the nobleman and Antonio should be using with each other.

11. *Aragón*: a province in northeastern Spain.

12. *Sterncastle: castillo de popa*; in contrast to the forecastle, where the crew bunked, the sterncastle contained living quarters for the officers and gentlemen on board.

13. *Boat or dinghy*: this dual style (often giving the reader two nouns, adjectives, verbs, adverbs, etc., that may either say the same thing in more than one way or imply that the reader may want to choose one or the other) is Cervantes' own and does not indicate indecision on the translators' part.

14. *The things I've kept for you*: the reader discovers later just what these things are that Cloelia hands to Auristela.

BOOK I, CHAPTER 6

1. *And apparently some of them had gone over*: Cervantes simply says "some of them had gone over," *algunos se habían pasado,* but since Ricla is soon described as surprised that no barbarians went to the island, the idea that this observation is only apparently true needs to be added. Did Cervantes or perhaps his publisher mean to put instead *ningunos*—"none" had gone over?

2. *Transila*: this is the first time we hear the name of the Polish-speaking captive who interpreted at the time of Periandro's purchase by the barbarians.

3. *Tuscan*: the best-known dialect of Italian.

Book I, Chapter 7

1. *League*: a distance of approximately three nautical miles.
2. *Watches*: night on board ship was divided into three four-hour watches, the first watch (8 P.M. to 12 midnight), the midwatch (12 midnight to 4 A.M.), and the morning watch (4 A.M. to 8 A.M.). It is curious that Antonio should estimate the time by Polaris, the only star whose change of position during the night would be very difficult to detect without instruments.

Book I, Chapter 8

1. *Wolf*: stories of people turning into beasts go back to antiquity. Popular belief in werewolves was prevalent throughout the Europe of Cervantes' time.
2. *Norway*: in seventeenth-century Spain, Norway and darkness were almost synonymous terms. See Avalle-Arce, *Los trabajos de Persiles y Sigismunda* (Madrid: Clásicos Castalia, 1969), p. 92.

Book I, Chapter 9

1. In the translated poem we have reproduced the external form of the sonnet in Spanish and in English (fourteen lines—two quartets and two tercets) plus the iambic pentameter of English sonnets, but not the rhyme.

Book I, Chapter 10

1. *Manuel de Sousa Coutinho*: both the first name and last names of this character are very common in Portugal; however, there was a Portuguese gentleman of this same name who was captive in Algiers at the same time as Cervantes (1577–1579). In 1613, after twenty-eight years of marriage, he and his wife Magdalena separated—according to legend because Magdalena's first husband (thought to have been killed in battle) reappeared—and Sousa later entered into the Dominican order and called himself Fray Luis de Sousa, while his wife entered a nunnery. He became known in Portuguese literature for his *Vida de Dom Frei Bartolomeu dos Mártires* (*The Life of Friar Don Bartholomew of the Martyrs*), 1619.
2. *King . . . forts he has in Barbary*: the references to Portuguese troops in Barbary (the North African states) seem to indicate that this story is taking place before the annexation of Portugal by Phillip II of Spain in 1580, though the chronology of the book is not rigorously historical.

3. *Cloth of gold*: cloth of gold or gold tissue has been a prized fabric worn by nobility and the royal houses of Europe from the early middle ages. The material was woven from a warp of flat gold threads with a silk weft. The silk weft in this case was green in color.

4. *Who is better than God*: a paraphrase of a biblical verse, Exodus 15:11: "Who is like unto Thee, O Lord, among the gods? who is like Thee, glorious in holiness, fearful in praises, doing wonders?" (King James Version).

5. *Maria optimam partem elegit*: "Mary has chosen the best part." This is Jesus' answer to Martha when she complains that her sister Mary is not helping her with the work of serving her guests but is sitting at the feet of Jesus listening to him talk. The full quote from the King James Version of the Bible is: "But one thing is needful; and Mary hath chosen that good part, which shall not be taken away from her." Luke 10:42.

BOOK I, CHAPTER 11

1. *Scapular*: two small pieces of cloth joined by strings passing over the shoulders and worn under ordinary clothing as a badge of affiliation with a religious order or as a token of devotion.

2. *Order of Christ*: a Portuguese military order founded in 1317 by King Diniz, known in English as Denis or Dionysius. The gentlemen of the order wore a badge in the shape of a silver cross superimposed on a red one.

3. *Golandia*: possibly Gotland. This island is described by Olaus Magnus (1490–1557) in his *Historia de gentibus septentrionalibus* (1555) (known in English as *A Compendious History of the Goths, Swedes, and Vandals and Other Northern Nations* [London: J. Streeter, 1658]) as an island situated in the Baltic sea. It also appears on the maps in his *Carta marina* (1539) and is probably part of modern-day Sweden.

BOOK I, CHAPTER 12

1. *Hibernia and Ireland*: Cervantes uses both the ancient name "Hibernia" and the modern designation "Ireland" as if they referred to two different places.

2. *Barnacle*: a European goose that breeds in the arctic. The description Cervantes gives was considered factual and very probably has its source in Olaus Magnus' *Historia de gentibus septentrionalibus* (1555). The description of the bird's symbiotic relationship with rotting logs resembles that of the crustacean known as the barnacle with this same material, of course. This crustacean is the principal food of the barnacle goose and, indeed, gives it its name.

3. *Mauricios*: Cervantes is probably alluding to the very famous Fitzmaurice family of Ireland.

371

4. *Looking for the true faith in other peoples' opinions*: this is most likely a reference to the Protestant heresy.

BOOK I, CHAPTER 14

1. *I should say, filthy rose, for you never were clean*: this line in Spanish is a play on the name Rosamunda, which from the Latin means "clean" or "pure rose." Clodio insists that she is instead a *rosa inmunda*, an "unclean rose." The common pun *mundo–inmundo*, "unclean world," is also relevant here since Rosamunda is a very worldly person.
2. *Rosamunda*: historically this is probably Rosamond Clifford (d. 1176), mistress of Henry II of England (1133–1189). A considerable body of legendary material was written about Rosamond by later chroniclers. The best-known stories are variations on a tragic death. She was supposedly murdered at Woodstock by Eleanor of Aquitaine, either by poison, stabbing, beheading, or being bled to death in her bath.
3. *When this woman was on top of the world and had firmly seized the moment*: literally, "she was at the top of her wheel and had fortune by the forelock," which reflects the traditional view of Fortune's wheel on which Opportunity rides. In order to insure the continuation of good fortune, one needed to seize opportunity by its single forelock while it was at the top of the wheel, thereby preventing the wheel from turning further and changing one's luck. Compare the Spanish proverb: *A la oportunidad la pintan calva y con un solo pelo* ("they picture opportunity bald with just one hair").
4. *Treason pleases but the traitor displeases*: the policy expressed in this maxim was considered prudent in Cervantes' time, as shown by the execution of the rebel soldier in the last act of Calderón's *Life Is a Dream* (1635).
5. *King Midas' reeds appear there*: a reference to the legend of King Midas, who in Greek mythology befriended Silenus, the oldest of the satyrs; as reward Dionysus granted him his famous power to turn everything he touched into gold. In another legend, however, Midas was given donkey ears by Apollo for preferring Pan's music to Apollo's own. Midas hid his shame from all but his barber, who wishing to tell the secret, whispered it into a hole in the ground. The reeds that grew out of that hole, however, murmured the secret whenever the wind blew through them.

BOOK I, CHAPTER 15

1. *Peneus' daughter when the swift runner Apollo was pursuing her*: in Greek mythology a reference to Daphne, daughter of the river-god Peneus.

When pursued by Apollo, who wanted her to become his love, she prayed to Mother Earth for aid and was turned into a laurel tree.

BOOK I, CHAPTER 18

1. *Mauricio and Transila*: in the 1617 edition the names of Mauricio and Transila are repeated at the beginning and at the end of this list. It seems that Periandro and Auristela's names should have been included in one of these places, for they are on board Arnaldo's ship.

2. *Suckerfish*: in Spanish *rémora*, and in English "remora"; a species of fish characterized by an oval sucking disk on the top of the head. With this apparatus the remora, or suckerfish, attaches itself to sharks, swordfishes, marlins, sea turtles, etc., feeding on scraps from the prey of these larger creatures and in some cases on their crustacean parasites. Remoras sometimes attach themselves to small boats and, in sufficient numbers, were thought capable of changing a boat's course to theirs. See Sebastián de Covarrubias Orozco, *Tesoro de la lengua castellana o española* (Madrid, 1611; reprint, Barcelona: S. A. Horta, 1943), p. 903.

3. *Fate*: in the Spanish, *Parca* (*Parcae* in Latin and *Moirae* in Greek), one of the three fates of classical mythology.

4. Once again, the poem in Spanish is a sonnet. We have reproduced the form of the stanzas (two quartets and two tercets) and the meter in English, but not the rhyme.

5. *Nascitur*: "is born." It comes from the Latin saying: *Nascuntur poetae, fiunt oratores,* "poets are born but orators are made," and points to the difference between natural gifts and learned skills which Mauricio is stressing.

6. *Lycanthropy*: Cervantes' source here is Olaus Magnus' *Historia*. Like the belief that harmful animals could not stand English soil, belief in werewolves was an accepted fact in the Europe of Cervantes' time, although the tradition was not strong in Spain.

7. *Pliny*: Pliny the Elder (c. A.D. 23–79), the great Roman naturalist and author of the *Historia naturalis,* to which the book and chapter references refer. The Arcadians mentioned in the next line are from an interior and isolated region of ancient Greece proverbially associated with the ideal of a natural, simple pastoral life.

8. *King Arthur of England*: a reference to one element of the Arthurian cycle of legends, which were disseminated across Europe through medieval balladry and romance, including the English *Morte d'Arthur* (1485) by Sir Thomas Malory, holding that King Arthur, though fatally wounded by Mordred in battle, was carried away to Avalon, where his wounds would heal and from which he would someday return to his people. Although Arthur's turning into a crow does not appear in Malory, Cervantes mentions this same incident twice in the *Quixote* (part I, chaps.

13 and 49). It can also be noted that one of the Celtic gods, Bran, whose name means "crow," represents a divinity from the other world, a master of life and death.

9. *You shall not divine nor observe dreams*: Leviticus 19:26 (Douay translation from the Latin Vulgate, 1609).

10. *Son*: Venus' son was Cupid (also called Love or Eros), against whose arrows there is no defense, either in Heaven or on earth.

11. *Tethys*: in Greek mythology, a Titan and the wife of Ocean. Ocean, also a Titan, was lord of the River Ocean, the sea being thought of as a great river encircling the earth.

BOOK I, CHAPTER 19

1. *Crassus*: an ancient Roman family. Its best-known member, Marcus Licinius Crassus (d. 53 B.C.), became Rome's principal landowner and formed part of the First Triumvirate with Pompey and Caesar.

2. *Phineus' table*: in Greek mythology, Apollo, the truthteller, gave Phineus the gift of prophecy and he foretold unerringly. Zeus, who liked to wrap his deeds in mystery, was displeased and inflicted a terrible punishment on the old man. Whenever he was about to dine, the Harpies, called "the hounds of Zeus" and who were horrible flying creatures with women's heads and the body and claws of vultures, would swoop down and pollute the food, leaving it so foul that no one could bear to be near it, much less eat it.

3. *Egyptian*: a reference to the wife of Potiphar, an officer of Pharaoh; in Genesis 39:7–12 she tried unsuccessfully to seduce Joseph, her husband's slave.

BOOK I, CHAPTER 20

1. *Duel*: the Toledo Council of 1473 had forbidden the burial of men who died in duels, and the edict was reaffirmed at the Council of Trent in Session XXV (1563).

BOOK I, CHAPTER 21

1. *Paphos, Cnossus, Cyprus, the Elysian Fields*: Paphos was an ancient city on Cyprus; Cnossus, an ancient city and capital of Crete; Cyprus, an island in the eastern Mediterranean sea where Mount Olympus is located; the Elysian Fields, situated in the distant west at the edge of the world, was the happy otherworld for heroes favored by the gods. All of these places are associated with Venus and therefore with love.

2. *Argus*: in Greek mythology, a being with a hundred eyes, some of which were always open; his name was often used to mean a zealous watchman.

3. *Anfriso*: in Greek mythology, Zeus punished Apollo for killing the Cyclopes by making him serve as King Admetus' slave for a year. Among his other duties he diligently watched the king's sheep by the river Anfriso.

4. *Ireland, or to Hibernia*: remember that Cervantes uses these names as if they referred to different places. (See n. 1 to book I, chap. 12.)

BOOK I, CHAPTER 23

1. *Palm branches*: in classical antiquity the traditional crown of victory was made of palm branches or laurel.

BOOK II, CHAPTER 1

1. This is Cervantes' way of distancing himself from the narration, similar to his introduction of an imaginary Moorish author of the chronicles of Don Quixote, and not a comment by the present translators.

BOOK II, CHAPTER 2

1. *Policarpa*: the 1617 edition has "Policarpo" but Policarpa agrees more logically with the statement regarding the location of Auristela's room.

BOOK II, CHAPTER 3

1. *Falling in love with a bull*: Poseidon, the god of the sea, gave Minos a very beautiful bull to be sacrificed to him, but Minos could not bear to slay it and kept it for himself. To punish him, Poseidon made Pasiphae, Minos' wife, fall uncontrollably in love with the bull. The offspring of her love was the Minotaur.

2. *Banana tree*: this Spanish saying refers to a man who loved a banana tree so much he cared for it and treated it as if it were a beautiful woman. The legend may have its beginnings in the love Apollo felt for Daphne even after she was turned into a laurel tree by her father, a river god, while she was fleeing Apollo's advances.

3. *Cynthia*: in Greek mythology another name for Diana, the hunter. Because she is associated with the forest and animals, Cynthia was also a very common name for shepherdesses in Renaissance pastoral literature.

4. Once again we have reproduced the basic external form of the sonnet's stanzas, using iambic pentameter in English but not attempting assonance or rhyme.

BOOK II, CHAPTER 5

1. *Ganymede*: in Greek mythology, a young and very handsome Trojan prince who was carried up to Olympus by Zeus' eagle to be cupbearer to the gods.
2. *Argus to Auristela's heifer*: in Greek mythology, when Zeus fell in love with Io, the beautiful daughter of Inachus, Zeus' jealous wife Hera threatened her, so Zeus changed her into a white heifer. Hera was not fooled by the metamorphosis and asked him to give her the little cow as a present. He had to give the heifer to her and she placed it in the charge of Argus, the watchman with a hundred eyes.
3. *The eleven circles of Heaven*: historically the most influential of the geocentric cosmological theories that placed the earth motionless at the center of the universe with all celestial bodies revolving around it. The system is named for the astronomer Ptolemy (second century A.D.); it dominated astronomy until the advent of the heliocentric Copernican system in the sixteenth century and was still the dominant theory in the Europe of Cervantes' time. The eleven circles of Christianized Ptolemaic cosmology were: (proceeding outward) Earth, Moon, Mercury, Venus, Sun, Mars, Jupiter, Saturn, the Sphere of the Fixed Stars, the Primum Mobile, and Heaven.

BOOK II, CHAPTER 8

1. *Cenotia*: a common name associated with a legendary and famous *morisco* (Muslim baptized as a Christian) witch in the Spain of Cervantes' time.
2. *Kingdom of Granada*: Even though Spain was officially a unified country by Cervantes' time, the memory of the several separate kingdoms that comprised it was (and is) very much alive. Cenotia refers to the Muslim kingdom in Southern Spain centered in the city of Granada, the last to be reconquered from the Moors (by Ferdinand and Isabel in 1492). Because of its Moorish character it has always been considered the most exotic of the Spanish regions.

BOOK II, CHAPTER 9

1. See n. 3 to book I, chap. 19, concerning Joseph's escape from seduction by Potiphar's wife.

Book II, Chapter 12

1. *Hercules*: according to Schevill and Bonilla, this is the Celtic (rather than the Greek) Hercules described by the Roman writer Lucian. He holds a club in his right hand and a bow in his left, keeping many people captive with delicate chains of gold and amber attached from his tongue to their ears. His captives do not try to flee, rather wish to stay near him and praise him. The god in this form, therefore, was a symbol of eloquence. (R. Schevill and A. Bonilla, *The Trials of Persiles and Sigismunda* [Madrid: Bernardo Rodríguez, 1914]).

2. *Harmful pens*: through Transila it seems Cervantes is alluding to the possibility of an inaccurate continuation of Periandro's interesting story by some writer wishing to profit from it, as did in fact happen to Cervantes when Avellaneda published a "false" continuation of *Don Quixote*. In Cervantes' own continuation in Book II, Don Quixote complains about the "inaccuracies" in that spurious version of the history of his life.

Book II, Chapter 13

1. *Begins anew*: Counter-Reformation writers stressed that suicide was a mortal sin punished by eternal damnation.

2. *Danea*: although maps of the period indicate that this country must be Denmark, Cervantes makes a distinction between Leopoldio's country (Danea) and the kingdom of which Arnaldo is the crown prince.

Book II, Chapter 15

1. "*Shipwrecks*": this marine monster is described by Olaus Magnus (*Historia,* book 21) using the name *physeter*. According to Schevill and Bonilla, Cervantes uses the name "shipwreck" (*náufrago* in Spanish) because he took it from captions labeling Italian engravings that depicted these monsters destroying ships.

2. *Tiber gold*: from the Italian river that flows through Rome, and in Cervantes' time synonymous with "fine gold."

3. *Oh, my soul's only consolation . . . any other season*: a paraphrase of two verses from "Sonnet X" by the Spanish Renaissance poet Garcilaso de la Vega.

Book II, Chapter 17

1. *It's better to marry than to burn*: see I Corinthians 7:9.

2. *Dido and Aeneas*: in Greek mythology, Aeneas was the son of Venus and

377

the most famous of the heroes who fought for the Trojans in the Trojan War. When the Greeks captured Troy he was able, with his mother's help, to escape from the city with his father and his little son and sail away to a new home in Italy. Because Juno hated the Trojans she went to Aeolus, the king of the winds, and asked him to sink the Trojan ships; then when Neptune prevented the capsizings she decided to have Aeneas fall in love with Dido, the founder of Carthage, so he would settle down there and never reach Italy. Venus, with the aid of Cupid, turned Juno's plan around and caused Dido to fall in love with Aeneas. She committed suicide when he was called by Jupiter to leave Carthage and go on to Italy.

3. *Rémora,* see n. 2 to book I, chap. 18, for an explanation of the belief that the suckerfish or *rémora* could, in sufficient numbers, retard the movement of a ship.

Book II, Chapter 18

1. *A long distance over their path*: This description of skiing came to Cervantes from Olaus Magnus.
2. *I answered*: it would appear Cervantes forgot he had taken back the narration from Periandro.
3. *The beloved disciple*: this is John, the beloved disciple who leaned on Jesus' breast at the Last Supper, who took care of Mary the Mother after the crucifixion, and whom scholars in Cervantes' time took to be the writer of the Gospel of Saint John and the person who had the apocalyptic vision found in The Revelation.

Book II, Chapter 19

1. *One of the free German cities*: one of the cities not belonging to the Holy Roman Empire, i.e., a Protestant city.
2. *Kind hands*: perhaps Mauricio is referring to the devout custom of people keeping hermits supplied with food so their solitary lives would be free from earthly cares.
3. *Charles V shut up in a monastery*: Charles left the throne of Spain and the Holy Roman Empire and lived in the monastery of Yuste from February 3, 1557, to his death on September 21, 1558; there he spent his time repairing clocks and rehearsing his funeral.

Book II, Chapter 21

1. *The abyss calling others down to it*: these words are an echo of Psalm 42 (41 in the Catholic Bible):6 and 7: "O my God, my soul is cast down

within me . . . deep calleth unto deep at the noise of thy waterspouts: all thy waves and thy billows are gone over me" (King James Version). The word "abyss" in this context was interpreted by Covarrubias in his *Tesoro de la lengua castellana o española,* p. 29: "It refers to tribulations compared to a great storm when one trial comes on the heels of another. This is how the verse in Psalm 41 is to be understood" (translation ours).

BOOK III, CHAPTER 1

1. *Ganymede*: see n. 1 to book II, chap. 5.
2. *Ecclesiastical indulgences*: a partial remission of the time of punishment in Purgatory which is still due for sin after absolution.
3. *Sangián*: according to Schevill and Bonilla, this is most likely Saint Julian castle, constructed at the mouth of the river Tagus during the reign of Philip II (sixteenth century).
4. *Holy monastery*: the magnificent monastery at Belém, on the north bank of the Tagus facing the sea, was built by Manuel I (early 1500s) to commemorate the discovery of the route to India by Vasco da Gama.
5. *Manuel de Sousa Coutinho*: see book I, chap. 10.
6. *Very skilled in writing them*: Portuguese humorous epitaphs were so popular that they constituted a literary subgenre.
7. *Two sailors*: Cervantes seems to have forgotten that in Periandro's dream in book II, chap. 15, only one sailor was swallowed by the sea monster.
8. *This canvas . . .* : Schevill and Bonilla remind us that traveling storytellers with similar scenic backdrops could still be seen in Spain early in this century.

BOOK III, CHAPTER 2

1. *The Spanish magistrate*: *Corregidor,* the royally appointed magistrate or mayor of a Spanish town.
2. *Mount Parnassus, Castalia, and Aganippes*: Parnassus was the mountaintop home of the Muses; Castalia was a spring sacred to both Apollo and the Muses and located below Mount Parnassus at Delphi; Aganippes was a nymph whose spring on Mount Helicon also was sacred to the Muses and gave poetic inspiration to all who drank from it.
3. *A man's short suit*: typical male courtly attire of the period consisted of a jacket, pants to the knee, and stockings.
4. *A play based on them*: Francisco de Rojas Zorrilla, a successful playwright in the style of Calderón de la Barca, did in fact write a play based on Cervantes' romance not many years after it was published.

5. *Servant to act as confidant and comic relief*: Spanish plays of Cervantes' time usually provided the leading characters with a servant to whom they could express their hidden feelings and whose practical and humorous remarks served as a foil for their masters' high-minded and often exaggerated adherence to stylized codes of behavior. Though not from the world of the theatre, Cervantes' own Sancho Panza is the best-known example of the type.

6. *Alchemy* . . . alchemists sought to change base metals into gold but were unable to do so. By analogy, potential patrons of the arts, as Cervantes knew from bitter personal experience, did not always "produce" gold for writers and other artists.

7. *They could have their honor and eat up their profits, too*: Cervantine irony. The proverb in Spanish actually says that an honorable man is not moved by thoughts of profit, i.e., honor and profit don't go together.

8. *The tail of his vanity and silly madness drooped low*: an allusion to the legend that the peacock, on looking down at his feet, found them so ugly that his beautiful tail drooped and closed up.

9. *Cephalus and Procris*: in Greek mythology, a married couple who swore eternal fidelity; but Aurora, goddess of the dawn, who had fallen in love with Cephalus, carried him off. Disgusted by his devotion to his wife, she finally dismissed him but persuaded him to test his wife's fidelity during his absence. Cephalus disguised himself and tempted Procris to commit adultery. When she did not oppose him firmly enough, he angrily deserted her. They were later reconciled. Procris, however, eventually became jealous and followed Cephalus one night while he was out hunting with a javelin she had given him, one that never failed to reach its mark. Mistaking his wife for an animal, Cephalus killed her. He then wandered for many years but was unable to escape his grief and finally leaped off a cliff to his death.

10. *Juan de Herrera de Gamboa*: according to Avalle-Arce nothing is known about this poet, but on the basis of the more literal and historical nature of the second half of the *Persiles,* most scholars believe he was a real person.

11. *Trujillo . . . Don Francisco Pizarro . . . Don Juan de Orellana*: these men did exist; they were brothers and the sons of Don Fernando de Orellana, magistrate of Trujillo in 1607. They were related to Cervantes by marriage, and the episode revolving around them and Feliciana of the Voice appears to have some basis in actual events. See Avalle-Arce, *Los trabajos de Persiles y Sigsimunda,* p. 288, for a more detailed explanation of the relationship.

BOOK III, CHAPTER 3

1. *Hidalgo*: see n. 7 to book I, chap. 5, regarding the history and origin of the hidalgo title. The fact that Feliciana's family would rather she mar-

ried a nobleman of modest means than a rich hidalgo (who later protests that he *is* noble) points to the general recognition of the relatively lower social status of the hidalgo class. Remember that arguing this same question of the social status of hidalgos in relation to old established noble families, and how a member of this class was to address a member of the other, also caused Antonio's original problems and his exile.

2. *Chance . . . offers us its forelock*: see book I, chap. 14, for an explanation of the significance of grasping Fortune's forelock.

3. *Dress became shorter*: a euphemism for being pregnant, inspired by an old Spanish ballad. See Avalle-Arce, p. 293, n. 308.

BOOK III, CHAPTER 4

1. *A fall of princes*: a reference to Giovanni Boccaccio's didactic biographies of famous men, *De Casibus Virorum Illustrium* (1355–1360), written in Latin and translated in 1495 into Spanish with the title *Caída de príncipes*.

2. *My father*: When Auristela's identity is later revealed, Cervantes only speaks of her having a mother (book IV, chap. 12).

3. *As has been said*: Cervantes seems to have forgotten that he didn't mention earlier that the shepherd's sister has also just given birth.

4. *Holy Brotherhood*: the *Santa Hermandad*, a kind of national highway patrol that functioned for many years in Spain. For a time it was virtually the army of the Inquisition. Today the *Guardia Civil* (the Civil Guard) continues the peace-keeping function it carries out in this episode.

5. *Order of Santiago*: one of the oldest and most respected of the Spanish Christian military orders. It was founded in 1170 and named after Saint James, the patron saint of Spain.

BOOK III, CHAPTER 5

1. *Holy image of the Empress of Heaven*: see the notes by Schevill and Bonilla (p. 297) for an overview of the history of this famous statue to which many miracles are attributed. It is thought to date from the sixth century.

2. *Purple cloth of Tyre*: Tyre was an ancient Phoenician city famous for its textile industry and particularly for its purple dye. On its site is present-day Sur in Lebanon.

3. *They went like this*: the poem that follows in Spanish consists of twelve eight-line stanzas with eleven-syllable lines rhyming ABABCC. We have attempted neither rhyme nor meter in English, but have merely kept the eight-line stanzas.

4. *The golden locks of the sun*: God's plan for the incarnation of Christ through Mary was formed even before the Creation.

5. *God built a house for Himself*: while she was with child the Virgin Mary

381

was the dwelling place of God, just as Solomon's Temple in the Old Testament was God's house.

6. *It soared . . . beneath its feet*: this vision reflects the traditional medieval Ptolemaic view of the universe, with earth, sea, wind, and fire corresponding to the four terrestrial elements, and the moon, whose sphere represents the frontier between the realms of air and aether, nature and Heaven, demons and gods, corruptibility and incorruptibility, and mutability and permanence. Putting the moon beneath the feet of God's house is simply stressing that we are speaking of God's realm and not the earthly one.

7. *Mary's shining star*: the second major image for the Virgin Mary in the hymn is a star that appears before the birth of Christ.

8. *Chain of ancient iron*: like the "ancient storm" mentioned later in the ninth stanza, this is a reference to the concept of original sin caused by Adam's fall from grace. In the next stanza the allusion is strengthened by mention of the serpent in Eden who represented the Devil. The subsequent reference to the mortal discord of God and man continues the theme of man's sinful condition, which was restored to harmony by Mary's son.

9. *Ester*: heroine of the biblical book bearing her name who, as queen, interceded with King Ahasuerus to save the Jews from extermination.

10. *The coming harvest*: refers to the salvation of mankind through Christ at the end of the world.

11. *Dove*: in addition to its association with peace between God and man at the end of the biblical great flood, it is traditionally a symbol for blessings and happiness in marriage.

12. *Payment*: Christ's sacrifice is the payment for Adam's original sin.

13. *Virtuous mission*: the archangel Gabriel was sent by God to announce to the Virgin Mary that Christ was to be made incarnate in her.

BOOK III, CHAPTER 6

1. *Monda*: See the notes of Schevill and Bonilla, pp. 298–303, for an extensive history and description of this originally pagan festival. The Virgin often visited in Talavera is Nuestra Señora del Prado, Our Lady of the Meadow.

2. *Nuestra Señora de la Cabeza*: the Sagrario of Toledo, el Niño de la Guardia, the Verónica of Jaén, and Nuestra Señora de la Cabeza, are all well-known sanctuaries containing religious relics.

3. *The ones who rob alms from the truly poor*: begging pilgrims were a common problem in medieval and Renaissance Spain.

4. *The court of the great Philip III had recently returned*: Philip III's court moved from Madrid to Valladolid in 1601 and returned in 1606.

BOOK III, CHAPTER 8

1. *Garcilaso de la Vega*: a Spanish Renaissance poet (1503–1536) very famous in seventeenth-century Spain and much admired by Cervantes not only for his poetry but also for the personal example he set in the combining of arms and letters. The Tagus River is often mentioned in his poems.
2. *'Here Salicio brought his song to an end'*: a quote from Garcilaso's first Eclogue, verse 225. Salicio is one of the most famous shepherds in the Spanish pastoral tradition.
3. *Goths*: The Visigoths, one of the Christianized Germanic tribes that overran the Roman Empire, settled in Spain in the fifth century only to be in turn conquered by the Moors in the early eighth century. Toledo was the Visigothic civil and religious capital.
4. *Clusters of girls*: these are the famous country girls of the village of Sagra, dressed in their typical folk costume. They were made famous in Tirso de Molina's play, *La villana de la Sagra* (*The girl from Sagra*).
5. *Purer or older Christian blood*: for centuries following the expulsion or forced conversion of the Jews in 1492—and that of the *moriscos* (Spaniards who had preserved their Islamic cultural heritage and were suspected of still maintaining their Moslem beliefs) about a century later—this *limpieza de sangre,* ancestry untainted by Semitic blood, was a powerful criterion for both official and unofficial social discrimination. Cervantes is a writer usually notable for his advocacy of tolerance and forgiveness in human relationships of all kinds. Therefore, while along with other admirers of Cervantes, we may regret his narrator's or his characters' expressions of obviously historically and culturally based anti-Semitism, we have been very careful neither to exaggerate nor to diminish the impact of these expressions.
6. *Ingenuity shown by the cranes . . . its being heard*: According to Schevill and Bonilla, Cervantes took this story from Plutarch, *Moralia,* Section X, although Plutarch's example used ducks, not cranes.

BOOK III, CHAPTER 9

1. *Nuestra Señora de Esperanza*: Our Lady of Hope, a monastery outside the walls of the town of Ocaña. It was destroyed during the battle of Ocaña in the War for Independence against Napoleon (1808).
2. *Potosí*: a city in central Mexico famous for the fabulously rich silver mines discovered and developed there in the sixteenth century.
3. *Salamanca*: located in the province of León, Salamanca is the home of the oldest Spanish university, founded around 1230 and prestigious both in Cervantes' time and now.
4. *Even the wind might desire me*: it is not uncommon in myths for the wind

to represent a sexually aggressive male that pursues young women. Federico García Lorca's poem "Preciosa y el viento" ("Preciosa and the Wind") is a well-known twentieth-century example.

Book III, Chapter 10

1. *Ransomed captives*: many Spaniards of the time, including Cervantes himself, were captured by pirates on the Mediterranean, held prisoner in North Africa, then ransomed by religious orders. On their return to Spain they wore distinctive clothing to show their gratitude to God and to the religious brothers.
2. *Beyond the plus ultra of the columns of Hercules*: the strait of Gibraltar. *Ne plus ultra* ("no further") was a label Hercules was said to have placed on that western-most point of the Mediterranean. *Plus ultra* was a change in the legendary phrase made in Cervantes' time by Charles V, who placed it on his coat of arms to remind the world that Spanish explorers *had* gone further.
3. *Stroke*: the member of the galley crew who sits nearest the stern; because his back is to all the other oarsmen he sets the tempo for the whole crew.
4. *Dragut*: a famous pirate from Algiers.
5. *Phalaris and Busiris, Sicilian tyrants*: contrary to what the wandering undergraduate says, Busiris was not Sicilian but a mythical Egyptian pharoah associated particularly with Hercules, who put an end to his atrocities. The early Sicilian mythologist Diodorus did write about him, however. Phalaris was in fact a Sicilian tyrant (sixth century B.C.) famous for roasting victims in a bronze bull.
6. *Don Sancho de Leiva*: a commander of galleys who operated out of Naples.
7. *Shershel*: in "The Captives Tale" from *Don Quixote*, this town is described by the captive as being "thirty leagues from Algiers on the Orán side" (Miguel de Cervantes, *Don Quixote*, the Ormsby Translation, ed. J. Jones and K. Douglas [New York: W. W. Norton, 1981], p. 320).
8. *Summum jus summa injuria*: Latin for "strictest law, greatest harm."
9. *Reales*: a real was a small silver coin.

Book III, Chapter 11

1. *At least eleven*: see n. 3 to book II, chap. 5, for an explanation of the eleven spheres of Heaven.
2. *Antipodes*: in the Middle Ages and early Renaissance, people living on the side of earth opposite Europe were commonly thought of by the uneducated as a strange race existing upside down.

384

3. *Morisco village*: Moriscos were Spaniards who had converted from the Moslem faith to Christianity, either by faith or to avoid the rigors of the Inquisition. They tended to uphold their Islamic cultural heritage and were exiled from Spain in 1609. The name is a derivation of *moro*, or Moor, a general term referring to the mixed Arab and Berber conquerors of Spain who crossed the Strait of Gibraltar from Morocco in the eighth century.

4. *Scythia*: an ancient region of Eurasia, extending from the Danube on the west to the borders of China on the east. The Scythians flourished from the eighth to the fourth century B.C. The Greeks considered them barbarians.

5. *Old Christians*: See n. 5 to book III, chap. 8, for an explanation of "old Christian" blood.

6. *Banish the Moriscos from the country*: beginning in 1609 Spain's Philip II of the Hapsburg dynasty had in fact banished the Moriscos from Spain, even though it appears here as a prophesied future event.

7. *Fears to reckon with*: there were legitimate economic concerns at the time that banishment of the *moriscos* would cause serious shortages of cheap and productive farm labor.

8. *Lilíes*: shrill ululant sounds commonly made by North Africans as war-cries or to express grief.

9. *Descendants of Hagar*: Hagar was the handmaid of Abraham's wife Sarah. She was also Abraham's mistress and mother of his eldest son, Ishmael. In Islam, the Arabs claim descent from him and traditionally have regarded Hagar with special veneration, considering her Abraham's lawful wife.

BOOK III, CHAPTER 12

1. *Charming language*: natives in the region of Valencia speak a local language that is not a dialect of the Castilian Spanish spoken in the central parts of the Iberian peninsula but is rather related to Catalán, the language spoken in the region surrounding Barcelona.

2. *Monserrate*: a mountain in northeast Spain about 4000 feet high and rising abruptly from a plain in Catalonia, northwest of Barcelona. On a narrow terrace more than halfway up its precipitous cliffs is a celebrated Benedictine monastery, one of the major religious shrines of Spain. The first monastery dates from the eleventh century, and during the Middle Ages the mountain was thought to have been the site of the castle of the Holy Grail.

3. *Aragón*: a former kingdom in northeastern Spain; in 1479 it was united with Castile when Ferdinand (of Aragón) married Isabel.

4. *Order of Alcántara*: one of the great military religious orders of Spain; it was established in the town of Alcántara in the province of Extremadura in western Spain in the thirteenth century.

5. *La Mancha*: a region of central Spain in New Castile. It was made famous as the scene of many of Don Quixote's adventures.
6. *Perpiñán*: capital of the old province of Rosellón, which was Spanish
until Louis XIII took it from Spain in 1642. It is now Perpignan, capital
of the department of Pyrénées Orientales in southern France.

Book III, Chapter 13

1. *In France there isn't a man or woman who doesn't learn the Spanish language*:
Cervantes is correct in reporting the popularity of the Spanish language
and all things Spanish in the France of the sixteenth and seventeenth
centuries.

Book III, Chapter 15

1. *Much as the treacherous Deianira sent the shirt to Hercules*: believing he was
in love with a captive maiden, Deianira sent her husband Hercules a
robe soaked in the blood of the centaur Nessus who before he died at
Hercules' hand had told her his blood could be used as a charm if ever
Hercules should love another woman more than her. The robe caused
Hercules agonizing pain but did not diminish his strength. Deianira
killed herself after hearing what her gift had done to him, and Hercules
finally had to commit suicide on a giant pyre to escape the unbearable
pain.
2. *A new Europa*: in Greek mythology Zeus, smitten by the beautiful
Europa, daughter of the king of Sidon, changed himself into a handsome bull to attract her. When she got on his back to ride him he raced
across the sea to Crete with her and kept her there to bear him children.

Book III, Chapter 16

1. *Whom Heaven has only called "the beautiful"*: it was commonly believed
that women fortunate enough to be beautiful were often unlucky in
other matters.

Book III, Chapter 17

1. *Holofernes' ferocity didn't frighten the humble Judith*: in the Old Testament
of the Bible of some traditions and in the Aprocrypha of others, the
story of Judith is told in the book of the same name. It tells of an attack
on the Jews by an army led by Nebuchadnezzar's general Holofernes.

A besieged Jewish city is about to surrender when Judith, a Jewish widow of great beauty and devotion, enters the enemy camp, gains Holofernes' favor, and while sleeping with him cuts off his head. Judith returns to the city with his head, and the Jews rout the enemy army.

2. *Medusa's shield*: in Greek mythology, Medusa was the most famous of the three monstrous Gorgon sisters. Once a beautiful woman, she offended Athena, who changed her hair into snakes and made her face so hideous that all who looked at her were turned to stone. Perseus was able to kill her by looking at her reflection in a highly polished bronze shield Athena had given him. Cervantes has somewhat reversed the imagery.

Book III, Chapter 18

1. *Valiant youth . . . brave pirate*: Schevill and Bonilla (vol. 2, p. 312) think this pirate may be Alí Pashá, commander of the Turkish fleet at Lepanto, whose head was said to have been cut off and presented to the victorious Don Juan of Austria.

2. *Crescent moons*: the emblematic representation of a star with the crescent moon incorporated ancient Byzantine symbols and was later used as the standard of the Ottoman Turks after their capture of Constantinople.

3. *Another crowned young man*: King Don Sebastián of Portugal, the son of Prince Juan of Portugal and Juana, the daughter of Charles I of Spain (Charles V of the Holy Roman Empire). He was killed in 1578 in the battle of Alcazarquivir, Morocco.

Book III, Chapter 19

1. *Mask*: it was usual for travelers of Cervantes' time to wear masks to protect themselves from the dust and the sun.

2. *Blanca*: a copper coin of very little value.

3. *Vulcan himself has installed his own there*: Vulcan was the god of fire in Roman mythology. The Greeks knew him as Hephaestus. He fashioned ornaments, weapons, and magical contrivances for the gods and heroes at his huge forges.

4. *Academy of the Elite*: the real *Academia degli Intronati* (1525–1751)—literally, "The Academy of the Enthroned"—was established in Siena and was the first of its kind.

5. *Lucca . . . princes that would like to control it, too*: the capital of the province of the same name in north-central Italy. From its earliest beginnings as a Roman settlement (sixth century) it had been a prosperous capital and a free state. In the seventeenth century it still kept its independence even though much of Italy was under the domination of the Holy Roman Empire, ruled by Charles V of Spain.

BOOK III, CHAPTER 20

1. *Castrucha*: when referring to a woman, Spanish surnames ending in "o" were sometimes changed to end in the feminine "a."

BOOK III, CHAPTER 21

1. *Midsummer's morning just as the sun came up*: June 24, celebrated as the feast of the birth of Saint John the Baptist (which, incidentally, also happens to be Andrea's father's name). Both midsummer's day and midsummer's night (Saint John's Eve), because they mark the summer solstice, have been associated with solar ceremonies since long before Christianity. It was considered the one night of the year when supernatural beings (like Isabela's "devil") were abroad, and the importance of this night for lovers is undoubtedly a survival of fertility rites.
2. *Vade retro, exi foras*: Latin for "go back, get out."
3. *No matter how well-swept and clean you may find it*: popular belief held that sweeping the house and conjuring up the Devil went together.

BOOK IV, CHAPTER 1

1. *[Caves] to shelter us*: the word in Spanish in the 1617 edition seems to be *afos*, whose meaning is unknown. In some Spanish editions it is replaced by the word *hatos*, flocks or herds. The dictionary of the Royal Spanish Academy gives *afo* the same meaning as *hoyo*, "a hole or pit." We have used "cave" here since it seems to make sense in the context and is reminiscent of other scenes in the novel.
2. *The Flower of Unusual Aphorisms*: in Spanish, *Flor de aforismos peregrinos*. *Peregrino*, as well as being an adjective meaning unusual, strange, or wonderful, is also the word for pilgrim in Spanish; thus the play on words in Spanish is at least twofold.
3. *Ermine*: any of several weasels that assume white winter fur; the word in Spanish is *arminio*, and Belarminia's name means "beautiful ermine."
4. *Diego de Ratos . . . Valladolid*: according to Avalle-Arce (n. 482, p. 418), and Schevill and Bonilla (vol. 12; nn. 204–210, p. 314) this has long been supposed to be an allusion to Alonso Fernández de Avellaneda whose counterfeit second part of the *Quixote* came out in Tordesillas in 1614. This is the only author quoted by the Spaniard (usually taken to be a thinly disguised Cervantes) who is not a character with whom we are already acquainted. Both Mary Gaylord Randel ("Ending and Meaning in Cervantes' *Persiles y Sigismunda*," *Romanic Review*, 74 [1983]: 155) and Diana de Armas Wilson ("Cervantes Last Romance," *Cervantes*, 3 [1983]: 110–111) speak against limiting the meaning here to a mere

reference to Avellaneda; they caution that approach might short-circuit richer possibilities for seeing Ratos and his aphorisms as an attempt by Cervantes to begin a summary of the meaning of the romance as a whole.

BOOK IV, CHAPTER 3

1. *For God's own City*: the New Jerusalem or Holy City prepared by God to reward those who survive the Last Judgment. The Revelation, chap. 21, describes it in great detail.
2. *A Spanish poet . . . illustrious inhabitants*: scholars do not know who the author of the sonnet was, but Avalle-Arce (vol. 2; n. 491, p. 426) mentions that at least one sonnet fitting this description has been found in three different (anonymous) manuscripts in the National Library in Madrid; Schevill and Bonilla (nn. 222–225, p. 314) remind us also that Quevedo, inspired by Juvenal, wrote a very famous sonnet against Rome.
3. *Lawns of Madama*: Schevill and Bonilla tell us (vol. 2, p. 315) that the villa of Madama, known for its gardens and considered a Renaissance jewel, was named for "my lady" (madama) Margaret of Parma (1522–1586), illegitimate daughter of Holy Roman Emperor Charles V; she was Spanish regent of the Netherlands, married first to Alexander of Medici, who died, and later to the Duke of Parma.
4. *Pópolo Gate*: the gate of the old Flaminia way, the chief highway leading north from Rome to Gaul.
5. *Portuguese Arch*: an arch dedicated to Marcus Aurelius; Pope Alexander II ordered it torn down in 1662 to widen the thoroughfare.
6. *Venus . . . Aeneas*: Aeneas was the son of Venus, the goddess of love. He was among the most famous of the heroes who fought the Trojan War. With his mother's help he escaped from Troy after its defeat and went to Italy. Romans traditionally considered him the true founder of their city.

BOOK IV, CHAPTER 5

1. *Tower of Nona*: according to Avalle-Arce (n. 497, p. 432), the "Tor di Nona" was the chief Roman jail of the time. It was torn down in 1690.
2. *Penitentiaries*: a tribunal in Rome appointed by the pope and dealing with cases concerning the private spiritual good of individuals.
3. *His fall into the abyss with a third of the stars*: this fall is described in the Bible, The Revelation 12:3 and 4: "And there appeared another wonder in heaven; and behold a great red dragon, having seven heads and ten horns, and seven crowns upon his heads. And his tail drew the third part of the stars of heaven, and did cast them to the earth."

BOOK IV, CHAPTER 6

1. *Banchi*: The *Via dei Banchi*, near the Tiber River.
2. *Touchstone*: a type of black stone formerly used to test the purity of gold or silver by the streak left on it when it was rubbed with the metal.
3. *Walking tour of the seven churches*: the seven churches traditionally considered as most important to visit in Rome were the following: the Basilica of Saint Peter, the Basilica of Saint Paul, the Basilica of Saint Sebastian, the Church of Saint John Lateran, the Church of the Holy Cross, the Basilica of Saint Laurence, and the Basilica of Saint Mary Major. (*Ye Solace of Pilgrimes: A Description of Rome circa* A.D. *1450, by John Capgrave, An Austin Friar of King's Lynn*, ed. C. A. Mills [London, New York: H. Frowde: 1911].)
4. *Torcuato Tasso*: Tasso (1544–1595) was an Italian Renaissance poet whose Christian epic, *Jerusalem Delivered*, was immensely admired in Cervantes' time.
5. *Zárate*: Francisco López de Zárate (1585?–1658), a Spanish poet and playwright whose work influenced that of both Calderón and Cervantes. He was the author of *The Heroic Poem of the Discovery of the Cross by the Emperor Constantine*, dealing with the official conversion of the Roman Empire to Christianity.
6. *Francisco López Duarte*: an obvious misprint in the first edition for "Zárate."
7. *Ferrara*: a city in northern Italy.

BOOK IV, CHAPTER 7

1. *Flora of old*: perhaps a reference to the Roman goddess of flowers and fertility. Her festival, the Floralia, April 28–May 1, was celebrated with great gaiety and licentiousness. So, at least in literature, Flora also has been a name commonly used by women of easy virtue.
2. *Calabrian*: from Calabria, the province in southern Italy that forms the toe of the Italian "boot."
3. *Parrhasius, Polygnotus, Apelles, Zeuxis, and Timanthes*: these are all Greek painters of antiquity (from the third and fourth centuries B.C.) but now known only through written descriptions of their works.
4. *Hesperides*: in Greek mythology the Hesperides were the daughters of Atlas. They lived in a fabulous garden located at the western extremity of the world. There with the aid of the dragon Ladon they guarded a tree that bore golden apples.
5. *The sorceress Falerina*: a character in the Italian Renaissance romance *Orlando Innamorato* by Boiardo, and the subject of plays by Rojas Zorrilla, Coello, and Calderón in Renaissance Spain.
6. *New Egyptian temptress*: another allusion to the wife of Potiphar, who

tried to seduce Joseph; when she couldn't, she tried to use the cloak she had stolen from him to prove he was guilty of adultery (Genesis, chap. 39.) In book I, chap. 19, of *Persiles* Antonio compares Rosamunda to her also.

BOOK IV, CHAPTER 9

1. *Auristela, his angel of light . . . into one of darkness*: Lucifer, chief among angels and whose name meant "light bearer," rebelled against God, was cast out, and became Satan, the Prince of Darkness. The name "Auristela" ("golden star") is related to this Christian imagery of light and contrasts in this passage with the image of the Angel of Darkness, associated with death, the realm of Satan.
2. *The duke*: the 1617 edition has *el conde*, "the count," which seems to be an oversight by Cervantes.

BOOK IV, CHAPTER 10

1. *Everything on earth . . . even parents and husbands or wives*: an echo of the New Testament praise of giving up all and dedicating oneself to God. In Luke 18:29 and 30, Jesus tells the disciples: "Verily, I say unto you, there is no man that hath left house, or parents, or brethren, or wife, or children, for the kingdom of God's sake, who shall not receive manifold more in this present time, and in the world to come life everlasting."

BOOK IV, CHAPTER 11

1. *His beloved's fine mind*: literally, her mental faculties, that is, her memory, understanding, and will.

BOOK IV, CHAPTER 12

1. *That latitude*: the Ptolemaic cosmology included a "nineteenth climate" in the far north having six months of day and six of night.
2. *Thule*: often seen in the Latin phrase, *ultima Thule*, "farthest Thule." Although in ancient geography and poetry this was often a reference to a rather nonspecific northernmost region of the world (possibly modern Iceland, Norway, or the largest of the Shetland Islands), in the next chapter Cervantes specifically calls it "Iceland."
3. *Ac tua nautae/Numina sola colant: tibi serviat ultima Thule*: by the Roman poet Virgil, the *Georgics* is a long poem in Latin about the life of farm-

ers. The lines quoted mean, "May your holiness be adored only by sailors; may farthest Thule serve you."

4. *Frisland*: apparently not to be confused with Friesland in the Netherlands, or the Frisian Islands in the North Sea off the coast of the Netherlands and Germany, this island appears on maps of the far north of Europe dating from the fourteenth century.

5. *The Straits of Hercules*: the Straits of Gibraltar.

6. *Tinacria*: a form of the Latin name for Sicily, *Trinacria*.

7. *Parthénope*: a name for Naples recalling the siren in Greek mythology who threw herself into the sea after her songs failed to lure Ulysses into a shipwreck.

8. *Terrachina*: a town on the Appian Way about seventy miles southeast of Rome. Nearby Lautulae Pass marked the frontier between the Papal States and the Kingdom of Naples.

9. *The disease that comes with the stifling weather here*: Avalle-Arce points out (n. 554, p. 468) that in Cervantes' *Master Glass* there is a reference to "the period of unseasonable weather, bad and harmful for all who at that time enter or leave Rome." This seems to be a reference to the dog days of late summer, a period that in the Mediterranean coincides with extremely hot weather plagued by disease and discomfort.

BOOK IV, CHAPTER 13

1. *Nicholas Temo the Venetian*: this is undoubtedly Nicholas Zeno, whose book about a trip to northern Europe was published in 1558 but included a map dated 1380. The book seems to be largely invention with some reference to earlier histories and manuscripts. See Schevill and Bonilla (vol. 2, pp. 319–324) for a detailed discussion of this geography.

2. *Saint Thomas . . . Latins*: this legendary monastery appears in Nicholas Zeno's work and Cervantes has imaginatively elaborated on it even further. Tuscans are natives of the province of Tuscany in north-central Italy. The Tuscan spoken language became the literary language of Italy after Dante, Petrarch, and Boccaccio wrote in it. In ancient times the Latins were the inhabitants of Latium in central Italy. Early on, Rome became the capital of this province and its conquests spread the Latin language over Italy and the vast Roman Empire.

APPENDIX

1. *Maravedí*: a small coin of which thirty-five were worth a real.

2. *Doña Catalina de Salazar*: she and Cervantes were married on December 12, 1584, in Esquivias, her hometown, in the province of Toledo. She died in Madrid on October 31, 1626. They had no children.

3. *San Lorenzo*: the royal palace–monastery of San Lorenzo del Escorial built not far from Madrid by Philip II.

4. *Children*: the reference here is to his literary works, although scholars believe that Cervantes probably had at least one illegitimate daughter.

5. *Saint Jerome . . . Origen's commentary*: Origen, a third-century Egyptian scholar who wrote in Greek, was the most influential theologian of the early Greek church. Saint Jerome admired his work and translated his homily on the biblical book *The Song of Solomon* into Latin, and in that form it was widely read in medieval monasteries.

6. *Cum in omnibus omnes, in hoc seipsum superavit Origenes*: Latin for "While he surpassed all others' efforts in those [i.e., his other biblical commentaries], in this [*The Song of Soloman*] Origen outdid even himself."

7. *Unless, etc.*: Unless, that is, other church authorities should subsequently take a different view of the book.

8. *José de Valdivieso*: a prolific religious poet and the author of allegorical religious plays known as *autos sacramentales*. He also issued the religious approval for Cervantes' *Journey to Parnassus* and the second half of *Don Quixote*.

9. *Don Francisco de Urbina*: member of a Madrid family and nephew of the playwright Lope de Vega's first wife.

10. *Third Order of Saint Francis*: subsequent to the founding of the Franciscan Order, there were established a second order for women, the Poor Clares, and the so-called Third Order, a devotional association of laymen to which many distinguished Spaniards of the seventeenth century belonged. Cervantes joined shortly before his death. In some places there was an unofficial tradition that membership assured the soul's salvation.

11. *Epitaph*: the form of the poem in Spanish is a ten-line stanza with eight syllables per line and rhyming ABBAABBCCB. In general, in translating poems we have not attempted to use rhyme, keeping only the same number of lines and stanzas.

12. *Luis Francisco Calderón*: a clergyman, perhaps from Toledo, about whom little is known. As Avalle-Arce points out in his note (p. 44), two unknowns composed these poems in honor of Cervantes after his death, while Lope de Vega's death inspired two entire volumes in verse, one by Spanish writers and another by Italians.

13. *Sonnet*: in this as in other sonnets that Cervantes includes as part of his romance, we have reproduced the form of the four stanzas (two quartets and two tercets) and have put the lines in iambic pentameter whenever possible. We have not attempted to reproduce rhyme or assonance.

14. *Tagus*: the Tagus flows through central Spain and Portugal into the Atlantic. Spanish writers of the time enjoyed continuing the literary convention of claiming its sands were made of gold.

15. *Don Pedro Fernández de Castro*: to this patron of the arts Cervantes also dedicated his *Exemplary Novels*, his *Eight Plays and Eight Farces*, and the

second half of *Don Quixote*. He was the Spanish viceroy in Naples from 1610 to 1616, which explains the references in this dedication to a glorious return to Spain.

16. *Encomienda . . . and of the Order of Alcántara*: the *encomienda* was a Spanish institution especially prominent in the history of sixteenth- and seventeenth-century Latin America by which the king "entrusted" or granted estates to individuals or, as in the present case, to the prestigious military orders with religious overtones composed of powerful knights. The Order of Alcántara was founded in 1166.

17. *With almost the same words*: the well-known ballad verses that Cervantes here adapts to his own situation began as follows:

> With my foot already in the stirrup,
> In the agony of death,
> My Lady, I write you this,
> For I cannot leave here alive,
> Much less return to see you.

18. *"Weeks in a Garden," and the famous "Bernardo"*: both of these unfinished works by Cervantes have been lost.

19. *Galatea*: this example of the pastoral novel, a Renaissance genre typical of the sixteenth century, was Cervantes' first work. It was published in 1585, in spite of having been left by the author without a conclusive ending.